THE AUTHORITY OF INTERNATIONAL COURTS

Why do some international courts wield broad authority while others face pushback or fade into irrelevance? This book provides novel theoretical and empirical insights into this question. It offers a fresh, interdisciplinary perspective on the authority of international courts, drawing from law, political science and behavioural research.

It develops, in Part I, a theoretical model and analytical framework for assessing these questions. The model explains how authority relationships between courts and their audiences – such as states, NGOs, individual applicants, and domestic courts – are formed, maintained, or contested. In Part II, the book applies this analytical framework to in-depth case studies of two selected international courts: the European Court of Human Rights and the Court of Justice of the Economic Community of West African States. These studies not only provide deeper insights into the authority of these courts but also demonstrate how the analytical framework can be applied to other international courts to generate an enhanced understanding of international court authority.

The book sheds new light on why some courts enjoy enduring authority and others face pushback, offering powerful tools for understanding the behaviour of international courts and their audiences.

Volume 16 in the series Hart Monographs in Transnational and International Law

Hart Monographs in Transnational and International Law

Series Editor: Craig Martin Scott, Professor of Law, Osgoode Hall Law School of York University, Toronto

The objective of this series is to publish high-quality scholarship in public international law and private international law, as well as work that adopts "transnational law" as its thematic, theoretical or doctrinal focus. The series strives to be a leading venue for work of the following sort:

* critical reappraisals of foundational concepts and core doctrinal principles of both public and private international law, and their operation in practice, including insights drawn from general legal theory;

* analysis and development of conceptions of 'transnational law', including in relation to the role of unofficial law and informal processes in transnational regulation and in relation to theories and studies of 'governance' in transnational spheres; and

* empirical studies of the emergence, evolution and transformation of international and/or transnational legal orders, including accounts and explanations of how law is constructed within different communities of interpretation and practice.

In relation to the first of these categories, the series especially welcomes monographs that explore the interactions between the ever-integrating fields of public and private international law. Of special interest are explorations of the extent to which these interactions are structured by higher-order principles and policies, on the one hand, and by politics and the exercise of various forms of power, on the other hand.

The series is open to work not only by law scholars but also by scholars from cognate disciplines.

Recent titles in this series

The Institutional Problem in Modern International Law
Richard Collins

Liability for Transboundary Pollution at the Intersection of Public and Private International Law
Guillaume Laganière

Faith in Courts: Human Rights Advocacy and the Transnational Regulation of Religion
Lisa Harms

The Law's Last Frontier: The Private Dimension of International Law
Horatia Muir Watt

Manufacturing Sovereignty: International Law, Labour Struggle, and the Making of Iraq
Ali Hammoudi

The Authority of International Courts: A Behavioural Framework
Dana Burchardt

The Authority of International Courts

A Behavioural Framework

Dana Burchardt

• H A R T •
OXFORD • LONDON • NEW YORK • NEW DELHI • SYDNEY

HART PUBLISHING

Bloomsbury Publishing Plc

Kemp House, Chawley Park, Cumnor Hill, Oxford, OX2 9PH, UK

1385 Broadway, New York, NY 10018, USA

Bloomsbury Publishing Ireland Limited, 29 Earlsfort Terrace, Dublin 2, D02 AY28, Ireland

HART PUBLISHING, the Hart/Stag logo, BLOOMSBURY and the Diana logo are trademarks of Bloomsbury Publishing Plc

First published in Great Britain 2026

A catalogue record for this book is available from the British Library.

A catalogue record for this book is available from the Library of Congress.

Library of Congress Control Number: 2026936852

ISBN: HB: 978-1-50999-292-8
ePDF: 978-1-50999-294-2
ePub: 978-1-50999-293-5

Typeset by Compuscript Ltd, Shannon

Contents

PART II
APPLYING THE BEHAVIOURAL CONCEPT OF INTERNATIONAL COURT AUTHORITY

Introduction

THE PERFORMANCE OF international courts and tribunals is a key concern of international law and international relations scholarship. The number of courts has significantly increased in the past three decades, generating a judicialisation of the international order. This includes courts on a regional and sub-regional scale, as well as on a (quasi)universal scale. Conceptually, courts function as an important pillar of the international rule of law. They aim at guaranteeing a rules-based international order and provide an element of separation of powers within this order. They shape considerably both the legal and factual dimension of the international order. The activities of international courts have thus attracted much attention from those interested in the development of international law. At the same time, a considerable number of international courts have encountered pushback by states and other actors in recent years, even to a point that the existence of some of them is chequered. For example, beyond non-compliance with judgments, states have withdrawn from, announced that they are no longer to be subjected to, or have otherwise undermined the jurisdiction of the International Criminal Court, the regional human rights courts, the World Trade Organization (WTO) dispute resolution mechanisms and investment arbitration tribunals. Both these developments – judicialisation of the international order and pushback against courts – has spurred considerable interest in analysing the relationship between courts and their constituencies. The numerous approaches in scholarship include studies on compliance, effectiveness, legitimacy and authority, taking various analytical and normative, formalist and practical perspectives.[1]

THE NOTION OF AUTHORITY

In this book, I focus on the authority of international courts. Authority is a somewhat cross-cutting notion that also refers to aspects relevant for compliance, effectiveness and legitimacy of international courts. The notion of authority thus

[1] As a small selection, see, eg, KJ Alter, LR Helfer and MR Madsen (eds), *International Court Authority* (OUP 2018); N Grossman, HG Cohen, A Føllesdal and G Ulfstein (eds), *Legitimacy and International Courts* (CUP 2018); A Føllesdal, JK Schaffer and G Ulfstein (eds), *The Legitimacy of International Human Rights Regimes* (CUP 2013); T Squatrito, OR Young, A Føllesdal and G Ulfstein (eds), *The Performance of International Courts and Tribunals* (CUP 2018); JT Gathii (ed), *The Performance of Africa's International Courts: Using Litigation for Political, Legal, and Social Change* (OUP 2020); Y Shany (ed), *Assessing the Effectiveness of International Courts* (OUP 2014); LR Helfer and A-M Slaughter, 'Toward a Theory of Effective Supranational Adjudication' (1997) 107 *Yale Law Journal* 273; KJ Alter and LR Helfer, 'Nature or Nurture? Judicial Lawmaking in the European Court of Justice' (2010) 64 *International Organization* 563; F Zarbiyev, 'Saying Credibly What the Law Is: On Marks of Authority in International Law' (2018) 9 *Journal of International Dispute Settlement* 291.

captures a major part of the discussion about international courts. Authority as a concept is well suited for analysing the many interactions that international courts have with their constituencies. In particular, the interrelations that define an international court are more comprehensive than the mere compliance relationship towards the parties to a dispute. They include various practical and discursive modes of authority that go beyond compliance; and they concern a broad range of actors such as, inter alia, states, individuals, other courts, scholars and the general public. The authority concept can address all these dimensions. Moreover, authority as an analytical lens provides an objective yardstick. This contrasts with an effectiveness assessment which is necessarily based on a normative approach: whether one considers a court to be effective depends on the normative expectations that one has with regard to that court, particularly as to the functions that one considers a court to have.[2] This is not the case for analytical research on authority.[3] While the normative expectations of actors play a role for the assessment, no common normative basis is needed. An authority analysis addresses, and includes, the actors' diverging expectations as such.

RESEARCH QUESTION

On this basis, this book addresses an issue that has been controversially discussed among international courts scholars. When comparing international courts, authors have noticed the differences in the authority relationships that courts have – even when they are similarly designed – towards the relevant groups of actors. As a result, there has been a discussion as to the factors that determine these differences. Why have some courts broader authority than others? And why are some authority relationships robust while others fall prey to pushback by various actors? Authors have suggested different hypotheses on the matter. For example, it has been discussed to what extent the authority of international courts is determined by the design features of international courts or their judicial practice; by 'factors within the control of the judiciary' or other factors; by factors relating to the courts themselves or to the relevant actors; by formal legal factors or the political, social and cultural context in which the court and the actors operate. These potential factors are often assessed differently by legal scholars and political scientists when researching international courts.[4]

This book aims at advancing the research on this issue. The guiding question is the following: why do we see these differences in the authority relationships? What are the factors that determine whether and to what extent actors accept the authority of an international court and continue to do so over time without major pushback? In short: *what are the factors that determine the authority relationship between international courts and their relevant actors?*

[2] Speaking of an 'inescapable normative dimension' that is inherent 'to any study of the performance of international courts', T Squatrito, OR Young, A Føllesdal and G Ulfstein, 'A Framework for Evaluating the Performance of International Courts and Tribunals' in Squatrito et al (n 1) 3.

[3] As compared to normative reflections on authority, see ch 1.

[4] For an overview of the diverging views, see ch 1.

The book answers this question by providing insights in the interplay between factors for authority and the extent to which authority relationships can develop and remain robust. It engages with authority as an analytical concept and develops a framework that can be used for assessing the authority of every individual international court. It offers explanations as to how certain categories of factors interrelate and how this determines authority relationships. It does not, however, aim at determining 'global trends' regarding the extent to which international courts in general exercise authority or whether this authority is robust. The book also does not provide an inventory of all the international courts and their varying authority. Rather, it takes two selected courts as examples to demonstrate how, based on the suggested framework, the assessment of authority relationships can and should be conducted with the aim of understanding the determining factor for each context. The book further shows that authority relationships between an international court and its constituencies vary significantly among courts, among groups of actors, and across time periods.

RELEVANCE OF THE RESEARCH QUESTION

Understanding the factors that shape the authority relationship between international courts and the relevant actors is important for various reasons. In addition to the theoretical interest in conceptualising this relationship, it has practical significance. First, an understanding of these factors enables established international courts to develop strategies to enhance the acceptance of their authority. Previous strategies can be reassessed as to whether they effectively target the right factors for each group of actors. This can contribute to increasing the robustness of authority relationships even despite changing circumstances. Courts might address pushback tendencies more effectively or even avoid them to begin with. In a climate of repeated pushback against international courts, such insights are most valuable.

Second, for newly established and future courts, understanding the dynamics of authority relationships is crucial for building authority relationships towards their constituencies. Adopting strategies to gain broad acceptance requires courts to be aware of the relevant factors and their interplay. What is more, when creating future courts (such as, for example, a potential multilateral investment court), insights into the factors that contribute to robust authority relationships can help the constituting actors to make the appropriate design choices. As outlined in this book, institutional design aspects such as judicial independence or access rules to courts can be important factors for authority relationships.

BEHAVIOURAL APPROACH TO AUTHORITY

To assess the factors that determine the authority relationships of international courts, I take a perspective that so far has not been considered in much detail in the discussion about international courts: the perspective of behavioural research. With this notion, I refer to research on human behaviour broadly understood, a research field that combines findings from various disciplines such as psychology, sociology, economics and related disciplines. It focuses on the behaviour of actors that belong to the audiences of the authoritative entity. I use insights from this research to re-evaluate the factors discussed in the scholarship on international courts said to determine the authority relationship; and to shed light on – so far still somewhat obscure – additional factors.

From this perspective, I develop a novel conceptual and analytical framework for assessing the factors that determine the authority relationship and to compare them among different actors and settings. This framework is composed of three key elements: *motivation, opportunity and constraints* (the MOC framework). This framework makes it possible to structure the factors that shape authority relationships, highlight their way of functioning and take into account their interrelations. The behaviour of the relevant actors can be assessed both with regard to accepting the authority of international courts and with regard to rejecting it in case of pushback.

This framework consolidates the diverging suggestions in international law and political science research regarding possible explanations for the authority of international courts. It seeks to provide novel insights to scholars of both international law and international relations who engage with international courts, offering a 'three-pronged' interdisciplinary framework with elements of legal research, political science and behavioural research. The MOC framework makes it possible, first, to further develop the dialogue between legal and political science assessments of international courts; and second to explore international courts as a research object for behavioural research. While the former aspect contributes to understanding to what extent legal as opposed to non-legal factors shape court authority, the latter allows us to establish better comparability between different international courts. Rather than merely pointing to a context-dependency of these authority relationships, the framework suggested in this book makes it possible to conceptualise contextual factors and compare the behavioural factors among settings and regions.[5]

The framework thus provides a tool for assessing international court authority from a behavioural perspective and for understanding the factors that shape this authority as well as the interplay between these factors. It gives guidelines for such an assessment by offering a conceptual explanation as to the factors involved, and by highlighting the range of information necessary for fully understanding the various authority relationships between an international court and its constituencies.

STRUCTURE OF THE BOOK

This book is structured in two parts. The first part is conceptual in nature, while the second part is empirical.

The first part develops a conceptual and analytical framework for the authority of international courts. (The term international court is understood broadly; the

[5] I outline in detail the benefits of this approach in ch 3.

framework is also applicable to quasi-judicial bodies.) To construct this framework, the first part of the book engages with the conceptual basis of authority and connects it to behavioural research that provides insights for the relationship between international courts and their relevant actors.

Chapter one begins by giving an overview of the existing debate about authority in law, political science and sociology. It presents some guiding conceptual lines that are important for situating the present approach within the discussion about authority. Specifically, it points to the differences between normative and analytical, descriptive and explanatory, de jure and de facto, attributive and relational approaches to authority. Against this backdrop, the chapter points out that the concept of international court authority developed in this book is analytical and relational, that it focuses on the explanatory dimension of authority research and takes a de facto understanding of authority as a starting point. It argues for a contextualised notion of authority that takes the specificities of international courts into account. And it outlines a concept of authority of international courts that engages with the broad range of relationships between courts and their relevant actors.

Chapter two develops the analytical framework for the factors that shape authority relationships in general. To start with, I sketch out the broad lines of behavioural research on which this framework is build. I then introduce the above-mentioned three-pronged model which includes the factors motivation, opportunity and constraint. I show how this MOC framework can be operationalised in the context of authority. I highlight the relationship between the factors, showing how understanding this relationship can provide an explanation for why factors play out differently in different settings. I also adapt it to the specific situation of pushback against an authoritative entity. Finally, the chapter highlights the benefits of this framework for analysing the factors for authority.

Chapter three links the MOC framework to the particular case of international courts. I provide an overview of how the factors determining authority relationships with international courts can be assessed based on the behavioural model suggested in this book. I outline factors that influence the behaviour of actors when they accept the authority of international courts and I connect this framework to pushback against international courts. The aim is to reconceptualise, from a behavioural perspective, the factors that have been discussed as determining international court authority. Moreover, I describe strategies of international courts to improve the behavioural setting for actors to accept their authority and provide reference points for assessing the effectiveness of such strategies.

The second part of the book puts the MOC framework developed in Part I into practice. It assesses, for two selected international courts, the factors that determine whether relevant actors including, inter alia, member state governments, domestic courts, individuals, NGOs and regional institutions accept the authority of these courts. It also analyses the factors for (potential) pushback against these courts. And it outlines the strategies of the respective courts to enhance acceptance and reduce pushback, as well as assessing whether these strategies are expected to be effective in light of the given behavioural framework. For this assessment, Part II engages in depth with the legal framework in which the courts operate as well as with their jurisprudence. The impact of these legal factors on the acceptance of international court authority is evaluated. Further, they are linked to the broad range of non-legal factors that also contribute to shaping authority relationships. I explore these factors and highlight the interplay of legal and non-legal factors. This assessment is based on a meta-analysis of research findings in the scholarship on the respective courts as well as on my own primary research relating to the jurisprudence of these courts.

The international courts selected for this assessment are two regional courts: the European Court of Human Rights (ECtHR) and the Court of Justice of the Economic Community of West African States (ECOWAS Court).

Chapters four and five assess the authority relationship between the two selected courts and their respective audiences in turn. I focus on analysing the authority relationship with *(potential) applicants* and *(potential) respondents*. These terms are both understood broadly and also include, as applicants, actors such as NGOs that engage with the court via amicus curiae briefs and domestic courts in their role as initiators of preliminary reference procedures. And as respondent actors, I include all state actors (executive, legislative and judicial) that can potentially be involved in proceedings before the court or in the implementation of judgments. For both courts, I start by outlining the MOC factors for the (potential) applicants and evaluate which of the factors predominantly determine whether these actors accept the authority of the court. I then turn to the (potential) respondents, also showing the factors for the acceptance of authority and evaluating their effect for each group. In addition, for these actors, I assess the behavioural setting for pushback against the court. Finally, I outline the strategies that the respective courts have adopted to improve the conditions for their authority relationships and assess whether, according to the MOC framework, these strategies have the intended effect. This also includes, in separate sections, the strategies against pushback.

Chapter six provides a comparison of the findings in chapters four and five as well as a conclusion as to the MOC framework developed and operationalised in this book. First, it compares the MOC settings that shape the authority relationships of the ECOWAS Court and the ECtHR. Second, it addresses a specific category of factors: selected psychological factors that play a particular role for authority relationships. I outline how these factors have influenced the MOC setting in the two courts and how these courts have in turn engaged with these factors. Third, I link the findings of the book back to the discussion mentioned at the outset of this introduction as to what types of factors are predominantly responsible for stronger or weaker authority relationships. I specifically engage with the impact of legal factors on the one hand and of political factors on the other, as well as the development of the authority of international courts over time. In a final section, I provide concluding reflections on how to go forward when assessing the MOC setting for other international courts.

COURT SELECTION

I have selected the ECOWAS Court and the ECtHR for several reasons. Such regional courts make it possible to compare the behavioural setting not only for state actors such as domestic executive, legislative and judicial actors but also for institutional actors within the respective regional organisation, individuals, corporate actors, and civil society groups such as NGOs and bar associations. This enables me to compare the behavioural setting for different groups of actors vis-a-vis the same court, thus highlighting the heterogeneity and variability of authority relationships. And, of course, one can also compare the behavioural setting for the same group of actors vis-a-vis different courts.

It should be noted, however, that this selection does not mean that the behavioural framework developed in this book is only applicable to such 'new-style' international courts with access for non-state actors.[6] It is indeed applicable to all international judicial bodies, independently of the specific subject-matter jurisdiction, the compulsory or optional nature of its jurisdiction, access for state and/or non-state applicants and embeddedness into a regional or global regime. It is thus also applicable to 'old-style' international courts such as the International Court of Justice (ICJ) and the International Tribunal for the Law of the Sea (ITLOS).

Moreover, assessing the authority relationships of the two selected courts makes it possible to evaluate the effect of different socio-political settings on the relevant groups of actors. To engage with the question discussed in the international courts scholarship whether the socio-political setting is the most important factor for the acceptance of international court authority, it is useful for the present study to include a variety of such settings. In addition, the court selection makes it possible to compare, more generally, the European and the African experiences with regional courts. This comparative dimension can further contribute to addressing claims regarding the context-dependency of international court authority.

Finally, analysing the ECOWAS Court provides insights into a court that is so far not yet studied as much as other (older) international courts. The analysis in this book thus helps us to better understand this court, its jurisprudence and the varying nature of its authority relationships. In addition, as this court is still a relatively 'new' court, the analysis provided in this book makes it possible to gain substantial insights into the early phase of an international court's practice. Moreover, the comparison with a long-established international court such as the ECtHR brings out the similarities that exist regarding the development of international court authority over time. And it gives indications as to how the authority of younger courts might develop in the future.

*

In sum, the book presents an innovative theoretical concept for assessing the authority of international courts and it offers novel analytical insights into a set of selected authority relationships. It provides both a theoretical model which explains the interplay of the many factors that shape the behaviour of the relevant groups of actors, and a tool to analyse claims made in the legal and political science scholarship on international courts. In this way, it helps us better understand international courts and their development.

[6] On this notion in contrast to 'old style' international courts, KJ Alter, *The New Terrain of International Law: Courts, Politics, Rights* (Princeton University Press 2014) 81.

Part I

Developing a Behavioural Framework of International Court Authority

1

Conceptualising the Authority of International Courts: Setting the Direction

SCHOLARS HAVE DISCUSSED the concept of authority not only for centuries[1] but also from a multitude of perspectives. This has caused an abundance of – seemingly – alternative approaches as well as confusion as to how these approaches interrelate, and which question they address. In this chapter, I give an overview of the debate in political science, sociology and law. This allows me to situate the concept of authority suggested in this book within the existing debate and to highlight the features that will be important for the suggested concept.

The first section looks at authority from a general perspective. It presents guiding lines within the scholarly discussion about authority (section I). The second section considers international courts as authoritative entities and argues for a contextualised notion of authority that takes the specificities of international courts into account (section II).

I. CONCEPTUALISING AUTHORITY: GENERAL FEATURES

To capture the various approaches to authority existing in the scholarly debate, I categorise them according to the research question that they pursue. I emphasise those that are particularly relevant for situating the concept suggested in this book.

A. Normative vs Analytical

To start with, it is crucial to note that authority as a research object has various dimensions. Scholars have approached authority both from a normative and an analytical perspective. It is important to bear the diverging research focus of these perspectives in mind, and keep them conceptually distinct.[2]

[1] For a history of the concept of authority, see F Furedi, *Authority: A Sociological History* (CUP 2013).

[2] In contrast, arguing for a close interdependency between normative and analytical ('sociological') accounts of authority, N Roughan, 'From authority to authorities: bridging the social/normative divide' in R Cotterrell and M Del Mar (eds), *Authority in Transnational Legal Theory* (Edward Elgar 2016) 280.

The *normative perspective* asks about the reasons that can justify authority and the circumstances under which actors should accept an entity as authoritative. Raz has offered an influential account in answer to these questions.[3] His service conception of authority seeks to justify authority based on the claim that authoritative structures serve specific purposes for the subjects of authority concerned. According to Raz, actors should accept the authority of an entity when authoritative guidance is beneficial to these actors.[4] Others have built on this approach, including by adapting it to the international context. For example, the autonomy aspect inherent in Raz's service conception has been used as a basis for a democratic coordination-related account of authority of international law.[5] According to this approach, actors should accept the authority of international law considering the coordination benefit that it provides. Further, Raz's service conception has also been referred to for developing a normative account of the legitimate authority of international courts that asks when actors should defer to these courts and when non-compliance might be justified.[6]

Normative perspectives on authority are often linked to the notion of legitimacy.[7] Scholarship in this field reflects on when we *should* regard the exercise of authority as legitimate. (This is as opposed to the question linked to the analytical notion of legitimacy: when *do* certain actors regard the exercise of authority as legitimate.)[8] The normative perspective based on legitimacy provides abstract conceptual reasons for actors to accept the authority of an entity. It provides a general moral foundation for authority. Yet it does not enquire into the motivations that specific real-world actors in specific circumstances might have for accepting the authority of a specific entity.[9] In the context of international courts, and in addition to the above-cited authors that base their account of 'legitimate authority' on Raz's service conception, von Bogdandy and Venzke provide such normative reflections on the legitimacy of international courts' exercise of international public authority.[10] They discuss the basis on which one can justify the exercise of authority by international courts from the

[3] J Raz, 'The Problem of Authority: Revisiting the Service Conception' (2006) 90 *Minnesota Law Review* 1003, 1012.

[4] Raz, 'The Problem of Authority' (n 3) 1014. See also J Raz, *The Morality of Freedom* (OUP 1986).

[5] S Besson, 'The Authority of International Law – Lifting the State Veil' (2009) 31 *Sydney Law Review* 343.

[6] A Føllesdal, 'The Legitimate Authority of International Courts and Its Limits – A Challenge to Raz's Service Conception?' in P Capps and HP Olsen (eds), *Legal Authority Beyond the State* (CUP 2018) 188; S Wheatley, 'On the legitimate authority of international human rights bodies' in A Føllesdal, JK Schaffer and G Ulfstein (eds), *The Legitimacy of International Human Rights Regimes* (CUP 2013) 84.

[7] On the question whether there is a necessary connection between legitimacy and authority, HP Olsen, 'International Courts and the Building of Legal Authority beyond the State' in P Capps and HP Olsen (eds), *Legal Authority Beyond the State* (CUP 2018) 81. The notion of legitimate authority is also used when discussing the authority of international law, see eg, N Roughan, 'Mind the Gaps: Authority and Legality in International Law' (2016) 27 *European Journal of International Law* 329, 332.

[8] On the distinction between the normative and the analytical dimension of legitimacy, see I Hurd, 'Legitimacy and Authority in International Politics' (1999) 53 *International Organization* 379, 381; W Hinsch, 'Justice, legitimacy, and constitutional rights' (2010) 13 *Critical Review of International Social and Political Philosophy* 39.

[9] Raz, 'The Problem of Authority' (n 3) 1013–14.

[10] A von Bogdandy and I Venzke, 'In Whose Name? An Investigation of International Courts' Public Authority and its Democratic Justification' (2012) 23 *European Journal of International Law* 7; A von Bogdandy and I Venzke, *In Whose Name? A Public Law Theory of International Adjudication* (OUP 2014).

perspective of democratic theory. Further, an in-depth engagement with international court legitimacy is provided by interdisciplinary approaches to this topic.[11]

In contrast, an *analytical perspective* on authority studies how authority plays out in practice. It requires assessing how and when authority occurs in practice rather than how and when it should occur as a matter of conceptual justification. Such analytical research includes studying the entities that have, or claim to have, authority as well as the actors that recognise this authority (or not). And it includes enquiring why and under which circumstances authority is created and why and under which circumstances it reduces or disappears again.

In this book, I focus on the analytical rather than the normative perspective on authority. I do not discuss whether and when international courts should have authority. Instead, I seek to analyse whether and when they *do* have authority. As my focus is on the analytical dimension, the following reflections provide an overview of the existing analytical research on authority.

B. Describing vs Explaining

The analytical perspective on authority has in turn two dimensions: a descriptive and an explanatory dimension.

Research that focuses on the *descriptive dimension* aims at defining authority as a concept and measuring the authority of specific entities.

The question how to *define* authority is a complex one. In the first place, most modern concepts of authority engage with the notions of 'coercion' and 'persuasion', yet in different ways. These notions have been prominently invoked by Arendt who understands authority 'in contradistinction to both coercion by force and persuasion through arguments'.[12] In opposition to coercion by force, authority is considered to require 'complicity on the part of the subordinate subject', which is only possible if there is a certain freedom of the subject to decide how to behave.[13] At the other end of the spectrum, to differentiate between persuasion and authority, many authors use the distinction between content-dependence and content-independence of the actors' behaviour.[14] According to this criterion, authority exists when actors follow a directive independently of the content of the directive.[15] While Arendt and authors

[11] eg, N Grossman, HG Cohen, A Føllesdal and G Ulfstein (eds), *Legitimacy and International Courts* (CUP 2018).

[12] H Arendt, *Between Past and Future: Eight Exercises in Political Thought* (Penguin 1977) 93. For an example of a more recent use of coercion and persuasion as dual distinction, see eg, M Zürn, M Binder and M Ecker-Ehrhardt, 'International Authority and its Politicization' (2012) 4 *International Theory* 69, 86.

[13] G Simmel (trans and eds AJ Blasi, AK Jacobs and MJ Kanjirathinkal), *Sociology: Inquiries into the Construction of Social Forms* (Brill 2009) 130. Max Weber, *Economy and Society* (University of California Press 1978) 53, 212, speaks of a 'minimum of voluntary compliance'. See also on the distinction to force, A Kojève, *The Notion of Authority* (Verso 2014) 10.

[14] For a use of this distinction in the international law context, see eg, I Venzke, 'Between Power and Persuasion: On International Institutions' Authority in Making Law' (2013) 4 *Transnational Legal Theory* 354.

[15] On content-independence and command, HLA Hart, *Essays on Bentham: Jurisprudence and Political Philosophy* (OUP 1982) 261. See also AJ Simmons, 'Authority' in D Estlund (ed), *The Oxford Handbook of Political Philosophy* (OUP 2012) 23.

who adopt her approach see distinct dividing lines between coercion, authority and persuasion, others consider these distinctions as less clear-cut. For them, situations of authority can have elements of coercion and of persuasion.[16]

Moreover, there is a discussion about whether authority requires command and bindingness as defining elements, ie, whether authority is 'the exercise of binding powers to create formal obligations'.[17] This discussion reacts to the traditional understanding of authority as developed by Max Weber who construes authority based on commands and compliance.[18] Accounts of authority that refer to this understanding state, for example, that 'the ruler, A, commands a set of subordinates, B, to alter their actions'[19] and that 'authority always demands obedience'.[20] In contrast, the notion of 'deference' aims at going beyond command as the defining core of authority: actors 'defer' to an authoritative entity and this entity has 'the ability to induce deference in others'.[21] Regarding international relations, this discussion is linked to the question to what extent instances of 'liquid authority' as opposed to 'solid authority' constitute authority.[22] For Krisch, liquid authority is 'detached from ideas of command, delegation, and formally binding obligations' and 'it may appear in gradations, be dispersed over multiple actors, and its recognition based on a variety of sources, procedural or substantive'.[23] Similarly, Zürn's reflexive authority 'does not work exclusively with "commands to do x" but also includes "requests to consider y"'.[24] Suggestions such as Venzke's 'semantic authority' aim at decoupling the notion of authority from the notion of legal bindingness. Venzke defines semantic authority as 'actors' capacity to find recognition for their claims about international law and to establish reference points for legal discourse that others can hardly escape'.[25]

A further issue debated in the scholarship about authority is whether and, if so, how one should delineate the notion of authority from other notions. This discussion includes the relationship between authority and legitimacy. The question is in particular whether the notion of authority presumes legitimacy as a defining element, or alternatively, whether legitimacy is merely a possible explanatory factor for how

[16] eg, Zürn, Binder and Ecker-Ehrhardt (n 12) 87: 'A political authority may have both persuasive and coercive powers, but its power extends beyond the use of coercion and the need to be convincing in every instance'.

[17] N Krisch, 'Liquid authority in global governance' (2017) 9 *International Theory* 237. On authority beyond binding decisions by international bodies, see also F Zarbiyev, 'Saying Credibly What the Law Is: On Marks of Authority in International Law' (2018) 9 *Journal of International Dispute Settlement* 291.

[18] Weber (n 13) 53, 212.

[19] DA Lake, 'Relational Authority and Legitimacy in International Relations' (2009) 53 *American Behavioral Scientist* 331, 332.

[20] Arendt (n 12) 92.

[21] DD Avant, M Finnemore and SK Sell, 'Who Governs the Globe?' in DD Avant, M Finnemore, and SK Sell (eds), *Who Governs the Globe?* (CUP 2010) 1, 9; M Barnett and M Finnemore, *Rules for the World: International Organizations in Global Politics* (Cornell University Press 2004) 5.

[22] Krisch, 'Liquid authority' (n 17); N Krisch, 'Authority, solid and liquid, in postnational governance' in R Cotterrell and M Del Mar (eds), *Authority in Transnational Legal Theory* (Edward Elgar 2016) 25.

[23] Krisch, 'Liquid authority' (n 17) 243.

[24] M Zürn, *A Theory of Global Governance: Authority, Legitimacy, and Contestation* (OUP 2018) 47.

[25] I Venzke, 'Semantic Authority, Legal Change and the Dynamics of International Law' (2015) 12 *No Foundations* 1, 1–2. See also Venzke, 'Power and Persuasion' (n 14) 368; I Venzke, '"International Courts" De Facto Authority and its Justification' in KJ Alter, LR Helfer and MR Madsen (eds), *International Court Authority* (OUP 2018) 391, 395–97.

authority comes about.[26] A similar debate exists on the relationship between power and authority: whether authority is a form of power (eg, legitimate power) or whether power and authority are separate concepts.[27] In the context of international courts, this distinction between power and authority has played a role as well.[28] Although these issues frequently appear in the scholarship about authority, this debate becomes relevant only if the conceptual framework that a scholar suggests aims at engaging both with authority and with legitimacy/power.

In addition to the definition issue, the descriptive dimension of authority incorporates a further aspect: *measuring authority*. Such research is based on the assumption that authority is a matter of degree rather than an absolute category.[29] An entity can have no authority, narrow authority or broad authority – and anything in between. Measuring authority as a branch of research thus aims at determining the degree of authority that an entity exercises. This requires identifying indicators for broad or narrow authority. Several authors have made detailed suggestions on the methodology of measuring authority and the indicators that can be used for different contexts. For example, Hooghe et al have made such suggestions for measuring the authority of international organisations;[30] and Alter, Helfer and Madsen have developed indicators for measuring the authority of international courts.[31] Relatedly although not referring to the notion of authority, Shany developed a functions-based framework for assessing the 'effectiveness' of international courts,[32] while others such as Gathii argue for a broader approach to measuring international court performance that takes the societal impact of these actors into account;[33] and Squatrito suggests a framework and a methodology for measuring the 'outcome performance' and 'process performance' of international courts.[34]

The second dimension of the analytical perspective on authority goes beyond describing authority: it seeks to explain it. Research that addresses the *explanatory dimension* of authority is concerned with reasons for why authority comes about.

[26] On these two opposing approaches, see H Enroth, 'The Concept of Authority Transnationalised' (2013) 4 *Transnational Legal Theory* 336, 342–43; Zürn, Binder and Ecker-Ehrhardt (n 12) 82–83. Arguing that authority is always legitimate, Kojève (n 13) 11. For an account that distinguishes between authority and legitimacy in the context of international courts, see von Bogdandy and Venzke, *Investigation* (n 10) 8.

[27] For accounts of authority as a form of power, see eg, Weber (n 13) 212; DA Lake, 'Escape from the State of Nature – Authority and Hierarchy in World Politics' (2007) 32 *International Security* 47, 51; Zürn (n 24) 38. For an account that distinguishes power and authority, see eg, Arendt (n 12) 93.

[28] KJ Alter, LR Helfer and MR Madsen, 'How Context Shapes the Authority of International Courts' in Alter, Helfer and Madsen (eds), *International Court Authority* (n 25) 24, 52. Critical on the authority/power distinction in this contribution: A Føllesdal, 'Power or Authority; Actions or Beliefs' in Alter, Helfer and Madsen, *International Court Authority* (n 25) 412.

[29] See also Krisch, 'Liquid authority' (n 17) 242.

[30] L Hooghe, G Marks, T Lenz, J Bezuijen, B Ceka and S Derderyan, *Measuring International Authority* (OUP 2017).

[31] Alter, Helfer and Madsen, 'Context' (n 28) 34–36.

[32] Y Shany (ed), *Assessing the Effectiveness of International Courts* (OUP 2014). See also A von Bogdandy and I Venzke, 'On the functions of international courts: an appraisal in light of their burgeoning public authority' (2013) 26 *Leiden Journal of International Law* 49.

[33] JT Gathii (ed), *The Performance of Africa's International Courts: Using Litigation for Political, Legal, and Social Change* (OUP 2020).

[34] T Squatrito, 'Measurement and Methods: Opportunities for Future Research' in T Squatrito, OR Young, A Føllesdal and G Ulfstein (eds), *The Performance of International Courts and Tribunals* (CUP 2018) 373.

It studies in particular the motives that actors have when they accept authority. More broadly, explaining authority means determining factors that contribute to actors entering into an authority relationship. The elements of explanation that are suggested in the literature on authority are abundant. They include general explanations which claim to be applicable to various kinds of authoritative relationships; and specific explanations which only assess the factors that contribute to authority-building in specific contexts.

Examples for such general explanations are the habituation or internalisation model and the contract model, which are often presented as alternatives.[35] The habituation or internalisation model explains authority as adaptive behaviour of the subjects of authority. Actors get used to authoritative claims made by a certain entity and internalise that they are part of an authoritative relationship. According to Hurd, when an 'individual internalizes [a rule's] content and reconfigures his or her interests according to the rule', compliance becomes habitual.[36] Hurd associates the habituation approach to legitimacy as an explanatory factor.[37] The claim is that actors in practice have the 'normative belief' that an 'institution ought to be obeyed' and that they obey because of that belief.[38] Actors having internalised this belief is the key explanation in this approach, while the reasons for why actors accept this belief in the first place play less of a role.

An alternative explanation for authority is the contract model. For this model, authority is based on a contractual relationship between actors – the term 'contractual' understood as a non-legal notion. Actors enter an agreement according to which one actor accepts the authority of the other. This model is closely related to the idea of conferral or mandate given to an entity such as an international organisation or international court. For Lake, authority is founded on a 'social contract' by which authority is conferred and which serves the interests of the actors that are party to this contract.[39] The point of reference is an order that connects the parties to the contract: authority is 'a social contract in which a governor provides a political order of value to a community in exchange for compliance by the governed with the rules necessary to produce that order'.[40] This model thus provides an interest-related account of authority.

In addition to such general models of explanation, scholars have presented lists of context-specific factors that are said to contribute to the authority of specific entities. For international courts, these lists include, inter alia, formal or structural factors such as jurisdiction, access rules, personal and financial resources, independence and composition of the court, and the court's expertise; and factors relating to the courts' constituencies such as their interests, their commitment to the rule of law or the broader political context.[41] The various suggestions reflect diverging

[35] Hurd (n 8); Zürn (n 24) 41–45.

[36] Hurd (n 8) 388.

[37] Hurd understands legitimacy here as analytical rather than a normative notion: Hurd (n 8) 381.

[38] Hurd (n 8) 381.

[39] Lake, 'Escape from the State of Nature' (n 27); DA Lake, 'Rightful Rules: Authority, Order, and the Foundations of Global Governance' (2010) 54 *International Studies Quarterly* 587.

[40] Lake, 'Rightful Rules' (n 39) 589.

[41] eg, Alter, Helfer and Madsen, 'Context' (n 28) 36–52; Zarbiyev, 'Saying Credibly What the Law Is' (n 17); F Zarbiyev, 'Cutting off the King's Head: Rethinking Authority in International Law' (2023) 14

conceptual approaches, especially in the political science literature. For example, realist approaches argue that power dynamics among member states and the interests of states related to that are a determining factor for their acceptance of the authority of international courts; and that the interests of member states are particularly at stake in so-called high-politics areas so that building authority relationships is expected to be more difficult for international courts in these areas.[42] In contrast, an institutionalist perspective – which is also closely related to many approaches in the legal literature on international courts – focuses on the institutional design of international courts as potential explanatory factors for their authority.[43] Relevant features in this regard are the independence of international courts as well as jurisdiction and access rules, aspects also addressed in the present book. In addition, in particular, the legal assessment of international court authority considers the jurisprudential practice of international courts and their strategies and potential 'activism' as factors for creating and maintaining authority.

In the present study, I focus on the explanatory dimension of authority, taking a multicausal approach. I indicate this by the use of the term 'factors'.[44] The present study – as are other studies on the authority of international courts – is based on the assumption that various factors interact, together creating an authority relationship which is not determined by only one causal factor.[45]

C. De Jure vs De Facto

A further distinction that plays a central role in the discussion about authority is the distinction between de jure authority and de facto authority.[46] The notion of de jure authority is connected to an understanding of authority as a 'right to rule' or 'rightful

Journal of International Dispute Settlement 285; E Shirlow, *Judging at the Interface: Deference to State Decision-Making Authority in International Adjudication* (CUP 2021) 15–42. On the factors suggested in the context of the research on court effectiveness, Shany (n 32); LR Helfer and A-M Slaughter, 'Toward a Theory of Effective Supranational Adjudication' (1997) 107 *Yale Law Journal* 273. Similar factors have also been suggested in the research on sociological legitimacy, see HG Cohen, A Føllesdal, N Grossman and G Ulfstein, 'Legitimacy and International Courts – A Framework' in Grossman et al (n 11) 1.

[42] eg, E Posner and J Yoo, 'Judicial Independence in International Tribunals' (2005) 93 *California Law Review* 1. See also on the high-politics nature of disputes as explanatory factor, MR Madsen, P Cebulak and M Wiebusch, 'Backlash against international courts: explaining the forms and patterns of resistance to international courts' (2018) 14 *International Journal of Law in Context* 197; S Caserta and P Cebulak, 'Resilience Techniques of International Courts in Times of Resistance to International Law' (2021) 70 *International & Comparative Law Quarterly* 737.

[43] eg, Helfer and Slaughter, 'Toward a Theory of Effective Supranational Adjudication' (n 41); LR Helfer and A-M Slaughter, 'Why States Create International Tribunals: A Response to Professors Posner and Yoo' (2005) 93 *California Law Review* 899; RO Keohane, A Moravcsik and A-M Slaughter, 'Legalized Dispute Resolution: Interstate and Transnational' (2000) 54 *International Organization* 457. See also Shany (n 32). Arguing for institutionalism as the empirically most accurate approach, B Zangl, A Helmedach, A Mondré, A Kocks, G Neubauer and K Blome 'Between Law and Politics: Explaining International Dispute Settlement Behavior' (2012) 18 *European Journal of International Relations* 369.

[44] Also using this terminology, Alter, Helfer and Madsen, 'Context' (n 28).

[45] Alter, Helfer and Madsen, 'Context' (n 28) 36, pointing to the 'overlap and interdependence' between various contextual factors.

[46] See for an early account of this distinction, J Day, 'Authority' (1963) 11 *Political Studies* 257, 263.

rule'.[47] Studies of de jure authority assess authority from a formal perspective. They look particularly at the (legal) rules that provide the mandate for an entity to exercise authority.[48] The extent to which this mandate in practice actually translates into an authoritative impact on actors is not part of the de jure notion of authority. This question is studied as part of the notion of de facto authority. De facto authority represents the factual ability rather than the 'right to rule'. It captures the behaviour of actors in practice, such as actors recognising 'through actual behaviour' the authority of an entity.[49]

De facto and de jure authority are not mutually exclusive. These notions fulfil different analytical functions. They assess the formal (de jure) and the practical (de facto) recognition of authority by actors. They reflect different aspects of analysing authority: they 'direct their attention to different stages in the process of authority recognition'.[50]

Being aware of the distinct analytical functions that the notions of de jure and de facto authority fulfil is important when comparing different concepts of authority. However, some authors seem to suggest that the notions of de facto and de jure authority apply to different entities, ie, that some entities exercise de jure authority and others 'merely' de facto authority. For example, Simmons states that possessing de facto authority 'consists merely in claiming, exercising, or being generally believed (by those subject to the authority or by suitable officials) to possess those rights'.[51] A similar approach seems to underlie Krisch's distinction between 'solid' and 'liquid' authority. For actors with 'formal powers', authority is assessed from a de jure perspective only (solid authority) while for actors without 'formal powers', authority is based on a de facto assessment (liquid authority). Such approaches risk misrepresenting de jure and de facto authority as a matter of degree of authority rather than as the different analytical concepts that they are in fact. An entity which possesses de jure authority can be assessed with regard to whether and to what extent it also has de facto authority.

In this book, I take a de facto authority approach. The first reason is that international courts are an object of study for which de facto and de jure authority often diverge significantly. Merely assessing what is written in the treaty establishing a court does not tell us how the court and other actors use these rules in practice and to what extent the court actually influences the behaviour of these actors. As Alter, Helfer and Madsen put it,

> a court's capacity to actually exercise authority cannot be measured by legal competences alone. Even if an IC has been vested with the formal authority to rule and actually does rule, this does not mean that its rulings induce changes in behavior. In other words, the

[47] On this understanding and its alternatives, see Enroth (n 26) 342. Stressing the term 'rightful rule', Lake, 'Rightful Rules' (n 39). See also the related distinction between authority with and without 'special right with regard to the actions of others' as presented by Simmons (n 15) 24.

[48] eg, Hooghe et al (n 30).

[49] P-O Busch and A Liese, 'The Authority of International Public Administrations' in MW Bauer, C Knill and S Eckhard (eds), *International Bureaucracy* (Palgrave Macmillan 2016) 97, 108.

[50] Busch and Liese (n 49) 110.

[51] Simmons (n 15) 25.

> formal elements of legal authority at the center of many legal debates might not resonate with the real-world actions of the audiences of ICs.[52]

The second reason is that only certain actors such as mandate providers and parties to disputes before international courts are addressed by formal rules and de jure authority. Other actors such as civil society groups, other courts or the general public are not part of this formal framework of international court authority. Referring to de facto authority makes it possible to capture the influence of international courts with regard to all relevant groups of actors.

That said, assessing de facto authority does not mean excluding the de jure dimension. Instead, the de jure dimension plays a role in the explanatory analysis of de facto authority. The formal rules and thus the extent of de jure authority can be considered as one of the factors for de facto authority.[53] The present book thus takes the de jure dimension *indirectly* into account, ie, as one of the factors that contribute to the de facto authority of international courts.

D. Attributive vs Relational

A further distinction that shapes the debate about authority is the distinction between attributive concepts of authority and relational concepts of authority. Attributive concepts understand authority as an *attribute of an actor* while relational concepts understand authority as a *relationship between actors*.[54] For attributive approaches, the focus is on one actor only. Authority is understood as a 'certain quality' of an actor 'which make subordinates adapt their beliefs and behaviour'.[55] In contrast, relational approaches refer to several actors at the same time. They define authority as a relational link between actors.[56] According to this approach, certain actors recognise the authority of an entity and thus create an authoritative relationship between them and that entity.[57]

Depending on whether one takes an attributive or a relational approach, the descriptive dimension of authority is perceived differently.[58] Authority is defined and described from an attributive perspective, for example, as an ability to issue commands. This ability is an attribute of the authoritative entity and thus authority is measured by observing this entity. In contrast, a relational approach determines

[52] KJ Alter, LR Helfer and MR Madsen, 'International Court Authority in a Complex World' in Alter, Helfer and Madsen (eds), *International Court Authority* (n 25) 3, 6.

[53] See also Day who states that '"legal" authority … is a strong motive for people to obey'; Day (n 46) 263.

[54] On this difference, OJ Sending, 'Recognition and liquid authority' (2017) 9 *International Theory* 311, 312.

[55] Zürn (n 24) 38.

[56] Kojève (n 13) 8. For a non-attributional approach, see also Zarbiyev, 'Cutting off the King's Head' (n 41).

[57] On recognition as element of a relational approach, Sending (n 54) 313–14.

[58] Relational accounts of authority have also been applied to the normative dimension of authority, eg I Venzke and J Mendes, 'The idea of relative authority in European and international law' (2018) 16 *International Journal of Constitutional Law* 75; N Roughan, *Authorities: Conflicts, Cooperation, and Transnational Legal Theory* (OUP 2013).

authority by observing both this entity and the actors at which the authoritative behaviour is aimed. Focusing on recognition as a relational link, authority is, for example, described as actors recognising the directives of another actor as binding. From this perspective, measuring authority requires detecting such recognition.

The difference between the two approaches also has a significant impact on the factors that explain authority. From an attributive perspective, one can claim that authority is based on certain personal characteristics of an actor. This claim is inherent to Weber's notion of 'charismatic authority' according to which authority is 'resting on devotion to the exceptional sanctity, heroism or exemplary character of an individual person'.[59] Similarly, more recent concepts such as notions of authority that refer to the expert knowledge of an actor can be presented as attributive. This is the case if 'expert authority' is primarily explained as resulting from the expertise of the authoritative entity and linked to moral integrity or moral claims of the entity.[60] In contrast, from a relational perspective, the abilities and characteristics of an actor alone do not constitute an explanatory factor. Rather, the abilities and characteristics need to be put into relation to the expectations or interests of other actors. Applied to the example of 'expert authority' that means the following: a relational account builds on the observation that an actor has a certain expertise, *and* other actors have an interest in guidance by an expert body. The basis for authority in this account is thus a functional relationship between actors rather than the mere ability of one actor.

In this book, I take a relational approach. I conceive the authority of international courts as a relationship between courts and other actors. A key advantage of this approach is that authority as a relational construct is dynamic rather than static. Authority is not merely understood as a static 'structure that empowers and constrains actors', rather it is 'affected by actors and their actions'.[61] Actors constantly reassess this relationship which can lead to 'questioning and re-designing' of the relationship.[62] Authority as a relationship is thus subject to change. In other words: the dynamism of authority emanates from the relationship between actors. With regard to international courts, understanding authority in such a dynamic way is of particular importance.[63] If we want to understand how international courts build authority and how and why this authority develops over time to become broader, narrower or even disappear, a static notion by its very nature would not provide the tools for assessing such developments. The ability to capture dynamics is thus an essential benefit of the relational understanding of authority in the context of international courts.

What is more, a relational approach in general seems to be better suited for studying the factors that explain authority. Although attributive notions of authority include elements of explanations, these explanations have their limits. Focusing

[59] Weber (n 13) 215.

[60] Barnett and Finnemore (n 21) 24; Zürn (n 24) 52.

[61] Zürn (n 24) 42.

[62] Zürn (n 24) 46. For Krisch, dynamism also includes that different actors recognise different bodies as authoritative with regard to a specific subject matter, see Krisch, 'Liquid authority' (n 17) 244.

[63] See also Zarbiyev, 'Saying Credibly What the Law Is' (n 17) 310.

merely on an attribute of the authoritative entity makes it difficult to explain why some entities that possess a certain attribute have authority while other entities with the same attribute do not. Therefore, in order to understand the factors for authority, one needs to look at the relationship between actors. As Sending puts it:

> If we want to empirically capture how authority emerges and how it may stabilize ... and be transformed over time, we need analytical concepts that focus on the relations between actors rather than working with pre-defined categories of particular actors.[64]

Among relational approaches, one can find two variations. The most common is probably a dyadic approach: authority is conceived as a relationship between actor 1 who exercises authority and actor 2 who is the subject of this authority. Triadic approaches include a third (set of) actor(s). Here, authority is said to require acceptance by a broader community of actors or a broader 'social belief' among a group of actors that an actor should be able to exercise authority.[65] A triadic approach thus views authority as a relationship between actor 1 and a group of actors rather than as a relationship between two individual actors (as dyadic approaches do). This stresses the social dimension of authority. It also includes the costs that other social actors impose on an actor in case of non-compliance.[66]

The concept of authority suggested in this book combines both approaches. As a starting point, I focus on the relationship between a court and a specific actor, assessing the factors that shape this dyadic authority relationship. Yet among these factors, I also consider the impact of other actors which can have a supporting or a constraining effect on the authority relationship between the court and an individual actor. I consider this a crucial aspect of analysing court authority as it allows us to uncover and interlink the dynamics at play between several actors.

In addition, taking a relational approach gives us a choice between different perspectives from which one can study the authoritative relationship between actors. One can take the perspective of the entity that exercises authority or the perspective of the actors subjected to authority. Both perspectives are present in the research on authority. The classical analytical question as to why actors comply with the directives issued by a specific entity generally reflects the actors-perspective. Yet this issue can also be framed from a different perspective when scholars analyse the 'compliance pull' of norms or authoritative entities.[67]

In this book, rather than taking the court's perspective as a starting point, I take the perspective of the other actors. The question is thus: when do *actors accept* the authority of international courts? Given that the research on international courts has so far often taken a court-centred perspective, the actor-centred approach provides novel insights. Referring to the (potential) subjects of authority as a starting point allows me to include the impact of the broader group of actors in a systematic manner. For that, I use a framework that assesses the motivations, opportunities and

[64] Sending (n 54) 313.

[65] Venzke, 'Semantic Authority' (n 25) 13. Also considering the belief among the actors that recognise authority, Lake, 'Relational Authority' (n 19) 347.

[66] Krisch, 'Liquid authority' (n 17) 242.

[67] eg, T Franck, 'Legitimacy in the International System' (1988) 82 *American Journal of International Law* 705.

constraints for actors that can enter authority relationships with international courts. I develop this framework in chapters two and three.

As a dimension of a relational understanding of authority, it is important also to explore the close link between the factors for acceptance and rejection of authority. This is often not the case in the research on international courts. While the literature on pushback against international courts focuses on rejection,[68] the literature on effectiveness and authority of international courts focuses on acceptance.[69] The link between the two is not sufficiently analysed. This book aims at exploring this link further, highlighting both the differences and overlaps regarding the factors that determine whether actors accept or reject international court authority.

In this regard, a relational approach to authority also requires considering potential strategies of courts to address changing circumstances and pushback tendencies. As the analysis in this book highlights, court strategies that aim at avoiding or managing conflict directly influence the factors that contribute to acceptance and rejection of authority. Courts can be active subjects of the authority relationship and play a role in shaping it.

II. CONCEPTUALISING AUTHORITY OF INTERNATIONAL COURTS: SPECIFIC FEATURES

This section turns to the specific features of international court authority. It stresses the contextual nature of the notion of authority (II.A) and outlines the defining features of international court authority (II.B).

A. A Contextualised Notion of Authority

While the previous section demonstrates that the notions of authority used in different contexts share common features, they cannot – and should not – be entirely decontextualised. The concept of authority aims at describing, explaining and

[68] eg, Madsen, Cebulak and Wiebusch (n 42); KJ Alter, JT Gathii and LR Helfer, 'Backlash against International Courts in West, East and Southern Africa: Causes and Consequences' (2016) 27 *European Journal of International Law* 293; X Soley and S Steininger, 'Parting ways or lashing back? Withdrawals, backlash and the Inter-American Court of Human Rights' (2018) 14 *International Journal of Law in Context* (2018) 237; A Hofmann, 'Resistance against the Court of Justice of the European Union' (2018) 14 *International Journal of Law in Context* 258; TG Daly and M Wiebusch, 'The African Court on Human and Peoples' Rights: mapping resistance against a young court' (2018) 14 *International Journal of Law in Context* 294; MR Madsen, 'The challenging authority of the European Court of Human Rights: from Cold War legal diplomacy to the Brighton Declaration and backlash' (2016) 79 *Law and Contemporary Problems* 141; H Lovat, 'International Criminal Tribunal Backlash' in KJ Heller, F Mégret, SMH Nouwen, JD Ohlin and D Robinson (eds), *Oxford Handbook of International Criminal Law* (OUP 2020) 601; J Powderly, 'International criminal justice in an age of perpetual crisis' (2019) 32 *Leiden Journal of International Law* 1; on investment arbitration: D Caron and E Shirlow, 'Dissecting Backlash: The Unarticulated Causes of Backlash and Its Unintended Consequences' in A Føllesdal and G Ulfstein (eds), *The Judicialization of International Law: A Mixed Blessing?* (OUP 2018) 159.

[69] eg, Alter, Helfer and Madsen, *International Court Authority* (n 25); Shany (n 32); Helfer and Slaughter, 'Toward a Theory of Effective Supranational Adjudication' (n 41); KJ Alter and LR Helfer, *Transplanting International Courts: The Law and Politics of the Andean Tribunal of Justice* (OUP 2017).

assessing real-world phenomena. It serves specific functions that can differ according to the context. For example, a notion that has been developed for the domestic context has its limits for the international context. Accordingly, suggestions such as 'liquid authority' or 'international public authority' react to the specific requirements of the authority on the international level. Similarly, the notion of authority must be adjusted if it is used in the transnational context.[70] Further, a notion that has been developed to analyse the authority of certain (international) actors such as international organisations can have its limits with regard to international courts. Suggestions in international relations such as 'political authority', 'expert authority' or 'epistemic authority' are primarily designed to address phenomena related to different types of international organisations, formal expert bodies or informal (private) entities that contribute to international and transnational governance.[71] International courts do not play a major role in the development of these notions; and consequently these notions do not capture the authority of courts very well. In this literature, international courts are generally categorised as entities with 'solid' or 'formal' authority as they operate on a formal legal basis – without however considering the details of how, to what extent, in what form and with regard to which actors the authority of international courts is exercised. As a result, the research on international courts has developed its own notions of authority. For example, the notion of authority of international courts as suggested by Alter, Helfer and Madsen emphasises different features as compared with notions that address the authority of other international and transnational entities.[72]

The notion of the authority of international courts suggested in this book explicitly acknowledges this need for – at least partial – specificity. Here, I give a brief overview of these specific features.

A feature of the concept of authority that is particularly relevant for international courts is to differentiate between the various actors that can enter an authority relationship with these courts. While notions of authority often differentiate between certain kinds of entities that exercise authority, it is less common to differentiate (also) between the subjects of authority. In the context of courts, such a differentiation is particularly fruitful. International courts can exercise authority vis-a-vis a broad range of actors, including – but not limited to – states and individuals as litigants, other courts, civil society groups, scholars and members of the general public. To fully assess the authority of international courts, these groups of actors must be analysed individually. The authoritative relationship between a court and the different groups of actors are not uniform. For example, the authority relationship that exists between a court and the parties to a dispute is different from the authority relationship between a court and the general public. A uniform concept of court authority does not allow us to capture these variations.[73] What is more, the factors that contribute to whether these actors recognise the authority of

[70] Cotterrell and Del Mar (n 22); Roughan, *Authorities* (n 58).

[71] Zürn (n 24) 52; Zürn, Binder and Ecker-Ehrhardt (n 12) 86; Busch and Liese (n 49).

[72] Alter, Helfer and Madsen, 'Context' (n 28).

[73] See also the critique on this point by Venzke regarding the notion of authority used by Alter, Helfer and Madsen in Venzke, 'De Facto Authority' (n 25).

a court can vary as well depending on the kind of the actor. Analytically, it is thus useful to distinguish between these actors when assessing factors for international court authority.

To map these relationships between a court and other actors, I take a broad approach to the notion of authority. This is in line with the notions mentioned above that construe authority as going beyond issuing binding commands to the subjects of their authority. For international courts, this approach is useful to reflect the multiple ways in which a court can influence the behaviour of actors – not all of which are formally bound by the court decisions. Although such broader notions might be criticised, in some contexts, for risking to erode authority as a concept, they have considerable explanatory value especially for international courts.[74]

As a consequence, the concept of authority used in this book does not understand every authority relationship to be hierarchical. While some scholars consider a hierarchy between the entity that exercises authority and the subject of authority to be intrinsic to the concept,[75] such a hierarchical understanding is less pertinent when the notion of authority goes beyond command.[76] For the context of international courts, hierarchy is of limited explanatory value and might even distort the assessment. For example, when considering the relationship between an international court and domestic courts or other international courts, hierarchy does not describe the authority relationship that exists between these courts. These courts generally consider themselves to be independent actors.[77]

Linked to a broad understanding of authority that goes beyond command is a further specific feature of the authority of international courts: the discursive dimension of authority. International courts operate in the 'juridical field' of which discourse is an essential element.[78] International court decisions influence the legal and non-legal discourse of, and with, other actors: 'international judicial decisions usually enjoy an exceptional standing in semantic disputes about what the law means'; they 'redistribute argumentative burdens, and no participant in international legal discourse can easily escape the spell of precedents'.[79] For international courts, the discursive dimension requires closer scrutiny than might be the case for some other authoritative entities. As an explicit notion in this regard, Venzke's concept of 'semantic authority' aims at capturing this link between discourse and authority. It considers when establishing 'reference points for legal discourse' can be regarded

[74] B Peters and JK Schaffer, 'The Turn to Authority beyond States' (2013) 4 *Transnational Legal Theory* 315, 321.

[75] Arendt (n 12) 93: 'the authoritarian order … is always hierarchical'. Sending defines authority as a hierarchical relationship 'between a superordinate and a subordinate actor', Sending (n 54) 314. See also Lake, 'Escape from the State of Nature' (n 27). On the hierarchical understanding of authority in IR literature, Busch and Liese (n 49).

[76] Krisch, 'Liquid authority' (n 17) 241.

[77] For a non-hierarchical approach to legitimate court authority, see eg, S Hentrei, 'Generalising the Principle of Complementarity: Framing International Judicial Authority' (2013) 4 *Transnational Legal Theory* 419, 431.

[78] P Bourdieu, 'The Force of Law: Toward a Sociology of the Juridical Field' (1987) 38 *Hastings Law Journal* 814. On legal discourse, see also J Habermas, *Faktizität und Geltung – Beiträge zur Diskurstheorie des Rechts und des demokratischen Rechtsstaats* (Suhrkamp 1992).

[79] Von Bogdandy and Venzke, *Investigation* (n 10) 18–19.

as exercise of authority.[80] With regard to the influence of international courts on discourse, the present book takes this concept into account.

In sum, the concept of authority suggested in this book aims at grasping the particularities of international courts concerning two main aspects. It considers that the nature of, and factors for, authority can vary depending on the actors that enter an authority relationship. And it takes a broad approach to authority which goes beyond command and puts an emphasis on discourse.

B. Defining Features of International Court Authority

This last section takes a closer look at the defining features of international court authority. It outlines both the relevant groups of actors and the substantive core of an authority relationship.

As this book conceptualises authority relationships towards international courts from the perspective of the actors, it is crucial to identify who the relevant actors are. Here, I take a broad approach with the aim of capturing the diverse authoritative interactions of international courts. Building on the categories suggested by Alter, Helfer and Madsen for the constituencies of international courts, I differentiate between four groups of actors. The first group – which I call *level 1 actors* – are the parties to a dispute before a court and actors formally charged with implementing the court decision at hand. Immediate parties to a dispute before an international court can, for example, be state governments, individuals, corporate actors and NGOs (depending on the jurisdiction of the court). Actors that are in charge of implementation without being immediately involved as parties to a dispute include domestic courts and domestic administrative agencies. Unlike for some accounts of international court authority,[81] the focus here is thus not only on states – neither for level 1 actors nor for other groups of actors. *Level 2 actors* are future parties to disputes and actors in charge of implementation of future court decisions. They act in the framework of an authority relationship with an international court, for example, when domestic policies, jurisprudence or laws are changed in line with the court's jurisprudence although no dispute has been brought against the respective state (yet). *Level 3 actors* are members of the broader legal audience. Such members might include actors that generally cannot be level 1 or level 2 actors such as other international courts or institutions and legal academics. Moreover, actors that can be level 1 or level 2 actors in some contexts might in other contexts fall into the category of level 3 actors. These include civil society groups and bar associations depending on whether they have formal access to the court; and domestic courts if they refer to decisions of international courts to which their state is not a member. *Level 4 actors* are members of the broader non-legal audience, for example members of the general public. These categories of actors are ideal types serving as analytical tools only. They do not exclude that, in practice, the dividing lines

[80] Venzke, 'Semantic Authority' (n 25) 1–2.
[81] Strongly linking international court authority to states, eg, Olsen (n 7).

between these categories are sometimes blurry. Nonetheless, the categorisation into four levels provides a structure highlighting the different authority relationships which are relevant for international courts.

Turning to the substance of an authority relationship involving international courts, the defining features are twofold. An encompassing notion of authority that takes into account its social dimension and the perspectives of all the parties concerned combines *attitude* and corresponding *behaviour* for assessing the authority relationship. This is a dual approach authors have taken in various context, including in authority and norm compliance research, and specifically for international court authority.[82] Terminologically, I group these two elements together as *accepting authority*. Actors accept authority when they believe that they ought to self-constrain in view of an authoritative entity and when they implement this belief into corresponding behaviour in concrete interactions with the entity. Assessing, in the context of international courts, the factors that contribute to actors accepting the authority of international courts is the objective of this book. The framework outlined in chapters two and three provides the tool for that.

The authority-related attitude is characterised by the actor's belief that one ought to self-constrain in view of an authoritative entity. The corresponding behaviour implements this belief as 'observable acts of the subject'.[83] The key feature of this definition is self-constraint.[84] Self-constraint has two components. First, the authority relationship constrains the behaviour of an actor. From the sum of potential behavioural options available to the actor, several options are excluded, in the eyes of the actor, due to the authority relationship. The actor perceives their options of how to act in a certain situation as limited when being in an authority relationship as compared with not being in this authority relationship. Second, *self*-constraint means that the actor voluntarily decides to constrain their behaviour in view of the authority relationship.[85] This voluntary decision is often referred to as an actor's 'consent' to the authority relationship with an entity.[86] This is (ideal-typically) opposed to a situation in which the actor is coerced by force or punishment to behave in a certain way.[87] This aspect corresponds

[82] eg, Alter, Helfer and Madsen, 'Context' (n 28) 29; V Braithwaite, 'Dancing with Tax Authorities: Motivational Postures and Non-compliant Actions' in V Braithwaite (ed) *Taxing Democracy: Understanding Tax Avoidance and Evasion* (Routledge 2003) 15; more broadly, this dual approach is also advocated in norm robustness research: N Deitelhoff and L Zimmermann, 'Norms under Challenge: Unpacking the Dynamics of Norm Robustness' (2019) 4 *Journal of Global Security Studies* 2, 6.

[83] M Fishbein and I Ajzen, *Belief, Attitude, Intention, and Behavior: An Introduction to Theory and Research* (Addison-Wesley Publishing Company 1975) 13.

[84] Referring to 'willing constraint' and 'willing deference' to authority, J Jackson and J Gau, 'Carving Up Concepts? Differentiating Between Trust and Legitimacy in Public Attitudes Towards Legal Authority' in E Shockley, TMS Neal, LM PytlikZillig and BH Bornstein (eds), *Interdisciplinary Perspectives on Trust* (Springer 2016) 49, 51, 64.

[85] On this voluntary nature, see also Max Weber who speaks of a 'minimum of voluntary compliance', Weber (n 13) 212.

[86] eg, Jackson and Gau (n 84). S Milgram, *Obedience to Authority* (Harper & Row 1974) 141: 'in the case of voluntary obedience to a legitimate authority, the principal sanctions for disobedience come from within the person'.

[87] The ideal-typical distinction between voluntary compliance and coercion by force does not exclude that there can be 'grey zones' in which elements of both coexist.

to the classical distinction outlined above between authority and 'coercion by force'.[88]

This self-constraint has a general and a specific dimension. The general and specific dimension is related to what has been described as 'diffuse support' and 'specific support' for an entity: the former constitutes fundamental commitment to an entity while the latter relates to the satisfaction with the entity's performance at the moment.[89] This distinction is particularly important for such situations of disobedience in which an actor can lack specific support regarding a specific decision while at the same time maintaining general support for the entity. The actor would then believe that, in general, one ought to obey decisions of this court, however believing that in the specific case, circumstances are such that the actor ought not obey the decision at hand.

For the authority relationship to courts, it is useful to distinguish two variations of self-constraint. In the first scenario, the actor believes that one ought to align one's behaviour with the content of a judicial decision. The correspondent behaviour is practical content alignment such as classical compliance. In a compliance situation, an actor who is the addressee of a court decision implements the instructions contained in the decision. For these actors, the belief that one ought to align one's behaviour with the judicial decision is thus the belief that one ought to comply with the judgment. For other actors, content alignment can mean adjusting one's behaviour with the content of a judicial decision *as if* the decision was addressed to this actor. For example, potential future litigants can implement a decision that is not addressed to them but concerns a similar legal problem as the one they are facing. In both cases, the actors believe that they ought to adjust their behaviour to the instructions given by the court in the operational part of its judgment. In addition to these situations, an actor's belief that one ought to align one's behaviour with a judicial decision can also relate to the interpretation of a legal norm. Here, actors believe that they ought to adjust their interpretation of a legal norm to that given by the court. For example, this can be the case when one court adopts an interpretation provided by another court.

In the second scenario, the self-constraint does not relate directly to the content of the court decision. Rather, it concerns the role of this decision for legal discourse. This aspect reflects the specificities that exists for courts as authoritative entities. It takes up the notion of 'semantic authority' developed by Venzke.[90] In a judicial decision, a court establishes 'reference points for legal discourse that other actors can hardly escape'.[91] This relates to the observations that scholars of the performance of international courts have made: often, 'the power of international courts and tribunals lies not so much in their quantitative record as in their role in … shaping

[88] Arendt (n 12) 93.

[89] On these notions in the context of authority: J Gibson, 'Legitimacy is for Losers: The Interconnections of Institutional Legitimacy, Performance Evaluations, and the Symbols of Judicial Authority' in B Bornstein and A Tomkins (eds), *Motivating Cooperation and Compliance with Authority* (Springer 2015) 81, 82; on the original notions: D Easton, 'A re-assessment of the concept of political support' (1975) 5 *British Journal of Political Science* 435.

[90] I Venzke, *How Interpretation Makes International Law: On Semantic Change and Normative Twists* (OUP 2012) 57–63; Venzke, 'Power and Persuasion' (n 14); Venzke, 'Semantic Authority' (n 25).

[91] Venzke, 'Semantic Authority' (n 25) 1; Venzke, 'Power and Persuasion' (n 14).

discourse'.[92] Also for regional courts in particular, authors have argued for an understanding of court performance that takes into account the 'indirect' rather than only the compliance-related 'direct' impact of courts, including their discursive impact.[93] Within this facet of authority, self-constraint thus concerns the rules and dynamics of discourse. The actors believe that one ought to refer to the court. Referring here means that when discussing a certain legal question, the actor feels compelled to discuss the position of the court on the matter. Referring does not require that the actor adopts the position of the court: it is sufficient to explicitly take it into account. The actor is thus constrained in the discursive practice rather than the discursive outcome. This behavioural impact of a court decision can be termed 'discursive reference', as opposed to the content alignment described above.

Figure 1.1. summarises the potential elements of an authority relationship of actors towards courts. For both versions of authoritative belief – content-related and discourse-related beliefs – there is a corresponding behaviour: content alignment and discursive reference. Based on this understanding of authority, the remainder of the book assesses the factors that contribute to developing and maintaining authority relationships between international courts and their audiences.

Figure 1.1 Elements of an authority relationship between a court and an actor

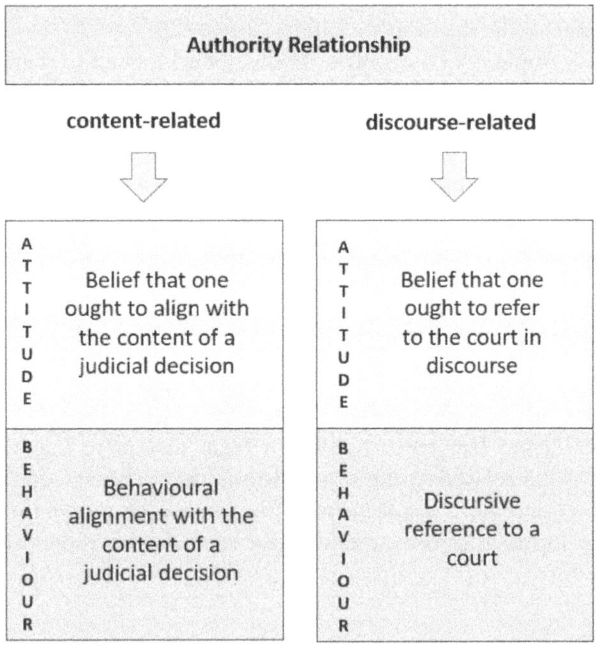

[92] C Stahn, 'Between "Faith" and "Facts": By What Standards Should We Assess International Criminal Justice?' (2012) 25 *Leiden Journal of International Law* 251.

[93] JT Gathii, 'Introduction – The Performance of Africa's International Courts' in JT Gathii (ed), *The Performance of Africa's International Courts: Using Litigation for Political, Legal, and Social Change* (OUP 2020) 1; ST Ebobrah and V Lando, 'Africa's Sub- Regional Courts as Back-Up Custodians of Constitutional Justice – Beyond the Compliance Question' in JT Gathii (ed), *The Performance of Africa's International Courts: Using Litigation for Political, Legal, and Social Change* (OUP 2020) 178.

2

The Factors for Authority: Introducing the MOC Framework

IN THIS CHAPTER, I develop a conceptual and analytical framework for the factors that shape authority. This framework implements the relational approach of authority which understands authority as a relationship between actors rather than the attribute of an entity (see chapter one). The suggested framework implements this approach by taking the perspective of the actors as a primary point of reference. The question that guides the analysis is: when do actors accept the authority of an entity? To answer this question, a behavioural perspective on authority offers valuable insights. It makes it possible to develop a framework that constructs authority from the perspective of the actors rather than from the authoritative entity. If we know under which circumstances an actor accepts the authority of an entity, we know when authority relationships develop and persist.

This chapter outlines the framework in general before chapter three links it in more detail to the context of international courts. In the first section, I sketch out the broad lines of behavioural research on which builds the suggested framework (section I). I then introduce the three-pronged structure of this framework which includes the factors motivation, opportunity and constraints (section II). I further develop this structure in a way that it can be operationalised in the context of authority (section III). In addition, I take a closer look at the specific situation of pushback against the authority of an entity (section IV). Finally, I highlight the benefits of this model for analysing the factors for authority (section V).

I. A BEHAVIOURAL PERSPECTIVE ON AUTHORITY

To develop a framework for authority, I draw on the research on human behaviour, a research field that combines findings from various disciplines such as psychology, sociology and economics and related disciplines. I use several general insights from that broad research field as a starting point for my approach.

At the core of the present approach is the key insight of behavioural research that behaviour is influenced by a plurality of factors. Based on the work of researchers such as Lewin, behaviour is classically understood as a function of both motivational forces stemming from the actors themselves and of environmental factors stemming from external circumstances.[1] This statement contains

[1] K Lewin, *Principles of Topological Psychology* (McGraw-Hill 1936).

multiple important aspects. To start with, it tells us that there are different kinds of factors, ie, behavioural factors can be grouped into categories that are diverging in nature. This implies that not all behavioural factors influence behaviour according to the same processes. Rather, one must consider for each category through which processes they influence behaviour.

Moreover, the above differentiation between motivational and environmental factors points to two important distinctions: the distinction between internal and external factors and the distinction between motivation and other factors. The former takes into account that the behaviour of an actor is not exclusively determined by this very actor; rather, it is also influenced by other actors and by material circumstances. The latter highlights the importance of motivational factors as a category, referring to the wealth of research that focuses on this aspect. Yet it also stresses that despite its importance, motivation is not the only factor. Only when assessing both these kinds of factors can one understand what drives an actor to behave in a certain way.

A further crucial insight related to the above approach is that behaviour is the result of the interaction of these factors. It is not sufficient to understand how each individual factor influences behaviour. Rather, one needs to take into account how the factors influence each other and whether (and under which circumstances) one factor might influence the behaviour more strongly than another factor or even trump it. Although behavioural research has been interested in this interrelation, there are still many unknowns – also specifically with regard to the context of authority. For international courts, this interaction has been debated, however so far without there being a convincing explanation of this interaction. This is a gap that this book will address.

Further, general insights stem from the research on behavioural change.[2] This line of research highlights that there might be different factors at play when assessing changing behaviour as compared with invariable behaviour.[3] Moreover, the notion of change emphasises the temporal dimension of behaviour. It relates to the question under which circumstances behaviour is invariable and a change in behaviour is durable. For example, some studies have shown that intrinsic and extrinsic motivational factors can diverge in how durable the behavioural change induced by them will be (an aspect further discussed below).[4]

Behavioural research – specifically social psychology – has examined behaviour in the context of authority. This includes two research questions: the factors for accepting authority and the factors for disobedience. Regarding the former, there has been a variety of studies on actors complying with norms, orders and decisions issued

[2] For an overview, see L Brennan, W Binney, L Parker, T Aleti, D Nguyen, *Social Marketing and Behaviour Change Models, Theory and Applications* (Edward Elgar 2014); T Chatterton, 'An introduction to theories of behaviour' in F Spotswood (ed), *Beyond Behaviour Change: Key Issues, Interdisciplinary Approaches and Future Directions* (University of Chicago Press 2016) 27.

[3] See also on the question whether changing circumstances as such (ie, independently of the way in which these circumstances change) can trigger a change in behaviour, C Engel, 'A Random Shock Is Not Random Assignment' (2016) 145 *Economics Letters* 45.

[4] W Binney, J Hall and P Oppenheim, 'The MOA framework and behavioural response' in *3Rs, Reputation Responsibility Relevance: Proceedings of the 2007 Australian and New Zealand Marketing Academy conference* 1144.

by political, judicial and executive entities. Here, the focus has been on motivation. An important issue in this regard has been the impact of procedural justice as a motivational factor. Scholars have specifically discussed the interrelation between procedural justice considerations and outcome favourability for determining whether actors implement decisions and, more generally, accept the authority of an entity.[5] This question highlights how factors within the same category (in this case motivation) interrelate. Furthermore, this line of research points to an aspect that is particularly important for international courts: the diversity of actors. It has shown that the behaviour of different groups of actors in an authority relationship is influenced by diverging factors.

While the research on obedience and the acceptance of authority more broadly has focused on motivation, studies on *dis*obedience have taken into account a wider range of factors.[6] Such factors include, for example, being 'prepared to disrupt the established social order', to be able to conceive of 'alternative definitions of the situation' and having the material resources to produce disobedience.[7] As I discuss below, these aspects are closely related to the suggested three-pronged model of factors that are relevant in authority relationships. This behavioural research on disobedience and the framework outlined in this book thus share a similar conceptual structure. More generally, the issue of disobedience is particularly relevant for assessing the pushback or resistance against authoritative entities – an issue that is important for international courts. The behavioural findings on disobedience can thus provide useful insights for this specific context. Furthermore, when studying courts, one can benefit from the behavioural research that takes a discursive take on disobedience. Studies on this aspect examine how communicative acts can shape a situation towards non-acceptance of authority.[8] This can contribute to understanding how actors influence each other through discourse resulting in pushback against courts.

Further, cognitive phenomena can influence the factors that determine authority relationships. This refers primarily to cognitive deviations from the rationality paradigm which characterises rational actor approaches in political science, economics and other fields of research. Such deviations include cognitive heuristics and biases

[5] TR Tyler and YJ Huo, *Trust in the Law: Encouraging Public Cooperation with the Police and Courts* (Russell Sage Foundation 2002); TR Tyler and A Lind, 'A Relational Model of Authority in Groups' (1992) 25 *Advances in Experimental Social Psychology* 115; J Brockner and BM Wiesenfeld, 'An Integrative Framework for Explaining Reactions to Decisions: Interactive Effects of Outcomes and Procedures' (1996) 120 *Psychological Bulletin* 189; T Stahl, J-W Van Prooijen and R Vermunt, 'On the psychology of procedural justice: reactions to procedures of ingroup vs. outgroup authorities' (2004) 34 *European Journal of Social Psychology* 173; PC Magalhães and L Aguiar-Conraria, 'Procedural Fairness, the Economy, and Support for Political Authorities' (2019) 40 *Political Psychology* 165. See also A Lind (ed), *Social Psychology and Justice* (Routledge 2020).

[6] In particular the experiments by Stanley Milgram and the related research, eg, S Milgram, *Obedience to Authority* (Harper & Row 1974); D Dolinski and T Grzyb, *The Social Psychology of Obedience Towards Authority: An Empirical Tribute to Stanley Milgram* (Routledge 2020); P Bocchiaro and P Zimbardo, 'On the dynamics of disobedience: experimental investigations of defying unjust authority' (2017) 10 *Psychology Research and Behavior Management* 219; P Bocchiaro and PG Zimbardo, 'Defying Unjust Authority: An Exploratory Study' (2010) 29 *Current Psychology* 155.

[7] HC Kelman and VL Hamilton, *Crimes of Obedience: Toward a social psychology of authority and responsibility* (Yale University Press 1989) 138.

[8] BL Parmar, 'Disobedience of Immoral Orders from Authorities: An Issue Construction Perspective' (2017) 38 *Organization Studies* 1373.

as described by prospect theory developed by Kahneman and Tversky and the subsequent research in the field of behavioural economics.[9]

A set of interrelated cognitive phenomena that are relevant for the assessment of authority relationships concern choices between behaviour as different options. First, the 'status quo bias' can influence these relationships. The status quo bias is a behavioural phenomenon that has been observed in a range of actors and situations. This term refers to people's tendency to place a higher value on any state of affairs that they consider to be the status quo than they would place on the same state of affairs if it were not the status quo.[10] This makes change less likely as the alternative situation is perceived as less valuable than the status quo. If the authority relationship is part of the status quo, this effect can contribute to perpetuating this relationship. A related notion is 'psychological inertia'. This is a phenomenon that also makes change less likely yet not because of a differently perceived value of the status quo but because change requires an additional and clear motivation for change.[11] If such a clear motivation for change does not exist, people perpetuate their current behaviour. Status quo bias and inertia are further linked to the default effect, a behavioural preference for the default option. Whether options are presented as opt-in or as opt-out, influences the likeliness that people decide for an option. It is more likely that they choose the option that happens to be presented as the default option.[12] Finally, a behavioural phenomenon that is used to explain some of the above effects but that can also stand alone is 'loss aversion'. This term describes the fact that people are more averse against a loss than an equivalent gain is attractive to them.[13] As a result, it is important for the choices an actor makes whether something is framed as a gain or a loss. Whereas a 'rational actor' would be expected to take the same decision irrespective of whether the choices are framed as a gain or as a loss, a decision-maker that is affected by loss aversion is less likely to decide in favour of a choice if it is presented as a loss scenario. This effect can become relevant in the discursive interaction between an authoritative entity and its audiences in which accepting authority can be framed as a gain or as a loss scenario.

A further important aspect of social psychology that is relevant in the authority context is group effects regarding behavioural conformity. Individuals are likely to conform with the behaviour of other members of a group when this behaviour is

[9] eg, D Kahneman and A Tversky, 'Prospect Theory: An Analysis of Decision under Risk' (1979) 47 *Econometrica* 263; D Kahneman and A Tversky, 'Judgment Under Uncertainty: Heuristics and Biases' (1974) 185 *Science, New Series* 1124; G Gigerenzer and R Selten (eds), *Bounded Rationality: The Adaptive Toolbox* (MIT Press 2002).

[10] W Samuelson and R Zeckhouser, 'Status Quo Bias in Decision Making' (1988) 1 *Journal of Risk and Uncertainty* 7; D Kahneman, J Knetsch and R Thaler, 'Anomalies: The Endowment Effect, Loss Aversion, and Status Quo Bias' (1991) 5 *Journal of Economic Perspectives* 193, 197–99; R Korobkin, 'The Status Quo Bias and Contract Default Rules' (1998) 83 *Cornell Law Review* 608.

[11] D Gal, 'A psychological law of inertia and the illusion of loss aversion' (2006) 1 *Judgment and Decision Making* 23.

[12] eg, EJ Johnson and DG Goldstein, 'Defaults and Donation Decisions' (2004) 78 *Transplantation* 1713; BC Madrian and DF Shea, 'The Power of Suggestion: Inertia in 401(k) Participation and Savings Behavior' (2001) 116 *Quarterly Journal of Economics* 1149.

[13] Kahneman, Knetsch and Thaler (n 10); E Zamir, 'Loss Aversion and the Law' (2012) 65 *Vanderbilt Law Review* 829.

perceived as being reflective of a social norm.[14] Social norms are 'rules and standards that are understood by members of a group and that guide and/or constrain social behavior without the force of laws'.[15] Conformity is a relevant factor for whether actors accept the authority of an entity or not. If an actor observes that other group members accept the authority of an entity, the conformity pull of the group effect makes it more likely that the actor will conform to this behaviour and also accept the authority of this entity. Inversely, less conformity among group members makes it less likely that an actor conforms with the majority behaviour. This is relevant both for accepting authority and for rejecting it. As to the latter, the 'true-partner effect' is an expression of this dynamic.[16] This term describes the behavioural phenomenon that actors are more likely not to conform with the majority of the group members when there is a second actor that shares their point of view as opposed to when all the other group members agree. The pressure towards conforming with the group is reduced when another actor also deviates from the majority approach.

On the individual level, a similar psychological factor that influences behaviour and can become relevant in the authority context is people's need for consistent behaviour. People have a tendency to behave in a manner that is consistent with previous behaviour.[17] This tendency can lead to a cognitive shortcut according to which decision-making is simplified by aligning with previous behaviour rather than assessing each situation anew.[18] Related to that is the notion of 'decisional inertia', that is 'the tendency to repeat previous choices independently of the outcome'.[19] For long-term relationships such as most authority relationships, these consistency-driven effects are important. They can contribute to maintaining existing authority relationships despite changing circumstances.

Finally, a behavioural phenomenon that can play a role for authority relationships is the 'foot-in-the-door' technique.[20] This technique uses the observation that 'once someone has agreed to a small request he is more likely to comply with a larger request'.[21] In an authority context, this technique compels actors 'to gradually escalate

[14] Early studies on this effect include M Sherif, *The Psychology of Social Norms* (Harper & Row 1936); S Asch, *Social Psychology* (Prentice-Hall 1952); S Asch, 'Opinions and social pressure' (1955) 193 *Scientific American* 31.

[15] RB Cialdini and MR Trost, 'Social Influence: Social Norms, Conformity, and Compliance' in DT Gilbert, ST Fiske and G Lindzey (eds), *The Handbook of Social Psychology* (McGraw-Hill 1998) 151, 152.

[16] For the first empirical study on this effect, see SE Asch, 'Effects of group pressure on the modification and distortion of judgments' in H Guetzkow (ed), *Groups, Leadership, and Men* (Carnegie Press 1951) 177. See also WN Morris and RS Miller, 'The Effects of Consensus-Breaking and Consensus-Preempting Partners on Reduction of Conformity' (1975) 11 *Journal of Experimental Social Psychology* 215. On physical proximity of another 'rebel' as factor for disobedience, Bocchiaro and Zimbardo, 'On the dynamics of disobedience' (n 6).

[17] RB Cialdini, *Influence: Science and Practice*, 5th edn (Pearson Education 2009) 51 et seq.

[18] ibid 54.

[19] C Alós-Ferrer, S Hügelschäfer and J Li, 'Inertia and Decision Making' (2016) 7 *Frontiers in Psychology* 169.

[20] JL Freedman and SC Fraser, 'Compliance without pressure: the foot-in-the-door technique' (1966) 4 *Journal of Personality and Social Psychology* 195; on the effect of this technique in 'unjust authority' situations, Bocchiaro and Zimbardo, 'Defying Unjust Authority' (n 6) 166.

[21] Freedman and Fraser (n 20).

their obedience'.[22] This effect is explained by different psychological processes, including the need for consistent behaviour.[23] For the person or entity making the requests, the foot-in-the-door effect thus means that it makes sense to first ask for something small before requesting something more intrusive or demanding. This technique can also work for obtaining high-cost behaviour by actors if the requests are increased gradually.[24] It can be linked to strategies of authoritative entities as to how to expand and strengthen their authority.

In this book, I make use of these insights to provide a behavioural model of authority that can further the understanding of international court authority. Analysing the factors that contribute to actors accepting authority or to reject it, I address the question: what are these factors and how do they interrelate? Through the MOC framework developed below, I categorise the factors that have been discussed in the context of authority and specifically court authority according to how they influence behaviour. This makes it possible to understand the functioning of the individual factors. At the same time, it provides a basis for analysing the interrelations among factors.

II. INTRODUCING THE MOTIVATION – OPPORTUNITY – CONSTRAINT (MOC) FRAMEWORK

In this section, I introduce the model on which the conceptual and analytical framework developed in this book is based. I have chosen this model because it is very well suited for explaining how and when authority relationships develop. Among its many benefits that I outline in more detail in section V, the framework inspired by this model makes it possible to include a range of relevant factors rather than focusing on one specific factor alone as well as to assess and uncover the relations between these factors. It further speaks to the relational character of authority and its 'social dimension' by taking into account the relationship between various (groups of) actors. And it makes it possible to assess and explain changes in authority relationships as well as providing a reference point for comparison among different authoritative entities.

A. The MOA Model

The framework for authority factors suggested in this book is based on the motivation–opportunity–ability model (MOA). I adapt this model to the authority context and complement it with further insights from behavioural research. The MOA model has been used for various analytical purposes, including explaining behaviour relating

[22] Bocchiaro and Zimbardo, 'Defying Unjust Authority' (n 6) 166.

[23] JM Burger, 'The Foot-in-the-Door Compliance Procedure: A Multiple-Process Analysis and Review' (1999) 3 *Personality and Social Psychology Review* 27.

[24] M Goldman, CR Creason and CG McCall, 'Compliance employing a two-feet-in-the-door procedure' (1981) 114 *Journal of Social Psychology* 259.

to social marketing, knowledge sharing, consumer choice and work performance.[25] Similar models also exist in other fields of research, such as criminology, that analyse the behaviour of actors.[26] The MOA model provides three categories of factors for behaviour: the motivation of the actor to adopt a certain behaviour; the opportunity that the actor has for this behaviour; and the ability to behave in this way. Each of these factors is necessary for the behaviour to materialise. One factor alone cannot induce the targeted behaviour (see also section III.D).

Motivation according to the MOA model is defined as goal-directed arousal.[27] Motivation can come in two variations: intrinsic and extrinsic motivation. Extrinsic motivation is understood as 'a type of motivation that is controlled by externalities that are not part of the activity or behaviour they are influencing'.[28] Such extrinsic motivation can emanate from extrinsic incentives such as financial rewards and recognition in the community.[29] In contrast, intrinsic motivation encourages 'behaviour for its inherent satisfactions rather than for some separable external consequence' (intrinsic motivation in the narrow sense)[30] or it is based on 'motives that are … intrinsic to the person – that is, where rewards are found within the person as distinct from some external source' (intrinsic motivation in the broader sense).[31] The former is, for example, the case when actors enjoy the behaviour as such; the latter when the behaviour is in line with one's values or is accepted as personally important.[32]

Opportunity 'represents the environmental or contextual mechanisms that enable action'.[33] Accordingly, 'lack of opportunity includes situations in which the individual wants to act but is unable to do so because there is no [mechanism enabling this action] at hand'.[34] Here, it is, for example, relevant whether technical preconditions are fulfilled. Some authors address these aspects as elements of a

[25] DJ MacInnis, C Moorman and BJ Jaworski, 'Enhancing and Measuring Consumers' Motivation, Opportunity, and Ability to Process Brand Information from Ads' (1991) 55 *Journal of Marketing* 32; M Blumberg and CD Pringle, 'The missing opportunity in organizational research: some implications for a theory of work performance' (1982) 7 *Academy of Management Review* 560; J Boudreau, W Hopp, JO McClain, LJ Thomas, 'On the interface between operations and human resources management' (2003) 5 *Manufacturing & Service Operations Management* 179; W Binney, J Hall and P Oppenheim, 'The nature and influence of motivation within the MOA framework: implications for social marketing' (2006) 11 *International Journal of Nonprofit and Voluntary Sector Marketing* 289; E Siemsen, AV Roth and S Balasubramanian, 'How motivation, opportunity, and ability drive knowledge sharing: The constraining-factor model' (2008) 26 *Journal of Operations Management* 426; Binney, Hall and Oppenheim, 'The MOA framework (n 4).

[26] On a model composed of the elements of motivation, opportunity and constraint, see D Kauzlarich and R Kramer, *Crimes of the American Nuclear State: At Home and Abroad* (Northeastern University Press 1998); DL. Rothe and CW Mullins, 'Toward a Criminology of International Criminal Law: An Integrated Theory of International Criminal Violations' (2009) 33 *International Journal of Comparative and Applied Criminal Justice* 97.

[27] MacInnis, Moorman and Jaworski (n 25) 34; ML Rothschild, 'Carrots, sticks and promises: a conceptual framework for the management of public health and social issues behaviour' (1999) 63 *Journal of Marketing* 24, 31.

[28] Binney, Hall and Oppenheim, 'The MOA framework' (n 4) 1144.

[29] ibid.

[30] ibid 1145; see also RM Ryan and EL Deci, 'Self-determination theory and the facilitation of intrinsic motivation, social development, and well-being' (2000) 55 *American Psychologist* 68, 71.

[31] D Beswick, *Cognitive Motivation: From Curiosity to Identity, Purpose and Meaning* (CUP 2017) 65.

[32] Ryan and Deci (n 30) 72–73; Beswick (n 31) 65–66.

[33] Siemsen, Roth and Balasubramanian (n 25) 427.

[34] Rothschild (n 27) 31.

'behavioural infrastructure'.[35] Although behavioural infrastructures are intended to enable behaviour, their concrete design can 'facilitate and/or prevent (create barriers to) specific behaviours from taking place'.[36] What is characteristic for the behavioural infrastructure that determines the opportunity for an actor is that the actor has no direct control over the elements of this infrastructure.[37] To illustrate: even if actors are motivated to recycle plastics, they cannot do so if there is no recycling system in place in their town. The opportunity factors are thus such that cannot be unilaterally changed, circumvented or ignored by the actors themselves.

The *ability* of an actor is determined by the actor's skills and personal resources (time, money etc) that are necessary for a certain behaviour.[38] This includes the ability of an actor to overcome constraints. Such constraints might be social pressure exercised by other actors; it can also be a habit of the actors themselves that is contrary to the targeted behaviour.[39]

B. From MOA to MOC

Referring to ability as a factor presents a challenge with regard to conceptualising constraints and their impact on behaviour. There is a difference between the existence of constraints on the one hand and the ability of the actor to overcome constraints on the other. Both are relevant – but both should be assessed individually. To illustrate: in a situation in which there are no constraints, it does not matter to what extent an actor has the ability to overcome constraints. The existence of constraints rather than the ability to overcome them is the primary behavioural factor. All other things being equal, without the existence of constraints, there would be no difference in the behaviour of an actor with a strong ability to overcome constraints and an actor with limited ability to overcome constraints. Similarly, low constraints are easier to overcome than high constraints – so overcoming low constraints would be possible even for such actors with limited ability to overcome constraints. The higher the constraints, the less actors might overcome them. For a comparative analysis of behaviour, the model should thus primarily refer to the existence of constraints. In many circumstances, constraints are also better observable than the ability to overcome them.

In this book, I therefore use a modified version of the MOA model. I rephrase the ability factor by focusing on its element of *constraint*. This includes primarily the existence of constraints and, only as a secondary aspect, the ability to overcome them. Constraints make it more difficult to engage in a certain behaviour. Narrow constraints thus mean that the respective actor has a high unconstrained ability to behave in

[35] L Brennan, W Binney, L Parker, T Aleti and D Nguyen, 'Behavioural models (conative models)' in Brennan et al, *Social Marketing* (n 2) 41, 61–64.

[36] ibid 61.

[37] Blumberg and Pringle (n 25) 565.

[38] Rothschild (n 27) 32. Instead of the term 'ability', some authors use the term 'capability', see eg, S Michie, MM van Stralen and R West, 'The behaviour change wheel: a new method for characterising and designing behaviour change interventions' (2011) 6 *Implementation Science* 42.

[39] Rothschild (n 27) 32.

the targeted manner. Mirroring the differentiation used for motivation, I distinguish between *intrinsic* constraints and *extrinsic* constraints. Intrinsic constraints refer to the actor's skills and personal resources. When actors do not have many personal resources such as time or money or they lack certain skills, they are limited in their ability to adopt certain behaviours. Extrinsic constraints are constraints exercised by other actors. This is, for example, the case if one actor puts pressure on the other with the aim of preventing a certain behaviour.

I thus refer to the factors *motivation*, *opportunity* and *constraints* as constitutive elements of what I call the *MOC framework*.

The MOC factors also have a subjective dimension that relates to the perception that the actor has regarding certain factors. For example, actors can have diverging perceptions of the social practice in their group which might lead one actor to perceive this social practice as more favourable than the other actor does.[40] Actors can also have diverging perspectives of how effective their behaviour would be. This aspect is at the heart of the 'self-efficacy model' which addressed the behavioural impact of an actor's perception that 'acting is worthwhile, likely to be effective'.[41] Further, in the context of the subjective dimension, the above-mentioned ability to overcome constraints becomes relevant again. In this regard, 'the one who perceives that they have the greatest ability to determine the outcomes will be the most likely to succeed'.[42] The subjective dimension can also be influenced by cognitive heuristics and biases as well as other psychological phenomena mentioned in the previous section. For example, actors can perceive motivational factors differently depending on whether they appear as the default option, in a loss framing or a gain framing. When assessing behaviour, this subjective dimension should be taken into account.

III. EXPLAINING AUTHORITY FROM THE PERSPECTIVE OF MOC

After having presented MOC as a framework for analysing behaviour in general, I now turn to its application to authority relationships. In what follows, I develop each of the MOC factors for the context of authority: the motivation to accept authority (III.A); the opportunity to accept authority (III.B); and constraints against accepting authority (III.C). I show how the factors interact and how to find out the determining factor for each specific MOC setting (III.D).

A. Motivation to Accept Authority

The individual factors that determine the motivation of an actor for accepting the authority of an entity can be manifold. These factors can contribute to both intrinsic and extrinsic motivation.

[40] See also I Ajzen, 'The Theory of Planned Behavior' (1991) 50 *Organizational Behavior and Human Decision Processes* 179, 188.

[41] Brennan et al, 'Behavioural models' (n 35) 43.

[42] Chatterton (n 2) 35.

Intrinsic motivational factors for accepting authority include a value-based motivation. Values such as, for example, procedural justice can motivate people to accept the authority of an entity. Intrinsic motivation is particularly important for authority as a long-term relationship. Actors who are intrinsically motivated to engage in a certain behaviour are 'more likely to maintain the practise without the presence of extrinsic rewards to motivate them to continue'.[43] For authority relationships that means, if actors accept the authority of an entity because of intrinsic motivation, they might be more likely to continue to show this behaviour in a durable manner.[44] Inversely, when actors are, for the most part, extrinsically motivated to accept authority, their behaviour is more vulnerable to varying external factors and thus more likely to change. With a view on assessing and developing strategies to motivate actors to accept authority, focusing on intrinsic motivation can thus be beneficial.

Extrinsic motivational factors include external incentives to accept authority. An actor can receive such external incentives from other actors, intentionally or unintentionally. Actors might promise benefits to an actor if the latter accepts the authority of an entity. For example, such a benefit could be the membership within a group to which accepting authority is made the explicit precondition. Taking into account extrinsic motivation implements the triadic approach to authority outlined in chapter one. This triadic approach considers the impact that actors have on each other with regard to their respective authority relationships with an entity.

Two motivational factors are of predominant importance in the context of authority relationships: values and interests. Although a clear-cut distinction between the two might not always be possible, using values and interests as analytical categories for motivational factors allows us to highlight the influence of structural and durable motivational factors such as values on the one hand as well as actor-specific and more variable motivational factors such as interests on the other.[45]

Values

Values are the first key factor for motivation. One can define values as 'enduring beliefs about desirable goals'.[46] These goals are of a structural kind and do not need to be in the immediate interests of the actor.

When values constitute an intrinsic motivational factor, accepting authority is a means to implement the actor's own values. To designate the extent to which entities and actors share values, I use the term *value-correspondence*. A high

[43] Binney, Hall and Oppenheim, 'The nature and influence of motivation within the MOA framework' (n 25) 292.

[44] Also emphasising the importance of intrinsic motivation for authority relationships, Tyler and Huo (n 5) 26–27.

[45] Pointing to the difference between individual interests on the one hand and, on the other, other values and shared understandings of social structures in the context of authority, M Zürn, *A Theory of Global Governance: Authority, Legitimacy, and Contestation* (OUP 2018) 44.

[46] L Brennan, W Binney, L Parker, T Aleti and D Nguyen, 'Emotional models (affective models)' in Brennan et al, *Social Marketing* (n 2) 79, 96 (Table 9.2).

value-correspondence can constitute a strong motivational factor for authority. In the scholarship on authority, the idea of value-correspondence is addressed as a relevant factor for the relationship between an authoritative entity and an actor. For example, Jackson and Gau refer to 'normative alignment' as a factor for cooperation with authoritative entities.[47] Actors evaluate whether entities 'act in ways that accord with societal values about how their power should be exercised'.[48] If an actor considers an entity to be aligned with the actor's values, 'this activates corresponding norms about how [the actors themselves] should behave' – thus fostering cooperative behaviour.[49] From a political science perspective, Zürn and colleagues have pointed out for 'political authority' that it 'depends on a common normative framework that provides a shared understanding of what the common good really is'.[50] In this statement, value-correspondence is seen as an essential factor for authority relationships. Similarly, Sending explains 'moral authority' as 'advance[ing] shared social and political objectives'.[51] Here, actors recognise an entity as 'moral authority' when they consider this entity to share their values and promote them. Regarding (domestic) courts, Christenson and Glick point to 'ideological congruence' between actors and courts as a factor that influences whether actors perceive courts as legitimate.[52] For the context of international courts, Achiume has developed a comparable notion.[53] She uses the terms 'socio-political dissonance' and 'socio-political resonance'. The former describes 'a state that results when a legal decision contradicts or undermines deeply held norms … that a given society or community forms on the basis of its social, political, and economic history'.[54] The latter describes 'the quality of affirming or according with a given society's norms as informed by its sociopolitical history'.[55] Sociopolitical dissonance and resonance illustrate whether the values reflected in the actions of the entity – that is, the jurisprudence of the international court – correspond to the values held by the relevant actors, here the society of the member states to the court. For Achiume, this is a determining factor for whether the authority of an international court is accepted or not. Similarly, contributions on specific value-bases such as for human rights courts have pointed to the importance of comparing the

[47] J Jackson and J Gau, 'Carving Up Concepts? Differentiating Between Trust and Legitimacy in Public Attitudes Towards Legal Authority' in E Shockley, TMS Neal, LM PytlikZillig and BH Bornstein (eds), *Interdisciplinary Perspectives on Trust* (Springer 2016) 49. Similarly, using the term 'moral alignment': J Jackson, B Bradford, M Hough, A Myhill, P Quinton and TR Tyler, 'Why Do People Comply With The Law? Legitimacy and the Influence of Legal Institutions' (2012) 52 *British Journal of Criminology* 1051, 1061; TR Tyler and J Jackson, 'Popular Legitimacy and the Exercise of Legal Authority: Motivating Compliance, Cooperation and Engagement' (2014) 20 *Psychology, Public Policy, and Law* 78.

[48] Jackson and Gau (n 47) 57.

[49] ibid.

[50] M Zürn, M Binder and M Ecker-Ehrhardt, 'International Authority and its Politicization' (2012) 4 *International Theory* 69, 87.

[51] OJ Sending, 'Recognition and liquid authority' (2017) 9 *International Theory* 311, 312.

[52] DP Christenson and DM Glick, 'Supreme Court's Legitimacy' (2015) 59 *American Journal of Political Science* 403.

[53] ET Achiume, 'The SADC Tribunal Sociopolitical Dissonance and the Authority of International Courts' in KJ Alter, LR Helfer and MR Madsen (eds), *International Court Authority* (OUP 2018) 124.

[54] ibid 125.

[55] ibid.

values reflected in domestic institutions and those represented and implemented by an international court.[56]

For assessing authority as a long-term relationship, it is relevant to consider that value-correspondence can increase or decrease over time. Values are not necessarily static: the values of the actors and/or the values of the authoritative entity can change. For a situation in which the values *of the entity* change, the above-mentioned notions of habituation and internalisation become relevant to explain stable value-correspondence. Habituation can explain why actors over time accept that authoritative entities have changed their values: actors get used to the new values of the entity. What is more, they might over time not only accept them as values of the entity but even internalise them as their own values.[57] If this is the case, actors do not perceive changed values of the entity as conflicting with the actor's own values: they have come to share the same values.[58] Of course, there is no guarantee that in each case in which an entity changes its values actors will in fact be habituated to these values or even internalise them. The alternative is decreasing value-correspondence which potentially weakens the actor's motivation for accepting authority.

For a situation in which the *actors* initially change their values, thus decreasing value-correspondence, strategies of the authoritative entity to address this issue become relevant. The entity might try to re-increase value-correspondence by adjusting its own values to the values of the actors. If successful, this balances out the changed values and, in sum, preserves value-correspondence. Such strategies of international courts are addressed in Part II of this book.

Although the values that can motivate actors to accept authority are manifold, I specifically highlight at this point a value that has been prominently discussed in behavioural scholarship on authority: procedural justice. Several studies have shown that procedural justice has a strong motivational impact both for compliance by level 1 actors and for acceptance of, and support for, authoritative entities by other actors.[59] The extent to which actors perceive an entity's decision-making process as fair significantly influences whether they accept this entity's authority. Importantly,

[56] B Çalı, A Koch and N Bruch, 'The Legitimacy of Human Rights Courts: A Grounded Interpretivist Analysis of the European Court of Human Rights' (2013) 35 *Human Rights Quarterly* 955.

[57] On actors 'internaliz[ing] the value that it is morally just to obey the law', Jackson et al (n 47) 1055.

[58] See also I Hurd, 'Legitimacy and Authority in International Politics' (1999) 53 *International Organization* 379, 388.

[59] Examples of studies on the matter include: Tyler and Huo (n 5); TR Tyler, JD Casper and B Fisher, 'Maintaining Allegiance toward Political Authorities: The Role of Prior Attitudes and the Use of Fair Procedures' (1989) 33 *American Journal of Political Science* 629; TR Tyler, A Lind and Y Huo, 'Cultural Values and Authority Relations – The Psychology of Conflict Resolution Across Cultures' (2000) 6 *Psychology, Public Policy, and Law* 1138; MD Ramirez, 'Procedural Perceptions and Support for the U.S. Supreme Court' (2008) 29 *Political Psychology* 675; M Kleine, P Langenbach and L Zhurakhovska, 'How voice shapes reactions to impartial decision-makers: An experiment on participation procedures' (2017) 143 *Journal of Economic Behavior & Organization* 241. On procedural justice as a factor for confidence in domestic courts, SC Benesh, 'Understanding Public Confidence in American Courts' (2006) 68 *Journal of Politics* 697. On the effect of procedural justice vis-a-vis an 'outgroup authority' as compared to an 'ingroup authority', T Stahl, J-W Van Prooijen and R Vermunt, 'On the psychology of procedural justice: reactions to procedures of ingroup vs. outgroup authorities' (2004) 34 *European Journal of Social Psychology* 173.

such an impact exists both for actors who benefit from an individual decision and actors who do not. In particular Tyler and colleagues have shown that there is a 'relationship between an individual's perception that a procedure was fair and his or her willingness to accept the outcome regardless of whether a favorable and unfavorable outcome was being delivered'.[60] This procedural justice value also constitutes a motivational factor for actors who are not directly addressed by the orders or decisions of an authoritative entity.[61]

Furthermore, procedural justice is a good example to highlight the following point: the more important a certain value is for an actor, the higher is the motivational potential of this value. For procedural justice, comparative cross-cultural studies emphasise this statement.[62] The procedural justice performance of an entity does not have the same motivational effect for all actors. The effect varies depending on the normative preference of an actor for a 'consultative' or 'autocratic' style of authority.[63] When comparing actors with these preferences, the former are more likely to put weight on procedural justice when evaluating dispute resolution. The importance that actors contribute to procedural justice as a value thus influences to what extent this value is a motivational factor for accepting authority despite negative outcomes.

Interests

The interests of an actor are the second key factor for motivation. Interests are often part of a behavioural analysis that takes a rational choice approach. According to this approach, actors behave in a rational and consistent manner in order to 'maximise utility'. This understanding of rational choice focuses on the 'maximization in pursuit of self-interest'.[64] It relates to immediate economic, social or political benefits. The interests of the 'rational actor' are used as a reference point for many behavioural models, including on behaviour change.[65] Interests are thus an important aspect to be included in the MOC framework.

In the political science literature on authority, interests are discussed as an element of a realist model of authority. This model presents authority as

> an instrumental and calculated assessment of the net benefits of compliance versus non-compliance, with an instrumental attitude toward social structures and other people. The task of the governing agent becomes to structure incentives so that community members find compliance the most rationally attractive option.[66]

[60] Tyler and Huo (n 5) 56.

[61] eg, Ramirez (n 59). However, according to some studies, personal experience with a court seems to increase the impact of procedural justice considerations, SM Olson and DA Huth, 'Explaining public attitudes toward local courts' (1998) 20 *Justice System Journal* 41.

[62] Tyler, Lind and Huo (n 59).

[63] ibid 1140.

[64] A Sen, 'Rational Behaviour' in SN Durlauf and LE Blume (eds), *The New Palgrave Dictionary of Economics*, 2nd edn (Palgrave Macmillan, 2008) 68 = *The New Palgrave Dictionary of Economics*, DOI 10.1057/978-1-349-95121-5_1568-2, at 3.

[65] For an overview of rational choice-based models on behaviour change, see L Brennan, W Binney, L Parker, T Aleti and D Nguyen, 'Rational economic models (cognitive models)' in Brennan et al, *Social Marketing* (n 2) 17.

[66] Hurd (n 58) 385.

At first glance, an interest-based behaviour of actors might seem opposed to an understanding of authority that is based on the actor's belief that one ought to align one's behaviour with an order or decision of an authoritative entity. It seems to describe mere 'instrumental compliance' where an actor assesses each decision about compliance or non-compliance only in view of self-interest – whether in gaining awards or avoiding punishment.[67] However, an interest-based understanding of authority is possible. It does not imply a 'continuous reassessment of every rule and relationship from an instrumental point of view' but rather a situation in which the actors base their acceptance of the 'existing structure of relations and institutions' on interests.[68] Thus, what matters for the MOC framework are the interests that motivate actors to be part of an authority relationship.

The interests that motivate the behaviour of actors can be manifold and strongly depend on the authority situation at hand. Broadly, possible interests include specific economic, social and political interests. Illustrations for such specific interests that are relevant in the context of international courts are provided in Part II of this book.

Interests can also be of a more general nature. For example, actors can have an interest in efficient decision-making. Actors can consider accepting the authority of an entity and following its instructions to be a more efficient way of decision-making than assessing every choice independently.[69] It is a way of outsourcing responsibility and reducing decision-making efforts.[70] A further general interest that can motivate actors to continuously accept the authority of an entity is the interest in consistent behaviour. As mentioned in section I, people are inclined to behave in a manner that is consistent with their previous behaviour.[71] This can be a relevant motivational factor for accepting authority in general and for specific kinds of behaviour within authority relationships. The latter include repetitive situations such as being a recurrent respondent before a court. The longer the behaviour is perpetuated, the more likely it is that actors perceive their interest in consistent decision-making as a substantial motivational factor for accepting the authority of the entity.

Values and Interests as Reflected in Other Concepts

In developing the motivational factor of MOC, I do not directly include the notion of legitimacy of the authoritative entity. This is a deliberate choice in the interest of analytical clarity. I acknowledge that, often, the legitimacy of an entity is discussed as a factor that would motivate actors to recognise the authority of the entity.[72]

[67] Jackson et al (n 47) 1055.

[68] Hurd (n 58) 386.

[69] Considering compliance as an instance of 'habitual or routinized behaviours' due to which actors do not have to make case-by-case judgments, Jackson et al (n 47) 1053, 1055.

[70] On responsibility perceptions as an aspect of obedience and disobedience, D Kaposi, 'The resistance experiments: Morality, authority and obedience in Stanley Milgram's account' (2017) 47 *Journal for the Theory of Social Behaviour* 382.

[71] Cialdini (n 17).

[72] For a legitimacy-related approach in the behavioural literature, eg, TR Tyler, *Why People Obey the Law* (Yale University Press 1990); Jackson et al (n 47); Jackson and Gau (n 47); J Gibson, 'Legitimacy Is for Losers: The Interconnections of Institutional Legitimacy, Performance Evaluations, and the Symbols

However, I consider that rather than referring to the notion of legitimacy, it is more fruitful for the present study to refer directly to the aspects that the notion of legitimacy comprises. In fact, what is at the core of the notion of legitimacy is interests and values. For example, legitimacy is defined as 'a generalized perception or assumption that the actions of an entity are desirable, proper, or appropriate within some socially constructed system of norms, values, beliefs, and definitions'.[73] In this definition, legitimacy is in essence described as value-correspondence. The values of the entity and the values of the actors that consider this entity to be 'legitimate' correspond. One of the advantages of referring directly to values and interests rather than referring to them by the detour of legitimacy is better observability. If the perception of legitimacy that actors have towards an entity is understood as a 'subjective feeling',[74] such a feeling would elude 'behavioural observation'.[75] In contrast, interests and values are also often reflected in statements and behaviour in contexts other than the authority relationship so that they are more easily observable.

A similar argument can be made regarding the notion of 'reputation'.[76] Several authors have argued that the reputation of an institution would be a factor for their authority. As in the case of legitimacy, using this notion leaves open when it is that actors would consider an institution to have a 'good' reputation. Yet, one can consider an institution to have a 'good' reputation when its actions are in line with the actors' values. Here again, values are the determinant aspect. Directly assessing these values makes this aspect more tangible and accessible as a factor for authority.

B. Opportunity to Accept Authority

As we saw above, opportunity 'represents the environmental or contextual mechanisms that enable action'.[77] Opportunity is provided by an infrastructure over which the actors have no direct control. An authority relationship depends on such an opportunity. Actors that potentially might accept the authority of an entity must have the opportunity to do so. This aspect is also highlighted by a strand of scholarship that has explored the 'legal opportunity structure' in which actors engage with entities such as courts.[78] Although this literature takes a broad approach as to what to address

of Judicial Authority' in B Bornstein and A Tomkins (eds), *Motivating Cooperation and Compliance with Authority* (Springer 2015) 81. See also A Føllesdal, 'Power or Authority; Actions or Beliefs' in Alter, Helfer and Madsen, *International Court Authority* (n 53) 412, 415. For a legitimacy-related approach in the political science literature, see ch 1.

[73] MC Suchman, 'Managing Legitimacy: Strategic and Institutional Approaches' (1995) 20 *Academy of Management Review* 571, 574.

[74] Hurd (n 58) 381.

[75] B Peters and JK Schaffer, 'The Turn to Authority beyond States' (2013) 4 *Transnational Legal Theory* 315, 329.

[76] Zürn (n 45) 52; on reputation as performance indicator for international courts, see Y Shany (ed), *Assessing the Effectiveness of International Courts* (OUP 2014) 59.

[77] Siemsen, Roth and Balasubramanian (n 25) 427.

[78] eg, L Vanhala, 'Legal Opportunity Structures and the Paradox of Legal Mobilization by the Environmental Movement in the UK' (2012) 46 *Law & Society Review* 523; B Wilson and JC Rodriguez Cordero, 'Legal Opportunity Structures and Social Movements: The Effects of Institutional Change

as opportunity, it refers, at its core, to various opportunity elements discussed here as part of the MOC framework, such as procedural parameters. The legal opportunity structure approach has also found its way into the scholarship on international courts, relating, inter alia, to the opportunity structure offered by formal rules on jurisdiction and access to courts.[79]

In a setting such as regarding the authority of an institution, formal rules play an important role in shaping opportunity. Formal rules determine which actors can engage with the authoritative entity and in what way. When formal rules give actors the possibility to engage with an entity, they provide an opportunity to accept this entity's authority. They provide the formal infrastructure. Inversely, when formal rules exclude certain actors from such engagement, this limits the opportunity for these actors to accept the authority of an entity. For example, a state that is a member state of an international organisation encounters a formal infrastructure to engage with this institution – an infrastructure that a non-member state or a private actor does not have. The infrastructure enables more, easier or more direct engagement with the institution. For courts, such formal rules that provide opportunity are, for example, access rules determining who can be a party to a dispute before the court. In this way, formal opportunity elements also contribute to delineating different groups of actors, in particular level 1 and level 2 actors as compared with other groups of actors.

The formal legal opportunity structure is complemented by a behavioural opportunity structure. Whether actors accept the authority of an entity is influenced by the social practice within the actors' reference group. The psychological effects of conformity and non-conformity outlined in section I are relevant in this regard. If members of a group accept the authority of an entity, this behaviour makes accepting authority salient and creates a social practice that makes it more likely for others to align with this behaviour due to group effects. Inversely, the behavioural opportunity structure is unfavourable if the majority of the members of the social group do not engage in the respective behaviour and the conformity pull supports non-compliance.

C. Constraints against Accepting Authority

Constraints are factors that make it more difficult, if not impossible, for actors to accept the authority of an entity. They have a disabling rather than enabling thrust.

Intrinsic constraints against accepting authority exist when entering an authority relationship requires certain skills or resources. On a very basic level, for such an authority relationship to form, an actor must be able to comprehend

on Costa Rican Politics' (2006) 39 *Comparative Political Studies* 325; EA Andersen, *Out of the Closets and Into the Courts: Legal Opportunity Structure and Gay Rights Litigation* (University of Michigan Press 2005).

[79] JT Gathii and JW Mwangi, 'The African Court of Human and Peoples' Rights as an Opportunity Structure' in JT Gathii (ed), *The Performance of Africa's International Courts: Using Litigation for Political, Legal, and Social Change* (OUP 2020) 211.

commands or other authoritative statements and to act according to these statements. To illustrate: forming an authority relationship towards a newborn child is not possible as the child will not be able to comprehend authoritative statements. Further intrinsic constraints can stem from a lack of information about the existence of certain institutions and their actions. This can, for example, be the case when individuals are not aware of certain judicial bodies before which they can file claims to enforce their legal rights; or when an expert body issues a guideline, but the relevant actors are not aware of this guideline. In terms of resources, financial resources can be an intrinsic constraint for (state and non-state) actors that want to engage with entities such as international organisations or courts.

Extrinsic constraints can be generated by other actors. This can be the case when an actor exercises influence on another actor in order for the latter not to accept the authority of an entity. For example, a governmental actor can threaten private actors or even other public actors such as judges with negative repercussions in case they accept the authority of an entity. Such attempts would constitute a constraining factor for the targeted actor.

A particularly interesting instance of extrinsic constraint is a situation in which two authority relationships are competing.[80] Authorities are competing when there is no clear hierarchy between them, and they both address the same actors. Here, accepting the authority of one entity necessarily means rejecting the authority of the other. For the actor facing both these entities, the authority claim of one entity is at the same time a constraint against accepting the authority of the other entity. This can be the case if different courts compete for authority because they have jurisdiction over the same subject matter and issue conflicting decisions. In such a situation, the constraint exists even if one entity's authority claim does not purposefully aim at undermining the other entity's claim.

As in the case of extrinsic motivation, taking into account extrinsic constraints implements the triadic approach to authority outlined in chapter one. Including the impact of other actors in both the motivational and the constraining factors shows that this impact can be both beneficial and detrimental to an authority relationship. Also, it is important to note that in a given situation, an actor can face, at the same time, extrinsic motivation *and* extrinsic constraints stemming from other actors. In most cases, an actor relates to a variety of other actors with diverse preferences, rather than a homogeneous group of actors. Some of these actors might support the authority relationship whereas others do not.

D. Relationship between the MOC Factors: Finding the Determining Factor

In this section, I turn to the interaction of the three MOC factors. This is a crucial analytical dimension of the MOC framework. I show that, based on this framework, it is possible to find out the determining factor for each specific MOC setting. The MOA research outlined in section II provides the basis for these insights.

[80] See also F Zarbiyev, 'Cutting off the King's Head: Rethinking Authority in International Law' (2023) 14 *Journal of International Dispute Settlement* 285, 297 et seq.

The first insight of MOA research on the relationship between the individual factors relates to the necessity of these factors. There seems to be consensus on the question that a certain behaviour does not take place when one of the three factors is nil.[81] If one of the factors does not exist at all, the behaviour is impossible as all factors are necessary elements for the behaviour. If there is no motivation, no opportunity or no ability, no behaviour takes place. In other words, all three factors are essential, and, in this regard, they are equal requirements. For the adjusted MOC framework, this means the following: with no motivation, no opportunity or maximum constraints on ability, the actor does not behave in the targeted way.

In addition, there is a second insight from MOA research relating to settings in which none of the three factors is nil, but they vary in their intensity. In such a setting, an actor has some motivation, some opportunity and some ability; but one of these factors is lower than the others. For example, an actor can have high motivation and broad ability but only narrow opportunity; or broad ability and opportunity but low motivation. The question then is whether an increase in one factor can balance out a low level in another factor. There are different models which aim at answering that question.

A 'complementarity model' of the relationship between the three factors would suggest that it is indeed possible for factors to balance each other out. According to this model, the outcome of behaviour is determined by the sum of the three factors and/or their multiplication.[82] The underlying assumption is that when one modifies one of the factors by increasing or decreasing it, this would necessarily impact the outcome of behaviour. For example, if an actor has moderate motivation and moderate constraints but narrow opportunity, the desired behaviour would increase if one increased the motivation factor. According to this model, the low level of one factor such as opportunity can be balanced out by the other factors. The 'complementarity model' has two variations on which it depends to what extent a low factor can be balanced out. In a 'multiplicative model', the low level of one factor strongly reduces the behaviour and only a major increase in the other factors would show a certain balancing effect. In contrast, in a 'linear model', all three factors would have an equivalent impact, and full complementarity is reached much more easily.

An alternative model is the 'constraining factor model'. According to this model, 'it is the minimum among the three factors of motivation, opportunity, and ability that ultimately determines behaviour'.[83] In this model, the factor with the lowest level determines the outcome in a way that cannot be balanced out by increasing the other two factors. The following 'bottleneck' metaphor describes this model:

> [O]ne can think of motivation as a flow of energy that has to pass through the neck of a 'bottle' in order to result in a particular action. But there are two potential bottlenecks: one defined through opportunity, the other through ability. If the flow of energy (motivation) is less than the capacity defined by the two potential bottlenecks, the flow itself is the constraining factor and increased motivation leads to stronger and/or more frequent action. If, however, it is either opportunity or ability that constrains the flow then that

[81] Siemsen, Roth and Balasubramanian (n 25) 429–31.
[82] eg, Blumberg and Pringle (n 25) 565.
[83] Siemsen, Roth and Balasubramanian (n 25) 431.

> factor becomes the bottleneck and determines the degree to which motivation can flow through the bottle – and therefore to what degree an action takes place.[84]

This model is in a way an extreme form of the 'multiplicative model' which considers the lowers factor as predominant while the other two factors only have a minor impact. Here, even this minor impact disappears.

As will be outlined further in chapter three, for the context of authority of international courts, the constraining factor model and the closely connected multiplication model have the most explanatory value. The relevant insight provided by these models is that the factor with the lowest level has predominant (multiplication model) or even exclusive (constraining factor model) impact on the outcome of behaviour. If, for example, an actor's motivation is low, a high level of opportunity and/or unconstrained ability cannot balance that out. Motivation becomes the determining factor. In the same way, narrow opportunity cannot be balanced out by a high level of motivation and/or ability; and a low level of ability cannot be balanced out by a high level of motivation and/or opportunity.

Based on these insights, it is possible to find out for each MOC setting in the authority context which factor determines whether an actor accepts the authority of an entity. For certain actors, the MOC setting might be such that motivation is at the lowest level among the three factors and thus determines the extent to which the actors accept the authority of an entity. For other actors, the MOC setting might be different, for example, with opportunity being at the lowest level of the three factors and thus determining the extent to which accepting the authority is possible for these actors. Finding the determining factor for each MOC setting thus helps us to understand the specifics and the dynamics of authority relationships.

IV. AN MOC SPOTLIGHT ON PUSHBACK AGAINST AUTHORITY

The previous section has outlined how the MOC framework can be used to conceptualise the factors that contribute to actors accepting the authority of an entity. The present section reverses the perspective. It considers the factors for pushback against an entity. Pushback refers to a situation in which an actor has initially accepted the authority of an entity before rejecting it or reducing the extent to which authority is accepted. If one does not look specifically at the factors that contribute to rejection, one might overlook some of the factors that are relevant for the authority relationship between an entity and its relevant actors. Although many aspects mentioned in the previous section contribute to understanding pushback as well, one can grasp some factors better when taking an explicit pushback perspective. Specifically, when applying the MOC framework, it becomes apparent that the factors for pushback are not merely a negative version of the factor for acceptance of authority.

As in the previous section, I refer here to a range of insights from behavioural research to add further substance to the three-pronged MOC scheme. The research on disobedience seems particularly helpful in this regard. For example, the Milgram

[84] ibid.

experiments and similar more recent studies can highlight the role of various factors relating to motivation, opportunity and constraint that lead actors to disobey.[85] Furthermore, behavioural research can help better understand how interactions among groups of actors increase or decrease the likelihood that actors push back against an authoritative entity.

A. Motivation

The motivational factors for pushback are closely linked to the motivational factors for accepting authority. Value-correspondence plays a crucial role here as well. The correlation is of course reversed: low value-correspondence is a motivational factor for pushback. When actors perceive the entity as reflecting values that diverge from their own values, this can motivate them not to accept the authority of the entity any longer. When the values of the actors and the entity increasingly diverge, this shift constitutes the motivational factor for pushback.

The aspect of decreasing value-correspondence is also reflected in many behavioural studies on disobedience. In particular, this research assesses disobedience against 'immoral authority' or 'unjust authority'.[86] In substance, these terms describe a situation in which actors perceive the entity as acting contrary to their values. An authoritative entity that is perceived as 'immoral' or 'unjust' does not embrace the values of the observing actor. Such studies thus allow us to closely observe the motivational effect of a lack of value-correspondence. They also show that *gradually* decreasing value-correspondence can motivate actors to push back against the authority of the entity. There is no need for a sudden shift.

Regarding interests as a motivational factor for pushback, one aspect deserves specific attention. This is the question whether a broadening authority relationship makes pushback more likely. Actors might perceive a broadening authority relationship as impacting their economic, social and political interests. As in the case of changing values, actors might accept a changing interest setting only until it reaches a certain tipping point. Interests would then constitute a motivational factor for pushback. In this context, the question arises whether a potential value-correspondence would be able to balance out such perceived negative interests. Here, the above-mentioned research on how procedural justice values and interest-based outcome assessments interrelate can provide insights for pushback as well.[87]

B. Opportunity

To start with, formal circumstances can constitute opportunity for pushback. This is, for example, the case when level 1 and level 2 actors accept the authority of an entity for

[85] Milgram (n 6). Critical on the conclusion in the former studies, Kaposi (n 70).
[86] Milgram (n 6); Parmar (n 8); Bocchiaro and Zimbardo, 'On the dynamics of disobedience' (n 6); Bocchiaro and Zimbardo, 'Defying Unjust Authority' (n 6).
[87] See studies at n 59.

a predetermined period of time, requiring renewed formal acceptance after this period has ended. In such a situation, the formal framework in which the authority relationship is integrated provides an opportunity for an actor to cease accepting the authority of the entity concerned. Further, for pushback that occurs within a certain procedural setting, the procedural rules constitute an element of the opportunity structure. If, for example, actors attempt to change the legal framework in which a court operates, rules regarding the necessary majority for an amendment of this framework shape the opportunity that smaller groups of actors have for pushing back.

When considering research on disobedience, a further aspect regarding opportunity seems to be particularly important for pushback: the actor's perception of opportunity. For actors to reject authority, they 'must be aware of – or be able to conceive of – alternative definitions of the situation and interpretations of its requirements'.[88] This means that actors must be aware that an opportunity for pushback exists. This is not always a given. Actors might not perceive pushback 'as an option when confronted with a situation which, objectively at least, offers such an opportunity'.[89] The perception of opportunity is likely to be influenced by both the personal experience of the actor, ie whether, in the past, the actor has already used an opportunity for pushback, and the social environment, ie, whether other actors disobey or push back against an entity in certain situations. Observing other actors' behaviour can make actors aware of opportunities and of modes of pushback.

A related aspect of the behavioural opportunity structure for pushback is the 'true partner effect'.[90] As mentioned in section I, this term describes the behavioural phenomenon that actors are more likely not to conform with the majority of the group members when there is a second actor that shares their point of view as opposed to when all the other group members agree. The social opportunity structure generated by the actor's social group thus becomes more favourable when there is a 'partner' with whom they can deviate together. In the authority context, critical actors are thus more likely to push back against an entity when other actors also do so.

Moreover, discursive interaction among actors can shape the extent to which these actors perceive situations as opportunity for pushback. Prolonged critical discourse influences how actors perceive a situation – in the sense of a self-reinforcing mechanism. With each critical communicative act, a situation is shaped more towards non-acceptance.[91] Discourse shapes the interpretation of a situation and, if this interpretation strengthens the perception of a pushback situation, it can make disobedience more likely.

C. Constraints

Extrinsic constraints against disobedience and other forms of pushback can be generated by actors that support the authority of the respective entity. Such *supporting*

[88] Kelman and Hamilton (n 7) 138.

[89] On non-compliance, Jackson et al (n 47) 1053.

[90] Asch, 'Effects of group pressure' (n 16); Morris and Miller (n 16). On physical proximity of another 'rebel' as a factor for disobedience, Bocchiaro and Zimbardo, 'On the dynamics of disobedience' (n 6).

[91] Parmar (n 8) 1381 (Figure 1).

actors can exercise pressure on an actor that is attempting to engage in pushback. For example, a supporting actor such as an influential civil society group can target a governmental actor with the aim to discourage the latter from pushing back against an institution. More generally, members of a group face a constraining social environment when they try to push back against an authoritative entity: they 'disrupt the established social order and the smoothness of social interaction and [have] to suffer the consequences of such disruption'.[92]

In addition, intrinsic constraints against pushback might include aspects such as the actor's personal skills and resources, including financial resources. As to the latter, it has been observed that: 'successful disobedience requires a certain level of resources. As long as individuals perceive that the authority figure has the greater resources (monetary and military), disobedience is unlikely to occur'.[93]

In conclusion, when conceiving the factors for pushback through the MOC lens, one can conceptualise the way in which the relevant factors operate. Moreover, the pushback perspective renders more visible certain factors that one would not necessarily detect when assessing authority relationships from the perspective of acceptance only.

V. THE BENEFITS OF THE MOC MODEL

Taking a behavioural approach to authority and specifically using the MOC model has several benefits.

Generally, a behavioural approach to authority takes the relational character of authority seriously. It does not only refer to the characteristics of an authoritative entity to explain why authority exists. Such an approach would, for example, struggle to explain why actors accept the authority of some entities but not of others although these entities have the same characteristics. Rather, a behavioural approach uses the actors' behaviour as a point of reference which leads to considering a broader range of factors and allows us to make use of the findings of behavioural research for explaining behaviour in the authority context. In this way, one can uncover causal relations and factors that a non-behavioural perspective on authority might not consider.

Assessing authority relationships based on the MOC framework is particularly well-suited for analysing behavioural factors for authority. It makes it possible to include a range of relevant factors rather than focusing on one specific factor alone. In particular, it sheds light on the factors beyond motivation which seem somewhat understudied for authority. What is more, attributing specific aspects to one of the three MOC elements has an analytical value in itself. It highlights the way in which each aspect influences the behaviour of actors and emphasises that not all factors function in the same way. For example, factors can be of an intrinsic or extrinsic nature; they can further or constrain behaviour; some factors can be influenced

[92] Kelman and Hamilton (n 7) 138.

[93] KS Bordens and IA Horowitz, *Social Psychology*, 2nd edn (Psychology Press 2001) 277, referring to Kelman and Hamilton (n 7).

by the entity and/or the actors while for others that is not possible. In this regard, MOC integrates various distinctions that have been proposed in the scholarship on the authority of entities such as international courts and makes it possible to consolidate them.[94]

Further, categorising factors according to the MOC framework allows us to assess and uncover the relations between these factors. It addresses the interaction among factors relating to motivation, opportunity and constraint. And it provides a framework for discussing the interrelation within categories, such as among various motivational factors. As outlined in section III.D, MOC helps determining whether, for certain authority relationships, there is one or several predominant factor(s); and how variations in one factor might influence the other factors.

The MOC framework is also well suited to conceptualise the 'social dimension' of authority.[95] The framework explicitly takes into account the relationship between various (groups of) actors. MOC adopts a triadic approach to conceptualising authority as a relationship. It provides a structure to highlight how actors influence each other concerning whether, how and when they accept the authority of an entity. MOC makes this possible by distinguishing between motivational and constraining factors as well as between intrinsic and extrinsic factors. The functioning of these extrinsic factors stemming from other actors is well captured by the MOC framework. This does more justice to these factors and to their role for behavioural outcomes than describing their effect, for example, as 'involuntary' acceptance of authority.[96] According to MOC, the existence of extrinsic motivational or constraining factors does not make deference 'involuntary'. Rather, these factors are integrated into a broader set of factors that determine the behaviour of an actor. MOC provides a more nuanced understanding of these factors, including of the interplay of 'voluntary' and 'involuntary' elements in behaviour.

More generally, the possibility to include both intrinsic and extrinsic factors in the MOC framework is a benefit. Unlike some other approaches, MOC does not consider that *either* aspects that are internal to the actors such as their interests *or* aspects that are external to them such as opportunity leads to the behaviour of actors. Instead, MOC includes both internal and external elements. Motivation and constraints can be of an intrinsic nature while extrinsic factors can exist as elements of motivation, opportunity and constraint. MOC allows us to conceptualise in theory and assess in practice the simultaneity of these factors and their interrelation. Further, it makes it possible to underline that intrinsic and extrinsic factors might have different effects. As noted above, intrinsic motivational factors can have a stronger effect for durable authority relationships than extrinsic motivational factors.

[94] See for a categorisation according to whether courts or other actors have control over a factor, LR Helfer and A-M Slaughter, 'Toward a Theory of Effective Supranational Adjudication' (1997) 107 *Yale Law Journal* 273; differentiating between institution-specific factors, constituency-related factors and factors relating to the political contexts, KJ Alter, LR Helfer and MR Madsen, 'How Context Shapes the Authority of International Courts' in Alter, Helfer and Madsen, *International Court Authority* (n 53) 36–52.

[95] N Krisch, 'Liquid authority in global governance' (2017) 9 *International Theory* 237, 242.

[96] ibid 242.

Relatedly, the MOC framework is pertinent for assessing and explaining changes within authority relationships. In this regard, it speaks to concepts of authority that emphasise the dynamic rather than static nature of authority (see chapter one). MOC makes it possible to measure which of the individual MOC factors increases and decreases instead of merely measuring whether authority overall does so. Notably, the MOC framework also makes it possible to highlight how the behaviour of the entities themselves can contribute to an increase or decrease in authority. As a result, it is possible to assess and explain pushback against entities such as international courts and the resilience of these entities.

Compared with certain political science models of authority, the MOC framework consolidates various approaches to authority that might appear incompatible. It combines them into a single model, integrating them into a structure and making the interrelations between these explanatory strands visible and their coexistence plausible. This is the case, for example, for voluntaristic and deterministic approaches to authority. As outlined in chapter one, the contract model of authority is an example of the former while the habituation/internalisation model leans towards a deterministic understanding of authority. The benefit of the MOC framework is that it does not have to side with one or the other. Instead, it includes elements of both. The foundation of MOC is voluntaristic as it rests on a freedom of actors to recognise authority or not. Among the elements of MOC, the motivation of the actor is of a voluntaristic nature. However, in MOC, the voluntarism is not 'excessive' as has been criticised for the contract model.[97] Its voluntarism is counterbalanced. Most notably the MOC element opportunity is a purely external factor that lies beyond the influence of the actor. Thus, MOC includes both elements of voluntaristic and deterministic approaches, which is not only in line with behavioural science but also creates a framework that is more balanced than some of the models of authority suggested from the perspective of political science alone.

Specifically for assessing the authority of international courts, the MOC framework offers additional benefits. First, it fosters interdisciplinary dialogue among existing strands of research on international courts. It allows us to consolidate the legal perspective on international courts which primarily focuses on the legal rules that shape the opportunity structure as well as on the jurisprudential strategies of courts and the political sciences approaches that emphasise motivational and contextual factors. The MOC approach integrates them into one framework, connecting them and highlighting their interrelations. Second, MOC offers a reference point for comparison among international courts. It makes it possible to go beyond merely noting a context-dependency of authority relationships. Rather, the context-related aspects are categorised and qualified, transposing them into comparable factors. By analysing international courts through the lens of the MOC framework, it becomes possible to compare and contrast their authority relationships and determine whether similar patterns as to contextual factors are at play for different international courts.

[97] Zürn (n 45) 42.

In conclusion, MOC is a framework to dissect authority relationships and the factors that contribute to their creation, preservation and decrease. It systematises the factors and highlights their variable effects and interrelations. Using MOC as a template for assessing authority relationships thus offers novel insights into how authority comes about. In the following chapter, I show how MOC can be applied to the relationship between international courts and the actors that accept their authority.

Before doing so, I address two possible concerns as to applying the suggested behavioural model to authority relationships.

A first possible concern about constructing a behavioural model of the factors for authority relates to its empirical foundation. Some of the findings to which this model refers have not yet been empirically tested within the context of authority relationships. However, the empirical research in this field has addressed a diverse set of behavioural settings which has shown that the above-mentioned models have explanatory value in a wide range of contexts. This is a strong indication that these findings also can illuminate behaviour in the context of authority relationships. Moreover, in the following chapters, I demonstrate that the suggested framework does indeed explain observations that researchers on the authority of international courts have made. This includes observations that might seem counterintuitive if one does not take behavioural research into account. The fact that such observations correspond to the predictions made by a behavioural model of authority speaks further for the significance of the existing findings also for authority relationships. Finally – and importantly – the framework can be used as an analytical template that, by choosing a novel perspective, makes it possible to uncover previously undetected causal links. The second part of this book implements this aspect. It assesses the causal links indicated by MOC by applying this framework to selected international courts and their authority relationship with their constituencies. This further substantiates the pertinence of the behavioural approach suggested in this book.

A second concern as to whether a behavioural approach is appropriate relates to a particularity of some authority relationships. Authority relationships can include actors other than individuals. This can be states, governmental or non-governmental organisations, courts, administrative entities, associations and many more. Assessing such actors from a behavioural perspective treats their actions as behaviour. Critics might object that these actors are not human beings and therefore do not 'behave' in the narrow sense of the term or that their decision-making processes are more complex than human behaviour and thus not comparable with the latter. Two points can be made in response to this objection.

First, a behavioural perspective has already been successfully used to address the actions of non-individual actors. For example, behavioural research has addressed corporate actors and shown that cognitive effects also influence the behaviour of these actors.[98] Certain strategies in behavioural economics such as nudging are addressed

[98] For an overview, see C Engel, 'The behaviour of corporate actors: How much can we learn from the experimental literature?' (2010) 6 *Journal of Institutional Economics* 445.

both at individual and non-individual actors.[99] Further, studies in behavioural law and economics have assessed states as actors that are affected by cognitive heuristics and biases.[100] Behavioural approaches to international law have established this behavioural perspective for assessing the full range of international actors.[101] And in international relations, 'behavioural international relations' has developed a sub-field that particularly assesses the behaviour of states and international organisations.[102] In other fields such as criminology, complex social phenomena which involve not only groups of individuals but also organisational structures within these groups have been addressed based on models that are closely related to the behavioural MOA model.[103] These examples show that behavioural insights can be applied beyond individual actors as well.

The second point that can be made in response to the above objection is that the decision-making of such actors is, in essence, determined by human beings. Although they might act, to a greater or lesser degree, within organisational structures, the individual or collective decision-makers that shape the actions of these actors are human in nature. As has been argued for a variety of such actors, inside the 'black box' of their social construction as a monolithic entity is human behaviour which should be analysed as such.[104] On the international level, the human actors within the black box of entities such as states or international courts include, inter alia, heads of state, diplomats or judges.[105] It is the behaviour of a group of individuals or of certain leaders within the group that shapes the outcome of such decision-making. Behavioural effects within groups have long been established.[106] Even if some behavioural phenomena might vary depending on whether one observes an individual or non-individual actor, many of the broad lines of behavioural research are observable in both contexts.

[99] On nudging, see C Sunstein, 'Nudges.Gov – Behaviorally Informed Regulation' in E Zamir and D Teichman (eds), *The Oxford Handbook of Behavorial Economics and the Law* (OUP 2014) 719; C Sunstein and R Thaler, *Nudge: Improving Decisions About Health, Wealth, And Happiness* (Yale University Press 2008).

[100] eg, J Galbraith, 'Treaty Options: Towards a Behavioral Understanding of Treaty Design' (2013) 53 *Virginia Journal of International Law* 309.

[101] eg, A van Aaken and T Broude, *Behavioral Economics and International Law* (OUP forthcoming); A van Aaken, 'Rationalist and Behavioralist Approaches to International Law' in J Dunoff and M Pollack (eds), *International Legal Theory* (CUP 2021) 261; A van Aaken, 'Behavioral International Law and Economics' (2014) 55 *Harvard International Law Journal* 421; T Broude, 'Behavioral International Law' (2015) 163 *University of Pennsylvania Law Review* 1099; D Teichman and E Zamir, 'Nudge Goes International' (2019) 30 *European Journal of International Law* 1263; S Puig, 'Debiasing International Economic Law' (2019) 30 *European Journal of International Law* 1339.

[102] A Mintz, 'Behavioral IR as a Subfield of International Relations' (2007) 9 *International Studies Review* 157; EM Hafner-Burton, S Haggard, DA Lake and DG Victor, 'The Behavioral Revolution and International Relations' (2017) *International Organization* 71 S1.

[103] Kauzlarich and Kramer (n 26); Rothe and Mullins (n 26).

[104] Making such an argument for courts and the judges composing them, JL Dunoff and MAPollack, 'International Judicial Practices: Opening the "Black Box" of International Courts' (2018) 40 *Michigan Journal of International Law* 47. Arguing that states should not be analysed as if they were monolithic entities, eg U Kischel, 'The State as a non-unitary actor: the role of the judicial branch in international negotiations' (2001) 39 *Archiv des Völkerrechts* 268.

[105] For this argument, see also van Aaken, 'Rationalist' (n 101) 275.

[106] For an overview, see Engel (n 98). For a comparison between individuals and groups, see NL Kerr, RJ MacCoun and GP Kramer, 'Bias in Judgment: Comparing Individuals and Groups' (1996) 103 *Psychological Review* 687.

In conclusion, the specific nature of authority relationships does not stand in the way of applying a framework that is based on behavioural insights. Rather, a behavioural perspective has the potential to reconceptualise the factors for authority and their interrelations and to shed light on factors that might otherwise be overlooked. Furthermore, it can be used to assess the effectiveness of authority-building strategies.

3

The Factors for Authority of International Courts: Contextualising the MOC Framework

IN CHAPTER TWO, I developed a conceptual and analytical framework that can be used to assess authority relationships. In the present chapter, I apply this framework to the specific context of international courts. The term 'international courts' is understood broadly, also including quasi-judicial bodies. The chapter gives a general overview of the MOC framework in the context of international courts, before Part II of the book turns to a detailed application of this framework.

First, I outline the MOC factors that influence the behaviour of actors when they accept the authority of international courts (section I). Second, I address strategies of international courts to enhance the factors that influence actors to accept their authority (section II). Third, I connect the MOC factors to the context of pushback against international courts (section III). The last section outlines the programme for the empirical studies in Part II of the book (section IV).

The examples I use in this chapter are illustrative rather than exhaustive. Here, I do not give an in-depth analysis of individual courts yet; rather, I refer to various courts to highlight that the MOC factors can take different shapes. This provides an overview before the in-depth MOC analysis of selected courts in Part II of the book.

I. FACTORS FOR ACCEPTING THE AUTHORITY OF INTERNATIONAL COURTS

To determine when actors accept the authority of international courts, the MOC framework structures the possible factors according to its three-pronged matrix: (I.A) motivation for accepting authority; (I.B) opportunity for accepting authority; and (I.C) constraints against accepting authority. Taking into account the interaction of these factors makes it possible to find out the determining factor for each group of actors (I.D).

Applying the MOC framework sheds light on controversially debated issues which are recurring in the scholarly discussion on international court authority. This includes the issue whether 'formal' factors such as jurisdiction or access rules play a less important role for international court authority as opposed to other factors such as the political context in which the court and the actors operate.[1] MOC offers a novel perspective on this question. According to MOC, it is not necessarily one of the two factors that determines the authority relationship between an actor and a court. Instead, the behavioural framework attributes these factors to different elements of the MOC structure. As I develop further in this section, the 'formal' factors primarily relate to opportunity while aspects relating to the political context can influence both motivation and constraints. The interplay of the factors determines for each actor which factor ultimately defines the behaviour.

A. Motivation for Accepting Authority

For the context of international courts, the aforementioned distinction between the two sets of motivational factors is useful: values and interests. I address both of them in turn.

Values

First, *institutional values* relating to the court and its functioning play a considerable role as motivational factors. A key institutional value is the rule of law.[2] It forms the foundation of court authority. Several authors have pointed to the fact that it is beneficial for the authority of an international court if all or most of the member states have an internal governance system that is based on the rule of law.[3] And empirical studies have demonstrated that authoritarian states are less likely to accept the authority of international courts.[4] More generally, the rule of law has

[1] For this view, see eg, KJ Alter, LR Helfer and MR Madsen, 'Conclusion – Context, Authority, Power' in KJ Alter, LR Helfer and MR Madsen (eds), *International Court Authority* (OUP 2018) 435, 439–41; S Caserta and P Cebulak, 'The limits of international adjudication: authority and resistance of regional economic courts in times of crisis' (2018) 14 *International Journal of Law in Context* 275; N Krisch, 'Liquid authority in global governance' (2017) 9 *International Theory* 237, 249. In contrast, other contributions put more emphasis on the formal legal framework when analysing the authority of international courts, see eg, LR Helfer and A-M Slaughter, 'Toward a Theory of Effective Supranational Adjudication' (1997) 107 *Yale Law Journal* 273.

[2] Arguing that people follow rules 'because they accept that it is morally right to abide by the law', J Jackson, B Bradford, M Hough, A Myhill, P Quinton and TR Tyler, 'Why Do People Comply With The Law? Legitimacy and the Influence of Legal Institutions' (2012) 52 *British Journal of Criminology* 1051, 1053, 1055.

[3] eg, KJ Alter, LR Helfer and MR Madsen, 'How Context Shapes the Authority of International Courts' in Alter, Helfer and Madsen (eds), *International Court Authority* (n 1) 24, 42; Y Shany (ed), *Assessing the Effectiveness of International Courts* (OUP 2014) 60; Helfer and Slaughter, 'Toward a Theory of Effective Supranational Adjudication' (n 1) 331–35; K Raustiala and A-M Slaughter, 'International Law, International Relations and Compliance' in W Carlsnaes, T Risse and BA Simmons (eds), *Handbook of International Relations* (SAGE Publications 2002) 538; TG Daly and M Wiebusch, 'The African Court on Human and Peoples' Rights: mapping resistance against a young court' (2018) 14 *International Journal of Law in Context* 294, 296; D Shelton, 'Performance of Regional Human Rights Courts' in T Squatrito, OR Young, A Føllesdal and G Ulfstein (eds), *The Performance of International Courts and Tribunals* (CUP 2018) 114, 146.

[4] T Ginsburg, 'Authoritarian International Law?' (2020) 114 *American Journal of International Law* 221.

also been shown to influence compliance with international treaties.[5] For actors who do not embrace the rule of law, the value-correspondence in relation to the international court is reduced.

A related institutional value that can influence motivation is an actor's expectation regarding judicial independence. Judicial independence is part of procedural fairness, an aspect that, as outlined in chapter two, is an important motivational factor for accepting authority. Judicial independence has been discussed as an element of, and a factor for, the performance of international courts in various contexts.[6] However, actors can have diverging opinions on the extent to which international courts should be independent from political influence. Depending on their expectation of judicial independence, actors can be motivated or discouraged from accepting the authority of an international court if they perceive this court as sufficiently independent or alternatively as too independent or too little independent. This conundrum is in fact reflected in the discussion about whether the independence of international courts contributes to 'effective' international courts or not: there is no 'one-size-fits-all' answer to this question; rather, it depends on the values and corresponding expectation of the actors.[7] Accordingly, 'the key issue is not which procedure is used, but whether the procedure matches the values of the disputants'.[8]

Another institutional value that can be a strong motivational factor for actors to accept a broad authority of an international court is the function attributed to courts by diverging domestic constitutional approaches. For example, Huneeus has highlighted for the Inter-American Court of Human Rights (IACtHR) how the approach of 'neo-constitutionalism' adopted in many member states of this court has contributed to the strong support by level 1, level 2 and level 3 actors in the member states concerned.[9] As 'neo-constitutionalism' attributes a strong role for courts domestically vis-a-vis the other constitutional powers, it facilitates the acceptance of a broad authority of the IACtHR.

The second set of values that can be the object of value-correspondence are *substantive values*. These values reflect the 'larger social and political purposes' which international courts are expected by their audiences to serve, and which influence the authority relationship between the courts and their audiences.[10] While the institutional values mentioned above are relevant for all international courts, the substantive

[5] eg, OA Hathaway, 'Between Power and Principle: An Integrated Theory of International Law' (2005) 72 *University of Chicaco Law Review* 469.

[6] See, eg, the process-related performance framework suggested by T Squatrito, OR Young, A Føllesdal and G Ulfstein, 'A Framework for Evaluating the Performance of International Courts and Tribunals' in Squatrito, Young, Føllesdal and Ulfstein (eds), *The Performance of International Courts and Tribunals* (n 3) 3. For a normative discussion of procedural fairness standards, see N Grossman, 'The Normative Legitimacy of International Courts' (2013) 86 *Temple Law Review* 61.

[7] On this discussion, see E Posner and J Yoo, 'Judicial Independence in International Tribunals' (2005) 93 *California Law Review* 1. LR Helfer and A-M Slaughter, 'Why States Create International Tribunals: A Response to Professors Posner and Yoo' (2005) 93 *California Law Review* 899.

[8] TR Tyler, A Lind and Y Huo, 'Cultural Values and Authority Relations – The Psychology of Conflict Resolution Across Cultures' (2000) 6 *Psychology, Public Policy, and Law* 1138, 1149.

[9] A Huneeus, 'The Inter-American Court of Human Rights How Constitutional Lawyers Shape Court Authority' in Alter, Helfer and Madsen (eds), *International Court Authority* (n 1) 196.

[10] KJ Alter and LR Helfer, 'Nature or Nurture? Judicial Lawmaking in the European Court of Justice' (2010) 64 *International Organization* 563, 587.

values diverge depending on the court at hand. These values can include, for example, human rights protection for regional human rights courts, international criminal accountability for the International Criminal Court (ICC), economic integration for the Andean Tribunal of Justice (ATJ), the Court of Justice of the European Union (CJEU), the East African Court of Justice (EACJ) or the Court of Justice of the Economic Community of West African States (ECOWAS) and free trade for the World Trade Organization (WTO) Appellate Body.

Interests

A first interest that can be a motivation for accepting the authority of international courts is dispute resolution. Level 1 and level 2 actors can be interested in using the court to enforce their legal rights or simply obtain (peaceful) dispute resolution. The following observation illustrates the motivational force of an actor's interest in resolving their own disputes. When actors do not perceive themselves as part of an actual dispute, as in the case of mere monitoring of international obligations, they often have a low motivation to engage with an international court. For example, in the CJEU context, member states are reluctant to take on such a monitoring function as complainants against other member states or against European Union (EU) organs in proceedings under Articles 259 and 263 of the Treaty on the Functioning of the European Union (TFEU).[11]

For actors of all levels, a possible interest for accepting the authority of an international court is the legal expertise of the court. As for other authoritative entities, the perception that these entities 'know better' can motivate actors to accept their authority in various forms.[12] This also includes expert knowledge as a motivational factor for cross-references between judicial (and quasi-judicial) bodies.

Further, political interests can constitute motivational factors for accepting the authority of a court. Political actors within the domestic sphere can use international courts for strategic purposes. This is, for example, the case when members of the political opposition use an international court to criticise the current or former government and exercise political pressure by obtaining court decisions against it, including after a regime change. This has happened, for example, in the case of the IACtHR and the ECOWAS Court, as is outlined for the latter in chapter five.[13] Similarly, domestic institutions can use international courts strategically against other domestic institutions. For example, in the case of the CJEU, domestic courts frequently make use of the 'judicial empowerment' vis-a-vis other domestic actors that follows from citing CJEU decisions and the preliminary reference procedure.[14]

[11] Article 259 TFEU had been used fewer than 10 times by 2021.

[12] M Zürn, *A Theory of Global Governance: Authority, Legitimacy, and Contestation* (OUP 2018) 43. On the aspect of expertise as normative reason for accepting authority, J Raz, *The Morality of Freedom* (OUP 1986) 75.

[13] On the development of the Inter-American human rights system during the areas of democratisation, X Soley, 'The Transformation of the Americas: The Rise of Human Rights and the Inter-American System' (Dissertation, University of Frankfurt 2021).

[14] On this 'judicial empowerment', JHH Weiler, 'The Transformation of Europe' (1991) 100 *Yale Law Journal* 2403, 2426. On the recent dynamics of domestic supreme courts reasserting control and limiting

More generally, the interest in effective behaviour constitutes a motivational factor for accepting the authority of an international court. This is particularly relevant for level 1 and level 2 actors. Actors are motivated to engage in a certain behaviour if they expect this behaviour to have the envisaged effect.[15] If actors expect, for example, that the court will hear their arguments, that the court will take a decision and do so within a reasonable time frame, and that the opposing party will implement a decision if they lose the case, the actors will consider it effective to bring a case to the court.[16]

This brief – illustrative rather than exhaustive – overview of possible motivations shows that the range of motivational factors is wide. Different actors generally would have diverging motivations, although some motivations such as institutional values might be shared by many actors. The case studies in Part II of this book illustrate the diversity of motivational factors further.

B. Opportunity for Accepting Authority

A key element of the opportunity structure is formal legal rules. First, the broader the subject-matter jurisdiction of an international court according to its founding legal document, the broader the opportunity for actors to engage with the court. As an example, the African Court on Human and Peoples' Rights (ACtHPR) has, compared with the ECtHR, a remarkably large de jure subject-matter authority not only on the African Charter on Human and Peoples' Rights but also on other regional and universal human rights instruments (ratified by the state parties concerned).[17] This creates the opportunity for actors to address the court with legal questions relating to all these instruments.

Second, formal rules shape the opportunity structure by determining the extent to which actors have access to the court.[18] Access rules decide which kinds of actors can enter a formal authority relationship with a court. For example, for human rights courts, the access of individuals is crucial to reach a wide number of actors. There are various possibilities for access rules in practice, including compulsory or optional jurisdiction for individual complaints or even no direct formal access at all. These rules provide a wider or narrower opportunity for individuals to engage with the court and to accept its authority. Another example for rules that shape opportunity are rules on preliminary reference procedures. They provide the opportunity for

the empowerment of lower domestic courts: T Pavone and RD Kelemen, 'The Evolving Judicial Politics of European Integration: The European Court of Justice and national courts revisited' (2019) 25 *European Law Journal* 352. On citation practice as element of empowerment: JA Mayoral, 'Judicial Empowerment Expanded: Political Determinants of National Courts' Cooperation with the CJEU' (2019) 25 *European Law Journal* 374.

[15] See also ch 2.

[16] Arguing that '[i]f a tribunal is ineffective, states will stop using it', Posner and Yoo (n 7) 28.

[17] Articles 3 and 4 of the Protocol to the African Charter on Human and Peoples' Rights on the Establishment of an African Court on Human and Peoples' Rights.

[18] Alter, Helfer and Madsen discuss this aspect under the notions of 'compulsory jurisdiction and multiple access points', Alter, Helfer and Madsen, 'How Context Shapes the Authority of International Courts' (n 3) 38.

domestic courts to directly address the international court. The high number of cases originating from preliminary reference procedures in the context of the CJEU as well as the frequent use of these procedures before the ATJ show that the possibility of preliminary references creates significant opportunities for a wide number of actors to reach an international court.[19] Moreover, formal rules can provide opportunity beyond a conventional litigant status. For example, if these rules allow for amicus curiae briefs, the concerned actors have a direct way to engage with the court and to accept the court's authority. The discussion around the possibility of amicus curiae briefs at the WTO Appellate Body demonstrates how important this issue can be for the authority of a court.[20]

Formal rules can also influence whether (and which) respondent actors have the opportunity to accept the authority of an international court. For example, rules on remedies influence whether a court can order financial compensation, an order that most likely would reach only the competent administrative agency as an actor in charge of compliance; or whether it can order the amendment of laws which addresses the domestic legislator. Such diverging rules on remedies create different opportunities for the actors addressed by these remedies to accept the authority of the court.

In addition to legal rules, the behavioural opportunity structure is also relevant. Depending on whether members of the same group of actors predominantly accept the authority or not, this constitutes a favourable or unfavourable behavioural opportunity. For example, the low number of African states that have accepted the jurisdiction of the ACtHPR for individual complaints and the recent tendency of several of the few states that initially had accepted it to withdraw their declaration under Article 34(6) of the Protocol to the African Charter on Human and Peoples' Rights creates a social practice that runs counter to accepting this jurisdiction. In this setting, states are less likely to make such a declaration than if the group practice was more favourable.

Finally, the opportunity structure can be influenced by domestic law. The way in which a domestic legal order conceives of the relationship between international and domestic law can shape the opportunity for actors to accept the authority of an international court. It makes a difference for domestic actors whether they have the opportunity to refer directly to decisions of international courts as legally binding within the domestic legal sphere or whether, in contrast, they can only do so if the legislator implements the decision into domestic law.

In sum, the MOC factor opportunity for accepting the authority of international courts is determined by a range of aspects that stem both from the international and the domestic sphere. This creates a cross-order opportunity structure. When

[19] eg, in 2019, 641 out of 1905 new cases brought to the CJEU were references for a preliminary ruling, see Annual Report 2019: curia.europa.eu/jcms/upload/docs/application/pdf/2020-05/ra_pan_2019_interieur_en_final.pdf. On preliminary references before the ATJ, KJ Alter and LR Helfer, *Transplanting International Courts: The Law and Politics of the Andean Tribunal of Justice* (OUP 2017) ch 3.

[20] Although many member states objected to the acceptance of unsolicited amicus curiae submissions under DSU Article 13 in the US Shrimp–Turtle case (Appellate Body Report, 8, WTO. Doc WT/ DS58/ AB/ R, adopted 12 October 1998), the Appellate Body has continued that practice and thus 'facilitated an increase in Member engagement and broadened the range of arguments and perspectives that it hears': G Shaffer, M Elsig and S Puig, 'The World Trade Organization's Dispute Settlement Body – Its Extensive but Fragile Authority' in Alter, Helfer and Madsen (eds), *International Court Authority* (n 1) 300, 317.

assessing the factors for the authority of international courts, it is necessary to take into account the interaction of these various infrastructural elements.

C. Constraints against Accepting Authority

Intrinsic constraints can result from a lack of awareness of an international court and insufficiently available information. Actors can lack information about certain international courts altogether or about certain aspects of their jurisdiction or procedure.[21] In particular, this is a risk for individuals as potential litigants before international courts. Lack of information can also be relevant for preliminary reference procedures by domestic courts. Here, domestic courts can either not be aware of the possibility altogether or of the circumstances in which such preliminary references are possible.

A further intrinsic constraint is related to the limited financial resources of an actor. For example, for private actors as potential litigants before investment arbitral tribunals, financial resources can be a significant constraining factor due to the high costs of these proceedings.[22] With regard to state actors, the high costs for proceedings before the WTO Appellate Body has been an important constraining factor for small developing countries with limited financial resources. Their solution was to enter into cooperation with large private companies to provide funding for these proceedings.[23] This example demonstrates the two elements of the constraint factor in MOC: the existence of constraints and the ability to overcome them.

Extrinsic constraints against accepting the authority of international courts can result from the behaviour of a constraining actor. Such constraints can come from political pressure exercised by governments on certain actors when they attempt to engage with an international court by filing a case or by supporting the court in discourse. For example, private companies seemed to fear retaliation from state governments if they filed a case before the Caribbean Court of Justice.[24]

Moreover, competing authority relationships are a potential constraining factor.[25] For example, such competing authority relationships are very prominent in the relationship between the CJEU and domestic constitutional courts, but also between domestic courts and the ECtHR and at times the International Court of Justice (ICJ).[26] Another example is the competing jurisdiction of the ICJ, the International Tribunal for the Law of the Sea and arbitral tribunals regarding law of the sea disputes

[21] Mentioning knowledge about a court as a factor for actors' attitudes towards courts, J Gibson, 'Legitimacy is for Losers: The Interconnections of Institutional Legitimacy, Performance Evaluations, and the Symbols of Judicial Authority' in B Bornstein and A Tomkins (eds), *Motivating Cooperation and Compliance with Authority* (Springer 2015) 81, 84.

[22] On these high costs as constraints and possible solutions, KE Boon, 'Investment Treaty Arbitration: Making a Place for Small Claims' (2018) 19 *Journal of World Investment & Trade* 667.

[23] Shaffer, Elsig and Puig (n 20) 311.

[24] S Caserta and MR Madsen, 'The Caribbean Court of Justice – A Regional Integration and Postcolonial Court' in Alter, Helfer and Madsen (eds), *International Court Authority* (n 1) 149, 160.

[25] Generally on competing international jurisdictions, Y Shany, *The Competing Jurisdictions of International Courts and Tribunals* (OUP 2004).

[26] eg, the disagreement between the ICJ and the Italian Constitutional Court on state immunity, Italian Constitutional Court judgment 238/2014: www.cortecostituzionale.it/documenti/download/doc/recent_judgments/S238_2013_en.pdf.

under Article 287 UN Convention on the Law of the Sea. Part II of the book explains such constraints further.

In sum, this overview of the MOC factors in relation to international courts has highlighted that, for each actor and each court, the specific MOC factors differ. Part II of this book illustrates these differences further.

D. Relationship between the MOC Factors: Finding the Determining Factor

A crucial question for understanding how the various factors influence the authority of international courts is to determine the relationship between the three MOC factors. Do they all have the same impact or is one of them more important than the others?

Answering this question would allow us to address a conundrum that the existing research on international court authority brought to the surface: the extent to which formal rules such as jurisdiction and access rules matter for international court authority. On the one hand, scholars have the intuition that these rules are likely to be very important to whether a court can develop authority.[27] On the other hand, studies such as conducted in the project by Alter, Helfer and Madsen have shown that the impact of other factors such as the motivation of actors or constraining contextual factors can be broader than that of formal rules.[28]

In the MOC framework, this issue can be phrased as a relationship between the three factors. As formal rules are an aspect of opportunity (see above), does the factor opportunity matter less than the factors of motivation and constraint? The findings by Alter, Helfer and Madsen seem to suggest this conclusion, despite its counterintuitive nature. However, when we consider the research on MOA in other fields of behaviour, we can develop an answer that reunites empirical findings and intuition. There is an explanation that is in line with both.

As outlined in chapter two, MOA research suggests that a certain behaviour does not take place when one of the three factors is nil.[29] With regard to the factors for accepting the authority of international courts, this means that all three factors are relevant. In particular, considering the debate in the literature on international courts, it is important to stress that opportunity is indeed a *necessary* factor for authority. The fact that opportunity factors such as jurisdiction and access rules are not by themselves sufficient for an actor to accept authority – because the other factors are necessary as well – does not lead to the conclusion that Alter, Helfer and Madsen seem to draw which is that they 'may be neither necessary nor sufficient for an IC to

[27] Helfer and Slaughter, 'Toward a Theory of Effective Supranational Adjudication' (n 1); Y Shany, 'Measuring Goal Attainment' in Shany (ed), *Assessing the Effectiveness of International Courts* (n 3) 49, 58, referring, inter alia, to formal rules as indicators for effectiveness. See also the initial hypothesis by Alter, Helfer and Madsen, 'How Context Shapes the Authority of International Courts' (n 3) 36, discussing the potential impact of institution-specific contextual factors.

[28] Alter, Helfer and Madsen, 'Conclusion' in Alter, Helfer and Madsen (eds), *International Court Authority* (n 1) 436.

[29] E Siemsen, AV Roth and S Balasubramanian, 'How motivation, opportunity, and ability drive knowledge sharing: The constraining-factor model' (2008) 26 *Journal of Operations Management* 426, 429–31.

gain de facto authority'.[30] Although they are indeed not sufficient, they are however necessary. Without any opportunity, actors will not accept the authority of courts.

Inversely, it needs to be emphasised again that all three factors being essential requirements for behaviour entails that none of these factors is sufficient by itself. This means that none of them guarantees that actors accept the authority of an international court. These behavioural findings are in line with empirical observations on international courts. For example, not every set of formal rules providing a broad opportunity for actors to accept court authority automatically translates into a broad de facto authority of this court. As Alter, Helfer and Madsen observe, such factors are 'important for some ICs, [while] other courts struggled to establish their authority notwithstanding these design features'.[31]

In addition to the fact that all three factors are not sufficient but necessary for behaviour to occur, MOA research indicates, as outlined in chapter two, that an increase in one MOC factor cannot balance out a low level of another factor if one adopts the constraining factor model or multiplication model. For international courts, this 'bottleneck effect' means that depending on the (group of) actor(s) and the level that each of the three factors reaches, a different factor – but only one – (predominantly) determines the authority relationship between the actor and the court. For example, if certain state actors have a low level of motivation, a high level of opportunity and/or unconstrained ability cannot balance that out. And despite a high level of motivation, for example, among certain groups of potential applicants to a court, these actors cannot engage with the court to a large extent if they have narrow opportunity and/or low ability to do so due to high extrinsic or intrinsic constraints.

This has several implications. First, it explains the conundrum mentioned above. It explains why aspects of opportunity such as formal rules seem to matter and not matter at the same time. They matter first of all as an essential element of MOC because without *any* opportunity, behaviour does not take place, ie, an actor does not accept the authority of an international court. Second, they matter to determine which of the three factors has the lowest level in a certain situation and thus the highest impact. When opportunity is at the lowest level, formal rules and other opportunity aspects become the determining factor. In such a situation, the extent of a court's authority depends on the extent of opportunity that these formal rules provide. However, if motivation or ability is the factor that is at the lowest level, they determine the authority relationship – and a high level of opportunity cannot balance that out. In the latter situation, increasing opportunity by adjusting the formal rules on jurisdiction or access does not change the extent of the court's authority. An example for this are the rules on preliminary references procedures before the CJEU, the ATJ, the EACJ and the ECOWAS Court. In all cases, domestic courts have had the opportunity to engage with the respective regional integration court. However, regarding the ATJ, only the courts in some member states use this instrument; and

[30] Alter, Helfer and Madsen, 'Conclusion' in Alter, Helfer and Madsen (eds), *International Court Authority* Conclusion (n 1) 441.
[31] ibid 439.

they almost exclusively use this for one single subject matter (intellectual property).[32] For the EACJ and the ECOWAS Court, the motivation of domestic courts for preliminary references is low so that despite the broad de jure opportunity, such references, practically, do not occur. In contrast, the motivation of domestic courts to address preliminary questions to the CJEU is higher and more widespread so that broad opportunity and high motivation translate into broad acceptance of the CJEU.

A second implication that deserves to be highlighted is that the factor that matters most for determining the relationship between an actor and an international court is not always the same. Rather, the determining factor needs to be assessed individually for each actor or group of actors. For example, in the context of human rights courts, the values and interests reflected in the idea of human rights adjudication are such that individuals as litigants are likely to have a high motivation to engage with the court and accept its authority. For these actors, opportunity or constraints are thus likely to be the determining factor. In comparison, the authority relationship between the same courts and other actors such as member states can be determined by a different factor. If the motivation of states to accept the authority of the court is low, even broad opportunity and low constraints will not make a difference. Here, motivation is at the lowest level of the three factors and thus has the biggest impact. In other words: for the authority of the same court, different factors can determine the authority relationships towards the various groups of actors.

This leads us to the third implication. If international courts use strategies that aim at enhancing their authority, these strategies can only be effective if they target the right factor for each actor. The right factor is the determining factor according to the MOC framework, that is the factor which is at the lowest level for the respective actor. There cannot be a one-size-fits-all strategy for all actors. For each actor, the MOC factors are different and, accordingly, for each actor, the lowest factor is not always the same. For some actors, motivation is at the lowest level so that motivation determines the behaviour. In this situation, only strategies that enhance motivation are effective. For other actors, opportunity is the lowest and thus the decisive factor. Here, only strategies that enhance opportunity are effective. For still further actors, ability is the lowest factor due to high constraints against accepting authority so that these constraining factors determine whether the actors accept authority or not. Only strategies that reduce such constraints are effective in this situation. Behavioural strategies thus require insights into which MOC factor is the most relevant for which actor. The following section outlines possible strategies of courts to enhance the acceptance of their authority.

II. STRATEGIES OF INTERNATIONAL COURTS TO ENHANCE THE ACCEPTANCE OF AUTHORITY

Each MOC setting is subject to change. It can become more favourable or less favourable for a certain behaviour. Part of the broader research on behavioural change is developing and assessing strategies to elicit more targeted behaviour.[33] Such strategies

[32] Alter and Helfer, *Transplanting International Courts* (n 19).

[33] See, eg, the overview of behavioural models of social marketing strategies, L Brennan, W Binney, L Parker, Tr Aleti and D Nguyen, 'Behavioural models (conative models)' in L Brennan, W Binney, L Parker,

for encouraging behavioural change relate to one of the recurring debates within the scholarship about international court authority. To what extent can courts influence whether they have broad or narrow authority regarding certain actors? Do factors for authority lie 'within the control' of international courts? And when are strategies to enhance authority and avoid pushback effective? In this scholarship, several authors have indeed argued that the behaviour of international courts can influence whether and to what extent actors accept their authority.[34] However, this literature leaves open how exactly the strategies of courts can contribute to fostering authority relationships and under which conditions they have a significant impact on actors.

The MOC framework sheds light on this question. One can assess how courts themselves can influence the behaviour of actors, to what extent certain courts do so (and others do not), and when such strategies are likely to be successful. As this section illustrates and Part II of the book demonstrates further, international courts can adopt different strategies to actively encourage actors to accept their authority. Courts can seek to increase the motivation of actors to accept their authority, increase the opportunities for actors to do so and reduce the constraints.

Before delving into an overview of possible strategies, it bears mentioning that this section is analytical rather than prescriptive. It highlights the strategies that courts can adopt and have adopted to influence the three MOC factors for their respective actors. These remarks do not contain the normative judgement that courts should adopt such strategies, prescribing such behaviour. Rather, it shows the possibilities that exist for courts to influence the MOC factors, engaging with the analytical discussion of whether courts can contribute to fostering authority relationships or not.

A. Increasing Motivation for Accepting Authority

Court strategies can address both the motivational elements outlined above: values and interests.

Values

A possible strategy of international courts is enhancing value-correspondence between the court and the actors. The following two examples illustrate such strategies.

A first potential target is the rule of law. International courts can attempt to strengthen the rule of law in their member states. Although not all international courts will be able to do so, some courts have a subject-matter jurisdiction that enables them to address structural rule of law-related issues within states. For example, the EACJ has a specific prong of its jurisdiction relating to the rule of law.[35] Further, human rights courts can target such structural issues in decisions on the right to a fair trial.

T Aleti and D Nguyen, *Social Marketing and Behaviour Change Models, Theory and Applications* (Edward Elgar 2014) 41.

[34] Helfer and Slaughter, 'Toward a Theory of Effective Supranational Adjudication' (n 1). See also Alter, Helfer and Madsen, 'How Context Shapes the Authority of International Courts' (n 3) 49 et seq.

[35] This prong is based on EACJ, *James Katabazi & 21 Others v The Secretary General of the East African Community & Another*, 1 November 2007, reference no 1/2007.

A second set of institutional values that international courts can target with strategies to increase value-correspondence are domestic constitutional approaches. A prominent example for a court that has adopted such a strategy is the IACtHR. The IACtHR has actively supported the 'neo-constitutional' approach in certain member states, including by developing the concept of 'conventionality control'.[36] The concept enables and obliges domestic courts to review legislation as to its compatibility with the American Convention on Human Rights as interpreted by the IACtHR.[37] This has strengthened the value-correspondence regarding a strong role for courts vis-a-vis other actors, which has contributed to actors accepting a broad authority of the IACtHR.

Further, international courts can address certain substantive values. An example for such a strategy is the CJEU's approach especially in its early decades to actively foster economic integration.[38] The integration friendly jurisprudence was favourable to economic actors within the common market, reducing possibilities for member states to adopt restrictive regulations concerning the four freedoms of the common market. By strengthening this value among economic actors, the CJEU created a shared value-basis between itself and these actors, enhancing value-correspondence as a motivational factor.

Interests

In addition to strategies addressing values, international courts can attempt to enhance the motivation of actors by addressing their practical interests. For example, if the interest of a considerable number of actors as in the inter-American context or the context of the ICC is to achieve transitional justice, a court can actively address this interest by providing special tools for that aim. Some of the special remedies designed by the IACtHR such as requests for public acts of apology, erection of memorials to deceased victims, or orders of investigation and punishment of those responsible for the violation, are designed by the court to address these interests.[39] By providing tools for actors to maximise their interests, a court can enhance the interest-based motivation of actors.

Further, the 'second order' interest of actors in effective behaviour is particularly susceptible for the strategies of international courts. For example, the CJEU has aimed at enhancing the motivation for the EU Commission to bring cases before the court by creating a 'strategic partnership' with the Commission concerning infringement procedures in which the Commission has a success rate of 90 per cent.[40] Here,

[36] Huneeus (n 9) 215.

[37] IACtHR, *Almonacid-Arellano et al v Chile*, 26 September 2006, (ser C) No 154, para 124: '[T]he Judiciary must exercise a sort of "conventionality control" between the domestic legal provisions which are applied to specific cases and the American Convention on Human Rights. To perform this task, the Judiciary has to take into account not only the treaty, but also the interpretation thereof made by the Inter-American Court, which is the ultimate interpreter of the American Convention'.

[38] On market integration as a goal of the CJEU, T Björnsson and Y Shany, 'The Court of Justice of the European Union' in Shany (ed), *Assessing the Effectiveness of International Courts* (n 3) 277, 286.

[39] For a list of categories of remedies, see GL Neuman, 'Inter-American Court of Human Rights (IACtHR)' in *Max Planck Encyclopedia of Public International Law* (2007) para 23.

[40] Björnsson and Shany (n 38) 289.

the court has actively addressed the Commission's interest in effective behaviour when introducing a procedure before the court. Further, as a more general strategy concerning actors' interests in effective behaviour, in order to avoid that proceedings are too lengthy and decisions come too late to effectively remedy the claimed violation of law, courts can, for example, streamline their decision-making by tools such as the 'pilot judgments' system adopted by the ECtHR.[41]

B. Increasing Opportunity for Accepting Authority

Courts can influence several elements of the opportunity structure. First, courts can influence their subject matter jurisdiction. They can interpret the formal rules of jurisdiction broadly, increasing the opportunity for actors to engage with the court. For example, the EACJ has constructed a human rights jurisdiction that was not included in the explicit mandate by the member states.[42] Reacting to expectations of human rights advocates, the court provided an opportunity for these actors to accept its authority.[43]

Second, courts can adopt strategies for broadening the access for level 1 and level 2 actors to the procedures before the court. The IACtHR, which initially faced a narrow opportunity for individuals to address the court, has developed cooperation with the Inter-American Commission to provide quasi-access for individuals to the court. According to their cooperation, the Commission generally brings a case before the court when individuals file a complaint before the Commission regarding a rights violation which is not remedied at the Commission level by the responding member state.[44] Moreover, although individuals cannot be formal parties to disputes before the IACtHR, the court has given them participation rights that come close to the position of a formal party.[45] The IACtHR has thus made individuals de facto level 1 actors which broadens the opportunity for these actors to engage with the court.

An additional way for international courts to influence opportunity is via the remedies that they order as well as via the scope of their review. To start with, depending on the remedies that courts choose, they can reach different groups of actors such as executive, legislative and judicial actors. For example, the ECtHR has, over time, taken a more far-reaching approach to remedies than in the early years, now also addressing domestic courts and legislators (see chapter five).

Further, courts can attempt to increase membership as an element that determines the opportunity of actors. An example of a strategy that influences membership concerns the notion of state. When the Committee on the Elimination

[41] On the pilot judgement procedure, M Fyrnys, 'Expanding Competences by Judicial Lawmaking: The Pilot Judgment Procedure of the European Court of Human Rights' (2011) 12 *German Law Journal* 1231.

[42] *James Katabazi & 21 Others v The Secretary General of the East African Community & Another*, 1 November 2007, reference no 1/2007.

[43] JT Gathii, 'The East African Court of Justice – Human Rights and Business Actors Compared' in Alter, Helfer and Madsen (eds), *International Court Authority* (n 1) 59.

[44] Article 45(1) of the Rules of Procedure of the Inter-American Commission on Human Rights.

[45] The autonomous procedural role for individuals is established by Article 25(1) of the Rules of Procedure of the IACtHR.

of Racial Discrimination (CERD) had to decide whether Palestine could file a complaint before it, the Committee had the chance to expand the membership via an interpretation of the notion of state.[46] The Committee could thus create the opportunity for the relevant Palestinian actors to engage with the Committee and accept its authority.

A final example of how international courts can enhance the opportunity for accepting their authority concerns the opportunity structure created by domestic law. For example, very early on in its jurisprudence, the CJEU adopted a strategy to limit the impact that the monist or dualist approach taken by member states would have on the opportunity for actors to accept its authority. By developing the doctrines of direct effect and primacy, the court has created a favourable infrastructure for the relationship between EU law and domestic law.[47] These doctrines aim at replacing the dualist approach of many member states, which would have jeopardised the uniform application of EU law within the member states. This jurisprudence has increased the opportunity for domestic actors to accept the authority of the court.

C. Reducing Constraints against Accepting Authority

The third factor that international courts can target are constraints against accepting authority. Such strategies can concern intrinsic as well as extrinsic constraints.

International courts can adopt strategies that address a lack of information as intrinsic constraints. This includes first and foremost the strategy to provide, on the court's website, information about the court, its procedure and its case law as well as engaging in outreach activities in relation to targeted audiences or interest groups. Another strategy addressing informational constraints among level 1 and level 2 actors but also certain level 3 actors relates to language. Having court decisions translated into other languages that might be relevant for the targeted audiences is a strategy that aims at reducing informational constraints for (potential) applicants as well as for level 3 actors regarding discursive authority.

As to financial constraints, international courts can also adopt some strategies. This includes the way in which they address cost orders, court fees and financial remedies. As to costs and fees, they can reduce the financial constraints for applicants, for example by refraining from cost orders to the disadvantage of applicants and by ensuring that there are no fees for bringing cases to court. As to respondents, they can decrease potential financial constraints by limiting the maximum amount of financial remedies. Further, international courts can encourage 'enabling' actors to help intrinsically constrained actors to overcome these constraints. For example, bar

[46] See CERD Committee, Inter-State communication submitted by the State of Palestine against Israel, 12 December 2019, CERD/C/100/5.

[47] On the de facto 'monism' postulated by the CJEU, see eg, M Kumm, 'The Moral Point of Constitutional Pluralism, Defining the Domain of Legitimate Institutional Civil Disobedience and Conscientious Objection' in J Dickson and P Eleftheriadis (eds) *Philosophical Foundations of European Union Law* (OUP 2012) 216, 227.

associations and NGOs can reduce lack of information or financial constraints that certain actors might face.[48]

Strategies against extrinsic constraints require that courts are able to influence the constraining actors. For example, if the government of a member state exercises pressure on other domestic actors such as individuals or domestic courts, the international court can adopt strategies to reduce the constraining behaviour of the government. The approach that the CJEU has taken on the issue of Polish judicial reforms serves as a case in point. By declaring certain measures to restructure the Polish judiciary unlawful (especially regarding judicial independence),[49] the CJEU attempts to limit the constraining effect of these measures on domestic courts, a constraining effect that impacts the ability of domestic courts to accept the authority of the CJEU.

In conclusion, although international courts might not be able to influence every parameter that contributes to the three MOC factors, the above examples have illustrated that there are nonetheless a variety of strategies that courts can adopt to enhance motivation, opportunity and the unconstrained ability of actors. Courts thus are not at the mercy of pre-existing circumstances. They can be active participants in a complex yet dynamic system of parameters that determine the authority relationship between these courts and other actors. However, it is also the case that not all strategies will be successful in enhancing the acceptance of court authority. Some strategies are effective, and others are not. Determining when they are indeed effective is the subject of the following section.

D. Effectiveness of MOC-Related Strategies

Assessing whether individual strategies of international courts to enhance the acceptance of their authority are effective presents a challenge. This is due to the many actors involved and the multiple factors at play that, in sum, create a complex web of interactions leading to a specific authority relationship between a court and an actor. However, the behavioural framework outlined in this book can offer insights on the matter. What is known about the relationship between the MOC factors as well as the effectiveness of behavioural strategies in other contexts can inform the assessment of court strategies.

First, it is important to reiterate that a strategy to enhance an MOC factor does not automatically lead to a change in the targeted behaviour. Not every increase in one of the MOC factors leads to a higher acceptance of the authority of the court. Rather, as outlined in chapter two, the 'bottleneck effect' requires that, for a change of behaviour, the factor with the lowest level of behaviour support is increased. For example, increasing opportunity does not show a significant effect if the actor's motivation is

[48] Alter, Helfer and Madsen, 'How Context Shapes the Authority of International Courts' (n 3) 51. Highlighting the role of NGOs as such 'enablers' for the ACtHPR, Daly and Wiebusch (n 3) 302.

[49] eg, CJEU, Case C-192/18, 5 November 2019, ECLI:EU:C:2019:924; Joined Cases C-585/18, C-624/18 and C-625/18, 19 November 2019, ECLI:EU:C:2019:982; Joined Cases C-748/19 to C-754/19, 16 November 2021, ECLI:EU:C:2021:931.

the MOC factor that is at the lowest level. The effectiveness of MOC-related strategies is thus *actor-specific*. In other words, a strategy that is always effective for all courts vis-a-vis all actors does not exist. One can only assess the effectiveness of a strategy for the specific relationship between a certain court and a certain actor. In Part II of this book, I provide examples of such a court-and actor-specific assessment of court strategies to improve the MOC setting.

Second, when analysing the effectiveness of court strategies, the adverse effects of such strategies play a role as well. Such effects can concern the other MOC factors for the same actor ('intra-actor' effect). They can also concern the interrelation between MOC factors of multiple actors ('inter-actors' effect). An example of a situation in which a court targets one factor and adversely affects another factor of the same actor ('*intra*-actor' effect) is the following: if a court adopts a strategy to enhance the opportunity for applicants, it is possible that this strategy inadvertently increases the extrinsic constraints on these applicants. This is the case if the broadened opportunity motivates external actors to exercise pressure on applicants not to bring cases to the court.

Adverse '*inter*-actors' effects, ie, the interrelation between MOC factors of multiple actors, work in a similar way. Increasing an MOC factor for one actor can directly affect a factor of another actor. For example, strengthening value-correspondence vis-a-vis one actor can undermine the value-correspondence vis-a-vis another actor. As a result, a strategy that aims at increasing the motivation of one group of actors leads to decreasing the motivation for another group of actors. This reflects the challenges stemming from the actor-specific nature of behavioural strategies. A strategy can negatively affect the MOC factors of other actors if the factors of both sets of actors are somewhat opposed. Consequently, the level of homogeneity among actors considerably influences the extent to which international courts can adopt effective behavioural strategies to enhance their authority.[50] It is thus decisive for effectiveness where the relevant audience of a court is situated on the spectrum between homogeneity and heterogeneity of actors' values and interests.

III. FACTORS FOR PUSHBACK AGAINST THE AUTHORITY OF INTERNATIONAL COURTS

As in chapter two, I conclude this chapter by reversing the perspective and taking a closer look at pushback against international courts. I consider the factors for why actors who initially accepted the authority of international courts push back against them. Rather than supportive behaviour, the point of reference here is the critical behaviour of actors. The analytical framework however remains the same: I discuss factors for motivation, opportunity and constraint relating to pushback. I also refer briefly to potential strategies of courts that aim at influencing such factors to avoid or mitigate pushback.[51]

[50] See also Helfer and Slaughter, 'Toward a Theory of Effective Supranational Adjudication' (n 1) 335.

[51] Differentiating between avoiding and mitigating pushback, MR Madsen, P Cebulak and M Wiebusch, 'Backlash against international courts: explaining the forms and patterns of resistance to international courts' (2018) 14 *International Journal of Law in Context* 197, 214.

In this book, I use the notion of *pushback* as an umbrella term for the different forms and intensities in which actors can challenge the authority of an international court. Although in the literature on international courts authors have suggested a variety of terminologies and classifications of such behaviour,[52] for many of them, the main thrust of differentiating between types of pushback is similar. It relates to the target of the pushback, for example targeting a single norm or rather the institution itself, and the aim of the pushback, for example critique with the aim of reform or rather a rejection, withdrawal from, or elimination of, the institution altogether.[53] Against the backdrop of these suggestions, I use the following terminology to differentiate between forms of pushback: structural pushback on the one hand, including *backlash* as its most intense form and *resistance* as a less intense form; and non-structural pushback on the other hand, including *norm contestation* and *objection* against a court decision in particular by non-compliance.[54]

Backlash is generally considered to be the strongest form of pushback against courts. It is characterised by the fact that it 'targets the institutions as such and their authority'[55] rather than contesting a certain legal norm or its interpretation by a court.[56] The actor that is lashing back aims at 'reduc[ing] the authority, competence, or jurisdiction of the court'.[57] Backlash is thus of a structural nature; it attacks the court as an institution rather than challenging its jurisprudence with regard to specific legal questions. Moreover, when engaging in backlash, actors ultimately reject the institution as a whole. It is 'actions taken in opposition to the system itself'.[58] This

[52] eg, Madsen, Cebulak and Wiebusch (n 51); M Breuer, 'The Concept of "Principled Resistance" to ECtHR Judgments: A Useful Tool to Analyse Implementation Deficits?' (2021) 12 *Journal of International Dispute Settlement* 250; M Breuer (ed), *Principled Resistance to ECtHR Judgments: A New Paradigm?* (Springer 2019); X Soley and S Steininger, 'Parting ways or lashing back? Withdrawals, backlash and the Inter-American Court of Human Rights' (2018) 14 *International Journal of Law in Context* 237; S Caserta and P Cebulak, 'Resilience Techniques of International Courts in Times of Resistance to International Law' (2021) 70 *International & Comparative Law Quarterly* 737; KJ Alter, JT Gathii and LR Helfer, 'Backlash against International Courts in West, East and Southern Africa: Causes and Consequences' (2016) 27 *European Journal of International Law* 293; A Hofmann, 'Resistance against the Court of Justice of the European Union' (2018) 14 *International Journal of Law in Context* 258; Daly and Wiebusch (n 3); MR Madsen, 'The Challenging Authority of the European Court of Human Rights: from Cold War Legal Diplomacy to the Brighton Declaration and Backlash' (2016) 79 *Law and Contemporary Problems* 141; H Lovat, 'International Criminal Tribunal Backlash' in KJ Heller, F Mégret, SMH Nouwen, JD Ohlin and D Robinson (eds), *Oxford Handbook of International Criminal Law* (OUP 2020) 601; J Powderly, 'International criminal justice in an age of perpetual crisis' (2019) 32 *Leiden Journal of International Law* 1; D Caron and E Shirlow, 'Dissecting Backlash: The Unarticulated Causes of Backlash and Its Unintended Consequences' in A Føllesdal and G Ulfstein (eds), *The Judicialization of International Law: A Mixed Blessing?* (OUP 2018) 159.

[53] In contrast, some others include also the – legally phrased – motivation for pushback into their definition, as in the case of 'principled resistance' proposed by Breuer, 'The Concept of "Principled Resistance"' (n 52).

[54] This terminology is most closely linked to the categorisation by Soley and Steininger (n 52) as well as to the differentiation between 'ordinary' and 'extraordinary resistence' [here pushback] by Madsen, Cebulak and Wiebusch (n 51).

[55] Madsen, Cebulak and Wiebusch (n 51) 203.

[56] For a definition of backlash that relates to the 'methods rather than the aims of the actors, see Lovat (n 52).

[57] W Sandholtz, Y Bei and K Caldwell, 'Backlash and International Human Rights Courts' in A Brysk and M Stohl (eds) *Contracting Human Rights* (Edward Elgar 2018) 159, 160.

[58] Caron and Shirlow (n 52) 160.

is, for example, the case when a member state withdraws from the jurisdiction of a court or when domestic actors including domestic courts entirely cease to procedurally engage with a court and to implement its judgments.

Resistance, although being structural in nature, does not fulfil the second feature that defines backlash. Resistance also targets the court as an institution rather than merely a norm or a decision. But actors that resist a court do not reject the institution as such. Instead, an actor that resists an international court without lashing back 'is still invested in the institution and seeks to reform it from within'.[59] Examples of such resistance are member states that aim at reforming the court in a manner that would reduce its jurisdiction or the access opportunity for applicants.

Norm contestation targets a specific norm rather than the institution. Yet it goes beyond the context of a specific judicial decision, in contrast to objection (see below). Instead, it 'primarily targets the norm(s) that are embodied in the decision'.[60] As norm contestation goes beyond the individual judicial decision, actors often challenge a specific norm repeatedly. Further, norm contestation can concern the content of a norm, its validity or its existence. Targeted norms can be both substantive norms applied by the court as well as procedural norms that determine jurisdiction and access to the court.

An *objection* against a court decision targets this decision without the structural component of challenging the institution. It does not have 'consequences on the structure and functioning of the [court]'.[61] Its strongest form is non-compliance with a decision, but state actors can also object against a decision by criticising it (more or less intensely).

Differentiating between the forms of pushback is relevant for assessing the MOC setting for pushback because this setting is not the same for all forms. In particular, the opportunity for pushback is inherently diverse for different forms. Further, as Part II of this book demonstrates, the determining factor according to the MOC framework can differ for the forms of pushback against the same court.

A. Motivation for Pushback and Strategies for Reducing Such Motivation

The motivation of actors to push back against an international court follows, for the most part, the rationale of the motivation for accepting authority. It can include a lack of value-correspondence, and it can concern practical interests. When the values of the actors and the entity increasingly diverge or when interests shift in a way that is detrimental to the existing authority relationship, this change constitutes the motivational factor for pushback. In this section, I provide a (non-exhaustive) overview of factors that can motivate pushback. Part II of this book expands on these factors when assessing pushback against the ECOWAS Court and the ECtHR.

[59] Soley and Steininger (n 52) 241. Different understandings of the term resistance are adopted by other authors, eg, Sandholtz, Bei and Caldwell (n 57) 160; Madsen, Cebulak and Wiebusch (n 51).
[60] Soley and Steininger (n 52) 240.
[61] ibid.

A lack of value-correspondence regarding both institutional and substantive values can motivate pushback. An institutional value that can be related to motivation for pushback is judicial independence. If, in the perception of certain actors, a court becomes 'too independent' or, inversely, 'too politicised' as compared with what it was before, such a structural shift can reduce value-correspondence. Accordingly, the ICC's 'proximity to state power' has triggered critique by such member states and other actors who value a higher level of judicial independence than that reflected in the ICC's practice.[62] Further, an example concerning substantive values is the lack of value-correspondence with regard to racial equality and post-colonial land reform in the context of the SADC Tribunal. This lack of value-correspondence has led to the backlash against the court.[63]

Further, pushback motivations can emanate from practical interests. For state actors, sovereignty-related interests are prominent in this regard. Such interests can, for example, be touched upon when the court broadens its jurisdiction, when it interprets procedural rules in a way that creates broader access for applicants or when it establishes principles such as direct applicability of the respective treaty norms in the domestic legal order or the primacy of these norms vis-a-vis domestic law. In addition, specific decisions on politically sensitive or socially controversial subject matters can motivate pushback. Scholars of international courts have argued that decisions in so-called high-politics areas are perceived as triggering more pushback than other more technical subject matters.[64] To what extent decisions on high-politics issues have in fact motivated pushback against the ECOWAS Court and the ECtHR is discussed in chapters four to six.

A specific group of actors that have been pushing back against international courts are domestic courts.[65] For these actors, there exist certain distinct motivational factors. In particular, domestic courts can perceive an international court as a threat to their own power. For example, domestic constitutional courts in the European region have to share competence for human rights matters both with the ECtHR and the CJEU, a fact that has created distributional conflicts. In this context, one can observe that the broadening authority especially of the CJEU in human rights matters has impacted the interests of domestic courts in a way that, at a certain point, has triggered pushback.[66]

[62] L Vinjamuri, 'The International Criminal Court – The Paradox of its Authority' in Alter, Helfer and Madsen (eds), *International Court Authority* (n 1) 331, 340.

[63] ET Achiume, 'The SADC Tribunal Sociopolitical Dissonance and the Authority of International Courts' in Alter, Helfer and Madsen (eds), *International Court Authority* (n 1) 124, 125.

[64] On human rights being a particularly likely field of high-politics issue areas providing opportunity to pushback, Madsen, Cebulak and Wiebusch (n 51) 215.

[65] See also generally on the role of domestic courts in the implementation of international obligations, R Kunz, 'Judging International Judgments Anew? The Human Rights Courts before Domestic Courts' (2019) 30 *European Journal of International Law* 1129; M Herdegen, 'General Overview' in S Kadelbach, T Rensmann and E Rieter (eds), *Judging International Human Rights: Courts of General Jurisdiction as Human Rights Courts* (Springer 2019) 345.

[66] See, eg, on the reaction of the German Constitutional Court to this jurisprudence, D Burchardt, 'Backlash against the Court of Justice of the EU? The Recent Jurisprudence of the German Constitutional Court on EU Fundamental Rights as a Standard of Review' (2020) 21 *German Law Journal* 1.

It bears mentioning that some motivations for pushback relate to the performance of the court while others are external to this performance.[67] The latter is the case in situations of political change when the values of the governing actors are shifting, for example with an increase in authoritarian structures. It also happens when actors question the values underlying the overall international legal regime of which the court is a part, including a rejection of multilateralism. Influencing such motivations is much more difficult, if at all possible, for a court as compared with motivations that are linked to the court's performance.

Courts can adopt a range of strategies to reduce pushback motivation. An important strategy in this regard is for a court to take an incremental approach to developing its jurisprudence.[68] An incremental approach can lower motivation for pushback due to the fact that it can be understood as a 'foot-in-the-door' technique outlined in chapter two.[69] Part II of this book will further exemplify that, in line with this technique, actors perceive the demanding jurisprudence of an international court as less intrusive – which in turn generates less motivation for pushback. As this technique can also work for obtaining high-cost behaviour, it is important for the context of international courts.[70]

Another key strategy of international courts is to use deference tools such as the margin of appreciation or a restrictive interpretation of their jurisdiction.[71] This strategy addresses the sovereignty-related interests of state actors and aims at reducing their pushback potential. In a similar vein, courts pair activist elements with state-friendly elements in order to reduce the pushback-motivating effect of the former. This is a way for courts to address diverging expectations, interests and values among their respective groups of actors. It is common for courts with diverse constituencies to attempt to find a middle ground between catering to one group or the other in order to reduce the pushback motivation for all groups of actors.

In addition to strategies that aim at reducing the pushback motivation in order to avoid pushback to begin with, courts also adopt strategies to manage ongoing pushback. For example, in the case of norm contestation, courts often have leeway to decide whether to escalate the conflict or not. One of the courts that has taken

[67] Pointing out that it can sometimes be difficult to distinguish whether 'backlash generates the cases, or if the cases generate the backlash', Alter, Helfer and Madsen, 'How Context Shapes the Authority of International Courts' (n 3) 42.

[68] On incrementalism as a factor, see Helfer and Slaughter, 'Toward a Theory of Effective Supranational Adjudication' (n 1) 314.

[69] JL Freedman and SC Fraser, 'Compliance without pressure: the foot-in-the-door technique' (1966) 4 *Journal of Personality and Social Psychology* 195; on the effect of this technique in 'unjust authority' situations, P Bocchiaro and PG Zimbardo, 'Defying Unjust Authority: An Exploratory Study' (2010) 29 *Current Psychology* 155, 166.

[70] M Goldman, CR Creason and CG McCall, 'Compliance employing a two-feet-in-the-door procedure' (1981) 114 *Journal of Social Psychology* 259.

[71] For an in-depth assessment of deference techniques, see E Shirlow, *Judging at the Interface: Deference to State Decision-Making Authority in International Adjudication* (CUP 2021). On the standard of review as a deference mechanism from a comparative perspective, V Lanovoy, 'Standards of Review in the Practice of International Courts and Tribunals' in G Kajtár, B Çalı and M Milanovic (eds), *Secondary Rules of Primary Importance in International Law: Attribution, Causality, Evidence, and Standards of Review in the Practice of International Courts and Tribunals* (OUP 2022) 42.

the latter approach to pushback management is the CJEU. It has generally shown an awareness of the political impact of its judgments and has taken into account the critique by member states or other actors. It was willing to change its jurisprudence to accommodate such critique as, for example, in the conflict with the Italian Constitutional Court in the context of the *Taricco* saga.[72] Such strategies have been termed 'legal diplomacy'.[73]

B. Opportunity for Pushback and Strategies for Reducing Such Opportunity

The opportunity for pushback against international courts differs depending on the forms of pushback. For backlash by withdrawal from the jurisdiction of the court, the opportunity structure is, inter alia, influenced by whether this jurisdiction is optional or mandatory for member states of the respective treaty regime. When a treaty regime contains such optional clauses, this makes it easier for member states to withdraw their declarations regarding these clauses. For example, concerning the ACtHPR as well as the pre-Protocol 11 ECtHR, such optional clauses have provided an opportunity for pushback.

Regarding resistance or backlash in the form of treaty amendments, the legal requirement as to who can initiate amendment proposals is a first element of the legal opportunity structure. A key opportunity feature is whether amendments require unanimity among all member states or whether it is possible to adopt protocols which can enter into force after the ratification of only some of the member states. The pushback opportunity is broader in the latter case than in the former. Further opportunity elements include procedural requirements such as temporal requirements to reduce the opportunity for rushed 'overnight' amendments and participation rights of other actors such as treaty institutions or civil society actors.

The legal opportunity structure for pushback in the form of norm contestation is shaped by procedural law. When respondents want to contest the jurisdiction of the court or the access possibility for applicants concerning their standing, a time limit or the exhaustion of domestic remedies, they often do so via preliminary objections. Whether the procedural framework allows for such objections more or less generously, contributes to shaping the legal discourse and potentially the outcome of the norm contestation. Furthermore, the behaviour of other actors is an element of the opportunity structure. When respondents observe other respondents to contest a norm in a certain way, this makes them aware of this particular opportunity for pushback. Other actors can thus shape the subjective perception that an actor has regarding the opportunity for pushback.[74]

The opportunity for non-compliance is the most multifaceted. To start with, the relationship between domestic law and the law of the respective treaty regime

[72] CJEU, C-42/17 (*Taricco II*), ECLI:EU:C:2017:936, and C-105/14 (*Taricco I*), ECLI:EU:C:2015:555; Italian CC, order 24/2017 and decision 115/2018.

[73] Madsen, Cebulak and Wiebusch (n 51) 214.

[74] On the subjective dimension of MOC, see ch 2.

is a feature of the legal opportunity structure for non-compliance. This relationship includes questions such as the direct applicability of the international legal norms and decisions, the primacy of these norms and decisions vis-a-vis domestic law, and the enforcement of the judgments of the international court. If there is no direct applicability, no primacy and no enforcement regime, the opportunity for non-compliance is broadest. Further, the scope of remedies that the international court can grant is part of the opportunity structure for non-compliance. When a court only issues declaratory decisions, there is – at least according to a formal understanding of compliance – no opportunity for non-compliance. The wider the range of remedies and the more demanding they are, the broader the opportunity for non-compliance. Another element of the opportunity structure is the (non-)existence of a monitoring mechanism. Considering that monitoring makes non-compliance salient, there is less opportunity for respondents not to comply without this being noticed. Finally, the behaviour of other actors is an element of the opportunity structure for pushback. For example, if one domestic court decides not to enforce the decisions of the international court based on a specific legal reasoning, this can make domestic courts in other member states aware of this form of pushback.

As part of the behavioural opportunity structure for pushback, the 'true partner effect' referred to in chapter two also becomes relevant in the context of international courts. When there is already another actor that is pushing back against the same aspect of the court's jurisprudence, the 'true partner effect' makes it more likely for the second actor to also engage in the same behaviour. Deviating from the majority approach of the social group is facilitated by this behavioural effect. Part II of this book provides examples of a pushback behaviour that one can interpret as an expression of this effect.

International courts can adopt a number of strategies to reduce the opportunity for pushback. With regard to resistance or backlash that involve treaty amendments, courts can, if this is part of their jurisdiction, shape the procedural and/or substantive conditions for such amendments. This can create a legal hurdle against such pushback. Regarding norm contestation, courts can adjust procedural rules to rein in certain gateways for contestation such as preliminary objections. To reduce the opportunity for objection in the form of non-compliance, courts can, for example, focus on declaratory decision-making and refrain from ordering respondents to take specific measures. In the same vein, courts can adjust the scope of their review, for example by excluding the review of domestic judicial decisions. Some courts such as the ECOWAS Court and the IACtHR have also established their own frameworks for monitoring compliance with their decisions, a strategy that, inter alia, reduces the opportunity for undetected non-compliance.[75]

[75] On the monitoring by the ECOWAS Court, see ch 4. On the IACtHR, see eg, IACtHR, *Baena Ricardo et al v Panama* (competence), 28 November 2003, Series C No 104; CM Bailliet, 'Procedure for Monitoring Compliance with Judgments and Other Decisions: Inter-American Court of Human Rights (IACtHR)' in H Ruiz Fabri and R Wolfrum (eds), *Max Planck Encyclopedia of International Procedural Law*: opil.ouplaw.com/display/10.1093/law-mpeipro/e2653.013.2653/law-mpeipro-e2653. On monitoring by human rights courts, see also Herdegen (n 65) 351.

C. Constraints against Pushback and Strategies for Increasing Such Constraints

Broad constraints against pushback can prevent actors from pushing back against the court even if they are motivated to do so and would have the opportunity for it. For such constraints, the relationship between the different actors or groups of actors plays an important role. An actor that is motivated to push back against an international court can be constrained by other actors who support the court and exercise pressure on the former. In this case, such supporting actors directly influence the ability of the actor that considers pushing back against the court.

Supporting actors can stem from the same group as the actor that is motivated to push back, and from a different group. As an example of the former, state actors can constrain pushback by other state actors. This is particularly the case in situations in which pushback would entail a treaty amendment or any other constellation in which it is necessary that other member states agree. The crucial role of supporting state actors in such situations has, for example, become apparent during the pushback attempts against the ECOWAS Court and the ECtHR (see chapters four and five). Further, as a second constellation, non-state actors can constrain state actors in their pushback attempt, ie, the constraints stem from a different group of actors. This can include civil society groups exercising pressure on a government that wants to withdraw from an international court, or academics and bar associations criticising a domestic court's pushback against an international court. Moreover, in a legal regime that, in addition to the court, has other strong institutions such as the Inter-American Commission on Human Rights, the support by these institutions can also have a constraining effect on pushback.

In addition to extrinsic constraints of supporting actors, there are several context-specific factors that can constrain pushback. Possible are knowledge-related intrinsic constraints. When actors have only low awareness of the court's activities, this makes it less likely for them to push back even though there would be objective motivational factors for them to do so. Further, a behavioural constraint against pushback is the status quo bias. As outlined in chapter two, there is a constraining effect of this tendency to place a higher value on any state of affairs that actors consider to be the status quo than they would place on the same state of affairs if it were not the status quo.[76] For example, certain features of the procedural law or of the substantive standards established by the court are valued more highly after they have been in existence for a certain time. To push back against these features at a later stage, state actors would have to overcome a status quo bias.

Strategies of international courts to increase constraints against pushback by some actors aim in particular at strengthening the support by other actors. When a court manages to gain the support of many actors, it is more likely that these actors will constrain attempts of other actors to pushback against the court. Such support would require that the constraining actors accept the authority of the court and that they are also willing to actively stand up against actors who push back. This aspect shows how closely the strategies regarding various actors are interwoven. Increasing

[76] See ch 2 section I.

motivation for accepting authority for one group of actors can double as a strategy to increase the constraints against pushback by another group of actors.

IV. TOWARDS AN MOC ASSESSMENT OF INDIVIDUAL INTERNATIONAL COURTS

After this chapter has given an overview of how the MOC framework can be applied to assess the authority of international courts, Part II of this book will put this framework into practice. It will assess the authority relationships of two selected courts: the ECOWAS Court and the ECtHR.

The present chapter has already foreshadowed the structure of this assessment. I will analyse the factors for accepting the authority of international courts as well as the factors for pushback. For both of these MOC settings, I will assess which of the factors predominantly determine whether the relevant groups of actors accept the authority of the courts. Further, I will outline the strategies that the respective courts adopt to improve the MOC setting and strengthen their authority relationships; and I will assess whether, according to the MOC framework, these strategies are effective. Unlike in the present chapter, this assessment will be *actor-specific*. The aim is to show what the MOC setting for each group of actors looks like. Only such an actor-specific approach makes it possible to evaluate the authority relationships and the factors for these relationships in sufficient detail. As mentioned in the introduction to this book, I focus on level 1 and level 2 actors, ie (potential) applicants and (potential) respondents, both broadly understood. Among these categories, I differentiate again among different actors that engage with the courts as applicants and as respondents. This can include member state governments, legislators and domestic courts, institutions of the respective regional organisation, individuals, corporate actors, NGOs and other civil society groups.

In terms of methodology, I base the assessment on a meta-analysis of research findings in the scholarship on the respective courts as well as on my own primary research. In particular for the ECOWAS Court for which there is not yet such a wealth of scholarship as in the case of the ECtHR, this is a crucial aspect of the analysis. I have analysed the decisions of these courts both as to their doctrinal content that shapes the legal elements of the behavioural setting in which actors potentially accept the authority of the court, and as to the strategies that these courts adopt to improve the MOC factors. This legal analysis is thus a key element of Part II. It is complemented with, and embedded in, findings on socio-political and practical factors that are part of the MOC setting.

It is part of the analysis to evaluate which of the factors predominantly determine the behaviour of these actors according to the MOC framework. As described in chapter two, the MOC factor that is the most unfavourable determines the behaviour of the relevant actors and thus the extent to which this actor accepts the authority of the international court ('bottleneck effect'). To find this factor, I classify, for each group of actors, their motivation, the opportunity and the constraints as being on a low, moderate or high level. If needed, I use intermediate levels such as low to moderate or moderate to high. This classification makes an approximate quantification possible, which in turn is used to compare the levels of each MOC factor and define the least favourable. This approximate quantification is, due to the interplay of factors and the necessary contextualisation, not always clear-cut. But it makes it possible to paint a general picture of the behavioural setting for each group of actors and to define the determining factor. Moreover, this quantification is used to illustrate the findings for each court and group of actors with diagrams that translate the favourability levels (low, moderate to low, moderate, moderate to high, high) into a scale of 0 to 5. These figures summarise the findings.

Finally, part of the methodology employed in Part II is to take into account the development of authority relationships over time. I thus highlight the changes in the MOC setting that have occurred during the practice of each court. For the ECtHR that is a rather 'old' court, these changes are numerous and spread over a long period of time. However, for the ECOWAS Court as a 'newer' court, such changes – including major ones – have also taken place, so that the temporal assessment is also important for understanding the development of its authority relationships with its audiences.

Part II

Applying the Behavioural Concept of International Court Authority

4

The Court of Justice of the Economic Community of West African States (ECOWAS)

I. INTRODUCTION TO THE ECOWAS COURT

THE ECONOMIC COMMUNITY of West African States (ECOWAS) is a regional organisation of currently 12 member states in West Africa which aims at promoting economic integration in the region. It was initially established in 1975 and, after a period in which it had somewhat fallen into irrelevance, relaunched in 1993 with the adoption of the Revised Treaty. The 12 member states of ECOWAS are Benin, Cabo Verde, Côte d'Ivoire, the Gambia, Ghana, Guinea (currently suspended), Guinea Bissau, Liberia, Nigeria, Senegal, Sierra Leone and Togo. Until recently, Mali, Niger and Burkina Faso have also been member states of ECOWAS. After their respective military coups and an ensuing conflict with ECOWAS, the three states however declared their withdrawal from the organisation in 2024.

Article 3(1) of the Revised Treaty provides that the aim of ECOWAS is to 'promote cooperation and integration, leading to the establishment of an economic union in West Africa in order to raise the living standards of its people, and to maintain and enhance economic stability, foster relations among Member States and contribute to the progress and development of the African Continent'. According to Article 6 of the Treaty, the institutions of the community include, inter alia, the Authority of Heads of State and Government, the Council of Ministers, the Community Parliament, the Commission (former Executive Secretariat)[1] and the Community Court of Justice (ECOWAS Court).

The ECOWAS Court of Justice was created by the Revised ECOWAS Treaty of 1993 and accompanying Protocol A/P1/7/91. It was inaugurated in 2001 and heard its first case in 2004. Shortly after the court started its activity, the procedural framework of the court was amended by Additional Protocol A/SP.1/01/05 (19/01/2005). The court's initial jurisdiction concerned, at its core, the interpretation and application of regional integration law. This jurisdiction has been broadened by the 2005 Protocol to matters relating to human rights. The ECOWAS Court is thus a hybrid regional court, ie, a court with a combined jurisdiction regarding regional

[1] ECOWAS Decision A/DEC.16/01/06 transformed the Executive Secretariat into a Commission.

integration and human rights protection. Both these strands of jurisdiction will be addressed in this chapter and assessed as to the MOC factors that contribute to actors accepting the court's authority. In addition, it is only briefly mentioned here that the court also has jurisdiction concerning various additional matters including disputes between ECOWAS and its employees; the function as an Arbitral Tribunal; and the competence conferred on it by an agreement of the parties (Article 10 of the amended Protocol).

The court's seat is in Abuja, Nigeria. It was originally composed of seven judges; since 2018 the number of judges has been reduced to five. Addressing initially 15 and currently 12 member states and ECOWAS institutional actors, the court has a considerable reach among level 1 and level 2 actors. According to the court's statistics, there have been more than 350 (reported) decisions of the court between 2003 and 2025.[2] Of these decisions, the vast majority concerns human rights matters. The number of decisions rendered each year has been increasing. Furthermore, as the analysis in this chapter will outline, the existing authority relationship towards level 1 and level 2 actors has been robust over time. Despite some instances of pushback in the early phase of the court's operational phase (see section II.B.ii), the extent of the authority relationship has not reduced. Rather, as the following sections demonstrate, it has broadened during the past 20 years.

This brief overview indicates that the ECOWAS Court is well suited to study developing authority relationships between the court and its audiences. It allows us to assess the MOC factors for applicants and respondents concerning the acceptance of authority as well as for pushback. The dual mandate also makes it possible to assess – and to contrast – how the MOC factors play out for human rights matters as compared with regional integration matters. With this aim, the human rights (section II) and regional integration law (section III) contexts are addressed in turn.

II. MOC IN THE CONTEXT OF HUMAN RIGHTS

As the MOC factors for level 1 and level 2 actors diverge for (potential) applicants on the one hand and (potential) respondents on the other, this section analyses these factors for both groups of actors individually (II.A and II.B). In addition, further distinctions are made where appropriate for sub-groups among these actors such as individuals, corporate entities, NGOs as well as governmental and judicial actors within the member states. This analysis aims at establishing how the MOC setting is shaped for each group of actors and, comparatively, how the MOC factors diverge among these groups. I then link these findings to the strategies of the court, showing where the court has influenced the MOC factors and, whether, according to the MOC framework, the court has indeed tackled the determining factor that will direct the behaviour of the relevant actors (II.C).

[2] An unofficial (non-exhaustive) repository of decisions is available at: ihrda.uwazi.io/.

A. MOC Factors for (Potential) Applicants

I start the assessment by exploring the factors that shape motivation (section II.A.i), opportunity (section II.A.ii) and constraints (section II.A.iii) in turn. This aims at determining the nature and extent of each MOC component. I then analyse which of the factors primarily determines whether (potential) applicants accept the authority of the ECOWAS Court (section II.A.iv).

i. Motivation

Motivational factors for (potential) applicants in human rights cases can both be related to these actors' values and interests. The following remarks provide an overview of the motivational factors that are relevant in the context of the ECOWAS Court.

Values

To start with, for (potential) applicants in human rights cases, the substantive value of human rights protection is a motivational factor. This factor is specifically important for actors that are not personally affected by a human rights violation such as NGOs who aim at improving the structural human rights situation in the ECOWAS member states. Such human rights promoting NGOs that have addressed the court include, inter alia, regional branches of Amnesty International, Avocat Sans Frontieres, the Centre pour la Défense des Droits de l'Homme et la Démocratie en Afrique, the 'Socio-Economic Rights & Accountability Project' (SERAP) and various local NGOs.[3] But other actors, including individuals, are also likely to be motivated by value considerations regarding human rights protection. Such motivational factors become particularly weighty when, as will be outlined below, the interest-related motivational factors are rather low with regard to the interest in dispute resolution and effective remedies. Upholding human rights as a value in legal and political discourse is an aim that, for value-motivated actors, can stand on its own.

Further, a relevant procedural value that can constitute a motivational factor for (potential) applicants is the independence of the ECOWAS Court. As human rights are for the most part directed against state governments, the independence of the ECOWAS Court from these governments is important for (potential) applicants. The institutional design of the ECOWAS Court reflects the value of judicial independence. Its independence is explicitly required by Article 15(3) of the Revised ECOWAS Treaty and Article 3(1) of the Protocol: 'Judges shall be independent, and the court shall execute its functions independently from the member states and the ECOWAS

[3] eg, *Registered Trustees of Avocat Sans Frontieres France v Nigeria*, 31 January 2014, ECW/CCJ/APP/14/13; *Amnesty International Togo and Others v Togo*, 25 June 2020, ECW/CCJ/JUD/09/20; *SERAP v Nigeria*, 19 June 2014, ECW/CCJ/JUD/16/14; *SERAP v Nigeria*, 14 December 2012, ECW/CCJ/JUD/18/12; *Centre for Democracy and Development, and Another v Mamadou Tandja & Niger*, 9 May 2011, ECW/CCJ/JUD/05/11; *SERAP v Nigeria and Universal Basic Education Commission*, 30 November 2010, ECW/CCJ/JUD/07/10; *Advocaid Ltd v Sierra Leone*, 7 November 2024, ECW/CCJ/JUD/33/24.

institutions'. The 2005 Protocol created a Judicial Council in charge of judicial appointments, replacing the former system in which Heads of States decided which judges to appoint. The Judicial Council is also competent for disciplinary matters, 'insulat[ing] judges from attempts by governments to remove them from office'.[4] Judges have diplomatic immunity (Article 6 of the Protocol). They shall not exercise any functions of a political, administrative or professional nature (Article 4(11) of the Protocol). Judges currently only have a comparatively short four-year term which is however non-renewable – as opposed to the initial design where judges were appointed for a renewable five-year term. Deliberations of the court are secret (Article 19(3) of the Protocol). In addition, the court is financially independent from foreign financing, in contrast to several other regional courts. Its budget is almost entirely provided by the ECOWAS member states via an ECOWAS Community levy and ECOWAS reserve fund.[5] In sum, the *de jure* independence of the court is relatively high.

The perception that (potential) applicants have of the court's *de facto* independence might however be influenced by additional aspects. This includes the fact that the judges of the ECOWAS Court are generally recruited from among members of the domestic judiciary and the domestic judiciary is in many member states not considered to be fully independent from state governments.[6] In particular in combination with the comparatively short four-year tenure, actors might have concerns about whether the judges are able to free themselves from the domestic culture of government deference that might exist in their home jurisdictions. Such concerns can however be overcome when actors consider the previous jurisprudence, especially the fact that the court has repeatedly decided against state governments, as well as when considering the emphasis that the court puts on presenting itself as independent (see also section II.A.iii).[7] As a result, although there is no evidence of major concerns as to the independence of the ECOWAS Court, actors might differ in how high they perceive the level of *de facto* independence to be.

Interests

Turning to interest-related motivational factors, dispute resolution is classically perceived as a key interest for (potential) applicants to engage with a court.[8] Considering the interest of actors in effective behaviour, dispute resolution is likely

[4] KJ Alter, LR Helfer and JR McAllister, 'A New International Human Rights Court For West Africa: The Ecowas Community Court of Justice' (2013) 107 *American Journal of International Law* 737, 760.

[5] D Abebe, 'Does International Human Rights Law in African Courts Make a Difference?' (2017) 56 *Virginia Journal of International Law* 527, 563.

[6] See in more detail on this aspect, section II.B.i.

[7] Independence and impartiality are presented as core values of the court, see: courtecowas.org/about_us/mission-vision/.

[8] On dispute resolution as a function of international courts, A von Bogdandy and I Venzke, 'On the functions of international courts: an appraisal in light of their burgeoning public authority' (2013) 26 *Leiden Journal of International Law* 49; A von Bogdandy and I Venzke, *In Whose Name? A Public Law Theory of International Adjudication* (OUP 2014); JE Alvarez, 'What are International Judges for? The Main Functions of International Adjudication' in CPR Romano, KJ Alter and Y Shany (eds), *The Oxford Handbook of International Adjudication* (OUP 2013) 159; Y Shany, *Assessing the Effectiveness of International Courts* (OUP 2014).

to be a goal for actors when they expect this goal to be achievable by bringing their dispute to the court. For disputes to be effectively resolved, the court would need to decide the case in substance (rather than dismissing it on procedural grounds); and the decision of the court would need to be effectively implemented by the respondent.

In the context of the ECOWAS Court, effectiveness considerations prevent actors from being strongly motivated by an interest in dispute resolution. In the first place, the implementation of ECOWAS Court decisions presents challenges. Especially in the initial phase of the court's practice, more than half of the enforceable decisions of the ECOWAS Court have not been implemented by states.[9] The reasons for that will be highlighted in more detail in section II.B. However, the following points serve as a preliminary illustration of the *legal* barriers to enforcement. First, although an enforcement mechanism exists for decisions containing an executable content according to Article 24 of the Protocol, this mechanism requires each member state to put the domestic enforcement structure in place. For that, states have to determine the competent national authority for the execution of decisions of the ECOWAS Court – which, for a long time, only a few of them had done.[10] Only very recently have the majority of member states designated a national enforcement authority.[11] Second, the lack of enforcement of ECOWAS Court judgments by domestic courts diminishes the effectiveness expectations of applicants. For example, the High Court of Ghana refused in its *Mba* decision to enforce an ECOWAS Court judgment[12] because the ECOWAS Treaty had not been given effect in domestic law by statutory enactment.[13] The ECOWAS Court has not addressed this issue by establishing direct applicability as a principle of ECOWAS law,[14] in contrast to the Court of Justice of the European Union (CJEU) that developed its jurisprudence on direct applicability to overcome the similar problem in the European context.[15] Relatedly, there is no legal regulation on the level of the member states as to how to integrate declaratory judgments

[9] ST Ebobrah and V Lando, 'Africa's Sub-Regional Courts as Back-Up Custodians of Constitutional Justice Beyond the Compliance Question' in JT Gathii (ed), *The Performance of Africa's International Courts: Using Litigation for Political, Legal, and Social Change* (OUP 2020) 178, 193.

[10] On this issue, M Happold and R Radović, 'The ECOWAS Court of Justice as an Investment Tribunal' (2018) 19 *Journal of World Investment & Trade* 95, 114. See also, regarding the fact that by 2021, 'only six of the 15 member states have complied with their obligation under Article 24 of the Protocol', the critical statement of the President of the ECOWAS Court at the opening of the 2021 external court session in Abidjan, Cote d'Ivoire, as reported in the media, see Oludare Richards, 'Non-enforcement of rulings threatens ECOWAS Court' *Guardian* (21 October 2021): guardian.ng/news/non-enforcement-of-rulings-threatens-ecowas-court/.

[11] 10 out of the currently 12 member states had done so by mid-2025. See statement at 'Inaugural Meeting of Competent National Authorities Responsible for Enforcement of ECOWAS Court Judgments Begins in Lagos, Nigeria': courtecowas.org/pending-cases-and-decisions/compliance/.

[12] *Chude Mba v Ghana*, ECW/CCJ/APP/01/13.

[13] High Court of Ghana, *In the Matter of an Application to Enforce the Judgment of the Community Court of Justice of the ECOWAS against the Republic of Ghana and In the Matter of Chude Mba v The Republic of Ghana*, Suit No. HRCM/376/15 (2016). On this case, RF Oppong, 'The High Court of Ghana Declines to Enforce An ECOWAS Court Judgment' (2017) 25 *African Journal of International and Comparative Law* 127.

[14] With the exception of the *Pinheiro* decision which includes an obiter dictum on direct applicability – see section III.C and *Kemi Pinheiro v Ghana*, 6 July 2012, ECW/CCJ/JUD/11112, para 50.

[15] Critical as to the ECOWAS Court's 'ostrich approach' regarding the relationship between Community and domestic law, ST Ebobrah, 'Critical Issues in the Human Rights Mandate of the ECOWAS Court of Justice' (2010) 54 *Journal of African Law* 1, 14.

in the domestic legal order. This also affects the effectiveness of ECOWAS Court decisions.[16]

A further aspect relating to effectiveness considerations is the nature of remedies that the court awards in cases of established human rights violations. Most of the remedies awarded by the court have been declarations of human rights violations and, in some cases, compensatory and/or moral damages, as well as occasionally an order to release a plaintiff from detention or to provide a speedy trial.[17] Initially, the court was rather hesitant to award financial compensation, let alone to award other, potentially more far-reaching, remedies as some other regional courts do. For example, when plaintiffs requested an order to investigate certain killings by the military in Niger, the court explicitly refused to do so.[18] This limited the expected effectiveness especially for applicants interested in combating structural human rights issues. As its jurisprudence developed, the court has however begun to broaden the range of remedies. This includes, in the second SERAP case, an order to take measures to restore a damaged part of the environment, to prevent such damages in the future and to hold the perpetrators responsible;[19] in the *Solomon Mfa* case concerning 'mass killings and destruction of properties', the court ordered the respondent state to investigate these killings and destruction and to 'identify and prosecute the perpetrators and redress the victims thereof';[20] and it even started to order the respondent state to amend the domestic law that the court found to be in violation of international human rights law (see also section II.B).[21]

Finally, there has been for a long time no institutionalized compliance monitoring for decisions of the court. States were not required to report about their compliance with ECOWAS Court decisions to the court itself or to another ECOWAS institution. This has further lowered the expected effectiveness of bringing cases to the court for dispute resolution reasons. Only recently, the court has instituted a monitoring structure. It now orders state respondents to report to the court the measures taken to implement the operational orders included in a decision (see also section II.B).[22] This is likely to increase expected effectiveness for applicants.

In addition to enforcement issues, various aspects of the jurisprudence of the ECOWAS Court can enhance or decrease to what extent applicants expect bringing a

[16] See also K Bado, *The Court of Justice of the Economic Community of West African States as a Constitutional Court* (Nomos 2019) 40.

[17] eg, *Ebrimah Manneh v The Gambia*, 5 June 2008, ECW/CCJ/APP/04/07; *Illia Malam Mamane Saidat v Niger*, 22 June 2021, ECW/CCJ/JUD/17/2021; *Alex Nain Saab Moran v Cape Verde*, 15 March 2021, ECW/CCJ/JUD/07/2021; *Aziagbede Kokou v Togo*, 3 July 2013, JUD/ECW/CCJ/JUD/07/13; *Assima Kokou Innocent v Togo*, 28 November 2013, JUD/ECW/CCJ/JUD/08/13; *Mr. Cherif Madi v Niger*, 1 April 2022, ECW/CCJ/APP/30/20.

[18] *Sidi Amar Ibrahim and Others v Niger*, 8 February 2011, ECW/CCJ/JUD/01/11.

[19] *SERAP v Nigeria*, 14 December 2012, ECW/CCJ/JUD/18/12.

[20] In *Rev. Fr. Solomon Mfa and Others v Nigeria and Others*, 16 February 2019, ECW/CCJ/JUD/06/19.

[21] *Amnesty International Togo and Others v Togo*, 25 June 2020, ECW/CCJ/JUD/09/20.

[22] eg, *Illia Malam Mamane Saidat v Niger*, 22 June 2021, ECW/CCJ/JUD/17/2021; *Diawara Oumar v Côte d'Ivoire*, 22 October 2021, ECW/CCJ/JUD/34/21; *Kodjo Alain Victor v Cote d'Ivoire*, 26 April 2021, ECW/CCJ/JUD/09/21; *Adam Latif and 4 Others v Togo*, 30 November 2023, ECW/CCJ/JUD/45/2023; *Oluwatimilehin Adebayo v Nigeria*, 3 December 2024, ECW/CCJ/JUD/44/24; *Jean Edoh Nunyava Oumolou v Togo*, 30 January 2024, ECW/CCJ/JUD/02/24.

case before the court to be effective. For example, the jurisprudence about the burden and standard of proof in human rights cases can influence such effectiveness perceptions. On the one hand, certain aspects of this jurisprudence enhance the expected effectiveness of dispute resolution interests of applicants. In particular, in arrest and detention cases as well as cases of alleged torture, the court has stated that the burden of proof shifts to the respondent state due to the particular nature of these cases.[23] Where the burden of proof is placed on the respondent, the applicants have reason to expect greater effectiveness in addressing the court with the aim of dispute resolution. On the other hand, the court has put in place a high standard of proof that can be perceived as a hurdle to effective realisation of applicants' interests.[24] To illustrate, this is the case when the court requires documentary evidence of physical violence in cases in which applicants are from rural areas and where written evidence is nearly impossible to obtain.[25] Similarly, in cases of alleged violations of undue delays in judicial proceedings, the court has required applicants to provide extensive proof of the existence and legal form of such delays (such as adjournment *sine die*), requiring documentation of internal judicial decisions that in certain cases might not be possible for applicants to obtain.[26]

Effectiveness considerations concerning dispute resolution also relate to how efficiently the court can handle the cases brought before it. So far, the ratio of judges/number of cases has not created issues. However, in light of the court's increasing workload the reduced number of five judges bears the risk of altering the court's effectiveness in the future,[27] possibly lowering the motivation of potential applicants to bring cases before the court.

Despite these effectiveness considerations concerning the applicants' interest in dispute resolution, the motivation to engage with the court is not generally at a low level. It is important to take into account that for some groups of applicants before the ECOWAS Court, dispute resolution is not a key expectation or motivational factor. As various observers have pointed out, 'litigants who go to the ECOWAS Court are not wedded to the traditional roles of the judicial system as dispute settlers'.[28] They pursue various other interests that I will outline in turn.

[23] Regarding arrest cases, see eg, *Dorothy Chioma Njemanze and Others v Nigeria*, 12 October 2017, ECW/CCJ/JUD/08/17, 32; *Ousainou Darboe v The Gambia*, 20 January 2020, JUD/ECW/CCJ/JUD/01/20, 23. See also ME Addadzi-Koom, 'Of the Women's Rights Jurisprudence of the ECOWAS Court: The Role of the Maputo Protocol and the Due Diligence Standard' (2020) 28) *Feminist Legal Studies* 155, 167.

[24] eg, *Saidykhan v Gambia*, 16 December 2010, ECW/CCJ/JUD/08/10, para 28 et seq; *Daouda Garba v Benin*, 17 February 2010, ECW/CCJ/JUD/01/10. On this issue also OC Okafor and OJ Effoduh, 'The ECOWAS Court as a (Promising) Resource for Pro-Poor Activist Forces – Sovereign Hurdles, Brainy Relays, and 'Flipped Strategic Social Constructivism'' in Gathii (ed), *The Performance of Africa's International Courts* (n 9) 106, 146.

[25] Critical on this issue, Fréderic Foromo Loua and Jonathan Kaufman, 'Molmou v Guinea: The ECOWAS Court of Justice at the Service of its Member States' (2017) 2 *Business and Human Rights Journal* 149, 154–55.

[26] eg, *Daniel Makolo Esq. v Nigeria*, 27 October 2021, ECW/CCJ/JUD/37/21, paras 64–70.

[27] M Happold, 'Investor–State Dispute Settlement using the ECOWAS Court of Justice: An Analysis and Some Proposals' (2019) 34 *ICSID Review* 496, 512.

[28] OD Akinkugbe, 'Towards an Analyses of the Mega-Political Jurisprudence of the ECOWAS Community Court of Justice' in Gathii (ed), *The Performance of Africa's International Courts* (n 9) 149, 176.

A first important aim of applicants before the ECOWAS Court is to flag out human rights violations. The interest here is to publicise certain violations that otherwise would be hidden by state governments. For example, in the *Manneh v Gambia* case which concerned an individual applicant who had been arrested by the Gambian police, held incommunicado after his arrest and detained without trial,[29] bringing the case to the court meant that

> the family of the victim and the victim's lawyers were able to publicly denounce the regime in the Gambia whilst putting out their story in the public and international domain. The publicity that the *Manneh* case received in the sub-region, particularly in the Gambia, Ghana, and Nigeria ensured that the allegations of the suppression of journalists and the violation of their rights could no longer be considered as speculations nor be ignored.[30]

On the one hand, such informational interests concern the specific situation of the applicants whose narrative and related evidence as to the human rights violation they have suffered can be confirmed by an official institution, a confirmation that might not be achievable for these applicants on the domestic level. On the other hand, by providing broadly and internationally available information about human rights violations, court proceedings before the ECOWAS Court can serve as a 'warning system to the regional and wider international community'.[31]

Along similar lines, bringing cases to the court can serve the related goal of unveiling broader structural rule of law issues in the respondent state. Such issues can become apparent through the reaction of the state to the proceedings before the ECOWAS Court. In the *Manneh* case, the Gambia's refusal as the respondent state 'to participate and the failure to comply showcased … the Gambian regime's disregard for the rule of law within its domestic legal system'.[32] Similarly in the *Saidykhan* case,[33] the proceedings before the court and the fact that the Gambia did not appear before the court reinforced 'the warning that the Gambian regime was authoritarian'.[34] As a consequence, 'attention was drawn to the situation in that state and the international community, particularly ECOWAS Member States became alerted to the need for intervention'.[35] Other examples in which applicants have drawn attention to structural human rights issues include the malfunctioning of the judicial system in Mali;[36] or a case reflecting continuing societal customs and structures that allow situations in which women are held in slavery in certain rural areas of Niger.[37] The latter case has also had a significant impact on addressing slavery issues in the member states.[38]

[29] *Ebrimah Manneh v The Gambia*, 5 June 2008, ECW/CCJ/APP/04/07.
[30] Ebobrah and Lando (n 9) 200.
[31] ibid 201.
[32] ibid 200.
[33] *Saidykhan v The Gambia*, 16 December 2010, ECW/CCJ/JUD/08/10.
[34] Ebobrah and Lando (n 9) 202.
[35] ibid.
[36] *Cheikh Abdoulaye Mbengue v Mali*, 7 October 2011, ECW/CCJ/JUG/08/11.
[37] *Hadijatou Mani Koraou v Niger*, 27 October 2008, ECW/CCJ/JUD/06/08.
[38] See HS Adjolohoun, 'The ECOWAS Court as a Human Rights Promoter? Assessing Five Years' Impact of the Koraou Slavery Judgment' (2013) 31 *Netherlands Quarterly of Human Rights* 342.

Further, for certain groups of applicants, strategic political interests present an important motivational factor. This is particularly the case for political actors belonging to opposition parties in the member states. They have approached the court repeatedly in cases that concern deficiencies in domestic electoral law and practice, using the court as an alternative political forum.[39] For example, in *Congrès pour la Démocratie et le Progrès v Burkina Faso*, the applicants – including various political parties – challenged the exclusion by the domestic Electoral Code of candidates belonging to an ousted regime.[40] In *Sule Audu*, the applicants claimed a violation of their election rights due to the fact that, after a candidate had died during the election process, their votes were transferred to another candidate, a process that, according to them, robbed the election of its nature as an expression of the will of the people.[41] Political actors have also used the court to call attention to their claims of suppression by governmental actors,[42] including in cases against domestic agencies invalidating the election of a member of Parliament[43] as well as allegations of arrest and arbitrary detention of opposition politicians.[44]

ECOWAS Court decisions 'have been used directly or indirectly to apply domestic and international pressure on governments to act differently', not only in the case at hand but also in the future.[45] In fact, deterrence has been prominent among the motivational factors of political active applicants before the ECOWAS Court. For example, in *Hope Democratic Party & Alhaji Haruna Yahaya Shaba v Nigeria* which concerned the unlawful use of public funds for the electoral campaign by the then President of Nigeria,[46] the applicants – an opposition party and its presidential candidate – 'wanted a ruling from the Court as a deterrent for future conduct of the Member State'.[47] This is evidenced by counsel's statement that the applicants continued to pursue a judgment despite the fact that the then president had lost the election and conceded defeat 'so as to serve as a deterrent to other would-be violators of the elections law on fairness and equality before the law'.[48] Similarly, in *Centre for Democracy and Development* in which the applicants challenged the attempt of the then President of Niger to change the Constitution so as to remain in this position for a third term in office,[49] the applicants' goal was that 'the ECOWAS Court's decision would help dissuade other officials who intended to manipulate the Constitutions

[39] Akinkugbe (n 28) 154, 176.
[40] *Congrès pour la Démocratie et le Progrès (CDP) and Others v Burkina Faso*, 13 July 2015, ECW/CCJ/JUG/16/15.
[41] *Sule Audu and Others v Nigeria*, 22 November 2017, ECW/CCJ/JUD/17/17.
[42] eg, *Khalifa Ababacar Sall and Others v Senegal*, 29 June 2018, ECW/CCJ/JUD/17/18.
[43] *Jerry Ugokwe v Nigeria and Others*, 7 October 2005, ECW/CCJ/JUD/03/05.
[44] eg, *Barthelemy Toye Dias v Senegal*, 23 March 2012, ECW/CCJ/JUG/05/12.
[45] ST Ebobrah, 'The ECOWAS Community Court of Justice – A Dual Mandate with Skewed Authority' in KJ Alter, LR Helfer and MR Madsen (eds), *International Court Authority* (OUP 2018) 82, 95.
[46] *Hope Democratic Party & Alhaji Haruna Yahaya Shaba v Nigeria and Others*, 14 October 2015, ECW/CCJ/JUD/19/15.
[47] Akinkugbe (n 28) 163.
[48] *Hope Democratic Party & Alhaji Haruna Yahaya Shaba v Nigeria and Others*, 14 October 2015, ECW/CCJ/JUD/19/15, para 9.1.
[49] *Centre for Democracy and Development, and Another v Mamadou Tandja & Niger*, 9 May 2011, ECW/CCJ/JUD/05/11.

of their country for a longer time while they were in power'.[50] To achieve that aim, applicants bring cases to the court even if they are aware that they will not be able to obtain a favourable judgment on the merits. The court has recognised deterrence as an aim for applicants, especially in public interest litigation,[51] even issuing orders to the respondent state that aim at future avoidance of human rights violations.[52] This further enhances the motivation of applicants interested in preventing future human rights violations.

For these aims, ie, flagging human rights violations and poor rule of law standards; strategies for opposition politicians within the political discourse; and deterrence considerations, the expected effectiveness is high. Proceedings before the court have been repeatedly used for these purposes, signalling to potential future applicants that such an engagement with the court is beneficial for their causes. What is more, these strategies have led to observable national and international reactions by actors including other member states, international institutions, NGOs, other civil society actors and the media in the relevant states, supporting the interests and aims of the respective applicants.[53] These aims thus have a strong motivational impact.

Finally, a further potential motivational factor for actors to engage with a court and accept its authority is the court's expertise.[54] For the ECOWAS Court there are, however, structural limitations to this factor. This is due to the requirements for judges to be appointed to the court which concern, on the one hand, the general legal expertise of the judges and on the other, the specific human rights expertise. As to the former, there have been initial doubts which were addressed by the creation of a Judicial Council 'to ensure that the Court is endowed with the best qualified and competent persons'.[55] The second aspect however remains an issue: the '[e]xperience or qualification in human rights is not a consideration for appointment as a judge of the ECCJ [… which] poses challenges for the credible exercise of its human rights mandate in terms of not requiring any specific human rights qualification for appointment'.[56] At least de jure, the *personal* expertise of judges thus cannot serve as a basis for a perceived human rights experience of the court. Yet prolonged practice of the court in human rights cases and the growing body of related jurisprudence can foster a perception of *institutional* expertise in this regard. Indeed, when studying the development of the human rights jurisprudence, one can observe a significant increase in the quality of the legal argument and the depth of the assessment. While at the beginning of the court's operational phase, decisions engaged with the relevant legal questions in a rather cursory manner, more recent decisions show an in-depth evaluation of the legal issues at stake and a thorough (comparative) analysis of existing

[50] Akinkugbe (n 28) 172.

[51] *Rev. Fr. Solomon Mfa and Others v Nigeria and Others*, 16 February 2019, ECW/CCJ/JUD/06/19, para 63.

[52] ibid 31.

[53] For a detailed account of this impact, Akinkugbe (n 28); Okafor and Effoduh (n 24).

[54] See also F Zarbiyev, 'Cutting off the King's Head: Rethinking Authority in International Law' (2023) 14 *Journal of International Dispute Settlement* 285.

[55] ECOWAS Newsletter, 1 October 2006, cited by Alter, Helfer and McAllister (n 4) 760.

[56] Ebobrah, 'Critical Issues' (n 15) 10; see also Alter, Helfer and McAllister (n 4) 761.

international human rights jurisprudence. The motivational potential of the court's perceived human rights expertise has thus increased.

In conclusion, the impact of the individual motivational factors is thus varied. While the value-related factors are rather strong, the impact of interest-based motivation differs considerably depending on the interest at hand. For actors primarily interested in effective dispute resolution by the court, the impact ranges at the lower part of the spectrum in particular due to compliance issues. For actors interested in exposing human rights violations and in achieving political and discursive aims, the motivation is high.

ii. Opportunity

The opportunity for applicants to engage with the court is, first and foremost, shaped by the rules on jurisdiction and access to the court. Social opportunity elements and some practical aspects add to this opportunity structure.

Jurisdiction

The opportunity structure with regard to the subject-matter jurisdiction on human rights has changed during the court's time of operation. Initially, the 1991 Protocol did not confer human rights jurisdiction on the court. Potential applicants with human rights claims thus formally had no opportunity to engage with the court in substance. However, this did not stop applicants in the first case brought to the court, the *Afolabi* case concerning a unilateral border closure by Nigeria, to try and circumvent the unfavourable opportunity structure.[57] They claimed a violation both of regional integration law and of human rights (Article 12 of the African Charter on Human and Peoples' Rights), hoping that the court would interpret the existing jurisdictional rules in a way that would make it possible for human rights cases to be admitted.[58] While some regional courts acted according to such incentives and broadened their mandate,[59] the ECOWAS Court did not do so.[60]

In the 2005 Protocol, the member states extended the jurisdiction to the court to human rights cases. The new Article 9(4) as amended by the Protocol establishes 'jurisdiction to determine cases of human rights violations that occur in any member state'. This provision established one of the broadest opportunity structures as to subject-matter jurisdiction for human rights that (potential) applicants before regional courts can have. First, the jurisdiction is detached from the regional economic integration context which is at the core of ECOWAS. Human rights violations fall within the mandate of the court whether or not they are linked to economic integration or the implementation of ECOWAS measures. Further, the

[57] *Olajide Afolabi v Nigeria*, 27 April 2004, ECW/CCJ/JUD/01/04.

[58] In the second case brought to the court before the adoption of the 2005 Protocol, the applicant also claimed, inter alia, a human rights violation. However, this case was brought against an individual. See *Chief Frank Ukor v Rachad Laleye*, 27 May 2005, ECW/CCJ/APP/01/04.

[59] EACJ, *James Katabazi & 21 Others v The Secretary General of the East African Community & Another*, 1 November 2007, reference no. 1/2007.

[60] *Olajide Afolabi v Nigeria*, 27 April 2004, ECW/CCJ/JUD/01/04.

Protocol does not specify the legal instruments that the court can use as a yardstick for assessing human rights violations. Based on a literal understanding of Article 9(4), this norm provides the opportunity for applicants to claim a violation of any human rights instrument deemed suitable. In practice, applicants have made use of this opportunity and 'have invoked a wide range of international human rights instruments in their claims against ECOWAS Member States'.[61] However, as a matter of practice, the ECOWAS Court has limited this opportunity somewhat by taking the African Charter on Human and Peoples' Rights as a primary point of reference. The court refers to the Charter in virtually all human rights cases. Only as an additional set of legal rules does it invoke other universal and regional human rights instruments. For example, it regularly mentions the (non-binding) Universal Declaration[62] and the International Covenant on Civil and Political Rights.[63] Occasionally, it also refers to other subject-specific instruments such as the Convention against Torture[64] or the Convention on the Elimination of All Forms of Discrimination Against Women and the Maputo Protocol on the Rights of Women in Africa.[65] For the applicants, the opportunity structure is thus still broad, but the predominance of the Charter makes it appear slightly narrower than the de jure formulation suggests.

A specific opportunity structure exists for human rights cases that touch upon election matters. Election-related cases are, prima facie, considered to constitute a different jurisdictional aspect. The protocol does not establish any explicit jurisdiction of the court regarding election matters with the effect that applicants cannot per se invoke irregularities during election procedures directly before the court. However, in many instances, election matters overlap with human rights issues and thus potentially involve the human rights jurisdiction of the court. Applicants have repeatedly made this argument and given a human rights framing to their claims. For example, in the *Ugokwe v Nigeria* case of 2005, a question regarding the validity of an election was presented as a violation of the right to a fair hearing before domestic courts

[61] Ebobrah, 'Dual Mandate' (n 45) 88.

[62] *Ameganvi Manvi Isabelle v Togo*, 7 October 2011, ECW/CCJ/JUD/09/11, para 67; *SERAP v Nigeria*, 14 December 2012, ECW/CCJ/JUD/18/12, para 35; *Bakary and Others v Mali*, 17 March 2011, ECW/CCJ/JUD/03/11; *Amouzou Henri and Others v Côte d'Ivoire*, 17 December 2019, ECW/CCJ/JUG/04/09, paras 57 and 62; *Sow Bertin Agba v Togo*, 11 June 2013, ECW/CCJ/JUD/05/13, para 36; *Assima Kokou Innocent v Togo*, 28 November 2013, ECW/CCJ/JUD/08/13, para 39; *Sule Audu and Others v Nigeria*, 22 November 2017, ECW/CCJ/JUD/17/17; *Daniel Makolo Esq. v Nigeria*, 27 October 2021, ECW/CCJ/JUD/37/21, para 46.

[63] eg, *SERAP v Nigeria*, 14 December 2012, ECW/CCJ/JUD/18/12; *Amouzou Henri and Others v Côte d'Ivoire*, 17 December 2019, ECW/CCJ/JUG/04/09, paras 57 and 62; *Badini Salfo v Burkina Faso*, 31 October 2012, ECW/CCJ/JUD/13/12, para 41; *Simone Ehivet and Michel Gbagbo v Côte d'Ivoire*, 22 February 2013, ECW/CCJ/JUD/03/13, para 54 et seq; *Sow Bertin Agba v Togo*, 11 June 2013, ECW/CCJ/JUD/05/13, para 36; *Assima Kokou Innocent v Togo*, 28 November 2013, ECW/CCJ/JUD/08/13, paras 40, 58, 82, 83; *SERAP v Nigeria*, 19 June 2014, ECW/CCJ/JUD/16/14, para 92; *Sule Audu and Others v Nigeria*, 22 November 2017, ECW/CCJ/JUD/17/17; *Daniel Makolo Esq. v Nigeria*, 27 October 2021, ECW/CCJ/JUD/37/21, para 58; *Illia Malam Mamane Saidat v Niger*, 22 June 2021, ECW/CCJ/JUD/17/2021, para 228 et seq; *Djedjey Deret Ives Marcel v Côte d'Ivoire*, 29 May 2024, ECW/CCJ/JUD/12/24, para 51.

[64] eg, *Assima Kokou Innocent v Togo*, 28 November 2013, ECW/CCJ/JUD/08/13, para 60; *Dorothy Chioma Njemanze and Others v Nigeria*, 12 October 2017, ECW/CCJ/JUD/08/17, 41.

[65] eg, *Aminata Diantou Diane v Mali*, 21 May 2018, ECW/CCJ/JUD/14/18, 3; *Dorothy Chioma Njemanze and Others v Nigeria*, 12 October 2017, ECW/CCJ/JUD/08/17, 41.

deciding on the matter.[66] However, the court decided in this case that 'no provision, whether general or specific, gives the Court powers to adjudicate on electoral issues or matters arising therefrom'.[67] In this early jurisprudence, the court has thus limited the opportunity structure for human rights cases by excluding situations that concern domestic elections. In contrast, in its more recent jurisprudence the ECOWAS Court has mitigated its initial stance. In *Congrès pour la Démocratie et le Progrès v Burkina*, a decision of 2015 concerning the amendment of domestic electoral law, the court has stated that it is open to consider election-related cases which concern (alleged) human rights violations.[68] However, the initial approach is still part of the court's case law, so that the extent to which the court actually provides an opportunity for applicants to bring election-related human rights cases depends on the court's understanding of when such a case is of a human rights nature. For example, in *Sule Audu v Nigeria* decided in 2017, the court dismissed an election-related case at the jurisdictional level based on a very cursory assessment of whether it involved a potential human rights violation.[69] The opportunity structure regarding such cases has thus been somewhat ambivalent. In recent cases, the court has however accepted its jurisdiction in such matters.[70]

A further aspect influences the opportunity structure regarding the ECOWAS Court's jurisdiction. This concerns the nature of the member states' actions that applicants can challenge before the court. Article 9(4) of the Protocol speaks of human rights violations 'that occur in any member state'. This does not limit the jurisprudence of the court to specific state institutions or forms of state action. However, the ECOWAS Court itself has curtailed its jurisdiction in this regard: for about a decade, it was very reluctant to review judicial decisions at all. In the *Ugokwe v Nigeria* case as well as in the *Keita v Etat de Mali* case, it declared that, as it is not a court of appeal or cassation, it does not have the competence to reverse the judgments of domestic courts.[71] It stated that:

> Appealing against the decision of the National Court of Member States does not form part of the powers of the Court; … the kind of relationship existing between the Community Court and these national courts of Member States are not of a vertical nature between the Community and the Member States, but demands an integrated Community legal order. The ECOWAS Court of Justice is not a Court of Appeal or a Court of cassation.[72]

Based on this jurisprudence, the court refused to assess potential human rights violations in cases that had previously been brought before a domestic court, referring to the above-cited phrase.[73] With this application of its jurisdiction, the court did not

[66] *Jerry Ugokwe v Nigeria and Others*, 7 October 2005, ECW/CCJ/JUD/03/05.

[67] ibid para 19.

[68] *Congrès pour la Démocratie et le Progrès (CDP) and Others v Burkina Faso*, 13 July 2015, ECW/CCJ/JUG/16/15, para 19.

[69] *Sule Audu and Others v Nigeria*, 22 November 2017, ECW/CCJ/JUD/17/17, 16.

[70] *Akolly Hanou Woetru v Togo*, 6 June 2024, ECW/CCJ/JUD/23/24.

[71] *Jerry Ugokwe v Nigeria and Others*, 7 October 2005, ECW/CCJ/JUD/03/05, para 32; *Keita v Mali*, March 2007, ECW/CCJ/APP/03/07, para 30.

[72] *Jerry Ugokwe v Nigeria and Others*, 7 October 2005, ECW/CCJ/JUD/03/05, para 32.

[73] eg, *Cheikh Abdoulaye Mbengue v Mali*, 7 October 2011, ECW/CCJ/JUG/08/11, para 38; *Bakary and Others v Mali*, 17 March 2011, ECW/CCJ/JUD/03/11, paras 29–31.

distinguish between a review of these decisions based on international human rights law as opposed to a review based on domestic law, as well as between the effect of a declaratory judgment regarding a domestic decision as compared with an annulment of such a decision. This legally unconvincing approach considerably reduced the opportunity for (potential) applicants to successfully bring such cases to the ECOWAS Court.[74]

More recently, however, the court has started to consider explicitly the abovementioned distinction between a human rights and a domestic law yardstick for review. In the 2014 case *Avocat Sans Frontières France v Nigeria*, the court differentiated between grounds that 'are based on violation of human rights' as compared with 'grounds of appeal against the conviction and sentence',[75] confirming that a 'case for alleged violation of human rights under Article 9(4) of the Supplementary Protocol is within the jurisdiction of this court and does not amount to an appeal from the decision of the National Court'.[76] In the *Mahamadou* case of 2016, it stated more explicitly that

> lorsqu'une décision de justice est, en elle-même attentatoire aux droits de l'homme, il va de soi que le juge communautaire, qui a reçu mandat de protéger les droits des citoyens de la communauté, ne saurait avoir d'autre choix que d'intervenir et dénoncer cette violation; Qu'il ne saurait rester inerte face à une violation flagrante des droits de l'homme, peu importe l'acte qui est à l'origine de cette violation; Qu'il ne s'agit pas pour lui ici de contrôler la légalité d'une décision rendue par une juridiction nationale mais de constater la violation manifeste des droits de l'homme contenue dans un acte judiciaire.[77]

Since these decisions, the court has further consolidated this jurisprudence by differentiating between its (lack of) 'jurisdiction to examine the decisions of national courts and its jurisdiction to hear cases of human rights abuses arising therefrom'.[78] While it upholds its jurisprudence that it is not competent to review domestic judicial decisions in an appellate court capacity, it acknowledges that allegations of human rights violations provide a sufficient basis for admissibility.[79] This approach now seems to

[74] Criticising this approach: A von Staden, 'Subsidiarity, exhaustion of domestic remedies, and the margin of appreciation in the human rights jurisprudence of African sub-regional courts' (2016) 20 *International Journal of Human Rights* 1113, 1121; ST Ebobrah, 'Litigating Human Rights Before Sub-Regional Courts in Africa: Prospects and Challenges' (2009) 17 *African Journal of International and Comparative Law* 79, 99. However, even in the early years, the court occasionally decided a case that involved domestic courts, such as in *Ameganvi Manvi Isabelle v Togo*, 7 October 2011, ECW/CCJ/JUD/09/11.

[75] *Registered Trustees of Avocat Sans Frontières France v Nigeria*, 31 January 2014, ECW/CCJ/APP/14/13, para 51.

[76] ibid para 53.

[77] *Farimata Mahamadou and Others v Mali*, 17 May 2016, ECW/CCJ/JUD/11/16, paras 45–46 (translation: 'When a judicial decision, in and of itself, infringes human rights, it goes without saying that the Community judge – who has been entrusted with the mandate to protect the rights of the Community's citizens – can have no choice but to intervene and denounce this violation. He cannot remain inactive in the face of a flagrant violation of human rights, regardless of the act that gave rise to that violation. In doing so, he is not reviewing the legality of a decision handed down by a national court, but rather noting the manifest violation of human rights contained in a judicial act').

[78] *Finance Investment & Development Corporation Inc v Liberia*, 4 July 2018, ECW/CCJ/JUD/23/18, 10; also *Daniel Makolo Esq. v Nigeria*, 27 October 2021, ECW/CCJ/JUD/37/21, para 75; *Mr. Cherif Madi v Niger*, 1 April 2022, ECW/CCJ/APP/30/20, paras 84–85; *La Ligue Senegalaise Des Droits Humaines & Amnesty International Senegal Section v Senegal*, 31 March 2022, ECW/CCJ/JUD/22/22, paras 47–49.

[79] ECCJ, *Khalifa Ababacar Sall et Autres v Senegal*, 29 June 2018, ECW/CCJ/JUD/17/18, 22–24, 28.

converge with the jurisprudence of other human rights courts on the matter. The opportunity for (potential) applicants to bring cases relating to fair trial rights in judicial proceedings has thus broadened.

A final determinant for the jurisdiction-related opportunity structure is the temporal applicability of the Protocol. Although this aspect concerns only a few cases, it is significant for the practice of the court. Here again, the opportunity structure has changed over time. Initially, the court decided in *Chief Frank Ukor* – a case filed before the Protocol amendment, but decided subsequently – that the 2005 Protocol had no retroactive effect.[80] However in a decision in 2012 the court interpreted Article 9(4) of the Protocol in a more wide-reaching manner. It decided that the effect of the Supplementary Protocol of 2005 is retroactive, so that human rights violations that occurred before the Supplementary Protocol entered into force can also be brought to the court.[81] For such cases, the temporal opportunity structure has thus been rather broad. More recently, however, the court seems to have returned to a narrower approach. In the *Mado* case of 2022 and subsequent decisions, the court rejected the retroactive applicability of the 2005 Protocol for situations in which there is no continuous human rights violation.[82]

Access Rules

The rules regulating access to the court influence the opportunity structure for the various groups of (potential) applicants differently. For individual applicants, the 1991 Protocol initially did not provide any access. In this phase, the opportunity for such applicants to engage with the court was thus very limited. Accordingly, only two cases were filed by individual applicants in this period of the court's existence.[83] In the *Afolabi* case, the applicants tried to entice the court to create individual access.[84] Yet the court refused to create individual access by way of expansive jurisprudence. However, shortly after this decision, member states created individual access by the 2005 Protocol. This Protocol inserted a new Article 10 into the existing provisions which states that access to the court is open to 'individuals on application for violation of their human rights' (Article 10(d)).

To have access to the court, ie, for their case to be admissible, individuals have to demonstrate that they have been the victim of an alleged human rights violation.[85] The individual applicant has to establish the status of a direct victim or an indirect victim,[86] the latter being however applied restrictively as to the required proof of

[80] *Chief Frank Ukor v Rachad Laleye*, 27 May 2005, EC\V/CCJ/APP/01/04, para 20.

[81] *Falana and Another v Benin and Others*, 24 January 2012, ECW/CCJ/JUD/02/12, para 28.

[82] *Mado Fidegnon Frederic v Togo*, 30 March 2022, ECW/CCJ/JUD/21/2022; *Woamede Tedevi Kokou v Togo*, 13 March 2023, ECW/CCJ/JUD/05/23; *Jean Edoh Nunyava Oumolou v Togo*, 30 January 2024, ECW/CCJ/JUD/02/24.

[83] *Olajide Afolabi v Nigeria*, 27 April 2004, ECW/CCJ/JUD/01/04; *Chief Frank Ukor v Rachad Laleye*, 27 May 2005, EC\V/CCJ/APP/01/04.

[84] *Olajide Afolabi v Nigeria*, 27 April 2004, ECW/CCJ/JUD/01/04, para 23.

[85] *Alhaji Muhammed Abrahim Hassan v Govenor, Gombe State & Federal Government of Nigeria*, 2012, ECW/CCJ/RUL/07/12) para 46.

[86] *Amnesty International Togo and Others v Togo*, 25 June 2020, ECW/CCJ/JUD/09/20, para 33; *Abayomi Babalola v Côte d'Ivoire*, 6 June 2024, ECW/CCJ/JUD/21/24, para 59.

relationship with the direct victim.[87] Moreover, for exceptional circumstances, the court has broadened the opportunity for individual applicants to bring a case before the court. In *Congrès pour la Démocratie et le Progrès v Burkina Faso*, the court acknowledged that 'it may occur that in specific circumstances, the risk of a future violation confers on an applicant the status of a victim'.[88] In situations of 'violations which have not yet occurred, but are very imminent', applicants thus can seize the court before an actual prejudice has arisen.[89] This approach has been endorsed and specified in the subsequent jurisprudence.[90] Although the court also decided that this jurisprudence does not apply to violations by future legislative acts that are not yet adopted or in force,[91] it broadens the opportunity for applicants to bring cases to the court, especially in cases of (alleged) systemic violations of human rights.

Moreover, in its recent jurisprudence, the court has also created the opportunity for an *actio popularis* by individuals – a possibility initially only recognised for NGOs (see below). In *Patrick Eholor v Nigeria* (2023), the court set out three criteria for an *actio popularis* that it applies to individuals. The court stated that

> in granting an individual the capacity to bring an actio-popularis application, the following conditions must be fulfilled; 1) the rights allegedly violated must be established to be capable of being held by the public and not a private right. 2) The reliefs sought must be exclusively for the benefit of the public to the exception of personal interest of the Applicant … 3) The victims while not determinable, must for purposes of award of reparation be capable of being envisioned or envisaged by the Court.[92]

This jurisprudence broadens the access opportunity for individuals further. However, the court applies these three criteria very restrictively, so that the extent of this possibility for *actio popularis* is limited.[93]

Although it is not explicitly mentioned in Article 10 of the Protocol, the court has also granted access to NGOs as applicants.[94] This is a stance that the court has taken early on from the first cases brought to it by NGOs: the SERAP cases. It stated that

> an NGO duly constituted according to the national law of any ECOWAS Member State, and enjoying observer status before ECOWAS institutions, can file complaints against Human Rights violation in case that the victim is not just a single individual, but a large group of individuals or even entire communities.[95]

[87] eg, *Mahawa Cham and Sarjo Cham v The Gambia*, 5 July 2023, ECW/CCJ/JUD/26/23.

[88] *Congrès pour la Démocratie et le Progrès (CDP) and Others v Burkina Faso*, 13 July 2015, ECW/CCJ/JUG/16/15, para 17.

[89] ibid para 16.

[90] *Kenneth Roberts and Others v Nigeria*, 27 October 2021, ECW/CCJ/JUD/38/21, paras 62 and 65.

[91] *Jacob Abdulahi & 5 Others v Nigeria & 2 Others*, 29 March 2022, ECW/CCJ/JUD/18/22.

[92] *Patrick Eholor v Nigeria*, 7 December 2023, ECW/CCJ/JUD/51/23, para 52.

[93] eg, *Incorporated Trustees of Media Rights*, 30 May 2023, ECW/CCJ/JUD/15/24; *Incorporated Trustees of Prince & Princess Charles Offokaja Foundation Nigeria and Another v Nigeria*, 14 February 2025, ECW/CCJ/JUD/06/25.

[94] However, this concerns only NGOs from ECOWAS member states, see eg, *Incorporated Trustees of Prince & Princess Charles Offokaja Foundation Nigeria and Another v Nigeria*, 17 March 2025, ECW/CCJ/JUD/14/25.

[95] *Registered Trustees of the Socio-Economic Rights & Accountability Project (SERAP) v President of Nigeria and Others*, 10 December 2010, ECW/CCJ/APP/07/10, para 61. See also *SERAP v Nigeria*, 27 October 2009, ECW/CCJ/APP/0808, para 33.

This has created a broad form of *actio popularis* as NGOs could bring (any) cases in which individuals are the victims of human rights violations.[96] However, in its later jurisprudence the court has limited that broad access. First, it has distinguished between the following two situations. For cases of collective interest (public interest litigation) which the court defined as concerning 'victimized groups who ordinarily are without sufficient means of access to legal services or justice', the SERAP jurisprudence on *actio popularis* applied.[97] In contrast, for cases in which 'the alleged victims are well determined', the victims were 'expected to access the Court by themselves'.[98] Here, NGOs did not have standing on *actio popularis* grounds. This approach has recently been replaced by the above-mentioned three-pronged test established in the *Ebolor* case. The *Ebolor* jurisprudence and its narrow application further reduce the *actio popularis* possibility for NGOs. However, it bears mentioning that an NGO can also bring cases on behalf of direct victims when it is mandated by the victims to do so.[99] And NGOs can engage with the court via amicus curiae briefs.[100] In sum, despite the above-mentioned limitations, the jurisprudence creates a rather broad opportunity for NGOs to engage with the court.

For another group of (potential) applicants – corporations and other legal persons – the opportunity structure was until recently somewhat unclear. Over many years, the jurisprudence of the court varied as to whether it granted access to such applicants under its human rights jurisdiction or not. In several cases such as *Starcrest Investment* and *Ocean King Nigeria*, the court decided that, in general, legal persons do not have standing.[101] This outcome was based on the wording of Article 10(d) of the Protocol which refers, in the English language version, to 'individuals' only.[102] In contrast, in other cases, the court had interpreted Article 10(d) of the Protocol in a different manner. Referring to the French language version of the provision which mentions 'toute personne victime' and thus does not distinguish between natural and legal

[96] See for a more recent case that engages in detail with this jurisprudence, *Federation of African Journalists and Others v The Gambia*, 13 February 2018, ECW/CCJ/JUD/04/18, 16 et seq. See also *Rev. Fr. Solomon Mfa and Others v Nigeria and Others*, 16 February 2019, ECW/CCJ/JUD/06/19, para 60 et seq.

[97] *The Incorporated Trustees of Fiscal and Civic Right Enlightenment Foundation v Nigeria and Others*, 7 June 2016, ECW/CCJ/JUG/18/16, 15. See also *SERAP v Nigeria and Another*, 13 February 2014, ECW/CCJ/RUL/03/14, para 15; *The Reg. Trustees of Jama'a Foundation & 5 Others v Nigeria & The Attorney General and Minister of Justice of the Federation*, 20 March 2020, ECW/CCJ/JUD/04/20, paras 56–60; *La Ligue Senegalaise Des Droits Humaines & Amnesty International Senegal Section v Senegal*, 31 March 2022, ECW/CCJ/JUD/22/22, paras 65–67.

[98] *SERAP v Nigeria and Another*, 13 February 2014, ECW/CCJ/RUL/03/14, para 16.

[99] ibid para 14; *The Incorporated Trustees of Fiscal and Civic Right Enlightenment Foundation v Nigeria and others*, 7 June 2016, ECW/CCJ/JUG/18/16, 15. A similar rationale seems to have already guided the decision in *Centre for Democracy and Development* in which the Court rejected the standing of NGOs given that they were registered in member states other than the respondent state and could thus not act on behalf of the people of Niger. See *Centre for Democracy and Development, and Another v Mamadou Tandja & Niger*, 9 May 2011, ECW/CCJ/JUD/05/11, para 29.

[100] See, eg, the amicus curiae brief by Amnesty International in *SERAP v Nigeria*, 19 June 2014, ECW/CCJ/JUD/16/14, para 12.

[101] *Starcrest Investment Ltd v ECOWAS Commission and Others*, 8 July 2011, ECW/CCJ/JUD/06/11, paras 15–17; *Ocean King Nigeria v Senegal*, 8 July 2011, ECW/CCJ/JUD/07/11, paras 46–50.

[102] ibid para 49.

persons, the court concluded that legal persons could file human rights complaints.[103] According to this jurisprudence, legal persons have standing if they are victims of a human rights violation. Finally, to consolidate these diverging approaches, the court used the case of *Dexter Oil Ltd v Liberia* in 2019 to spell out the access rules for legal persons. It takes up a distinction between human rights and fundamental rights already mentioned in the *Ocean King* case,[104] stating that it

> hereby departs from all decision wherein corporate body are accommodated under Article 10 (d) of the [Protocol]; and affirms only individuals have access for Human Rights violation except in internationally accepted conditions … The established exceptions under which corporate bodies can ground an action are rights that are fundamental rights not dependant on human rights and they include right to fair hearing, right to property and right to freedom of expression.[105]

Legal persons thus have an acknowledged opportunity to engage with the court in human rights cases, yet this opportunity is, as in the *Dexter Oil* case, limited to claiming violations of the right to a fair hearing, the right to property and the right to freedom of expression.[106] This narrow approach has since then determined the decision-making of the court.[107]

In this context, it bears mentioning that the court has also explicitly acknowledged that political parties – which are often set up as legal persons – can have standing before the court in cases relating to the right to participate in political elections. In *Congrès pour la Démocratie et le Progrès v Burkina Faso*, the court stated that 'it would be purely artificial and unreasonable for the Court to deny political parties the right to bring their cases before it, once the rights relating to their assigned mission of participating in the electoral race are violated'.[108] Here again, the court recognised an issue-specific standing for such applicants, creating an opportunity to engage with the court.

For all of the aforementioned groups of applicants, a further – important – aspect shapes the opportunity structure as to access to the court. Unlike other access provisions before regional courts, the Protocol that regulates access to the ECOWAS Court does not mention a requirement to exhaust domestic remedies before filing a case at the court. Article 10(d) of the Protocol only demands that the application should not be submitted 'whilst the same matter has been instituted before another International Court for adjudication'.[109] The court has repeatedly emphasised the literal reading of

[103] *National Co-ordinating Group of Departmental Representatives of the Cocoa-Coffee Sector (CNDD) v Côte d'Ivoire*, 17 December 2009, ECW/CCJ/JUD/05/09, para 23; *SYNECOCI and Others v Côte d'Ivoire*, 19 February 2018, ECW/CCJ/JUD/07/18, 6.

[104] *Ocean King Nigeria v Senegal*, 8 July 2011, ECW/CCJ/JUD/07/11, para 51.

[105] *Dexter Oil Ltd v Liberia*, 6 February 2019, ECW/CCJ/JUD/03/19, paras 71, 72.

[106] For an overview of how the jurisprudence on access of legal persons developed over time, see also Happold (n 27) 502 et seq; P Wiater, *Internationale Individualkläger – Ein Vergleich des Zugangs zu Gericht im Wirtschaftsvölkerrecht* (Mohr Siebeck 2020) 303 et seq.

[107] eg, *Amnesty International Togo and Others v Togo*, 25 June 2020, ECW/CCJ/JUD/09/20, para 35. See also *La Société Bedir SARL v Niger*, 1 July 2020, ECW/CCJ/JUD/11/20, paras 41–43; *True Whig Party v Liberia*, 24 November 2023, ECW/CCJ/JUD/44/23, para 52.

[108] *Congrès pour la Démocratie et le Progrès (CDP) and Others v Burkina Faso*, 13 July 2015, ECW/CCJ/JUG/16/15, para 20.

[109] The court has decided that this does not include the African Commission on Human and Peoples' Rights, see *Ms. Rose Breivogel and Another v Nigeria*, 21 March 2022, ECW/CCJ/JUD/05/22, para 40.

Article 10(d) and confirmed that applicants can file human rights cases even if domestic remedies have not been exhausted.[110] The opportunity structure in this regard is thus broad.

Furthermore, the opportunity structure has been ambivalent as to whether human rights cases before the court can be time-barred. The point of reference for this issue is Article 9(3) of the Statute according to which an action is time-barred after three years 'from the date when the right of action arose'. The jurisprudence of the court is inconsistent as to whether this provision is applicable in the human rights context. Both in the early and the recent jurisprudence of the court, there are instances in which the court rejected the applicability of this provision in human rights cases.[111] In the 2018 case *Federation of African Journalists*, the court even said that any opposing decisions 'are hereby overruled'.[112] This is, according to the court, due to the wording of the French version of the Protocol that does not include a time limit for cases against member states. This is a very permissive stance that broadens the opportunity for applicants considerably. However, in contrast to these decisions but without engaging with them, the court has, both in the years before and after this decision, applied Article 9(3) of the Protocol to human rights cases.[113] This had in turn limited the opportunity for applicants to bring such cases to the court. In recent cases, the court has however reiterated again its stance taken in *Federation of African Journalists* so that the extent of the access opportunity remains somewhat unclear, however with a tendency towards the non-application of the time limit.[114]

Yet when applying the time limit, the court has also established exceptions to this rule. In *Femi Falana*, the court distinguished between ordinary human rights violations and gross human rights violations: while the three-year rule is applied to the former, the latter are not affected by it.[115] In addition, the court has taken up the concept of 'continuous violations' to which various other human rights courts also refer. The court has recognised that for continuous violations, 'the statute of limitation shall only begin to run from the time when such unlawful conduct or omission ceases'.[116] This means that even when the court does apply Article 9(3) of the Protocol, the opportunity for applicants to access the court is somewhat broadened. The jurisprudence on time limitations and the resulting

[110] eg, *Etim Essien v Gambia*, 14 March 2007, ECW/CCJ/APP/05/05, paras 20–27; *Hadijatou Mani Koraou v Niger*, 27 October 2008, ECW/CCJ/JUD/06/08, paras 36–49; *Ocean King Nigeria v Senegal*, 8 July 2011, ECW/CCJ/JUD/07/11, paras 37–41; *Sikiru Alade v Nigeria*, 11 June 2012, ECW/CCJ/JUD/10/12, para 29 et seq; *Hans Capehart Williams SR v Liberia and Others*, 30 November 2015, ECW/CCJ/JUD/25/15, 11–13.

[111] *Federation of African Journalists and Others v The Gambia*, 13 February 2018, ECW/CCJ/JUD/04/18, 20; *Djot Bayi Talbia & 14 Others v Nigeria & 4 Others*, 28 January 2009, ECW/CCJ/JUD/01/09, para 30.

[112] *Federation of African Journalists and Others v The Gambia*, 13 February 2018, ECW/CCJ/JUD/04/18, 20.

[113] For a subsequent case, see *Umeh and Others v Nigeria*, 1 July 2020, ECW/CCJ/JUD/10/20, paras 26–33.

[114] *Incorporated Trustees of Center for Peace and Conflict Management in Africa and Rethink Africa Foundation & 7 Others (Consolidated) v Nigeria*, 29 March 2022, ECW/CCJ/JUD/17/22, paras 68–71; *Oluwatimilehin Adebayo v Nigeria*, 3 December 2024, ECW/CCJ/JUD/44/24, paras 28–29; *Jean Edoh Nunyava Oumolou v Togo*, 30 January 2024, ECW/CCJ/JUD/02/24, para 34.

[115] *Falana and Another v Benin and Others*, 24 January 2012, ECW/CCJ/JUD/02/12, para 30.

[116] *SERAP v Nigeria*, 14 December 2012, ECW/CCJ/JUD/18/12, para 62. See also *Umeh and Others v Nigeria*, 1 July 2020, ECW/CCJ/JUD/10/20, paras 29–33.

opportunity structure thus oscillates between a very permissive and a somewhat permissive stance.

Social Opportunity Elements

In addition to the legal opportunity structure, there is a social opportunity structure that also contributes to the MOC setting for applicants. Social opportunity is shaped by group effects such as the tendency of actors to conform to the social norm within the group of actors of whom they consider themselves to be a member, and situations in which the actions of other members of this social group can be perceived as an opportunity for an actor's own behaviour. Among the applicants to the ECOWAS Court, human rights NGOs are more likely to perceive themselves as part of the group of regional NGOs as compared with individual applicants or corporate actors. Conformity tendencies as behavioural factors as well as opportunity enhancing network effects are thus most relevant for NGOs.[117] As mentioned above, there is indeed a wide range of NGOs that have engaged with the court both as applicants and as amicus curiae.

Practical Opportunity Elements

In addition to jurisdiction and access rules, the opportunity structure is also influenced by the practical capacities of the court. The more cases the court can manage based on its personal and financial capacities, the broader the practical opportunity for actors to engage with the court. This aspect is closely related to the motivational factor effective behaviour, as discussed above. But the emphasis here is on the de facto capacity of the court rather than the perception of actors about this capacity. In particular the limited number of judges risks limiting the practical opportunity for bringing increasing numbers of cases to the court.

To sum up, the opportunity structure for (potential) applicants to the ECOWAS Court in human rights matters is favourable since the changes introduced by the 2005 Protocol. While there was virtually no opportunity for applicants to engage with the court in human rights cases before the amendment, the revised Protocol has created a broad opportunity regarding jurisdiction and access rules, particularly in the absence of a catalogue of invocable human rights instruments and of an exhaustion of domestic remedies rule. The jurisprudence of the ECOWAS Court has somewhat reduced this very broad structure, most prominently so by refusing in the early years to review decisions of domestic courts. At the same time, the court has created at least a moderate opportunity for applicants that are not explicitly mentioned in Article 10(d) of the Protocol. This concerns NGOs and corporate entities, with the opportunity structure for the former being more favourable than for the latter. Yet it is also important to note that, with regard to various elements of the opportunity structure, the jurisprudence of the court has been, or still is, fluctuating. Finally, the de facto capacity of the court so far does not limit the opportunity of applicants.

[117] On conformity as group effect, see ch 2.

iii. Constraints

(Potential) Applicants face both intrinsic and extrinsic constraints.

Intrinsic Constraints

Awareness of the court and knowledge about its jurisprudence in human rights matters has been, and still is, a relevant constraint for potential applicants. It is however useful to consider the differences among groups of potential applicants. For certain groups of actors including bar associations and NGOs, there is a higher level of awareness than for the 'ordinary citizenry'[118] in the West African region so that lack of awareness has been, especially in the earlier years, a considerable constraint for potential individual applicants.[119] However, for member states against whom the court has decided high-profile cases in the past two decades, the court and its human rights jurisdiction has become more present in the domestic discourse. High-profile cases have generated considerable press coverage of the court in states such as Nigeria and Liberia[120] and enhanced general awareness of the court: what 'grab[s] headlines … significantly enhance the Court's salience and visibility across West Africa'.[121] Moreover, in Nigeria, the state in which the ECOWAS Court has its seat, the awareness is naturally higher than in other states. For this state, it has been observed that 'a healthy level of awareness and interest in the human rights mandate' of the court exists. This includes the introduction of courses on the ECOWAS Court in the Nigerian Law School and lectures on the court at the Nigerian Bar Association.[122] In line with this higher awareness, there are far more applicants filing cases against Nigeria compared with other member states. In addition to being aware of the court at all, knowledge about, and accessibility of, the court's jurisprudence is an issue. Not all court decisions are available on the court's website, and the decisions that are available are scanned versions of hard copies and not searchable documents. This makes it difficult for applicants to identify the lines of jurisprudence of the court on selected issues, a fact that constitutes a constraint for applicants wanting to engage with this jurisprudence.

A further intrinsic constraint that is relevant for (potential) applicants before the ECOWAS Court is financial in nature. For many (potential) applicants in some of the poorer and/or more remote areas of West Africa, the costs of a procedure before the court is a considerable constraint to engaging with the court. This includes costs that occur for attending a hearing in Abuja, the seat of the court, given the vastness of the West African region. The latter costs have been occasionally reduced when the court decides to sit in another state (see section II.C.i). Moreover, there are no court fees for applicants (Article 13 Practice Directions 2012). In fact, this 'reduction, however modest it might seem, still confers a significant benefit to all-too-many

[118] Okafor and Effoduh (n 24) 145.
[119] A Banjo, 'The ECOWAS Court and the Politics of Access to Justice in West Africa' (2007) 32 *African Development* 69, 77.
[120] Ebobrah, 'Dual Mandate' (n 45) 96.
[121] Alter, Helfer and McAllister (n 4) 765.
[122] Ebobrah, 'Dual Mandate' (n 45) 96.

citizens in a developing sub-region such as West Africa'.[123] A further way of reducing cost lies in the option to hold virtual court sessions. During the Covid 19 pandemic, Article 5 of Practical Direction 2020 created that possibility. Such a practice can contribute to further decreasing financial constraints for applicants.

Intrinsic constraints as to knowledge and financial ability are much more pronounced for individual applicants in the West African region than for other groups of applicants such as NGOs and corporate entities. NGOs have, by way of their human rights-related activities, an expertise in the field which generates knowledge about the court and its jurisprudence. For corporate actors, having the financial means to retain lawyers with relevant expertise is also likely to reduce knowledge-related constraints more than is the case for many potential individual applicants. And the very diverging impact of financial constraints for individual and non-individual applicants is an obvious consequence of the still considerable part of the population with low income in West Africa.[124]

Extrinsic Constraints

An extrinsic constraint that is relevant for some (potential) applicants in human rights cases are competing authority relationships. For potential applicants from several member states, the African Court of Human and Peoples' Rights (ACtHPR) is (or has been) a competing forum for human rights matters. Among the ECOWAS member states, for Ghana and the Gambia (and for the former member states of Burkina Faso and Mali), a declaration under Articles 5(3) and 34(6) of the Protocol establishing the ACtHPR is currently in force which enables individuals and NGOs to access the court. For Benin and Côte d'Ivoire, this possibility existed until these states withdraw their Article 34(6) declarations in 2020.[125] In such situations of competing jurisdiction, the ECOWAS Court might appear as the less attractive forum. This is exemplified when comparing cases brought against Benin and Côte d'Ivoire. A numeric comparison is possible as the courts started to operate in human rights matters at a similar time. By 2020, the time of withdrawal of their declarations, there had been only about 11 (reported) ECOWAS Court decisions against Benin but 43 cases before the ACtHPR; there had been only about 13 (reported) ECOWAS Court decisions against Côte d'Ivoire but 38 cases before the ACtHPR.[126]

Comparative aspects that potential applicants might consider include the jurisdictional scope, access rules regarding time-barred cases or exhaustion of domestic remedies, content of established jurisprudence about the substance of human rights

[123] Okafor and Effoduh (n 24) 135.

[124] According to the World Bank income categories, the ECOWAS member states are, at the time of writing, classified as follows: Low income: the Gambia, Guinea, Guinea Bissau, Liberia, Sierra Leone, Togo (and former member states Burkina Faso, Mali and Niger); Lower middle income: Benin, Côte d'Ivoire, Ghana, Nigeria, Senegal; Upper middle income: Cabo Verde. Data available at: datahelpdesk.worldbank.org/knowledgebase/articles/906519-world-bank-country-and-lending-groups.

[125] On these withdrawals, see also section II.B.ii.

[126] The statistical sources used here are, on the one hand, the official statistic of the ACtHPR available on its website at: www.african-court.org/cpmt/statistic; and on the other hand, the informal statistics of the Institute for Human Rights and Development in Africa at: ihrda.uwazi.io/.

protection, compliance expectations of member states, costs and distance, familiarity with the institutions etc. As potential applicants are likely to assess some of these aspects more in favour of the ECOWAS Court than others, the extent to which the competing ACtHPR jurisdiction is perceived as a constraining factor will depend on their preferences. Potentially, the constraining effect of this competing authority can be high. In addition to preference, the expected constraining effect also differs among the groups of applicants. For example, the access rules before the ACtHPR differ for individuals, NGOs and corporate entities and depending on how favourable they are for each group, the competing effect with the ECOWAS Court diverges.

The withdrawals of the Article 34(6) declarations by Benin and Côte d'Ivoire in 2020 make it possible to assess how the applicants' behaviour is affected when the constraining effect of competing authority relationships is removed. Since the withdrawal, there has been an increase in cases brought against Côte d'Ivoire to the ECOWAS Court as compared with the period when individual access to the ACtHPR was still possible. There have been at least nine (reported) decisions against Côte d'Ivoire in the five years after the withdrawal as compared with about 13 (reported) decisions in the previous 15 years. This can be taken as an indication that, while direct access to the ACtHPR was still possible, the competing authority relationship regarding this court had constrained the (potential) applicants' behaviour as to bringing cases to the ECOWAS Court. For Benin, the statistics are less indicative with at least four (reported) decisions against Benin in the last five years as compared with 10 (reported) cases previously.

Further, a relevant competing authority relationship exists between the ECOWAS Court and domestic courts. Especially given that the Protocol does not require an exhaustion of domestic remedies, there is a situation of 'competing competences' in which the ECOWAS Court and domestic courts appear as alternative fora.[127] The competition among these courts is more pronounced than that between the ECOWAS Court and the ACtHPR. Applicants cannot only choose between these fora, they can also file cases to the ECOWAS Court and a domestic court simultaneously.[128] The court has explicitly recognised that 'pendency of the suit before a domestic court cannot oust its jurisdiction to determine this case on alleged human rights violation'.[129] In such situations conflicting judgments are thus a very real possibility, creating a constraining authority competition not only for the applicants but also for the other actors involved. However, given the structural deficits as to the independence of the judiciary in many member states, potential applicants might consider the ECOWAS Court forum as being more attractive. As mentioned above, the 'institutional failure of national systems' is a motivational factor for ECOWAS Court applicants which has 'led citizens to seek alternatives outside their national judicial systems'.[130] Where, and as long as these institutional deficits in the domestic judiciary

[127] E Ojomo, 'Competing Competences in Adjudication: Reviewing the Relationship between the ECOWAS Court and National Courts' (2014) 7 *African Journal of Legal Studies* 87, 118.

[128] This is not possible before the ACtHPR, see Article 10(d) of the Protocol.

[129] *SERAP v Nigeria*, 19 June 2014, ECW/CCJ/JUD/16/14, para 76.

[130] Ojomo (n 127) 118. See also AY Kane, 'The Relationship between Institutional Design and the Efficiency of a Jurisdiction – Focus on the Court of Justice of the Economic Community of West African States' (2020) 24 *Max Planck Yearbook of United Nations Law* 282, 301.

persist, the constraining impact of the competing authority relationship between the ECOWAS Court and domestic courts is rather low.

In conclusion, the intrinsic constraints regarding knowledge about the court and financial abilities to file cases before it are still considerable in the ECOWAS context, however more so for individuals than for other groups of applicants. Further, competing authority relationships to the ACtHPR and domestic courts constitute extrinsic constraints which are higher for applicants that have access to the ACtHPR than for those who do not. However, at present they do not create a major structural constraint for most applicants.

iv. Assessment of MOC Factors

The above analysis of MOC factors for (potential) applicants in human rights cases has painted the following picture.

In the period between the court's inauguration in 2001 and the 2005 Protocol amendment, there was virtually no opportunity for any of the groups of potential applicants to engage with the court. The court neither had jurisdiction in human rights matters nor was access possible for these actors. In addition, some of the constraining factors were high, especially as to the lack of knowledge of the court. However, actors were motivated to bring cases to the court as several of the motivational values and interests outlined above already existed at the outset. Among the MOC factors, opportunity was thus at the lowest level which, according to the MOC framework, made this the key determining factor for the behaviour of potential applicants. In fact, despite the existing motivation, the lack of opportunity resulted in only one human rights case against a member state – the *Afolabi* case of 2004 – brought to the court by this group of potential applicants in this period.

Since the 2005 Protocol, the MOC factors play out differently from the initial phase of the court's practice. They also diverge among the groups of (potential) applicants. For NGOs, the MOC factors are generally favourable. The change in the MOC setting is illustrated by Figure 4.1. NGOs are strongly motivated both by human rights values and by strategic interests as to exposing human rights violations and achieving discursive aims. The opportunity structure is rather broad with access rules that allow to file cases on behalf of groups of individuals and even enabling an *actio popularis*. NGOs furthermore profit, like the other groups of applicants, from the absence of an exhaustion of domestic remedies rules and the ambivalent but rather lenient time limit to file cases. The same is true for the broad jurisdiction on human rights cases that make it possible, at least in principle, to invoke any human rights instrument relevant to the case. Initially, a major caveat has been the refusal of the court to review decisions by domestic courts, but, as outlined, the court has expanded its approach over time. The social opportunity structure adds a favourable dimension to the opportunity for NGOs. Finally, the intrinsic constraints as to knowledge and financial ability as well as the extrinsic constraints concerning competing authority relationships are rather low for NGOs. The latter is due to the structural deficit in the domestic judiciary and, although there is a competing authority relationship for NGOs from states that have made a declaration under Article 34(6) of the Protocol establishing the ACtHPR, the ACtHPR does not have a major comparative advantage with regard to access opportunity for NGOs from the West African region. This favourable MOC situation for NGOs has indeed translated into a variety of NGOs bringing cases to the court.

Figure 4.1 Development over time of the MOC setting for NGOs as applicants before the ECOWAS Court in human rights cases[131]

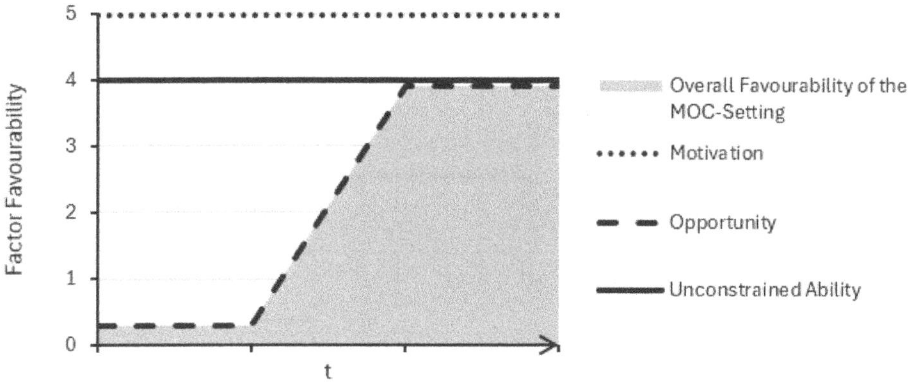

When assessing the current relationship among the MOC factors for NGOs, none of the factors stands out clearly as the lowest. Motivation, opportunity and unconstrained ability are well developed, however with slightly more limitations as to opportunity and ability. The latter two factors are thus, according to the MOC framework, likely to determine the behaviour of NGOs as (potential) applicants. If the court's strategy was to further enhance the likeliness that NGOs engage with the court, increasing opportunity and decreasing constraints is, based on the MOC framework, expected to lead to the desired outcome.

For individual applicants the MOC assessment is, considering the diversity of this group, less uniform. On the one hand, there are certain individual applicants for whom the MOC factors are rather favourable, ie, political actors (see Figure 4.2). For these actors, strategic interests as motivational factor are strong; compliance by the respondents is not their primary goal so compliance deficits do not noticeably reduce the level of motivation. Opportunity for these individuals is broad due to the favourable jurisdiction and access rules, with the exception of election-related cases for which the human rights jurisdiction is not always exercised. Constraints can be rated as moderate. While this group of actors initially had a limited knowledge of the court and of the possibility to pursue strategic interests before it, they have over the years become increasingly aware of this possibility. Financial constraints are likely to be lower than for many other individual applicants in the region. The competing authority relationships towards the ACtHPR and to domestic courts is relevant for these actors, in particular as these actors seem to address domestic courts more frequently than NGOs before filing

[131] The illustrations in this chapter translate the quantification used for the assessment in this book – low, moderate to low, moderate, moderate to high, high – into a scale of 0 to 5.

a case before the ECOWAS Court. In this regard, constraints are likely to present the determining MOC factor for the behaviour of these actors in the human rights context. Strategies that reduce these constraints can thus lead to these actors engaging with the court more.

Figure 4.2 Development over time of the MOC setting for political actors as applicants before the ECOWAS Court in human rights cases

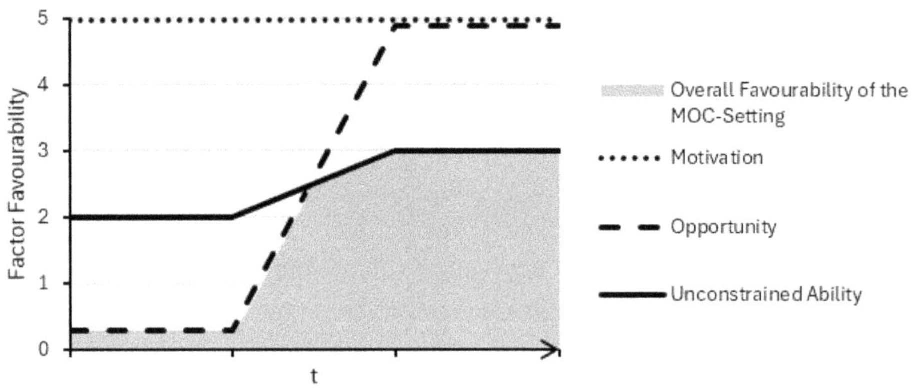

On the other hand, there is the large group of 'ordinary citizens' of ECOWAS states for whom the MOC assessment appears still much more unfavourable (see Figure 4.3). For these potential applicants, motivation is already significantly lower. Although they can have an interest in exposing human rights violations of which they have been the victim, and in obtaining recognition of their victim status, they are less likely to be motivated by structural interests such as the discursive effects of cases before the court and regional awareness raising and deterrence. Moreover, given the existing compliance deficits, the interest in dispute resolution including obtaining financial compensation for human rights violations can only have a limited motivational impact. For this group of individual actors, the expected effectiveness of their engagement with the court as to dispute resolution is however likely to be an important factor. The level of motivation is thus moderate at best. In contrast, the opportunity structure for this group of potential applicants is favourable. Very broad access rules and broad jurisdiction – with the notable exception of the court initially not reviewing decisions of domestic courts – would make it possible for these actors to engage with the court in a wide range of cases. Yet the constraints for these actors are rather high. This is in particular due to intrinsic constraints such as knowledge of the court and the financial means of bringing cases to the court, despite some improvements over time. The (unconstrained) ability to engage with the court would be, for a considerable number of individual applicants, the lowest and thus determining factor, while a low motivation might be determining for others. This means that motivation and constraints are the MOC factors that, at present, are most relevant for whether these actors engage with the court. To significantly enhance the likeliness that this group of actors engages with the court, both motivational and constraining factors would need to be addressed.

Figure 4.3 Development over time of the MOC setting for individuals as applicants before the ECOWAS Court in human rights cases

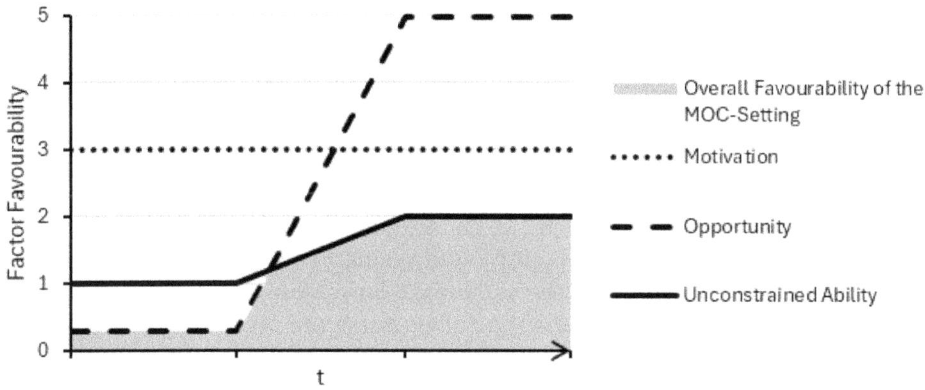

Finally, for corporate entities, the MOC assessment shows yet again different determining factors (see Figure 4.4). Motivation can be expected to be moderate – similar to what has been said for individual applicants, however with strategic interests such as deterrence of member state authorities being a more probable motivation for these actors than for individual applicants. Opportunity is limited given that the court does not consider these applicants to have general access to the court. Yet as the rights for which the court does exercise jurisdiction regarding corporate entities – right to fair hearing, right to property and right to freedom of expression – are significant rights, the opportunity can nonetheless be termed as moderate. Constraints are lower than for many individual applicants because financial constraints for corporate entities are much less prevalent than for individuals and knowledge about the court is at least more easily available for these actors than for individuals, although knowledge deficits are likely to exist here as well. In sum, motivation and opportunity appear to be the lowest of the MOC factors for corporate entities so that these factors are expected to determine whether these actors engage with the court or not.

Figure 4.4 Development over time of the MOC setting for corporate entities as applicants before the ECOWAS Court in human rights cases

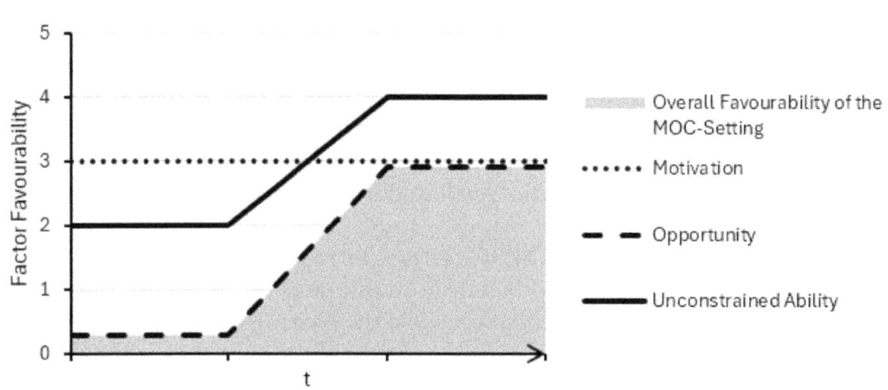

This assessment shows that for the various groups of (potential) applicants, MOC conditions differ. For some, the constraints, alone or in combination with motivation or opportunity, are decisive; for others, motivation and opportunity determine the behaviour. As a consequence, when the ECOWAS Court implements strategies to enhance its authority, it has to address different factors for different actors. Whether it has successfully done so is discussed in section III. What is more, the above assessment illustrates that certain claims made in the literature as to what influences the authority relationship between an international court and its audiences are not generalisable. First, it shows that the political context in which the court operates does not necessarily define the extent to which authority relationships with the court's audiences exist. Even in the absence of a well-established rule of law practice in the member states, there can be strong authority relationships with certain groups of actors. Rule of law deficits in certain member states can even constitute a motivational factor for actors to engage with the court, as well as limiting the constraining effect of competing authority relationships. This also points to another observation: compliance considerations and potentially existing deficits such as in the ECOWAS context only limit the motivation of certain actors. For others, expected compliance deficits do not hinder an engagement with the court because other interests and values can constitute a sufficient motivational basis. Moreover, the above assessment highlights when *legal* factors (as opposed to political factors) shape the actors' MOC setting in a decisive manner. For (potential) applicants for whom opportunity is the decisive factor, such as NGOs and corporate entities in the ECOWAS context, legal norms as to access and jurisprudence determine the extent to which these actors engage with the court. Here, lack of engagement with the court can be attributed to the legal framework. For other actors, legal aspects have an indirect effect on their behaviour. For example, rules on procedural costs can be decisive depending on the financial situation of the potential applicant, a situation that is likely to be the case for a considerable section of potential individual applicants before the ECOWAS Court. This also shows how the actors' behaviour is influenced by an interrelation between legal and non-legal factors.

B. MOC Factors for Respondents

After having assessed the MOC setting for applicants before the ECOWAS Court in human rights cases, I now turn to the respondents. In human rights cases, the respondents are the ECOWAS member states. To take into account the various relevant state actors, this section understands the term 'respondent' actors broadly. Where appropriate it distinguishes among the state actors and considers not only state governments but also domestic courts and legislative actors in charge of applying ECOWAS Court decisions.

The section first analyses the MOC factors for the acceptance of the authority of the ECOWAS Court (III.B.i). It then turns to instances of pushback, assessing the MOC factors for state actors' pushback against the court (III.B.ii).

i. MOC Factors for Acceptance of the Court's Authority

a. Motivation

Motivational factors for state actors to accept the authority of the ECOWAS Court in human rights matters are related to both these actors' values and interests.

Values

For state actors in the ECOWAS context, value correspondence regarding the substantive value of human rights protection is rather well developed. Human rights values can thus present a solid motivational factor for ECOWAS member states to accept the authority of the ECOWAS Court in human rights matters. There is a high commitment to human rights in this region and these states 'stand out as the most committed to the African human rights system'.[132] The 1993 ECOWAS treaty already includes the 'recognition, promotion and protection of human and peoples' rights' as a fundamental principle of the ECOWAS community (Article 4g). Due to states reorienting their values during the humanitarian interventions in this region in the 1990s, state governments strengthened their support for human rights values even if this meant limiting the sovereignty of the state.[133] The ECOWAS Protocol on Democracy and Good Governance from 2001 re-emphasised these values. Article 1(h) requires that the 'rights set out in the African Charter on Human and Peoples' Rights and other international instruments shall be guaranteed in each of the ECOWAS Member States'. All member states are indeed parties to the Charter. Further, Articles 34 and 35 include provisions on the promotion, protection, monitoring and enforcement of human rights in the territories of the member states, both by the states themselves and the ECOWAS institutions.

Despite this aspirational commitment to human rights values among all member states, the extent to which these values are also reflected in the human rights practice of the member states diverges among the states. As an indication of this divergence, the Freedom House ratings as to political rights and civil liberties are insightful. Although this rating only partly addresses the scope of human rights matters, it sheds some light on the human rights practice in this region. Table 4.1 shows that for most ECOWAS member states, the ratings range mid-table with states being classified as 'partly free'. Negative outliers are Guinea as well the three former member states which are classified as 'not free, while Cabo Verde and Ghana are rated above average as 'free'. Given this diverging and mostly moderate human rights practice, keeping the commitment to human rights values salient among state actors might be a challenge. This can affect the extent to which certain state actors subjectively embrace the formally existing value-correspondence as a motivational factor.

Further, there is a certain level of value-correspondence between the court and the member states as to institutional values relating to the rule of law. The rule of law, and specifically judicial independence, are endorsed by member states in their constitutive documents. According to Article 1(a) of the ECOWAS Protocol on Democracy and Good Governance from 2001, judicial independence is part of the 'constitutional

[132] Ebobrah, 'Dual Mandate' (n 45) 87.
[133] Alter, Helfer and McAllister (n 4) 771.

principles shared by all Member States'. The Protocol specifies this independence requirement also in the context of human rights. Article 33(1) of the Protocol emphasises that member states 'recognize that the rule of law involves not only the promulgation of good laws that are in conformity with the provisions on human rights, but also a good judicial system'. Furthermore, its Article 35 provides that member states 'shall establish independent national institutions to promote and protect human rights', a provision that arguably also includes judicial institutions. From the time of the inauguration of the ECOWAS Court, there has thus been a general commitment of member states to the values of the rule of law and judicial independence, constituting the basis for value-correspondence between the member states and the ECOWAS Court.

However, despite this general commitment these values are not shared, as a matter of practice, by all ECOWAS member states to the same extent. In several member states, the rule of law practice and the independence of the judiciary show considerable deficiencies. Table 4.1 provides an overview of how the ECOWAS member states are ranked according to selected rule of law and judicial independence indices. This can directly affect the authority relationship between these states and the ECOWAS Court. For example, with regard to the Gambia, which was ranked as non-free during the regime of Yahya Jammeh who was president of the country from 1996 until 2017,[134] value-correspondence as to the relationship between courts and governmental actors was rather weak. As an observer put it: Yahya Jammeh had 'conquered his own judiciary' and thus 'refused to be bound by a court in Abuja [i.e. the ECOWAS Court]'.[135]

Table 4.1 Standards of the rule of law as well as political rights and civil liberties in the ECOWAS member states[136]

Member State *(former member state)*	Freedom House Report 2025: overall score and status	Freedom House Report 2025: judicial independence	WJP Rule of Law Index 2024 *Overall score and global rank [among 142 assessed states]*	Worldwide Governance Indicators: rule of law [for 2023] *Estimate of governance (−2.5 to +2.5) and percentile rank among countries*
Benin	60 – Partly Free	2/4	0.48–93	−0.51–33.02
Cabo Verde	92 – Free	4/4	n/a	0.40–61.79
Côte d'Ivoire	49 – Partly Free	1/4	0.45–104	−0.46–35.38
the Gambia	47 – Partly Free	2/4	0.49–87	−0.37–38.21
Ghana	80 – Free	2/4	0.55–62	−0.10–49.53

(continued)

[134] eg, Freedom House Report of 2017 on the Gambia (with a score of 20/100): freedomhouse.org/country/gambia/freedom-world/2017.

[135] Statement by a West African human rights lawyer in an interview of 10 February 2011 conducted by, and cited according to KJ Alter, JT Gathii and LR Helfer, 'Backlash against International Courts in West, East and Southern Africa: Causes and Consequences' (2016) 27 *European Journal of International Law* 293, 297.

[136] Data available at: freedomhouse.org/country/scores; https://worldjusticeproject.org/rule-of-law-index/global; www.worldbank.org/en/publication/worldwide-governance-indicators.

Table 4.1 *(Continued)*

Member State *(former member state)*	Freedom House Report 2025: overall score and status	Freedom House Report 2025: judicial independence	WJP Rule of Law Index 2024 *Overall score and global rank [among 142 assessed states]*	Worldwide Governance Indicators: rule of law [for 2023] *Estimate of governance (−2.5 to +2.5) and percentile rank among countries*
Guinea	30 – Not Free	1/4	0.41–119	−1.11–14.15
Guinea Bissau	41 – Partly Free	1/4	n/a	−1.44–7.08
Liberia	64 – Partly Free	1/4	0.44–109	−1.03–16.98
Nigeria	44 – Partly Free	2/4	0.40–120	−0.89–20.28
Senegal	69 – Partly Free	2/4	0.55–60	−0.27–42.92
Sierra Leone	59 – Partly Free	2/4	0.43–110	−0.83–22.17
Togo	41 – Partly Free	2/4	0.45–106	−0.53–32.08
Burkina Faso	*25 – Not Free*	*1/4*	*0.46–98*	*−0.74–24.53*
Mali	*24 – Not Free*	*1/4*	*0.39–124*	*−0.98–18.40*
Niger	*30 – Not Free*	*1/4*	*0.43–114*	*−0.71–25.00*

Interests

Various interests can constitute motivational factors for member states to accept the authority of the ECOWAS Court. To start with, as for actors in other human rights regimes, a strategic interest for accepting the authority of a human rights court lies in being favourably perceived by other international actors. States care about their reputations which thus becomes a motivational factor.[137] Indeed, some ECOWAS member states have even translated their reputational concerns into legal claims by requesting the court to award the state damages for 'atteinte a son image et à son honorabilité'[138] or for the 'prejudice morale' caused by the applicant's claim that the state has violated human rights.[139]

Further, monitoring makes it more likely that other actors become aware of non-compliance by a respondent, thus motivating for compliance with the aim of avoiding reputational disadvantages or even formal sanctions.[140] Yet, for most of the court's practice there has been no generalised monitoring infrastructure. In particular, the Treaty does not assign a monitoring function to any of the ECOWAS institutions.

[137] On reputational effect in the international sphere, A van Aaken and B Simsek, 'Rewarding in International Law' (2021) 115 *American Journal of International Law* 195; R Brewster, 'Reputation in International Relations and International Law Theory' in JL Dunoff and MA Pollack (eds), *Interdisciplinary Perspectives On International Law and International Relations: The State of the Art* (CUP 2012) 524; GW Downs and MA Jones, 'Reputation, Compliance, and International Law' (2002) 31 *Journal of Legal Studies* 95.

[138] *Cheikh Abdoulaye Mbengue v Mali*, 7 October 2011, ECW/CCJ/JUG/08/11, paras 39–40.

[139] *Marie Molmou and Others v Guinea*, 17 May 2016, ECW/CCJ/JUD/16/16, 11.

[140] DT Welsh and LD Ordóñez, 'Conscience without Cognition: The Effects of Subconscious Priming on Ethical Behavior' (2014) 57 *Academy of Management Journal* 723.

Respondents thus were not as likely to expect reputational costs for non-compliance than if there had been such compliance monitoring. And the obligations enshrined in the operational part of the court's decisions have not been kept salient by compliance reports. More recently, however, the court has created its own monitoring mechanism. It now orders states to 'report' within a specified time frame about 'the measures taken to implement the orders' imposed in the judgment.[141] For this purpose, it has created, in its decisions, a section entitled 'compliance and reporting'. The court thus acts as a monitoring body. This novel mechanism enhances the motivation of respondents to comply.

For state governments, an interest in dispute resolution is a relevant motivational factor to accept the authority of the court. This interest is likely to be higher the more publicised and/or politically impactful is the dispute. When political actors such as opposition politicians bring a case to the court, government actors have an interest in this dispute being resolved so that it no longer shapes the public discourse. For cases brought by NGOs that might be well covered in the media and that influence public discourse, states have a similar interest. In contrast, for disputes with individuals that have less discursive influence and whose cases are not as often mediatised, the interest in dispute resolution is lower. This difference might contribute to the relatively low compliance rates of member states regarding the payment of damages ordered by the court to individual victims of human rights violations.

As an effectiveness consideration, state governments are of course interested in the court deciding in their favour. For states, the interest in winning a case was a strong motivational factor to engage with it especially in the early days of the court. In the early cases, the court did not often decide against the respondent states. Many cases were either ruled inadmissible or the court found that no human rights violation could be established. This high success rate 'encourage[ed] State Parties to continue to participate in proceedings which they mostly won'.[142]

Another interest-based motivational factor for accepting the court's authority can result from the fact that state actors are more likely than many applicants in human rights cases (with the exception of some NGOs) to repeatedly engage with the court. Such repeated engagement can have two implications relevant for the present context. To start with, repeated engagement can trigger the actors' interest in consistent behaviour.[143] As actors tend to opt for consistent behaviour, their past behaviour leads to an interest in upholding the preferences reflected in this behaviour. In the ECOWAS context, it was easy for states to engage with the court in the initial cases as the chances of the court finding a violation were low. In later cases which were more open as to their outcome, the previous behaviour of states and their interest in behaving consistently would have constituted a motivational factor for engaging with the court again. This effect however is likely to be stronger for states such as Nigeria and

[141] eg, *Illia Malam Mamane Saidat v Niger*, 22 June 2021, ECW/CCJ/JUD/17/2021; *Diawara Oumar v Côte d'Ivoire*, 22 October 2021, ECW/CCJ/JUD/34/21; *Kodjo Alain Victor v Cote d'Ivoire*, 26 April 2021, ECW/CCJ/JUD/09/21; *Adam Latif and 4 Others v Togo*, 30 November 2023, ECW/CCJ/JUD/45/2023; *Oluwatimilehin Adebayo v Nigeria*, 3 December 2024, ECW/CCJ/JUD/44/24; *Jean Edoh Nunyava Oumolou v Togo*, 30 January 2024, ECW/CCJ/JUD/02/24.

[142] Ebobrah, 'Dual Mandate' (n 45) 91.

[143] See ch 2.

Togo that are at the top of the list of cases brought against them than for states that only seldomly were in the role of respondent.

What is more, inertia and the status quo bias – two behavioural effects outlined in chapter two – can influence the motivational setting. Over time, repetitive situations appear to a lesser extent as requiring a choice. Active motivational assessments with an actor's full range of interests and values become less likely. When repeatedly engaging with the ECOWAS Court in human rights matters, state actors will question less and less whether to accept the authority of the court in the case at hand but rather perpetuate the behaviour adopted on earlier occasions – as an expression of inertia. As preferences can be merely perpetuated, there is less cognitive engagement aimed at reflected decision-making. In addition, the status quo bias is likely to enhance the value that actors attribute to the preferences expressed by previous behaviour.[144] In situations in which actors engage in decision-making beyond mere inertia, it is thus more likely that they decide to adopt the behavioural choice that they perceive as akin to the status quo. For example, even the Gambia during the Jammeh regime has, since it gave up in the *Saidykhan* case its previous strategy of non-appearance, engaged with the court in subsequent cases.[145]

In contrast to the above interests that are mostly relevant for governmental actors, the interests of *domestic courts* to accept the authority of the ECOWAS Court are less pronounced. First, the interest in consistent behaviour can become a motivational factor in the future – however this is not the case yet, as there has been only a limited number of cases in which domestic courts have implemented ECOWAS Court decisions. Further, a possible motivating interest can result from the domestic courts' relationship with their state government. Domestic courts are interested in their decisions being implemented and complied with by government actors. Hindering the implementation of decisions by the ECOWAS Court would potentially undermine the overall compliance practice regarding judicial decisions. To avoid such an effect on their own decisions, domestic courts can have a strategic interest in supporting implementation of ECOWAS Court decisions. However, it seems that it is not so much the relationship towards the state government that prevails in the motivational assessment of domestic courts. Rather, especially for apex courts, their interest in being the supreme judicial decision-maker determines whether or not to implement decisions of the ECOWAS Court. As will be outlined below, this opposing interest has led domestic courts to resist against implementing these decisions.

In conclusion, the motivation differs only somewhat for governmental actors as compared with domestic courts. For governmental actors, motivation is at a moderate level. This results primarily from the discrepancy between the well-developed aspirational value-correspondence as compared with the, at least partially deficient, de facto rule of law and human rights situation in many member states. The rather low interest in dispute resolution cannot counterbalance these motivation-limiting effects. For domestic courts, the motivation is even only low to moderate, while being

[144] On the status quo bias, see ch 2.

[145] *Saidykhan v Gambia*, 16 December 2010, ECW/CCJ/JUD/08/10. Later cases (still during the Jammeh regime) include *Omar Jallow & Amadou Scattred v The Gambia*, ECW/CCJ/APP/33/16; *Federation of African Journalists and Others v The Gambia*, ECW/CCJ/APP/36/15.

higher within the member states in which the rule of law and judicial independence is well developed. In particular, domestic courts are not very much motivated by interests such as strategic interests vis-a-vis other domestic actors or regarding an overall compliance practice.

b. Opportunity

The opportunity structure for (potential) respondents to accept the authority of the court is legally determined by the Protocol's provisions on the capacity of being sued for human rights violations. According to Article 9(4) of the Protocol, the jurisdiction of the court concerns cases of 'violation of human rights that occur in any Member State'. The wording of this provision is somewhat ambiguous as it speaks about violations *in* member states rather than *by* member states. This has made it necessary for the court to determine who can be a formal defendant before the court, and which kinds of acts of defendants can be reviewed.

First, the court has recognised that member states are the natural respondents in human rights cases. Formal respondents are only the states as such, rather than administrative entities within the state as some applicants had considered.[146] Further, given the ambiguous formulation of Article 9(4), applicants have tried to bring cases against private actors in human rights cases. The court has, however, decided that private actors cannot be respondents in human rights matters before the court.[147]

With regard to state actors, the court has distinguished between acts of the executive, judicial and legislative branches as objects for a human rights assessment. As already outlined in section II.A, the court initially merely reviewed executive acts. And even in these cases, it took a narrow approach as to the remedies that it ordered, primarily issuing declaratory decisions and only gradually expanding the cases in which it granted financial compensation or other remedies such as releasing a person from prison (see section II.A).

Further, it expanded the application of its jurisdiction to assessing human rights violations stemming from the conduct of domestic courts. In cases such as *Avocat Sans Frontières France v Nigeria* and *Mahamadou*, it abandoned its initial approach that equated a human rights review with a cassation court function that it does not possess.[148] The review of domestic judicial decisions is meanwhile well established.[149]

[146] eg, *SERAP v Nigeria*, 19 June 2014, ECW/CCJ/JUD/16/14, paras 67–68.

[147] eg, *Registered Trustees of the Socio-Economic Rights & Accountability Project (SERAP) v Nigeria and Others*, 10 December 2010, ECW/CCJ/APP/07/10, para 65 et seq; *Centre for Democracy and Development, and Another v Mamadou Tandja & Niger*, 9 May 2011, ECW/CCJ/JUD/05/11, para 31; *Marie Molmou and Others v Guinea*, 17 May 2016, ECW/CCJ/JUD/16/16, 6–7 (also citing further unreported decisions on the matter); on this issue see also ST Ebobrah, 'A rights-protection goldmine or a waiting volcanic eruption? Competence of, and access to, the human rights jurisdiction of the ECOWAS Community Court of Justice' (2007) 7 *African Human Rights Law Journal* 307, 321–22; K Bado, 'Good governance as a precondition for subsidiarity: human rights litigation in Nigeria and ECOWAS (2019) 57 *Commonwealth & Comparative Politics* 242, 251–54.

[148] *Registered Trustees of Avocat Sans Frontières France v Nigeria*, 31 January 2014, ECW/CCJ/APP/14/13; *Farimata Mahamadou and Others v Mali*, 17 May 2016, ECW/CCJ/JUD/11/16.

[149] eg, *True Whig Party v Liberia*, 24 November 2023, ECW/CCJ/JUD/44/23.

It does not only broaden the opportunity for applicants (see above), but it also broadens the opportunity for domestic courts to accept the authority of the ECOWAS Court. Domestic courts now can formally implement decisions of the ECOWAS Court, especially in relation to the procedural rights of litigants before domestic courts.

Unlike acts of the executive and the judiciary, acts of the legislature have not been addressed by the court in the first decade of the court's practice. The court has not engaged with claims regarding domestic legislation or even ordered the domestic legislator to amend laws that constitute or enable human rights violations brought before it, despite applicants requesting such orders.[150] This has limited the opportunity for legislative actors to accept the authority of the court. More recently, the court has however broadened this opportunity. In its decision in *Congrès pour la Démocratie et le Progrès v Burkina Faso* in 2015, the court assessed whether a domestic law provision (the Burka Faso Electoral Code) led to a violation of the applicants' rights, explicitly acknowledging that it has the power to decide by stating that 'the interpretation or application of the national text aims at depriving the citizens of rights embedded in international instruments'.[151] In the decision in *Federation of African Journalists*, the court explicitly granted non-declaratory remedies and ordered the respondent state 'to immediately repeal and/ or amend its laws'.[152] And in its *Umeh* decision, the court reaffirmed this jurisprudence even for cases in which domestic constitutional law is at stake, summarising its stance as follows:

> [T]his Court shall, where a case is brought before it, examine impugned legislations to ascertain whether or not the application of that impugned legislation constitutes a violation of human rights with the view to directing a review … [This Court] holds that it has the competence to compel member states to conform or meet their international and community obligations, and it does so where necessary by examining any impugned national laws with the view to ascertaining whether indeed any human rights violations have occurred.[153]

In the recent practice of the court, the domestic legislator is thus directly addressed by order to amend domestic legal provisions.[154] The court now puts legislative acts and domestic judicial decisions on an equal footing, reviewing both such state actions,

[150] See for such requests, eg, *Hadijatou Mani Koraou v Niger*, 27 October 2008, ECW/CCJ/JUD/06/08, para 28: 'Demand that the authorities of Niger introduce a new legislation which actually protects women against the discriminatory customs in issues of marriage and divorce'; *Registered Trustees of the Socio-Economic Rights & Accountability Project (SERAP) v Nigeria*, 10 December 2010, ECW/CCJ/APP/07/10, para 27: 'An order directing the government of Nigeria to establish adequate regulations for the operations of multinationals in the Niger Delta'.

[151] *Congrès pour la Démocratie et le Progrès (CDP) and Others v Burkina Faso*, 13 July 2015, ECW/CCJ/JUG/16/15, para 27.

[152] *Federation of African Journalists and Others v The Gambia*, 13 February 2018, ECW/CCJ/JUD/04/18, 57.

[153] *Umeh and Others v Nigeria*, 1 July 2020, ECW/CCJ/JUD/10/20, paras 43, 48.

[154] See for such orders also *Kodjo Alain Victor v Cote d'Ivoire*, 26 April 2021, ECW/CCJ/JUD/09/21; *Isaac Olamikan and Another v Nigeria*, 24 November 2023, ECW/CCJ/JUD/43/23; *Advocaid Ltd v Sierra Leone*, 7 November 2024, ECW/CCJ/JUD/33/24.

and declaring that: 'where human rights violations are raised by the laws or judgement of a court of a Member State, it will exercise jurisdiction over same'.[155]

Further, the practical opportunity for state respondents to engage with the court in human rights cases has increased continuously since the creation of the human rights jurisdiction in 2005. While there were only about 20 (reported) decisions between 2005 and 2010, the number has increased to about 140 (reported) decisions between 2020 and 2025.[156] These cases have provided an opportunity to engage with the court during the proceedings. And the by now considerable number of cases in which the ECOWAS Court has indeed found a human rights violation and issued an order (such as payment of damages, release from detention, conduct of a fair and speedy judicial proceeding, amendment of legal provisions etc) also create the opportunity to implement these decisions domestically.

For executive actors and domestic courts, the opportunity structure for implementing ECOWAS Court decisions is also shaped by the fact that, in several member states, there are no domestic legal provisions giving legal effect in domestic law to the Treaty and Protocol establishing the ECOWAS Court. As a consequence, executive actors and domestic courts in these member states do not have the opportunity to invoke and implement ECOWAS Court decisions directly. Furthermore, the absence of the enforcement framework required by Article 24 of the Protocol has, until recently, limited the opportunity structure for most of these actors. Given that many states had not determined the competent national authority for the execution of decisions of the ECOWAS Court,[157] domestic actors did not have the opportunity to enforce decisions due to the absent legal framework.

An example is the jurisprudence of domestic courts in Ghana refusing the enforcement of ECOWAS Court decisions. In the *Mba* case of 2016, the High Court of Ghana was asked to enforce an award in damages and costs from the ECOWAS Court for the violation of the applicant's human rights.[158] The court noted that in the absence of a statutory enactment in Ghana of the Treaty and the Protocol, there is no legal basis to directly implement ECOWAS Court decisions. It then went on to consider whether an implementation is possible according to the statutory regime for enforcing foreign judgments in Ghana.[159] But the High Court dismissed this option as well, given that these provisions do not state the ECOWAS Court as one of the courts to which the legislation applies. The court also excluded any other basis for enforcing the ECOWAS Court decisions such as an enforcement according to common law – which observers have criticised as unconvincing.[160]

[155] *Kodjo Alain Victor v Cote d'Ivoire*, 26 April 2021, ECW/CCJ/JUD/09/21, para 48.

[156] These figures are again based on the informal repository of IHRDA which is, however, not fully exhaustive (see n 126).

[157] See section II.A, as well as Happold and Radović (n 10) 114; and statements at nn 10 and 11.

[158] High Court of Ghana, *In the Matter of an Application to Enforce the Judgment of the Community Court of Justice of the ECOWAS against the Republic of Ghana and In the Matter of Chude Mba v The Republic of Ghana*, Suit No. HRCM/376/15 (2016). The applicant requested the enforcement of the ECOWAS Court decision in *Chude Mba v Ghana*, ECW/CCJ/APP/01/13.

[159] This refers to the Courts Act 1993 (Act 459), the High Court (Civil Procedure) Rules 2004 (CI 47) and the Foreign Judgments and Maintenance Orders (Reciprocal Enforcement) Instrument 1993 (LI 1575), see Oppong (n 13) 130.

[160] Oppong (n 13) 138.

The above-mentioned jurisprudence of the High Court of Ghana also constitutes an unfavourable *social opportunity structure* for domestic courts. A domestic court's choice to implement an ECOWAS Court decision is influenced by the relevant social practice within its group, here of domestic courts in other member states. If the High Court of Ghana or another domestic court had used the common law enforcement regime for ECOWAS Court decisions, this would have created a social opportunity structure in which this approach would have been made salient and acceptable within this group of actors. In contrast, the social practice among domestic courts in the ECOWAS region was one-sidedly directed against such enforcement and undermined this opportunity on the level of group practice. For domestic courts as members of their group of actors, the tendency to conform with this behaviour was strong – with a conformity pull that is unfavourable for accepting the authority of the ECOWAS Court.[161]

What is more, the question of a common law-based enforcement of ECOWAS Court decisions illustrates that regarding the effect of social practice, the relevant social group needs to be considered. For the behaviour of domestic courts regarding common law-based enforcement of ECOWAS Court decisions, the relevant social group is constituted by the courts in ECOWAS member states. Social practice outside this group seems to be perceived as less significant for these courts. In fact, in the context of the Tribunal of the Southern African Development Community (SADC), the Constitutional Court of South Africa has used a common law approach to enable the domestic enforcement of a decision of the Tribunal. In *Government of Zimbabwe v Louis Karel Fick and Others* in 2013, the Constitutional Court stated that

> the common law [must be] developed, so as to grant the right of access to our courts to facilitate the enforcement of the decisions of the Tribunal in this country. This … will be achieved by regarding the Tribunal as a foreign court, in terms of our common law.[162]

This (perceived out-group) practice has not shaped the behaviour of the domestic courts of ECOWAS member states.

To conclude, the opportunity for executive, legislative and judicial actors has broadened over time. For legislative and judicial actors, the opportunity was initially narrow when the court did not review legislative and judicial acts. It broadened when the court changed its stance on the matter and is now at a moderate level. For domestic courts, especially the lack of direct applicability of the Treaty as well as, for a long time, the lack of an enforcement framework according to Article 24 of the Protocol, has limited this opportunity. In contrast, for executive actors, the opportunity started off at a moderate level and became moderate to high when the court expanded the scope of remedies that addresses these actors. The increasing number of cases before the court adds to the de facto opportunity.

[161] On conformity as group effect, see ch 2.

[162] *South-African Constitutional Court, Government of Zimbabwe v Louis Karel Fick and Others* (CCT 101/12) [2013] ZACC 22; 2013 (5) SA 325 (CC); 2013 (10) BCLR 1103 (CC) (27 June 2013) para 69.

c. Constraints

For executive actors, and in an accessory manner also legislative actors, the intrinsic constraints for accepting the authority of the ECOWAS Court are low. Unlike for applicants, knowledge-related constraints do not play a role. Whether financial constraints exist depends on the practice of the court as to the damages awarded. Although the court does in fact order financial compensation, the compensation is not so high as to present a serious financial challenge for the state. In particular, awarded damages are only compensatory in nature. The ECOWAS Court has rejected claims of punitive damages with reference to the practice of other regional human rights courts.[163]

In terms of extrinsic constraints, member states can be faced with a competing authority relationship between the ECOWAS Court and the ACtHPR. As outlined above, this is a factor for Ghana and the Gambia (and it was the case for the former member states of Burkina Faso and Mali), for which a declaration under Articles 5(3) and 34(6) of the Protocol establishing the ACtHPR is currently in force. For Benin and Côte d'Ivoire, this declaration was in force until 2020. However, so far there seem to be no occurrences in which these courts have issued conflicting decisions in the same case against a member state. With regard to government actors, the constraining effect of a competing authority relationship towards the ACtHPR is – at least at the moment – only of a limited nature.

In contrast, the competing authority relationship towards domestic courts constitutes a more prominent constraining factor for executive actors. In the absence of an exhaustion of local remedies rule, applicants can bring their cases simultaneously to the domestic and international forums.[164] As a result, diverging decisions on the same case by domestic courts and the ECOWAS Court can occur. For executive actors, this means that they must choose between following the decision of the domestic court or that of the ECOWAS Court. The authority relationship towards the respective domestic court can thus constrain the implementation of the ECOWAS Court decision.

For domestic courts, the constraining factors are also primarily extrinsic in nature. First, given the deficiencies as to the independence of the judiciary in many ECOWAS member states (see Table 4.1), it is possible that government actors influence domestic courts in cases in which the implementation of ECOWAS Court decisions is at stake. Such potential governmental pressure constitutes a constraining factor for domestic courts that otherwise would accept the authority of the ECOWAS Court. Second, a constraining effect can result from the competing authority relationship that exists between lower domestic courts and their apex court. If the ECOWAS Court decides differently from a domestic (apex) court,

[163] *Ebrimah Manneh v The Gambia*, 5 June 2008, ECW/CCJ/APP/04/07, para 39. See also *Saidykhan v Gambia*, 16 December 2010, ECW/CCJ/JUD/08/10, para 43.

[164] The court has explicitly decided that it exercises its jurisdiction even if a suit on the same matter is pending simultaneously before a domestic court. *SERAP v Nigeria*, 19 June 2014, ECW/CCJ/JUD/16/14, paras 75–76.

this creates competing authority relationships for the other domestic courts. They must choose which decision to follow and are, when they consider implementing the ECOWAS Court decision, thus constrained by their authority relationship towards their (apex) court.

To sum up, the constraints for executive and legislative actors are thus low to moderate, also depending on the specific member state. The constraints for domestic courts are higher. They are currently at a moderate level for most member states, while being lower for courts in member states with more solid judicial independence.

d. Assessment of MOC Factors

The above assessment of the MOC factors for state actors shows the following result.

For *executive actors*, the initial MOC setting was characterised by a moderate motivation and opportunity and a moderate to high unconstrained ability to accept the authority of the court. Motivation and opportunity thus conjointly determined the behaviour of these actors. This setting changed somewhat over time when the opportunity broadened to a moderate to high level (see Figure 4.5). As a result, motivation is currently the determining MOC factor as it is at the lowest level among the three factors. Although there are several values and interests that can motivate governmental actors to accept the authority of the ECOWAS Court, the level of motivation is moderate. This is in particular due to the challenges that the value-correspondence is facing due to practical rule of law and human rights issues in the member states, as well as to the fact that the states' interest in dispute resolution in human rights cases is structurally low. Against this backdrop, time-related behavioural effects such as inertia and the status quo bias can become important elements for providing stable motivation for accepting the authority of the ECOWAS Court. The initial acceptance thus translates into a motivating factor for government actors in the long run. Opportunity is moderate to high because governmental actors are the 'classical' formal respondent in human rights cases before the ECOWAS Court and, as regards implementation of court orders, many such orders are addressed to the executive branch of member states. The ECOWAS Court's rather restrictive stance as to remedies as well as its lack of direct applicability of the Treaty and the Protocols, and, for a long time, the lack of an enforcement framework has reduced the de jure opportunity for these actors. The increasing number of human rights cases brought before the court constantly broadens the practical opportunity structure for these actors to engage with the court and, given the number of decisions that find for the applicants, to implement its decisions. Constraints are low to moderate for executive actors which means that their ability to accept the authority of the ECOWAS Court is moderate to high. The few existing constraints primarily stem from competing authority relationships towards other international and domestic courts.

Figure 4.5 Development over time of the MOC setting for executive actors as respondents before the ECOWAS Court in human rights cases

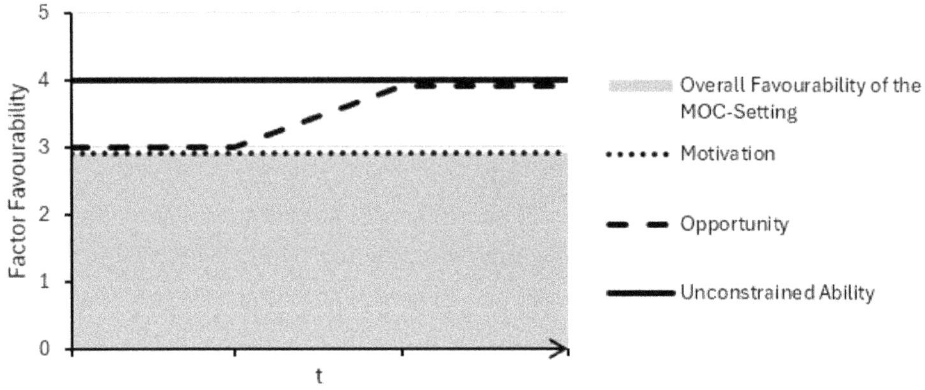

For *legislative actors*, the MOC setting is similar to that of executive actors. As for the latter, motivation is moderate, and the unconstrained ability is moderate to high. The opportunity structure is however different. It was initially narrow and broadened over time when the court reviewed legislative acts and even ordered legislative amendments. In the early phase, opportunity was thus the determining factor because it was at the lowest level. In later years, motivation and opportunity have both been at the same moderate level so that they conjointly determine the behaviour of these actors.

For *domestic courts*, the MOC setting has also changed over time (see Figure 4.6). Initially, opportunity was the determining factor. It was only at a low level while motivation was moderate to low and constraints were moderate. The narrow opportunity structure resulted in particular from the fact that, for a considerable time period, the ECOWAS Court refused to review decisions of the domestic judiciary. After the ECOWAS Court changed its approach and engaged in such review, the opportunity has increased to a moderate level. As a result of the increase, opportunity is no longer the determining factor. Instead, motivation is now at the lowest level among the MOC factors. Rule of law and independence issues on the domestic level limit value correspondence with the ECOWAS Court. Courts also have no significant (strategic) interest in accepting the authority of the ECOWAS Court. Specifically, their interest in an overall compliance practice regarding judicial decisions is not perceived as a strong motivational factor. In addition, interests in consistent behaviour as well as time-related behavioural effects could not have developed significantly so far, given that the number of court decisions that review domestic judicial decisions is still not very high and that an enforcement of ECOWAS Court decisions by domestic courts has not occurred. Against this backdrop, as a strategy to strengthen the authority relationship between the ECOWAS Court and domestic courts, it would not suffice only to further enhance opportunity. Rather, as motivation is currently the factor that determines the behaviour of domestic courts, motivation would need to be increased as well.

Figure 4.6 Development over time of the MOC setting for domestic courts as respondents before the ECOWAS Court in human rights cases

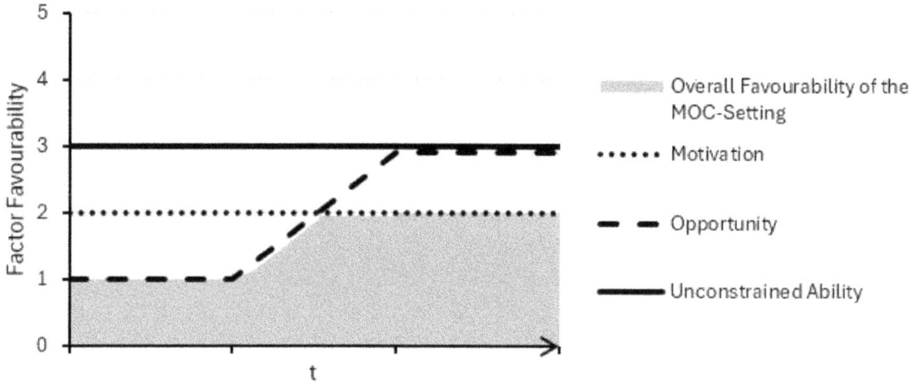

ii. MOC Factors for Pushback against the Court's Authority

After having analysed the MOC factors for the acceptance of the authority of the ECOWAS Court, I now turn to the opposite behaviour: pushback against this court. The aim is to assess the MOC factors that determine whether state actors challenge the authority relationship towards the ECOWAS Court.

The court itself has not faced any pushback by the withdrawal of member states. The withdrawals by Mali, Niger and Burkina Faso from the ECOWAS was not a reaction to the activities of the court. In its early years, and again, more recently, there have however been some instances of non-appearance or non-participation before the court by states such as the Gambia,[165] Nigeria,[166] Sierra Leone,[167] Togo[168] and Benin.[169] There has also been a major incident of structural resistance by the Gambia in 2009. The state tried to bring about an amendment to the Protocol. This attempt aimed, inter alia, at creating an exhaustion of domestic remedies requirement, a shorter time-limit to bring cases to the court and a limited catalogue of human rights including only instruments ratified by the respondent state. This attempt failed so that the broader provisions of the 2005 Protocol remain in place. The following reflections analyse this attempt further. Moreover, they address other instances of pushback such as non-implementation of ECOWAS Court decisions by state governments and domestic courts as well as norm contestation with regard to certain access rules. Motivational factors for potential pushback in the future are pointed out as well.

[165] *Ebrimah Manneh v The Gambia*, 5 June 2008, ECW/CCJ/APP/04/07; *Essien v Gambia*, 29 October 2007, ECW/CCJ/JUD/05/07.
[166] *Chukwuemeka Edeh v Nigeria*, 14 November 2024, ECW/CCJ/JUD/36/24.
[167] *Hassan Kargbo and 7 Others v Sierra Leone*, 14 October 2024, ECW/CCJ/JUD/37/24.
[168] *Abiguime Maguiliwè and 52 Others v Togo*, 10 July 2024, ECW/CCJ/JUD/26/24; *Afanvi Akuyo v Togo*, 17 March 2025, ECW/CCJ/JUD/11/25.
[169] *Sunday Igboho v Benin*, 5 December 2023, ECW/CCJ/JUD/50/23. See also generally, C Lentz, 'A party's non-participation in proceedings before the African Court on Human and Peoples' Rights and other regional courts in Africa', *African Human Rights Yearbook* 7 (2023) 137.

a. Motivation for Pushback

For *governmental actors*, there are manifold motivational factors to challenge the authority of the ECOWAS Court. To start with, low value-correspondence can motivate member states to push back. For some states, value-correspondence has been moderate or low in certain time periods. For example, the lack of value-correspondence regarding judicial independence has been a motivational factor for the Gambia during the Jammeh period. The lack of judicial independence on the domestic level reflected a value that influenced the stance that the governmental actors took towards the ECOWAS Court when attempting in 2009 to limit individual access to the ECOWAS Court. In fact, various NGOs in the region considered that this attempt was meant to 'depriv[e] citizens of free access' to an 'independent judicial instrument that is not usually available in many countries' in states 'where the judiciary is an arm of the executive'.[170]

A further motivational factor for pushback is the interest of states to exercise their sovereignty as extensively as possible. This can motivate governmental actors to resist against broad jurisdiction and access rules. First, the broad human rights jurisdiction of the court that is not limited by a catalogue of rights can be a factor for pushback based on this interest. Governmental actors might perceive the lack of a list of the human rights instruments that the ECOWAS Court can apply as causing an unpredictable and potentially expansive human rights jurisdiction. States may see this as 'overbroad delegation to interpret expansively this rapidly evolving area of international law'.[171] In fact, the 2009 resistance by the Gambia illustrates this concern. The state (unsuccessfully) suggested including an explicit provision into the Protocol stipulating that the Court should only have jurisdiction in cases arising from international instruments ratified by the respondent state.

The fact that states have accepted the broad human rights jurisdiction of the court in the 2005 Protocol and refused to amend it in 2009 does however limit the pushback-motiving potential of this broad jurisdiction. In contrast to the East African Court of Justice (EACJ) and the SADC Tribunal which established their respective human rights jurisdiction by way of expansive interpretation of their mandate, there is no lack of formal consent to the broad jurisdiction that could motivate or justify pushback against the formally stipulated jurisdiction of the ECOWAS Court under Article 9(4) of the Protocol. Yet the de facto confirmation of the Protocol in 2009 does not fully exclude that the human rights jurisdiction might motivate governmental actors to push back. These actors might consider the ECOWAS Court's human rights jurisdiction in action to turn out differently – and broader – than they had expected when creating it. Indeed, the fact that several states have challenged access rules such as the non-existing exhaustion of domestic remedies rule indicates that – at least some – member states were not fully aware of the implications that the new formulation of Articles 9 and 10 of the Protocol would have (see below). Similarly, respondents have

[170] 'Four IFEX members, civil society groups fear Gambia proposal will prevent ECOWAS Court from ruling in Saidykhan case', 28 September 2009: ifex.org/four-ifex-members-civil-society-groups-fear-gambia-proposal-will-prevent-ecowas-court-from-ruling-in-saidykhan-case/.

[171] Alter, Helfer and McAllister (n 4) 754.

challenged, via preliminary objection, the review of domestic judicial decisions and of domestic legislation by the ECOWAS Court.[172]

Second, in addition to jurisdictional rules, access rules can cause – and have caused – pushback against the ECOWAS Court. In particular, the lack of an exhaustion of domestic remedies rule before the court has triggered pushback by member states. Several member states have repeatedly, and specifically during the first decade of the court's practice, raised objections during court proceedings in cases in which domestic remedies were not exhausted. This includes states such as the Gambia, Niger, Nigeria and Senegal.[173] Raising this objection to admissibility can be categorised as norm contestation against an access rule. The Gambia however went a step further first by non-appearance before the court after a preliminary objection relating to non-exhaustion of domestic remedies was rejected by the court;[174] and then by trying to translate this resistance into a Protocol amendment. Its 2009 amendment initiative included the suggestion to insert an exhaustion rule in the procedural law framework of the court. As this initiative failed, the absence of an exhaustion rule has remained a motivational factor for pushback. Indeed, several states have occasionally raised such preliminary objections after the de facto confirmation of this rule in 2009.

However, the absence of an exhaustion of domestic remedies rule in the ECOWAS context takes into account the deficiencies as to judicial protection of human rights in many member states, particularly due to judicial independence issues (see Table 4.1). For those among the state actors who are willing to take this consideration into account, the absence of an exhaustion rule neither appears unreasonable nor might it constitute a major motivational factor for pushback.[175] Yet in the long run, this rationale itself can turn into a factor that motivates pushback. Its downside is that it reflects mistrust towards the member states as it assumes that they cannot provide effective domestic remedies. Although this is accurate for many member states at this time, this does not take into account potential positive changes. It also does not consider the current situation in some member states such as the already high level of judicial independence in Cabo Verde[176] as well as the fact that at least a certain level of judicial protection of human rights exists in the majority of member states.[177] Further future improvements in their judicial systems might lead states to perceiving

[172] eg, *Mr. Cherif Madi v Niger*, 1 April 2022, ECW/CCJ/APP/30/20; *La Ligue Senegalaise Des Droits Humaines & Amnesty International Senegal Section v Senegal*, 31 March 2022, ECW/CCJ/JUD/22/22.

[173] *Etim Essien v Gambia*, 14 March 2007, ECW/CCJ/APP/05/05, para 3; *Hadijatou Mani Koraou v Niger*, 27 October 2008, ECW/CCJ/JUD/06/08, para 29; *SERAP v Nigeria*, 30 November 2010, ECW/CCJ/JUD/07/10, para 10; *Sidi Amar Ibrahim and Others v Niger*, 8 February 2011, ECW/CCJ/JUD/01/11, para 26; *Ocean King Nigeria v Senegal*, 8 July 2011, ECW/CCJ/JUD/07/11, para 7; *Sikiru Alade v Nigeria*, 11 June 2012, ECW/CCJ/JUD/10/12, para 16; *Hans Capehart Williams SR v Liberia and Others*, 30 November 2015, ECW/CCJ/JUD/25/15, 8; *Federation of African Journalists and Others v The Gambia*, 13 February 2018, ECW/CCJ/JUD/04/18, 24 et seq.

[174] *Essien v Gambia*, 29 October 2007, ECW/CCJ/JUD/05/07, para 16. The Gambia also did not appear before the court in *Ebrimah Manneh v The Gambia*, 5 June 2008, ECW/CCJ/APP/04/07.

[175] See also on the rationale of this rule, Bado, 'Good governance' (n 147) 250.

[176] Freedom House report 2025 on Cabo Verde: freedomhouse.org/country/cabo-verde.

[177] Thus arguing for an exhaustion of domestic remedies requirement, AO Enabulele, 'Sailing Against the Tide: Exhaustion of Domestic Remedies and the ECOWAS Community Court of Justice' (2012) 56 *Journal of African Law* 268, 287 et seq.

the absence of an exhaustion rule as more and more inappropriate and this can present a potential motivation for pushback.

In addition to design features of the ECOWAS Court, its jurisprudence can create a motivation for pushback. It has been observed that, until recently, 'neither "subsidiarity", the "margin of appreciation", nor "deference" appear anywhere in the [court's] judgments'.[178] These notions that various regional courts use as important tools to prevent and manage state resistance, did not exist in the jurisprudence of the ECOWAS Court. However, even without explicitly referring to these notions the court's approach has been, at least with regard to some matters, an expression of deference and subsidiarity. This is, for example, the case when the court refused, before the 2005 Protocol amendment, to create a human rights jurisdiction by way of jurisprudential development, and when it restrictively decided on issues such as the jurisdiction in election cases, the access of corporations, and the jurisdiction over human rights violations by domestic courts. With regard to the latter, the court stepped back at least in its initial jurisprudence considerably, even going beyond subsidiarity as practised by other regional courts. In contrast, for matters such as access in *actio popularis* contexts, on the issue of time-limitations as admissibility criterion and on the exhaustion of domestic remedies, the court shows less deference. As a consequence, the mixed account in the court's jurisprudence as to subsidiarity and deference has led to a moderate-scale motivational factor for pushback.

More recently, however, the court has started to refer explicitly to the deference-inspired notions used by other regional courts. In its *Umeh* decision of 2020, the court used the notion of 'margin of appreciation' when interpreting the term 'in accordance with the law' in provisions such as Article 13(1) of the Charter regarding the right to participate in elections.[179] The court stated that

> it is also commonly agreed in all jurisdictions of the world that national or state parties enjoy a very wide margin of appreciation/flexibility/leverage in the application of their laws in the determination of what is in accordance with the law (so long as the law is not arbitrarily applied), because national authorities know and understand their citizens and territory better.[180]

In other cases, the court also speaks of the 'discretion' of the state to interfere with rights as long as this interference is proportionate.[181] The use of these terms has a twofold effect. On the one hand, such notions are a tool for the court to actually give more deference to states when deciding whether a state has violated human rights provisions. On the other hand, this language has a symbolic effect, signalling to the states that the court takes their sovereignty-related interests seriously. This framing can impact the perception that states have of the extent of deference given to them by

[178] von Staden (n 74) 1120.

[179] Article 13(1) stipulates: 'Every citizen shall have the right to participate freely in the government of his country, either directly or through freely chosen representatives in accordance with the provisions of the law'.

[180] *Umeh and Others v Nigeria*, 1 July 2020, ECW/CCJ/JUD/10/20, para 55. See also *Kenneth Roberts and Others v Nigeria*, 27 October 2021, ECW/CCJ/JUD/38/21, para 88.

[181] *Illia Malam Mamane Saidat v Niger*, 22 June 2021, ECW/CCJ/JUD/17/2021, para 103.

the court. As a result, the recent development reduces the pushback-motivating effect of the courts jurisprudence.

Further, especially in a post-colonial setting, states can be motivated to resist against the court when it is perceived as determined by extra-regional actors. This includes both political and legal influences on the court. Concerning the former, the ECOWAS Court does not provide much motivation for pushback. For example, little influence is exercised by non-ECOWAS states on the court via financial means, given that the court's budget is almost entirely provided by the ECOWAS member states. There has been, however, some foreign funding such as by the Ford Foundation and further cooperation with extra-regional organisations such as the Konrad Adenauer Foundation.[182] Furthermore, to have access to the court, actors must be connected to the ECOWAS context, in particular with NGOs having to be 'duly constituted according to the national law of any ECOWAS Member State and enjoying observer status before ECOWAS institutions'.[183] This prevents states perceiving the court as a platform for foreign actors. In contrast, there is more basis for states perceiving the jurisprudence of the court to be influenced by extra-regional *legal* sources. States might be critical of the court when it refers in its jurisprudence too extensively to non-African legal sources. Accordingly, the court's frequent references to the jurisprudence of the European Court of Human Rights (ECtHR),[184] occasionally to the Inter-American Court of Human Rights (IACtHR)[185] and, for some matters, to the CJEU[186] or to non-African domestic law,[187] has at least the potential to contribute a motivational factor for pushback.

[182] See, eg, the 2007 Annual Report and the 2009–2011 Annual Report of the ECOWAS Court: courtecowas.org/media-and-publications/publications/annual-reports/.

[183] *Registered Trustees of the Socio-Economic Rights & Accountability Project (SERAP) v President of Nigeria & Others*, 10 December 2010, ECW/CCJ/APP/07/10, para 61.

[184] For references to the ECtHR, see eg, *Dorothy Chioma Njemanze and Others v Nigeria*, 12 October 2017, ECW/CCJ/JUD/08/17, 34, 37; *Finance Investment and Development v Liberia*, 4 July 2018, ECW/CCJ/JUD/23/18, 9; *Koraou v Niger*, 27 October 2008, ECW/CCJ/APP/0808, para 39; *Ebrimah Manneh v The Gambia*, 5 June 2008, ECW/CCJ/APP/04/07, para 34 et seq; *Saidykhan v Gambia*, 16 December 2010, ECW/CCJ/JUD/08/10, para 43; *Jerry Ugokwe v Nigeria and Others*, 7 October 2005, ECW/CCJ/JUD/03/05, para 23; *Mme Aziablevi Yovo and Others v Société Togo Telecom and Togo*, 31 January 2012, ECW/CCJ/JUG/04/12, para 16; *Simone Ehivet and Michel Gbagbo v Côte d'Ivoire*, 22 February 2013, ECW/CCJ/JUD/03/13, para 66 et seq; *Baldé and Others v Senegal*, 22 February 2013, ECW/CCJ/JUG/04/13, para 68; *Congrès pour la Démocratie et le Progrès (CDP) and Others v Burkina Faso*, 13 July 2015, ECW/CCJ/JUG/16/15, para 36; *Kenneth Roberts and Others v Nigeria*, 27 October 2021, ECW/CCJ/JUD/38/21, paras 91, 93; *Umeh and Others v Nigeria*, 1 July 2020, ECW/CCJ/JUD/10/20, paras 30, 47, 57, 58; *Alex Nain Saab Moran v Cape Verde*, 15 March 2021, ECW/CCJ/JUD/07/2021, para 78; *Diawara Oumar v Côte d'Ivoire*, 22 October 2021, ECW/CCJ/JUD/34/21, para 73; *Illia Malam Mamane Saidat v Niger*, 22 June 2021, ECW/CCJ/JUD/17/2021, paras 67, 71, 78, 90; *Chukwuemeka Edeh v Nigeria*, 14 November 2024, ECW/CCJ/JUD/36/24, paras 38, 39.

[185] eg, *Dorothy Chioma Njemanze and Others v Nigeria*, 12 October 2017, ECW/CCJ/JUD/08/17, 39; *Finance Investment and Development v Liberia*, 4 July 2018, ECW/CCJ/JUD/23/18, 8; *Sidi Amar Ibrahim and Others v Niger*, 8 February 2011, ECW/CCJ/JUD/01/11, para 51; *Registered Trustees of Avocat Sans Frontieres France v Nigeria*, 31 January 2014, ECW/CCJ/APP/14/13, para 42; *Umeh and Others v Nigeria*, 1 July 2020, ECW/CCJ/JUD/10/20, paras 37, 79; *Isaac Olamikan and Another v Nigeria*, 24 November 2023, ECW/CCJ/JUD/43/23, paras 92, 93.

[186] eg, *Olajide Afolabi v Nigeria*, 27 April 2004, ECW/CCJ/JUD/01/04; *Jerry Ugokwe v Nigeria and Others*, 7 October 2005, ECW/CCJ/JUD/03/05, para 31; *Essien v Gambia*, 29 October 2007, ECW/CCJ/JUD/05/07, para 30.

[187] eg, *Federation of African Journalists and Others v The Gambia*, 13 February 2018, ECW/CCJ/JUD/04/18, 38; *The Incorporated Trustees of Fiscal and Civic Right Enlightenment Foundation v Nigeria and Others*, 7 June 2016, ECW/CCJ/JUG/18/16, 16; *Saidykhan v Gambia*, 16 December 2010, ECW/CCJ/JUD/08/10, para 28 et seq; *Ablogui and Others v Guinea*, 31 October 2023, ECW/CCJ/JUD/38/23, para 46.

Finally, the governmental actors' interest in effective behaviour can impact the motivation for pushback. Whether actors consider that their pushback will lead to the desired outcome influences whether they will resist at all. Prior successful instances of pushback can increase the expected effectiveness of a new pushback attempt, enhancing motivation for such attempts. Inversely, when a court has previously withstood pushback, it appears less likely that future attempts will succeed. In the ECOWAS context, there has been only one case of structural resistance by a member state – the Gambia's attempt to limit the court's jurisdiction in 2009 – and it did not succeed. This failure has reduced the expected effectiveness of future resistance. As a result, '[h]aving survived this attempt to curb its jurisdiction, the Court's human rights authority now rests on a more solid foundation than when the member states first gave the Court that authority in 2005'.[188]

The impact of expected effectiveness is also demonstrated by the norm contestation regarding the rule on exhaustion of domestic remedies. The practice of member states to raise preliminary objections in cases without exhausted domestic remedies has changed over time. When, at the beginning of the court's practice, no or little pronouncements of the court on the matter existed and the legal question thus seemed rather open, states would have expected that their preliminary objections would have some chances of success. Respondents thus raised such objections repeatedly in the first years.[189] Yet as the court reaffirmed time and time again its jurisprudence that an exhaustion of domestic remedies is not a requirement, the expected likelihood of a successful objection reduced significantly. And indeed, in recent years, states have generally not raised such objections any more (with only a few exceptions).[190] This decrease shows that when the effectiveness expectation varies, the motivation for this form of pushback also changes.

In contrast to the above forms of pushback, effectiveness considerations regarding non-compliance are however high. Many human rights decisions of the ECOWAS Court have not been implemented by governmental actors, without major consequences for these states. Governmental actors are thus likely to perceive non-compliance as effective behaviour.

Regarding *domestic courts*, the competing jurisdiction of the ECOWAS Court is a potential motivational factor for pushback. Due to the non-existing exhaustion of domestic remedies rule, the ECOWAS Court is competing with domestic courts on every level of the domestic judiciary.[191] This is different from settings with an exhaustion rule in which the competition mainly occurs between domestic apex courts on

[188] Alter, Helfer and McAllister (n 4) 765.

[189] *Etim Essien v Gambia*, 14 March 2007, ECW/CCJ/APP/05/05, para 3; *Hadijatou Mani Koraou v Niger*, 27 October 2008, ECW/CCJ/JUD/06/08, para 29; *SERAP v Nigeria*, 30 November 2010, ECW/CCJ/JUD/07/10, para 10; *Sidi Amar Ibrahim and Others v Niger*, 8 February 2011, ECW/CCJ/JUD/01/11, para 26; *Ocean King Nigeria v Senegal*, 8 July 2011, ECW/CCJ/JUD/07/11, para 7; *Sikiru Alade v Nigeria*, 11 June 2012, ECW/CCJ/JUD/10/12, para 16.

[190] See for such exceptions: *Hans Capehart Williams SR v Liberia and Others*, 30 November 2015, ECW/CCJ/JUD/25/15; *Federation of African Journalists and Others v The Gambia*, 13 February 2018, ECW/CCJ/JUD/04/18; *Portia Otto Alagba and 2 Others v Nigeria*, 6 June 2024, ECW/CCJ/RUL/01/24.

[191] The court has explicitly decided that it exercises its jurisdiction even if a suit on the same matter is pending simultaneously before a domestic court. *SERAP v Nigeria*, 19 June 2014, ECW/CCJ/JUD/16/14, paras 75–76.

the one hand and the regional international court on the other. This feature holds 'the potential for a disruptive conflict with the legal systems of member states'[192] and to 'pitch the Community Court against municipal courts, which of course are known to guard their jurisdiction very jealously'.[193] But even in the ECOWAS context, the motivation for pushback is strongest for high courts. In the domestic system, the decisions of these courts cannot be overturned. The fact that the ECOWAS Court could challenge their decisions is not in line with these courts' self-perception as apex courts. Preserving their institutional power is thus a motivational factor for pushback by these courts. However, the restrictive stance of the ECOWAS Court that initially did not review domestic court decisions and only gradually expanded its assessment to potential human rights violations by domestic courts, mitigated the extent to which the competing jurisdiction could motivate pushback.[194] Yet as this jurisprudence developed, the more competitive and potentially conflicting the setting has become in which domestic courts and the ECOWAS Court interact. The motivational potential has thus increased as compared with what it was in the early years of the court's practice.

In addition, the lack of expertise of the ECOWAS Court as perceived by the domestic courts especially in the early years of the ECOWAS Court constituted a further potential motivation for pushback. Domestic high courts 'were upset that judges with less qualifications and experience than they had could issue rulings that would be final and binding on them'.[195] However, as outlined in section II.B.i, states have adjusted the institutional design in order to increase the expertise of the judges at the ECOWAS Court, and the institutional expertise of the court based on its developing body of jurisprudence also relativises these concerns. Lack of expertise as a motivational factor for pushback by domestic courts thus is less impactful than the interest of domestic courts in guarding their jurisdictional power.

In sum, the pushback motivation for state actors is overall at a moderate level, while diverging somewhat among member states. In particular the value-correspondence is different for state actors depending on the rule of law standard within their respective member state. Important motivational factors that can concern actors in all member states include the broad human rights jurisdiction of the court and the absence of a requirement to exhaust domestic remedies. The ambivalent deference level within the jurisprudence of the court adds to these motivational factors, however with some changes over time. Regarding the expected effectiveness of pushback, this factor can most prominently motivate non-compliance, while being of a more limited effect for resistance and norm contestation. For pushback by domestic courts, the (perceived) rivalry with the ECOWAS Court that results from the absence of an exhaustion requirement is the key motivational factor leading at least to a moderate level of pushback motivation.

[192] Ebobrah, 'A rights-protection goldmine' (n 147) 328.

[193] AO Enabulele, 'Reflections on the ECOWAS Community Court Protocol and the Constitutions of Member States' (2010) 12 *International Community Law Review* 111, 131–32.

[194] On this development, see section II.A.ii).

[195] Statement from an Interview with ECOWAS Legal Affairs Directorate A by Alter, Helfer and McAllister (n 4) 760.

b. Opportunity for Pushback

The opportunity structure for pushback against the ECOWAS Court has legal and non-legal elements. These elements vary for the different forms of pushback. The legal opportunity structure for pushback in the form of Treaty and Protocol amendments is shaped by the formal rules regarding the amendment procedure of the ECOWAS Treaty. According to Article 35(1) of the Protocol, 'any member state [can] submit proposals for the amendment of the Protocol'. An amendment procedure can thus be easily initiated by any member state on their own. The Gambia made use of this opportunity in its 2009 attempt at resistance. However, to adopt such amendments, the other member states must agree according to Article 9 of the ECOWAS Treaty and ratify the amendment. While the legal opportunity structure to initiate amendments is thus broad for the individual state, this is – as is common in international institutional settings – not the case for successfully translating this initiative into an amended legal framework. In addition to the necessary consent of the other member states, transparency as a procedural feature of the amendment process also limits the opportunity for such pushback. Such transparency was an important factor in the Gambia's attempt to limit the jurisdiction of, and access to, the court. It enabled various groups of actors (see section II.C) to campaign against the proposed amendment. This stands in contrast to, for example, the rather clandestine amendment of the legal framework of some other regional courts.[196]

Further, as part of the social opportunity structure, states can perceive the behaviour of other states as an opportunity for pushback in the form of Treaty amendment. In the ECOWAS context, the amendment initiative of the Gambia created an opportunity for the other member states to limit the human rights jurisdiction of the court and its access rules. Although the other member states did not take up this opportunity, the amendment proposal by the Gambia formally involved them and provided a situation in which states had to normatively assess the existing rules on jurisdiction and access.[197]

For pushback in the form of norm contestation, the legal framework for preliminary objections has provided an opportunity for state actors. Article 87 of the Rules of the Court regulates this procedure that makes it possible for respondents to file such objections. As mentioned above, respondents have used this legal opportunity repeatedly to contest the admissibility rule concerning the non-exhaustion of domestic remedies. Moreover, the opportunity structure for such norm contestations also has a social element. Observing the norm contestations by other member states enables state actors to recognise a situation as an opportunity for such pushback. When the Gambia first raised a preliminary objection as to the exhaustion of domestic remedies in the *Essien* case,[198] this behaviour made preliminary objections as a tool for pushback in this matter salient to other states. An opportunity for those states had thus been pointed out and states such

[196] eg, regarding the EACJ in 2007.
[197] See also Alter, Gathii and Helfer (n 135) 299.
[198] *Etim Essien v Gambia*, 14 March 2007, ECW/CCJ/APP/05/05, para 3.

as Niger, Nigeria and Senegal used this opportunity to raise preliminary objections repeatedly.[199]

An opportunity for pushback in the form of non-compliance is provided by the enforcement system established by Article 24 of the Protocol. It requires member states to put a domestic enforcement structure in place and give notification of the competent domestic authority for enforcing ECOWAS Court decisions. This additional step provides an opportunity for states to hinder enforcement. Merely by not putting this mechanism in place, states can undermine the enforcement of ECOWAS Court decisions. As already mentioned, many member states had indeed not created this domestic enforcement structure for a long time and only very recently designated the competent domestic authority.

In addition, the changing setting as to institutional monitoring is also an element of the opportunity structure for non-compliance. As outlined above, there has been no such monitoring for most of the court's practice, thus contributing to a favourable opportunity structure for non-compliance. In contrast, when the court developed its own monitoring mechanism in the recent jurisprudence, this has reduced the opportunity for non-compliance. It makes non-compliance more salient which leads to less opportunity for respondents to disregard the court's decisions without other actors noticing it.

Further, an opportunity for non-compliance can result from the domestic legal framework of the member states. The constitutions of many (current and former) ECOWAS member states take a dualist approach to the relationship between domestic and international law.[200] Such dualism provides an opportunity for non-compliance. It requires that states incorporate the ECOWAS Treaty and Protocols by way of statutory enactment to give legal effect to these provisions in the domestic legal order. As the jurisdiction of the ECOWAS Court is based on these international legal instruments, their incorporation is considered a precondition for a domestic legal effect of ECOWAS Court decisions. The fact that many member states have not done so provides an opportunity for domestic judicial and administrative actors not to give effect to the court's judgments.[201]

In specific contexts, constitutional provisions have become relevant opportunity factors for non-compliance because of a regime change that a member state experienced. To avoid compliance with the *Ayika* decision of the ECOWAS Court from 2012, the Liberian government argued that this decision is not binding on it given that the Protocol had been ratified during the time of the National Transition Government, a transitional regime in place after the civil war and before the

[199] See n 173.

[200] eg s 12(1) of the Nigeria Constitution 1999; Article 96 of the Constitution of Senegal 2001; Article 78 of the Constitution of Mauritania; Article 138 of the Constitution of Togo; Article 149 of the Constitution of Burkina Faso; Article 115 of the Constitution of Mali; Article 145 of the Constitution of Benin; Article 120 of the Constitution of Cote d'Ivoire; Article 75 of the Constitution of Ghana; Article 77 of the Fundamental Law of Guinea; Article 169 of the Constitution of Niger. See also Enabulele, 'Reflections on the ECOWAS Community Court Protocol' (n 193) 124; M Adigun, 'Enforcing ECOWAS judgments in Nigeria through the common law rule on the enforcement of foreign judgments' (2019) 15 *Journal of Private International Law* 130, 155.

[201] See on this issue in Nigeria, Adigun (n 200) 155.

democratically elected administration in place since 2006. Based on this argument, the Liberian government brought a case before its domestic judiciary which led the Liberian Supreme Court to decide that the *Ayika* decision was indeed not binding on the current government.[202] Although Liberia has since then (re)ratified the Protocol, this incident further highlights how the domestic legal framework can provide an opportunity for pushback.

In addition, it is mentioned here for completeness that the number of decisions that the court issues against a member state is part of the de facto opportunity structure for non-compliance – at least in absolute terms. With more decisions, there is more opportunity not to comply. The initially low number of cases before the ECOWAS Court that has been increasing considerably over the last years thus reflects an expanding opportunity structure in this regard. However, from a relative perspective, the number of cases does not of course affect the pro rata opportunity structure.

Finally, the fact that the ECOWAS Court takes decisions in high-politics areas is an element of the opportunity structure for pushback.[203] Decisions of the court in high-politics cases create the opportunity for state actors to reproach the court with being a political actor and to pushback against it in various forms. While courts with a human rights jurisdiction generally face the risk that their cases have high-politics implications, this is, for the ECOWAS Court, especially to be expected in cases in which opposition politicians use the court as a regional forum for their cause as well as in the election cases repeatedly brought to the court (see section II.A). However, so far, the behaviour of state actors in the ECOWAS context does not show any clear pattern in this regard.

To sum up, the opportunity structure has been, for a long time, more favourable for non-compliance than for the other forms of pushback. Until the creation of the new monitoring mechanism as well as the implementation of the Article 24 enforcement structure, the opportunity for non-compliance was broad. It has now decreased. For pushback in the form of Treaty and Protocol amendments, the opportunity is on a moderate level, depending significantly on social opportunity elements shaped by the behaviour of other actors.

c. Constraints against Pushback

Extrinsic constraints against pushback in the ECOWAS context result primarily from supporting actors. An important group of supporting actors are NGOs. In the case of Gambia's resistance, NGOs strongly opposed the proposed amendments.[204]

[202] *Supreme Court of Liberia, Republic of Liberia v Ayika* [2013] LRSC 39 (15 July 2013): 'as the Protocol upon which the ECOWAS Community Court of Justice relies for the exercise of jurisdiction over the Republic of Liberia, not having been ratified by the Liberian Legislature, a mandatory requirement of the Liberian Constitution for the Protocol to be binding on the Republic, the said Protocol is not binding on the Republic of Liberia'.

[203] On the relevance of high-politics cases on pushback, see also ch 3 as well as MR Madsen, P Cebulak and M Wiebusch, 'Backlash against international courts: explaining the forms and patterns of resistance to international courts' (2018) 14 *International Journal of Law in Context* 197, 215.

[204] von Staden (n 74) 1119–120; Alter, Helfer and McAllister (n 4) 764.

They did not only campaign against the amendment proposal in the media but also took legal steps, including addressing the ECOWAS Court with an ex parte motion requesting an emergency order against an amendment of the Protocol.[205] In addition, they demanded to participate in the relevant ECOWAS meetings in order to put their arguments forward and ensure that the appropriate procedure was respected.[206] This pressure from NGOs is unsurprising given that NGOs had advocated against an exhaustion of domestic remedies rule in the first place.[207] NGOs had also been key supporters of the introduction of a human rights jurisdiction and had thus lobbied for the 2005 Protocol. This stance had naturally not changed in 2009.

Constraints to the Gambia's resistance came also from ECOWAS institutions. This included an 'overt and tacit support of individuals within the ECOWAS Commission'.[208] As the suggested amendments would have hindered the development of the ECOWAS Court, an institution in which the ECOWAS Commission (the then Executive Secretariat) was invested, it opposed the limitations to jurisdiction and access to the court as proposed by the Gambia.[209] It contributed to supporting the court and opposing the amendment proposal by 'information sharing and indirect coalition building'.[210] Specifically, it informed the judges of the ECOWAS Court of the ongoing attempt and provided advance information about meetings of the member states, enabling civil society groups to prepare for, and participate in, the meetings.[211]

Finally, and also as a result of the former, a constraining effect came from other member states. What played a role in this regard was that the self-interested intention of the Gambia was apparent to the other member states. The fact that the attempt was related to the *Manneh* decision of 2008 against the Gambia that the state opposed,[212] put the Gambia's initiative in an unfavourable light. This led member states to oppose the Gambia's amendment proposal.[213] This reaction illustrates that the extent to which such an attempt is perceived as honest by other actors can influence whether they resist the attempt or not.

Extrinsic constraints also exist against non-compliance. Civil society actors, international organisations and other governments have exercised pressure to achieve compliance with the ECOWAS Court's decisions. Specifically, regarding the Gambia that did not implement a number of decisions including *Ebrimah, Saidykhan, Hydara Jr* and *Manneh*, diverse actors such as the Media Foundation for West Africa, the African Commission on Human and Peoples' Rights and foreign governments have repeatedly demanded compliance.[214] Another example is the *Ayika* case against Liberia. The media coverage of the case condemning

[205] Alter, Gathii and Helfer (n 135) 299.
[206] ibid.
[207] Alter, Helfer and McAllister (n 4)757.
[208] Alter, Gathii and Helfer (n 135) 299.
[209] ibid 300.
[210] ibid 319.
[211] ibid.
[212] *Ebrimah Manneh v The Gambia*, 5 June 2008, ECW/CCJ/APP/04/07.
[213] von Staden (n 74) 1119; Alter, Helfer and McAllister (n 4) 763–64.
[214] Ebobrah, 'Dual Mandate' (n 45) 92.

Liberia's non-compliance was considerable and foreign governments such as the Nigerian government also urged Libera to comply.[215] Even where these attempts do not lead to compliance, such pressure by other actors increases the constraining factors against non-compliance and is able to reduce resistance of state actors with a lower level of motivation for pushback.

Finally, a behavioural constraint against pushback can originate from inertia and the status quo bias. As mentioned above, actors seem to have initially perceived certain features of the ECOWAS Court such as the human rights jurisdiction and the absence of an exhaustion of domestic remedies rule as provisional or experimental. However, over time, these features appear as a 'fait accompli'.[216] The mere fact that these features have existed for a continuous period of time has created a behavioural setting in which states are likely to uphold these features due to inertia. In addition, due to the status quo bias, these features are likely to be perceived as more valuable as compared with when they were initially introduced. Actors thus would also have to overcome a status quo bias to generate a behaviour that would qualify as pushback. The above-mentioned decrease in preliminary objections against cases without exhausted domestic remedies suggests that such behavioural constraints have played a role in the ECOWAS context (in addition to the effectiveness considerations relevant for motivation).

In sum, the constraints against pushback are on a moderate to high level, especially concerning pushback by formal amendments and by non-compliance. A strong and active group of supporting actors limits the ability for pushback considerably.

d. Assessment of MOC Factors

The analysis of MOC factors for pushback against the ECOWAS Court by governmental actors and domestic courts shows the following result.

For *governmental actors*, the pushback motivation is overall at a moderate level, with some differences among the forms of pushback. For norm contestation and structural resistance or even backlash, the motivation is moderate, while being moderate to high for non-compliance. Pushback motivation results in particular from the broad design of the human rights jurisdiction and of the access rules, especially regarding the exhaustion of domestic remedies. However, in practice, these features can motivate resistance, backlash or norm contestation only to a limited extent because the failed pushback attempts have lowered the expected effectiveness of such pushback. This is different with regard to non-compliance for which the expected effectiveness of the behaviour is high. In addition, for some member states, low value-correspondence regarding judicial independence can motivate pushback. In contrast to such structural motivational factors, the jurisprudence of the ECOWAS Court provides only a few reference points for pushback. Although the court only very recently started to refer to a margin of appreciation, the court's decision-making practice has been characterised by a considerable level of de facto deference. Despite some elements of expansive jurisprudence, the jurisprudence of the court thus is not a major motivational factor.

[215] ibid 93.
[216] Alter, Helfer and McAllister (n 4) 757.

As to the opportunity for pushback against the ECOWAS Court, the opportunity structure diverges significantly depending on the form of pushback. To start with, several structural factors have led to a broad opportunity for non-compliance that has only recently narrowed somewhat to a moderate to broad level. This includes the enforcement system established by Article 24 of the Protocol which, even to be operationalised in the first place, requires active state involvement and thus made it easy for states not to set up this system. Opportunity for non-compliance has also been broad as a result of the lack of a monitoring mechanism – and only with the recent monitoring approach by the court, this opportunity element has become less favourable for non-compliance.

In contrast to the broad opportunity for non-compliance, there is only a moderate level of opportunity for resistance in the form of Treaty and Protocol amendments and for norm contestation. The formal rules for such amendments only provide a limited opportunity as they might be easy to initiate but the adoption procedure is legally and politically demanding. Further, it is the behaviour of other actors that has shaped the pushback both in the form of amendments or the contestation of procedural norms such as access without exhaustion of domestic remedies. When initiating an amendment procedure or raising preliminary objections against the non-exhaustion of domestic remedies, the Gambia has created an opportunity for the other member states to push back. Considering this fluctuating social opportunity element, the opportunity structure for such forms of pushback is thus more volatile than in the case of non-compliance.

The constraints against pushback are moderate to high due to the active and diverse groups of supporting actors. This leads to a moderate to low ability for successfully pushing back in this way. Several groups of actors such as the ECOWAS institutions, NGOs and other member states have constrained the 2009 resistance by the Gambia. Similarly, when member states did not comply with ECOWAS Court decisions, actors such as other member states, the African Commission on Human and Peoples' Rights and civil society actors have exercised pressure on the relevant governments to implement these decisions. The fact that these supporting actors have intervened repeatedly against instances of pushback indicates that this support structure is rather stable. In addition, a factor that is independent of such actor support is the behavioural effect generated by inertia and the status quo bias. This effect which of course did not exist at the beginning of the court's operational phase has, over time, become more important. Perceiving certain design features such as the absence of an exhaustion rule as status quo reduces the likeliness of pushback against it.

As a result, the MOC settings for the forms of pushback by governmental actors differ only somewhat. Figure 4.7 illustrates these differences. For non-compliance, the motivation is moderate to high, the opportunity has been broad and has recently narrowed to a moderate level and the ability is moderate to low due to the existing constraints. This means that ability is at the lowest level so that constraints are the determining factor. As to structural resistance by formal amendments and norm contestation, motivation and opportunity are on a moderate level while the ability is moderate to low. As a result, ability also determines the extent to which actors engage in these forms of pushback.

Regarding *domestic courts*, the pushback motivation is the determining factor. It is moderate and thus at the comparably lowest level among the MOC factors (see Figure 4.7). The competitive setting created in particular by the absence of an exhaustion of domestic remedies rule is the key factor for the pushback motivation for courts in all member states. It has the potential to motivate pushback by apex courts as well as lower-level domestic courts. However, so far, this potential has only materialised partially. This is due, on the one hand, to the only recently increasing number of ECOWAS Court decisions which would at all make domestic courts aware of the competing jurisdictions. On the other hand, motivation for pushback has been reduced by the fact that the ECOWAS Court has only gradually developed a human rights review of domestic judicial decisions. This has resulted in the moderate motivation for domestic courts to push back. Yet this motivation is likely to increase with the growing body of ECOWAS Court decisions that review domestic judicial decisions. In contrast, doubts about the expertise of the court have, although present at the beginning of the court's operational phase, a rather low motivational effect at present. Further, the opportunity for non-compliance by domestic courts in many member states is still moderate to broad. This is due to the lack of legal structure for the application of ECOWAS court decisions from the perspective of domestic law because of dualist constitutional provisions; and, until recently, it was even broader relating to enforcement due to the Article 24 regime. In addition, domestic courts have, as a social opportunity element, generated opportunity for non-compliance by other domestic courts when they did not enforce decisions of the ECOWAS Court based on domestic law considerations. Last, constraints against pushback by domestic courts can be classified as low to moderate. Although the ECOWAS Court benefits from a strong network of supporting actors that have also addressed non-compliance, this constraining effect is less pronounced for domestic judicial actors as compared with governmental actors. As a result, the ability to engage in such pushback is moderate to high.

Figure 4.7 Comparison of the current MOC setting for pushback against the ECOWAS Court in relation to the human rights jurisdiction

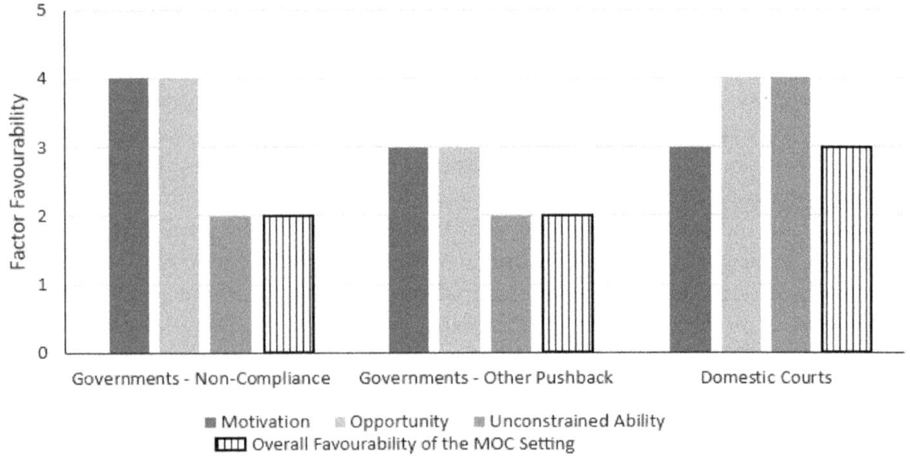

C. Assessing the Court's Strategies to Influence MOC

After having analysed how the MOC factors for accepting the authority of the ECOWAS Court play out for (potential) applicants and respondents, as well as, with regard to the latter, the MOC factors for pushback, I now turn to assessing whether the court itself has influenced these factors. I first evaluate to what extent the court has attempted to increase the MOC for accepting its authority and whether these attempts were successful, taking into account the insights on the interrelationship among MOC factors (II.C.i). The second part of the section then conducts this analysis with regard to efforts of the court to avoid and manage pushback (II.C.ii).

i. Increasing MOC for Accepting the Court's Authority

a. Enhancing Motivation

Enhancing the Motivation of Respondents

To start with, the court has engaged with aspects that shape the level of value-correspondence between the court and the member states. First, several aspects of the court's jurisprudence address rule of law values.[217] A strategy to strengthen these values and to emphasise that member states have committed to them, is to refer, in its judgments, to the ECOWAS Protocol on Democracy and Good Governance from 2001. The court has repeatedly invoked this Protocol to give rule of law-related considerations additional weight.[218] This jurisprudential use keeps the values enshrined in this instrument salient, potentially both in legal and political discourse. The court also points out that these values are not only enshrined in this international legal instrument but also in the constitutions of the member states. It states that 'the Court is of the view that the grand principles of separation of powers, democracy, good governance and constitutional convergence, etc, as stated in the Protocol, are principles enunciated in the constitutional texts of the States'.[219]

With this assertion, the court explicitly underscores value-correspondence, highlighting that the values of member states as reflected in their constitutions and the values operationalised by the court correspond. However, the court does not go as far as it could with regard to operationalising, and thus strengthening, these values. It does not consider that the above-cited rule of law principles are justiciable as such. It holds that 'in as much as disregarding any of said principles does not violate any specific human right, it would be difficult to assess the extent to which the States observe those principles'.[220]

Yet the court has found ways to include rule of law elements in its review. It has, for example, addressed issues regarding the separation of powers in certain member

[217] On the rule of law strategies of the court, see also Kane (n 130) 312–20.

[218] eg, *Baldé and Others v Senegal*, 22 February 2013, ECW/CCJ/JUG/04/13, para 51; *Congrès pour la Démocratie et le Progrès (CDP) & Others v Burkina Faso*, 13 July 2015, ECW/CCJ/JUG/16/15, para 31; *Sule Audu & Six Others v Nigeria*, 22 November 2017, ECW/CCJ/JUD/17/17.

[219] *Baldé and Others v Senegal*, 22 February 2013, ECW/CCJ/JUG/04/13, para 53.

[220] ibid.

states. In *Kodjo v Côte d'Ivoire*, the court was faced with a situation in which the executive branch of the state did not implement a domestic judicial decision.[221] It declared that

> the Court of Appeal of the Respondent … chose to order the release of the Applicant … The respondent … cannot submit itself to the jurisdiction of the Court and still decide on its own motion to disregard the order of the Court by arrogating to itself the powers of interpretation and application of the law, a responsibility that is clearly reposed in the Courts.[222]

The court has also addressed value-correspondence as to judicial independence. It assessed allegations of lack of independence of the domestic judiciary. Here, the court however seemed to have taken, at least in its earlier jurisprudence, a rather narrow approach as to the notion of judicial independence. It apparently required explicit governmental pressure or orders given to the judiciary for violations of the principle of judicial independence.[223] However in more recent jurisprudence, the court has conducted a more in-depth review which has found at least case-specific (if not structural) issues of judicial independence and impartiality.[224] It also emphasised the value of judicial independence in general, by adopting a statement that is well established in the independence-related jurisprudence of the ECtHR regarding the importance of perceptions of independence by the parties to the dispute and the general public.[225] It noted that '[c]e qui est en jeu, c'est la confiance que les tribunaux, dans une société démocratique, doivent inspirer au public, y compris à un accusé'.[226]

Further, the court links rule of law and democratic values, stressing their importance and their role for assessing whether human rights limitations are justified. The court said that

> in a democratic society based on the rule of law, political ideas that challenge the existing order and whose realization is advocated by peaceful means must be given an adequate opportunity for expression through the exercise of the right of assembly. This national security cannot be claimed to justify limitations to avoid merely local or relatively isolated threats to law and order.[227]

In *Amadou Cellou Dalein Diallo v Guinea*, the court defended democratic values by declaring a constitutional amendment with the aim of allowing for a third term of office for the President of Guinea to be in violation of the principles of democratic

[221] *Kodjo Alain Victor v Cote d'Ivoire*, 26 April 2021, ECW/CCJ/JUD/09/21.
[222] ibid para 71.
[223] eg, *Barthelemy Toye Dias v Senegal*, 23 March 2012, ECW/CCJ/JUG/05/12, para 22. Also *Cheikh Abdoulaye Mbengue v Mali*, 7 October 2011, ECW/CCJ/JUG/08/11, para 34.
[224] eg, *Diawara Oumar v Côte d'Ivoire*, 22 October 2021, ECW/CCJ/JUD/34/21, para 82: 'La cour constate donc que les actes dudit juge sont clairement révélateurs et motives par la partialité, les préjugés et la mauvaise foi'.
[225] ECtHR, *Sramek v Austria*, 22 October 1984, application no. 8790/79, para 42; *Ramos Nunes de Carvalho e Sá v Portugal*, 6 November 2018, application nos. 55391/13, 57728/13 and 74041/13, para 149; *Sacilor Lormines v France*, 9 November 2006, application no. 65411/01, para 60; *Kleyn and Others v the Netherlands*, 6 May 2003, application nos. 9343/98, 39651/98, 43147/98 and 46664/99, para 191.
[226] *Diawara Oumar v Côte d'Ivoire*, 22 October 2021, ECW/CCJ/JUD/34/21, para 74.
[227] *Illia Malam Mamane Saidat v Niger*, 22 June 2021, ECW/CCJ/JUD/17/2021, para 124. Similarly: *Federation of African Journalists and Others v The Gambia*, 13 February 2018, ECW/CCJ/JUD/04/18, 32.

change of government enshrined in the African Charter on Democracy, Elections and Governance.[228] And in *Mohamed Bazoum and Others v Niger*, the court declared the 2023 coup d'état against the elected president to be a violation of Protocol A/SP1/12/01 on Democracy and Good Governance and ordered the respondent to reinstate Mohamed Bazoum to office.[229]

Further, the court took up the requirement that rights limitations must not only be in accordance with domestic law but also 'necessary in a democratic society'.[230] This formulation (which is also inspired by the jurisprudence of the ECtHR) does not only refine the legal yardstick used by the court but also gives a further value-related connotation to its jurisprudence. This contributes to keeping these values salient and to stress value-correspondence.

The court has also strengthened the rule of law value by upholding the required rule of law standard even in state of emergency situations during regime change. It emphasised that the rule of law is such an important value that its minimum requirements must be upheld even during times in which the transitioning member state is in a state of emergency.[231] The court also made it clear that a regime change does not justify not applying rule of law or human rights standards to members of the ousted regime after the regime change has been completed. It decided that is prohibited to exclude members of the ousted regime from participation in elections as this would amount 'to an offence for holding an opinion, which is obviously unacceptable'.[232]

Moreover, the court has adopted a specific strategy for strengthening human rights protection as a value. This value is specifically fostered when the court addresses 'systemic human rights violations'. While the court did not make any statements as to structural issues in its earlier jurisprudence, limiting any declarations – including obiter dicta – strictly to the case at hand, it has meanwhile started to call out such issues. It 'takes judicial notice' of structural deficiencies such as 'the slow criminal justice delivery system' in Côte d'Ivoire.[233] And it makes general statements a to the negative impact of systemic human rights violations: 'the systemic violation of human rights … undermines real national security and can jeopardize international peace and security'.[234] The latter aspect also speaks to the member states' practical interests (in addition to values) as to why human rights should be protected by the court.

Another set of strategies targets the motivation of member states to comply with the decisions of the ECOWAS Court. They aim at increasing the visibility of the legal obligation to implement the court's decisions. A higher visibility of a behavioural norm increases the tendency of actors to behave in accordance with this norm.[235] The

[228] *Amadou Cellou Dalein Diallo and 50 Others v Guinea*, 6 June 2024, ECW/CCJ/JUD/18/24.
[229] *Mohamed Bazoum and Others v Niger*, 15 December 2023, ECW/CCJ/JUD/57/23.
[230] *His Lordship Justice Paul Uuter Derry and Others v Ghana*, 29 April 2019, ECW/CCJ/JUD/17/19, para 74.
[231] *Simone Ehivet et Michel Gbagbo v Côte d'Ivoire*, 22 February 2013, ECW/CCJ/JUD/03/13.
[232] *Congrès pour la Démocratie et le Progrès (CDP) and Others v Burkina Faso*, 13 July 2015, ECW/CCJ/JUG/16/15, para 28.
[233] *Kodjo Alain Victor v Cote d'Ivoire*, 26 April 2021, ECW/CCJ/JUD/09/21, para 69.
[234] *Illia Malam Mamane Saidat v Niger*, 22 June 2021, ECW/CCJ/JUD/17/2021, para 126.
[235] eg, N Belle and P Cantarelli, 'What Causes Unethical Behavior? A Meta-Analysis to Set an Agenda for Public Administration Research' (2017) 77 *Public Administration Review* 327, 333.

court has used both legal and non-legal techniques to pursue this aim. In its outreach activities, the court has repeatedly urged the member states to comply with its judgments, and as a precondition for domestic enforcement, to fulfil their obligations under Article 24 of the Protocol regarding the establishment of a domestic enforcement infrastructure. For example, in a statement at the opening of the 2021 external court session in Abidjan, the President of the Court appealed to 'the high political and judicial authorities of Cote d'Ivoire to discharge its treaty obligation by appointing such an authority as soon as possible'.[236]

Further, the court has taken in its recent jurisprudence a novel approach to enhance compliance by legal means. The court has created its own compliance monitoring system. As mentioned above, it now orders states to 'report' within a specified time frame about 'the measures taken to implement the orders' imposed in the judgment.[237] Including such reporting obligations is a bold and explicit strategy to enhance the motivation for compliance. It does not only make compliance norms more visible to the respondents, but it also makes it more likely that other actors become aware of non-compliance, a fact that can have a motivating effect both with regard to actors seeking to avoid sanctions[238] and to actors concerned about reputational disadvantages.[239]

Yet, the court has not expanded its jurisdiction to take, as a second step, decisions regarding the enforcement of its own decisions. For example, in the *Mba* case of 2018, the applicant had requested the court to order member states to enforce a previous decision for the court against Ghana.[240] The court however dismissed the admissibility of this case, stating that it did not have the competence to rule on enforcement matters.[241] The court thus limits its enforcement-related decision-making to monitoring.

Another aspect of the court's practice that can increase the motivation of actors to accept the authority of the court relates to its human rights expertise. This expertise has developed considerably since its early years. To illustrate this development, the jurisprudence on arbitrary detention is a good example. In the first cases, the assessment as to whether a detention could be qualified as arbitrary was very cursory. The court would mainly defer to domestic courts by rejecting an arbitrary detention claim whenever there were judicial proceedings involved in the detention.[242] What is more, the existence of domestic law on which the detention decision could be based sufficed for the court to declare the detention as non-arbitrary. In comparison, the court's later jurisprudence is more nuanced. It engaged in detail with allegations of arbitrary detention, referring to certain international legal standards such as those

[236] Statement as reported by Richards (n 10).

[237] eg, *Illia Malam Mamane Saidat v Niger*, 22 June 2021, ECW/CCJ/JUD/17/2021; *Diawara Oumar v Côte d'Ivoire*, 22 October 2021, ECW/CCJ/JUD/34/21; *Kodjo Alain Victor v Cote d'Ivoire*, 26 April 2021, ECW/CCJ/JUD/09/21; *Adam Latif and 4 Others v Togo*, 30 November 2023, ECW/CCJ/JUD/45/2023.

[238] Welsh and Ordóñez (n 140).

[239] On reputation as a motivating element, see references at n 137.

[240] *Chude Mba v Ghana and others*, 11 December 2018, ECW/CCJ/JUD/30/18.

[241] ibid 14. See also *Kokou Aziagbede and Others v Togo*, 6 December 2016, ECW/CCJ/JUD/29/16, paras 18, 22; *Col. Mohammed Sambo Dasuki v Nigeria*, 6 June 2024, ECW/CCJ/JUD/19/24.

[242] eg, *Amouzou Henri and Others v Côte d'Ivoire*, 17 December 2019, ECW/CCJ/JUG/04/09, para 87; *Barthelemy Toye Dias v Senegal*, 23 March 2012, ECW/CCJ/JUG/05/12, para 20.

set out by the UN Working Group on Arbitrary Detention;[243] and it included, with reference to the African Commission, a reasonability assessment, ie, whether a detention is 'just, necessary, proportionate and equitable as opposed to unjust, absurd and arbitrary'.[244] More generally, while the court frequently referred in its earlier jurisprudence to domestic decisions and only occasionally decisions by international human rights courts and bodies, the court now engages in depth with the existing case law.[245] By doing so, it signals to its audiences expertise in the matter, thus enhancing their expertise-related motivation to accept the court's authority.

Enhancing the Motivation of Applicants

A second set of strategies aims at enhancing the motivation of applicants. To foster value-correspondence with applicants who seek to engage with an independent institution, the court has emphasised its own independence. In its self-representation, independence has a central role. On the court's website, independence, impartiality and integrity are highlighted as core values of the court.[246] Furthermore, on a previous version of its website, the court stated: 'It is this functional independence of the Court, which allows it to play a fundamental role in resolving conflicts between stakeholders in the Community'. The court thus also links this value to the actors' interest in dispute resolution. This illustrates the strategic intention of referring to judicial independence to enhance the motivation of actors to engage with the court.

Further, given that a key caveat to the motivation of (potential) applicants is the limited expected effectiveness regarding dispute resolution and implementation of remedies, a useful strategy is to enhance the potential applicants' perception in this regard. The court indeed addresses the effectiveness perception of applicants in various ways. First of all, the court is aware of the compliance deficits that exist with regard to several member states. When it addresses these deficits by the strategies outlined above, this also has implications for the extent to which (potential) applicants consider it effective to bring cases to the court.

As a further strategy, the court explicitly acknowledges the interests of applicants in remedies that go beyond a declaratory statement regarding human rights violations. It takes this interest into account when considering the remedies that it awards:

> The Court is … mindful that its function in terms of protection does not stop at taking note of human rights violation. If it were to end in merely taking note of human rights violations, the exercise of such a function would be of no practical interest for the victims, who, in the final analysis, are to be protected and provided with relief.[247]

[243] *Sow Bertin Agba v Togo*, 11 June 2013, ECW/CCJ/JUD/05/13, para 33.

[244] *Illia Malam Mamane Saidat v Niger*, 22 June 2021, ECW/CCJ/JUD/17/2021, para 154. See also *Kodjo Alain Victor v Cote d'Ivoire*, 26 April 2021, ECW/CCJ/JUD/09/21, para 37 et seq.

[245] Also, while the court was not reflective on why it should be able to refer to domestic law at all, it later was mindful of showing that it can refer to it according to international law. See eg, *Falana and Another v Benin and Others*, 24 January 2012, ECW/CCJ/JUD/02/12, para 34.

[246] See: courtecowas.org/about_us/mission-vision/.

[247] *SERAP v Nigeria*, 14 December 2012, ECW/CCJ/JUD/18/12, para 118.

Putting this approach into practice, the court has broadened the scope of remedies that it grants. Specifically, as has been outlined above,[248] the court has started to order the amendment of domestic law provisions when these provisions are not in line with the respondent state's human rights obligations. This shift is particularly relevant for (potential) applicants interested in future structural changes beyond the case at hand. For this group of applicants, the recent jurisprudence significantly enhances the motivation to bring cases to the court.

At the same time, the court has emphasised the importance of the declaratory elements of its decision-making as well as of non-pecuniary remedies. As to the latter, it has stressed repeatedly that 'la reconnaissance de la violation ou la présentation d'excuses pour celle-ci, peut contribuer grandement à la résolution des prejudices causés par la violation'.[249] While this statement might be, prima facie, addressed at member states, it also points out to applicants the benefits of such remedies.

Further, the court specifically speaks to NGOs and their motivation to approach the court not only as applicants but also as amici curiae. It encourages NGOs in doing so by expressly thanking them in judgments 'for the insightful submission that have assisted this Court in taking an informed Decision'.[250] Such statements do not only communicate to the amici curiae in the specific case that their arguments have been heard and considered but it also highlights the role of amici curiae in general, making this option for engaging with the court more visible also for other NGOs in the future.

b. Enhancing Opportunity

Enhancing Opportunity for Applicants

With regard to its human rights jurisdiction and access of individuals, the court has used a policy strategy to enhance the opportunity for (potential) applicants to engage with the court in human rights cases. The court decided not to create such a jurisdiction and access itself through activist jurisprudence, thus taking a different approach than the EACJ or the SADC Tribunal. In its *Afolabi* judgment in which it decided not to expand its jurisdiction, the court stated that

> the Article in question, as a whole, being so clear … the Contracting parties in our view envisaged only Member States, despite what may look like being harsh on individuals or nationals of the Community. The Court is not here to change the provision of the Protocol but to apply it when it is clear or interpret it when it is abstruse and ambiguous.[251]

[248] Section II.B.i.
[249] *Diawara Oumar v Côte d'Ivoire*, 22 October 2021, ECW/CCJ/JUD/34/21, para 125 (with further references).
[250] *Federation of African Journalists and Others v The Gambia*, 13 February 2018, ECW/CCJ/JUD/04/18.
[251] *Olajide Afolabi v Nigeria*, 27 April 2004, ECW/CCJ/JUD/01/04, paras 54–55.

Although the court did not increase the opportunity for human rights applicants itself, the court actively lobbied for a human rights jurisdiction on a policy level. Alter, Helfer and McAllister describe the various ways in which the court did so:

> [T]he judges raised expansive policy arguments outside the courtroom to lobby for an overhaul of the 1991 Protocol. On the same day that the Court released the Afolabi judgment, it also issued a press release urging governments 'to enable individuals to bring actions before the court as there are cases member states cannot bring on behalf of [their] nationals'. The Court also published a booklet that summarized the legal arguments of parties in Afolabi and the judgment dismissing the suit ... During the next several months, in meetings with lawyers, civil society groups, and government officials, and in statements to the news media, the judges continued to publicize the need to provide access for private litigants.[252]

Other actors also took part in this campaign, including the West African Bar Association, other NGOs and the ECOWAS Executive Secretariat (now the Commission).[253] In sum, it led to a successful broadening of opportunity for private applicants, as it resulted in the 2005 Protocol which established the human rights jurisdiction and individual access.

The court also adopted jurisprudential techniques (rather than only policy techniques) to shape the opportunity for applicants. Most prominently, the court broadened the access opportunity for NGOs which was, unlike, for example, in the context of the ACtHPR, not explicitly mentioned in the court's basic legal instruments. When it first created access in the SERAP cases, it spelled out its strategy for doing so. It considered that

> public interest litigation ... is a healthy development in the promotion of human rights and this court must lend its weight to it, in order to satisfy the aspirations of citizens of the sub-region in their quest for a pervasive human rights regime.[254]

And it '[took] into account the need to reinforce the access to justice for the protection of human and people rights in the African context', when it specified the conditions under which NGOs can bring cases to the court regarding human rights violations of a 'large group of individuals or even entire communities'.[255] These statements show that the court was strategically considering how best to promote human rights protection when providing a broad access opportunity for NGOs. Although the court has somewhat cut back the broad access given to NGOs that is akin to an *actio popularis* in its later jurisprudence (see section II.A), the strategic dimension of this access remains salient. The court however balanced it with other strategic considerations that will be addressed below with regard to avoiding and managing pushback.

The court also broadened the access opportunity for individual applicants. The recent jurisprudence on *actio popularis* for individuals did so most prominently.

[252] Alter, Helfer and McAllister (n 4) 750.

[253] ibid 751.

[254] *SERAP v Nigeria*, 27 October 2009, ECW/CCJ/APP/0808, para 33.

[255] *Registered Trustees of the Socio-Economic Rights & Accountability Project (SERAP) v President of the Federal Republic of Nigeria & Others*, 10 December 2010, ECW/CCJ/APP/07/10, para 61. See also *SERAP v Nigeria*, 27 October 2009, ECW/CCJ/APP/0808, para 33.

Further, the court broadened the access opportunity with regard to their victim status. The court acknowledged that, at least in specific circumstances, a future violation of human rights can confer the required victim status to an applicant (see section II.A).

As to the key feature of the ECOWAS judicial framework – the absence of an exhaustion of domestic remedies rule – the court's strategy has been to preserve this broad opportunity. Here, there was no need to expand opportunity but to 'defend' the broad access possibilities against pushback from member states. The court did so both on a policy level in the context of the 2009 attempt of the Gambia to amend the access rules, and on a legal level when it repeatedly spelled out all the legal arguments that support upholding the non-exhaustion rule (see section II.B). In addition, the court also *promotes* the broad access that the exhaustion-free admissibility offers. For example, in its 2021 statement referred to above, the President of the Court said that 'Community citizens, therefore, have the option of lodging complaints for human rights violations before their national courts or the ECOWAS Court of Justice without the need to exhaust local remedies'.[256]

Regarding certain other opportunity features, the court has initially taken a narrow approach, thus limiting the opportunity for applicants, before broadening the opportunity in its more recent jurisprudence. As outlined in section II.A, this includes election matters for which the court rejected jurisdiction in earlier years and only later acknowledged that the human rights dimension of election matters is justiciable before it. Similarly, the court reduced the opportunity for applicants considerably when it refused to review domestic judicial decisions and legislative acts during the earlier years. When it changed its stance on the matter, it broadened the opportunity for applicants to bring cases against judicial and legislative acts before the court. Moreover, the court has initially taken a restrictive stance as to the temporal applicability of the 2005 Protocol before being more permissive regarding a retroactive effect of this protocol in its later jurisprudence.

For yet another set of access elements, the court has, for a long time, not taken a clear position, oscillating between a restrictive and a permissive stance. The jurisprudence of the court has been ambivalent as to whether and to what extent legal persons have access to the court in human rights cases, and as to whether Article 9(3) of the Statute that established the three-year time limit is applicable in human rights case (see section II.A). Depending on the decision at hand as part of the oscillating approaches, the court had limited or broadened the access opportunity in this regard.

Enhancing Opportunity for Respondents

The court has significantly shaped the opportunity structure for legislative and judicial actors. As outlined, it initially refused to review legislative acts and judicial decisions and only later created an opportunity for legislative and judicial actors to implement decisions directly addressed at them. Regarding legislative actors, the court upheld its restrictive stance for about a decade. More recently, in decisions such as *Congrès*

[256] Statement as reported by Richards (n 10).

pour la Démocratie et le Progrès v Burkina Faso and *Umeh*, it has accepted to review legislative acts.

As to the opportunity for *domestic courts* to accept the authority of the court, the ECOWAS Court first reduced the opportunity for domestic courts by excluding a review of domestic judicial decisions from its jurisdiction. The court then broadened its approach gradually over the years. As to the court's initial stance, the reasons for why the court reduced the opportunity structure are multilayered. In addition to the strategic choice to avoid pushback (see below), the approach to reduce the opportunity structure was triggered by the limited human rights expertise of the court in its early years. Coming from the domestic judiciary, the judges related the role of the court – and of other regional courts such as the ECtHR – to the functions that courts can have in the domestic judicial system. The following statement illustrates that understanding:

> Unlike other international courts of justice, such as the European Court of Human Rights, the Community Court of Justice, ECOWAS, does not possess, among others, the competence to revise decisions made by the domestic courts of Member States; it is neither a court of appeal nor a court of cassation (cour de cassation) vis-a-vis the national courts, and as such, the action of the Applicant cannot thrive.[257]

The court seemed to somewhat misconstrue the impact of ECtHR decisions with regard to domestic decisions, apparently assuming that the ECtHR is close to being a cassation court. It did not differentiate between the cassation of judgments and the declaration that the judgment violates human rights law, and between using domestic law as a yardstick for review as compared with international human rights instruments. This was also a reaction to the way in which applications during the early years were framed. When the first applicants brought cases to the court, they approached it in the way they would have done if it was a domestic court. They treated the court as a cassation court asking it to declare domestic court decisions 'null and void'.[258] This naturally would have influenced how the – still inexperienced – court reflected upon the review of domestic court decisions. However, as the human rights expertise of the court developed, the court considered in a more nuanced and appropriate way the jurisprudence of other regional courts on assessing human rights violations by domestic courts. It thus re-expanded the opportunity for domestic courts to accept the authority of the court.

As to the relationship between the ECOWAS legal order and the domestic legal orders as an element of the opportunity structure for executive actors and domestic courts, it bears mentioning here again that the court did not decide to enhance this opportunity. In particular, it did not develop a direct effect doctrine akin to what the CJEU has done, a doctrine that would make it easier for executive and judicial actors within the member states to take into account ECOWAS Court decisions as part of this legal order. It seems to be another instance in which the court gave prevalence to its pushback-related strategies as compared with strategies to increase opportunity. This corresponds to the court's perception according to which the CJEU is an

[257] *Keita v Mali*, March 2007, ECW/CCJ/APP/03/07, para 30.
[258] eg, *Jerry Ugokwe v Nigeria and Others*, 7 October 2005, ECW/CCJ/JUD/03/05, para 14.

'activist' court whose 'decisions attracted criticisms'.[259] The ECOWAS Court wanted to distance itself from such an approach.

c. Limiting Constraints

Limiting Constraints for Applicants

The court has adopted strategies to address the intrinsic constraints of applicants that reduce the likeliness that potential applicants engage with the court. First, it has addressed the limited awareness of the court and its human rights jurisdiction among potential applicants. The court aimed at enhancing awareness with 'sensitisation missions' to member states. It has undertaken such missions since the early years and has continued to do so during its practice with a 'comprehensive outreach campaign'.[260] Further, a strategy of the court has been to get closer to the people. Article 26(2) of the Protocol enables the court to sit elsewhere than in Abuja where it has its seat. For example, the court went to Mali,[261] Niger,[262] Benin[263] and Côte d'Ivoire.[264] However, the court only irregularly shifts its temporary seat so that the effect of this strategy to raise awareness is limited.[265] But the court has used these sessions to promote itself to the relevant actors within the respective member states, as illustrated by the already cited opening statement of the President of the Court at the occasion of the 2021 external session in Abidjan (Cote d'Ivoire).

In contrast, the court has missed a chance to reduce constraints resulting from a lack of knowledge of its jurisprudence. The court has

> not taken steps to ensure that all its decisions are (promptly) published on its website [which] can only have exacerbated this awareness problem and its consequent failure to reap optimally the fruits that will come with greater public awareness of, and access to, its decisions.[266]

Indeed, it is still the case that not all decisions are available on the court's website. And the documents of the available decisions are, as already mentioned, not searchable scans of hard copies. The fact that the accessibility of decisions remains so limited thus suggests that the court is not cognisant of the importance of these features for its audiences.

Second, the court has adopted strategies to reduce the constraints resulting from the potential applicants' financial situations. The court's initiative to get closer to the people by conducting external sessions addresses this issue (in addition to being a strategy for increasing awareness). Getting closer to the applicants, potential

[259] *Olajide Afolabi v Nigeria*, 27 April 2004, ECW/CCJ/JUD/01/04, para 56.
[260] See Interim Report 2019 and 2004 Annual Report of the Court as well as the 'outreach missions' listed at: courtecowas.org/media-and-publications/media/.
[261] In *Keita v Mali*, March 2007, ECW/CCJ/APP/03/07.
[262] In *Hadijatou Mani Koraou v Niger*, 27 October 2008, ECW/CCJ/JUD/06/08.
[263] In *Ameganvi Manvi Isabelle v Togo*, 7 October 2011, ECW/CCJ/JUD/09/11.
[264] In *Marie Molmou and Others v Guinea*, 17 May 2016, ECW/CCJ/JUD/16/16.
[265] Okafor and Effoduh (n 24) 134.
[266] ibid 145.

witnesses and locations of the alleged human rights violations makes it possible to reduce costs. This might enable applicants who otherwise would not have been able to overcome their financial restraints on their own account to engage with the court.[267] Similarly, the option to hold virtual court sessions that the court created as a reaction to the Covid 19 pandemic has also limited the financial burden for applicants from other ECOWAS regions. In addition, the court has rejected any financial counter-claims that some respondents have made regarding their defence costs.[268] The court thus limits the financial risk for applicants.

Limiting Constraints for Respondents

The court has targeted extrinsic constraints for respondents. As to the competing authority relationship of state actors regarding domestic courts, the court initially adopted a strategy to limit this constraining factor. When the court refused to review domestic judicial decisions, it avoided situations in which domestic actors such as administrative actors or other courts are faced with conflicting decisions on the same matter, one from the ECOWAS Court and one from the domestic court. Later, the more it moved towards assessing human rights violations by domestic courts, the more it de facto gave up this strategy. However, even in its recent decisions, the court still stresses rhetorically the different spheres of competence between domestic courts and the ECOWAS Court.

In contrast, regarding the competing authority relationship towards the ACtHPR, the court seems to have chosen to embrace this situation. It has emphasised that the decisions of the ACtHPR are not binding on the ECOWAS Court. The latter thus can take a different approach as to the interpretation and application of human rights standards, despite the fact that both use the Charter as their formal yardstick. The court stated that

> [i]t is pertinent to quickly clarify that while this court draws inspiration from the rich, flourishing and persuasive jurisprudence of the African Court of Human Rights and other reputable International Courts, this Court is not bound to follow their decisions. This position is further strengthened where the circumstances and peculiarity of the cases differ in all material sense.[269]

For state actors, this means that conflicting decisions might occur in the future so that the ECOWAS Court's approach might lead to enhancing this constraining factor. However, in several cases the court has adopted the ACtHPR's legal position so that conflicting decisions have been avoided in these instances.[270]

Finally, specifically for domestic courts, the jurisprudence of the ECOWAS Court on independence of the domestic judiciary can contribute to reducing constraints that stem from (potential) pressure from their respective governments not to implement ECOWAS Court decisions. If this jurisprudence has a positive effect on the level

[267] See also ST Ebobrah, 'Litigating Human Rights Before Sub-Regional Courts in Africa: Prospects and Challenges' (2009) 17 *African Journal of International and Comparative Law* 79.

[268] eg, *Cheikh Abdoulaye Mbengue v Mali*, 7 October 2011, ECW/CCJ/JUG/08/11, paras 39–40; *Marie Molmou and Others v Guinea*, 17 May 2016, ECW/CCJ/JUD/16/16, 11.

[269] *Umeh and Others v Nigeria*, 1 July 2020, ECW/CCJ/JUD/10/20, para 81.

[270] eg, *Advocaid Ltd v Sierra Leone*, 7 November 2024, ECW/CCJ/JUD/33/24, paras 56–58.

of judicial independence within member states, it becomes less likely that judicial actors are constrained in this way.

d. Assessment of Strategies

The above overview of court strategies leads to a differentiated conclusion.

Regarding *applicants*, the court has only partially addressed the respective determining MOC factors. While pre-2005, the court tackled the virtually non-existent opportunity for all groups of applicants as the obvious hurdle for them to engage with the court, it did not always target, post-2005, the lowest factor of the MOC setting determining applicants' behaviour. For corporate actors, for which motivation and opportunity are the determining factors, the court has kept the opportunity structure on a moderate level by confirming its jurisprudence that corporate actors only have access to the court for selected rights violations. It did not enhance this opportunity. The court has however addressed the motivation of these actors when taking the above-listed measures to enhance compliance and thus to increase the perceived effectiveness of this group's engagement with the court – although the court did not target these measures explicitly at this group but to applicants in general. Regarding NGOs, the court has initially created a broad opportunity which it then has somewhat reduced, thus making opportunity one of the determining factors for NGOs (in addition to unconstrained ability which is at a similar level). Rather than enhancing the MOC setting, the court has thus, when reducing opportunity, restricted the likeliness that these actors engage with the court. The court also did not attempt to address constraints for NGOs as to competing authority relationships. In contrast, for individual actors for whom either motivation or constraints are the determining factor, the court's strategies aim at improving the MOC setting. The strategies to increase awareness and limit costs for applicants target constraints as a determining factor for many individual applicants. Specifically, the awareness-raising strategies also relate to the determining factor for political actors as a sub-group of individual applicants. Similarly, the strategies of the court to increase compliance and thus to boost the effectiveness perception of individual actors addresses a determining factor for many individual applicants. In sum, the court seems to address the determining factors when it wishes to do so – which is particularly the case for individual applicants. With regard to other groups of applicants, the court's strategy is to keep the MOC setting on a favourable level, yet without maximising it in the way it potentially could. Not to enhance certain factors here therefore is a deliberate choice rather than an unsuccessful attempt to increase MOC.

Concerning *respondents*, the court's strategy for governmental actors focuses on increasing their motivation. As motivation is indeed the determining factor for these actors, the court's strategies in this regard are well oriented. This includes the court's attempts to enhance value-correspondence and to increase the interest in compliance. For domestic courts, and to some extent for legislative actors, the ECOWAS Court had initially created the determining factor for this group of actors. It had designed the opportunity structure in a narrow manner when it refused to review domestic judicial decisions and did not engage with legislative acts. Later, when it decided to broaden this opportunity, it indeed addressed the determining factor. Doing so was a necessary step to enable these actors to accept the court's authority. However, considering that after this development in the MOC setting, motivation has become the determining factor for domestic courts, the strategies with which the court addresses this factor are well targeted. In particular, when the court aims at improving the rule of law and independence issues on the domestic level, it potentially contributes to enhancing a value-based motivation of judicial actors (as well as reducing constraints on domestic courts that are exercised by domestic governments). Such value-based strategies can thus also improve the MOC setting for domestic court behaviour.

To conclude, the above outline shows that it is possible for the court to influence the MOC setting that determines whether actors accept the authority of the court. The authority relationship and the behavioural framework that leads to it are thus neither invariable nor unable to be influenced by the court. But it has also become apparent that not all elements of the MOC setting can be influenced by the court to the same extent, or at all. While the court's strategies can have an impact, they cannot be a panacea for the authority relationship with all relevant actors. What is more, when the court targets an MOC factor that is not determining the relevant group's behaviour, this strategy is not effective.

ii. Avoiding and Managing Pushback

In this section, I highlight some of the strategies of the court to avoid or to manage pushback. Such 'resilience techniques' can be categorised according to the time relative to the pushback at which they occur.[271] Accordingly, I outline strategies that aim at avoiding pushback and strategies to manage pushback while it is taking place. The former includes both techniques to avoid an initial pushback and techniques to avoid repeated pushback after it has occurred previously.

a. Decreasing Motivation for Pushback

The court has adopted a range of general and specific techniques to decrease the motivation for pushback. A first occasion for the court to avoid creating motivation for pushback was the *Afolabi* case of 2004. The court chose not to provide such motivation by jurisprudentially developing a human rights jurisdiction and individual access as other courts have done. It clearly feared that member states would resist its authority if it were to change the institutional mandate itself. In contrast, with the non-legal or policy strategy that it adopted instead, the court did not risk creating any motivation for pushback – for various reasons.[272] First, the court limited itself to a discursive strategy which left the decision as to whether to amend the Protocol in the hands of member states. Second, the ECOWAS legal

[271] S Caserta and P Cebulak, 'Resilience Techniques of International Courts in Times of Resistance to International Law' (2021) 70 *International & Comparative Law Quarterly* 737, 749.

[272] On the differentiation between 'judicial' and 'extrajudicial' techniques, Caserta and Cebulak (n 271) 749.

instruments explicitly allow judges to propose changes to the Protocol.[273] The judges' lobbying campaign was thus expressly legitimised by member states. Third, in the context of its policy campaign, the court also sought the support of other relevant actors including the West African Bar Association, other NGOs and the ECOWAS Executive Secretariat (now the Commission).[274] This support from a wide range of actors further legitimised the policy strategy of the court. As a result, the campaign did not only succeed in substance but was also conducted in a way to minimise pushback against the court.

Further, and specifically in its early years, the court adopted several strategies to reduce the motivation for pushback by state governments in high-politics areas. The court used a restrictive construction of both procedural and substantive law principles to reduce the motivation for pushback. For example, in the 2005 *Ugokwe v Nigeria* case regarding the Nigerian elections, the court decided not to take jurisdiction on the matter, stating categorically that 'no provision, whether general or specific, gives the Court powers to adjudicate on electoral issues or matters arising thereof' and that they cannot take any measures 'against the execution of the Judgment already made by the Federal Appeal Court of the Member State of Nigeria'.[275] This clear refusal to accept electoral cases persisted for several years (until the case *Congrès pour la Démocratie et le Progrès v Burkina* of 2015).[276] It has been suggested that by taking this strong stance, the court 'wanted to send a clear message that they would not intervene in future election disputes' which are considered highly political in nature.[277] Moreover, and as an example of how the court uses a restrictive take on substantive law to limit the motivation for pushback, the above-mentioned strict burden of proof requirement is illustrative. The burden of proof on the applicants to demonstrate the facts relating to alleged human rights violations such as mandatory documentary evidence of physical violence makes it possible for the court not to decide against states in certain highly political cases, creating less incentive for them to resist against the court. This jurisprudence 'becomes one way in which the Court has cleverly managed its relationship to the high politics of the ECOWAS regional arrangement and the great political, social, and economic power relative to it that is projected by ECOWAS Member States'.[278]

A further strategy of the court to reduce the motivation for pushback is the incremental approach taken to develop certain lines of jurisprudence. This strategy is akin to a 'foot-in-the-door' technique that uses smaller initial demands as a first step to reduce the resistance against further broader demands.[279] An important example in this regard is the jurisprudence on the kinds of acts of member states that are reviewed

[273] The President of the Court has the right to submit proposals for amendments of the Protocol, according to Article 33(1) of the 1991 Protocol (now Article 35(1)).
[274] Alter, Helfer and McAllister (n 4) 751.
[275] *Jerry Ugokwe v Nigeria and Others*, 7 October 2005, ECW/CCJ/JUD/03/05, paras 19, 33.
[276] *Congrès pour la Démocratie et le Progrès (CDP) and Others v Burkina Faso*, 13 July 2015, ECW/CCJ/JUG/16/15. See on this jurisprudential development, section II.A.ii.
[277] Alter, Helfer and McAllister (n 4) 759.
[278] Okafor and Effoduh (n 24) 146.
[279] See ch 2, and JL Freedman and SC Fraser, 'Compliance without pressure: the foot-in-the-door technique' (1966) 4 *Journal of Personality and Social Psychology* 195.

by the court. From initially only reviewing acts of the executive branch to expanding to domestic judicial decisions and recently also to legislative acts, the court has step by step embraced its full jurisdictional reach. What is more, as part of this strategy, the court has developed its jurisprudence on the review of domestic judicial decisions in an incremental way. With this approach, the court ensured that the relevant domestic actors could slowly adjust to the authority of the court and accommodate the decisions of the court on their respective acts.

The incremental broadening of its authority is however not characteristic of the entire jurisprudence of the court. Rather, the court has combined this approach with an opposing strategy. In some fields, it has started off with a broad understanding and moderated it by its subsequent jurisprudence. In a first step, this approach has catered to the interests and expectations of applicants. As von Staden observed as to this initial strategy:

> [T]he main audience that the courts see themselves speaking to, and whose goodwill they seek to gain and maintain, are arguably not respondent states, but the civil society actors that provide them with cases and buttress their authority, and these audiences are generally less interested in cutting states some slack through judicial doctrines of deference, but rather in effectively reining in state power.[280]

In a second step, limiting the initially broad approach aims at reducing motivation for pushback by state actors. Examples of this approach include the court's take on access of NGOs and *actio popularis* which the court construed more extensively in its SERAP jurisprudence than in subsequent cases; and the court's use of notions that reflect deference to member states such as the term 'margin of appreciation' which the court took up only recently. In particular, this margin of appreciation jurisprudence is an explicit strategy to reduce the motivation of state actors for pushback.

In addition, the court uses discursive tools to reduce the potential motivation for pushback that might result from certain aspects of its jurisprudence. By explaining the legal-political rationale of its decisions, it tries to generate acceptance among the audiences that are negatively affected by this jurisprudence. For example, the court extensively explains the rationale of the concept of margin of appreciation and the deference given to member states. This can be seen as a strategy to reduce pushback – yet in this context from applicants and other interested audiences rather than from member states who benefit from this turn. The court explains:

> [T]he state party enjoys a wide margin of appreciation because they know best and they are in a better position to determine what is reasonable, practicable and applicable in their special circumstances. It is not in the place of the citizens to choose or determine what they think is best, because if everyone had that choice, the state of anarchy will set in and the test of what is necessary for the society would fail.[281]

Similarly, the court aims at reducing the motivation for pushback by member states when explaining the legal-political reasoning for its rather broad application of

[280] von Staden (n 74) 1126.
[281] *Umeh and Others v Nigeria*, 1 July 2020, ECW/CCJ/JUD/10/20, para 67.

access rules. For example, with regard to access of NGOs, it outlines the rationale as follows:

> With the same purpose to ease access to Justice on Human Rights issues by the most vulnerable individuals and by impoverished communities, which, most of time, do not have means to lodge a complaint by themselves, in particular when the opposite party is a very powerful entity, the ECOWAS Court of Justice has reiterated in many instances that, in case of serious human rights violation, a Non-Governmental Organization may enjoy standing to file a complaint on their behalf.[282]

Moreover, the court stresses the interests of member states as litigants in disputes before it as a further strategy to reduce the motivation for pushback against a broad interpretation of admissibility rules. It uses a framing that presents these access rules as advantageous for both parties to the dispute. For example, in *Kenneth Roberts v Nigeria* in 2021, the court declared that 'it is the duty of the Court to aim at doing substantial justice between the parties and not to let that aim be turned away by technicalities'.[283] This 'justice between parties' framing portrays a rule that, in legal terms, benefits the applicants as a feature that is in the interests of respondents as well. Moreover, this framing emphasises justice as a value, fostering a value-based motivation for accepting this jurisprudence rather than for contesting the norm.

A further jurisprudential strategy concerns the referencing of non-African legal sources. On the one hand, the court has used 'comparative legal reasoning' as a technique to enhance the persuasiveness of its argumentation.[284] Although such references have always been part of the reasoning of the court, the extent and quality of the engagement with the jurisprudence of other human rights courts has increased along with the human rights expertise of the court. This comparative approach makes it possible to anchor the court's decision-making in the broader human rights discourse. As a result, it becomes less likely that relevant actors perceive it as activism of the ECOWAS Court or that they perceive the court as a political actor. In this regard, the comparative reasoning of the court aims at reducing motivation for pushback. On the other hand, there is a risk, as outlined above, that referencing non-African legal sources can be perceived as the court being influenced by extra-regional actors. Aware of this risk, the court has adopted a strategy to reduce the pushback motivation that might originate from such references. For example, in the SERAP II case, the court explicitly engaged with the question of whether the extensive rule in the American Convention on Human Rights on access of NGOs is appropriate in the African context. In relation to this rule, it stated that '[t]his more liberal locus standi has been welcomed and recommended for the African Continent'.[285] And as to the persuasive impact of the Aarhus Convention (Convention on Access to Information, Public Participation in Decision-Making and Access to Justice in Environmental Matters), the court declares that

[282] *SERAP v Nigeria*, 19 June 2014, ECW/CCJ/JUD/16/14, para 61.

[283] *Kenneth Roberts & 4 Others v Nigeria*, 27 October 2021, ECW/CCJ/JUD/38/21, para 64.

[284] On this comparative technique, Caserta and Cebulak (n 271) 749.

[285] *Registered Trustees of the Socio-Economic Rights & Accountability Project (SERAP) v President of the Federal Republic of Nigeria and Others*, 10 December 2010, ECW/CCJ/APP/07/10, para 59.

> [a]lthough the convention is not a binding instrument on African States, its importance, as a persuasive evidence of an international communis opinion juris in allowing NGOs to access the Courts for protection of Human Rights related to the environment, cannot be ignored or underestimated by this court.[286]

The court thus explicitly limits the effect of these sources to being of a persuasive rather than binding nature and links back the legal approaches to the African region. This is a strategy that the court continues to adopt also in its more recent jurisprudence. To decrease motivation for pushback that might originate from citing jurisprudence from the ECtHR, the court explicitly legitimises this use and points to the persuasive effect rather than bindingness:

> [C]onsidering the relative younger age of this Court vis-a-vis other international courts, it has enormously benefitted from the external aids to interpretation particularly, foreign judgments i.e. judgments of other international courts and tribunals where the issues concern interpretation of provisions of statutes in pari materia. Though of persuasive effect, this Court has resorted to pronouncements of such courts of no mean standing like the European Court of Human Rights and African Court of Human Rights in carving its own jurisprudence.[287]

A related strategy is also reflected in how the court addresses the currency of awarded damages. As there is no unified currency in the ECOWAS region, the court has awarded damages in different currencies – including in US dollars. Yet mindful of the use of this currency potentially creating motivation for pushback against perceived foreign influence, the court engaged with this issue in 2013: 'The Court recalls that since the US Dollar is a currency which is foreign to the ECOWAS zone, the amounts of money asked for as damages must henceforth be evaluated in the currencies of the Member States'.[288] Although the court has since not been entirely consistent with this intention,[289] this statement shows however that the court aims at minimising motivation for pushback relating to perceived foreign influence.

In addition to strategies that aim at avoiding pushback in the first place, the court has also adopted strategies to manage existing pushback. To start with, the continuous norm contestation by several member states concerning the non-existing requirement to exhaust domestic remedies – that was also part of the 2009 resistance of the Gambia in the form of the failed attempt to amend the Protocol – has led the court to adopt a strategy to reduce the motivation of these states to continue their contestation. The court repeatedly confirmed the non-exhaustion rule, engaging on each occasion with the arguments brought forward by the respondents. This strategy is a double-edged sword. On the one hand, the court communicates that it consistently upholds its stance on the exhaustion issue, a signal that can lead to reducing the effectiveness expectations of respondents to raise preliminary objections on this issue in the future. And by providing an

[286] ibid para 58.

[287] *Umeh and Others v Nigeria*, 1 July 2020, ECW/CCJ/JUD/10/20, para 59.

[288] *Sow Bertin Agba v Togo*, 11 June 2013, ECW/CCJ/JUD/05/13, para 38.

[289] The court has subsequently awarded damages in $US, eg, in its decisions in *Deyda Hydara Jr and Others v The Gambia*, 10 June 2014, ECW/CCJ/APP/30/11; *Ousainou Darboe v the Gambia*, 20 January 2020, JUD/ECW/CCJ/JUD/01/20.

in-depth assessment of each argument brought forward by the respondents, the court ensures that the respondents consider themselves to be heard by the court rather than their objections being summarily rejected. This can strengthen the respondents' perception of procedural justice, a factor that contributes to accepting the authority of the court.[290] Yet on the other hand, when the court keeps engaging with the exhaustion question in such detail despite having confirmed it many times, it upholds the perception that this question is legally discussable. Even though the court tried to settle the matter in the *Ocean King* case of 2011 by 'setting the record straight once and for all',[291] it kept discussing this issue at length in later judgments. Rather than reducing the effectiveness expectation of respondents, this seemed to encourage these actors to continue to raise this objection. What is more, given that its jurisprudence on other aspects of jurisdiction and access rules has shifted over time and/or has been inconsistent (eg, regarding the access of corporate actors), this might also foster rather than reduce the motivation for norm contestation. Such inconsistencies on other issues invites attempts to convince the court to change its mind on the exhaustion matter as well.

Beyond the non-exhaustion rule, the court adopts a similar strategy for respondents' arguments and preliminary objections that have a strong sovereignty connotation. Even when such arguments seem fruitless from a legal point of view, the court considers them carefully and ensures respondents are heard and their interests taken seriously so that, here again, the benefits of a procedural justice perception can be harvested. The court states, for example, as to a preliminary objection regarding a matter touching upon the internal affairs of the respondent state:

> The respondent again contends in its Preliminary Objection that the subject matter of the suit relates to its internal affairs, and to that extent this Court has no jurisdiction. The Court reiterates the position succinctly espoused in its jurisprudence to the effect that a Member State who has ratified the African Charter has acknowledged the supra-nationality of the ECOWAS and therefore has an obligation to respect and protect the rights set forth in the Charter notwithstanding its domestic laws ... Perhaps it is needless to emphasise that every human right issue that comes before the Court in one way or the other strikes cords with the internal affairs of the Member State concerned. Whereas the Court is proscribed from examining the internal affairs of Member States *in abstracto*, where any impugned activities of any Member State is implicated in an application before the Court, the Court has an unfettered jurisdiction to examine the said activities with the view to ascertaining whether any human right violation has occurred.[292]

For other legal questions that are repeatedly raised by litigants, the court is less inclined to discursively engage with them. In fact, it often sounds rather impatient when matters that it considers settled are mentioned again. This conveys the point that any potential norm contestation will remain unsuccessful before the court. For example, the court said that 'this Court, *times without number made it clear* in its jurisprudence that its jurisdictional powers did not extend to hearing appeals from

[290] On the impact of procedural justice for authority relationships, see ch 2.
[291] *Ocean King Nigeria v Senegal*, 8 July 2011, ECW/CCJ/JUD/07/11, para 37.
[292] *Kenneth Roberts & 4 Others v Nigeria*, 27 October 2021, ECW/CCJ/JUD/38/21, para 38, 40.

the decision of national Courts';[293] that 'this court has *made it abundantly clear* that for any action by any individuals to succeed, the Applicant will be required as a matter of law to establish the status of either a victim or an indirect victim';[294] and that 'the Court *made it abundantly clear* that non natural persons can enjoy freedom of expression'.[295] Using this language, the court focuses its strategy to reduce the motivation for norm contestation on effectivness considerations: litigants are made aware that contesting these norms will not be effective, neither in the case at hand nor in the future.

b. Decreasing Opportunity for Pushback

Although the strategies of the court focus on reducing motivation for pushback, the court has also adopted strategies to decrease the pushback opportunity. This primarily concerns pushback in the form of non-compliance. In contrast, regarding the opportunity for pushback in the form of treaty amendments and norm contestation, the ECOWAS Court has not taken any measures to reduce this opportunity.

Concerning non-compliance, a strategy of the court has been, especially in the earlier years, to limit the extent and nature of remedies.[296] Declaratory decisions by their very nature do not necessitate implementation and thus do not pose any compliance issues. The court did not (or only rarely) issue orders regarding damages and non-pecuniary remedies such as an amendment of domestic law that led to human rights violations, the persecution of responsible persons, institutional improvements or other more far-reaching remedies that various other regional human rights courts order in similar cases. It has explicitly engaged with its restrictive stance on remedies, for example by stating that 'the Court has no jurisdiction to make orders of injunction to the [member state] in respect of its domestic laws and internal procedures'.[297] Yet this restrictive strategy has not been absolute as the court has occasionally issued specific orders such as regarding the speedy trial when the court found that there were prolonged proceedings,[298] or regarding investigations to be conducted by a member state.[299] Moreover, in its more recent jurisprudence the court has further broadened its approach to remedies. In particular by starting to order domestic law amendments, the court now issues remedies that are both practically and politically demanding. This increases the opportunity

[293] *Registered Trustees of Avocat Sans Frontieres France v Nigeria*, 31 January 2014, ECW/CCJ/APP/14/13, para 50 (emphasis added).

[294] *Kenneth Roberts & 4 Others v Nigeria*, 27 October 2021, ECW/CCJ/JUD/38/21, para 57 (emphasis added).

[295] *Amnesty International Togo and Others v Togo*, 25 June 2020, ECW/CCJ/JUD/09/20, para 35 (emphasis added).

[296] See also Alter, Helfer and McAllister (n 4) 766.

[297] *Baldé and Others v Senegal*, 22 February 2013, ECW/CCJ/JUG/04/13, para 77.

[298] eg, *Aziagbede Kokou v Togo*, 3 July 2013, ECW/CCJ/JUD/07/13; *Assima Kokou Innocent v Togo*, 28 November 2013, ECW/CCJ/JUD/08/13; *Ekundayo Idris v Nigeria*, 23 March 2022, ECW/CCJ/JUD/09/22.

[299] eg, *Assima Kokou Innocent v Togo*, 28 November 2013, ECW/CCJ/JUD/08/13, para 92. For more recent examples, see *Ousainou Darboe v the Gambia*, 20 January 2020, JUD/ECW/CCJ/JUD/01/20; *Rev. Fr. Solomon Mfa and Others v Nigeria and Others*, 16 February 2019, ECW/CCJ/JUD/06/19; *Hassan Kargbo and 7 Others v Sierra Leone*, 14 October 2024, ECW/CCJ/JUD/37/24.

for non-compliance. Restricting remedies is thus no longer used as a tool to reduce opportunity for non-compliance.

Further, the court has pursued the above-mentioned policy strategy to address the issue relating to Article 24 of the Protocol. It aimed at reducing the opportunity for non-compliance created by the Article 24 framework. During its outreach activities, the court has drawn attention to the obligation of member states to put in place the domestic enforcement structure for ECOWAS Court decisions and urged them to do so – a strategy that has recently been successful.

As to the opportunity for non-compliance resulting from domestic law and in particular from the dualist provisions in the domestic law of many member states regarding the effect of the ECOWAS treaty and protocols, as well as the decisions of the court in the domestic legal order, it bears mentioning here again that the court did *not* adopt any strategy to reduce this opportunity. The court's consideration here seems to be that such a strategy (as it has been adopted, for example, by the IACtHR, the CJEU and the EACJ) might, while attempting to reduce opportunity for non-compliance, increase the motivation for structural pushback against the court.

c. Increasing Constraints against Pushback

As to constraints against pushback, the possibilities of the court to increase these constraints are limited. Most of the constraints mentioned in section B.ii are beyond the court's reach. Nonetheless, the court has adopted one notable strategy. Given that it had to face an attempt at structural resistance early in its period of practice, it has been aware for some time of the importance of supporting actors in such circumstances. A key group of supporting actors are NGOs. The court has thus adopted a strategy that aims at designing an NGO-friendly jurisprudence. This includes in particular the court's approach on access rules for NGOs and its decisions on *actio popularis*. Especially in the earlier SERAP cases, the broad access provided to NGOs is mindful of their crucial supporting role. Even though the court has since then somewhat amended this jurisprudence, the court remains NGO friendly in its attitude. This also includes, as a non-legal tool, its appreciative and encouraging discursive reaction to amicus curiae briefs by NGOs.

d. Assessment of Strategies

For assessing the strategies of the court to avoid and manage pushback, it is useful to differentiate between strategies relating to structural resistance and norm contestation on the one hand and strategies relating to non-compliance on the other. This is the case because, as outlined in section II.B.ii.d, the MOC settings for these kinds of behaviour are different.

For structural resistance by formal amendments and norm contestation, ability is low to moderate while motivation and opportunity are on a moderate level. According to the MOC framework, as long as the pushback ability remains at this comparatively low level, being the determining factor, the likelihood that these forms of pushback will occur is limited. Further reducing motivation for these forms of pushback will, as the MOC setting currently stands, only influence the behaviour of the relevant actors if it is significantly reduced so that it would become the determining factor among the MOC factors. As long as the unconstrained ability remains the determining factor, a further reduction of pushback motivation will not be effective. However, it is useful for the court to adopt strategies to *maintain* the motivation at the current level rather than allowing it to increase. If actors are highly motivated to push back through structural resistance or norm contestation, they are more likely to overcome constraints against such pushback. Accordingly, the above-listed strategies regarding motivation are effective when understood as techniques for capping motivation.

Strategies to reduce non-compliance need to consider that the MOC setting for this behaviour is different for governmental actors as compared with domestic courts. For the former, ability is the determining factor. It is at a low to moderate level, while motivation is moderate to high, and opportunity has been broad before recently narrowing to a moderate level. The strategy of the court to foster its relationship with supporting actors is thus well targeted to keep the ability limited. In contrast, for domestic courts, pushback motivation is the determining factor. Based on the MOC framework, strategies to reduce this motivation are most promising. Further, for both groups of actors, the strategies of the court that address opportunity for non-compliance can be fruitful if they manage to significantly reduce this opportunity. If this succeeded, opportunity would be at the lowest level as compared with the other two MOC factors, turning it into the determining factor for non-compliance. In particular, the monitoring mechanism that the court created recently is a strategy that goes in this direction. Yet as the court can only do so much in reducing the opportunity for non-compliance, the effect of this strategy is limited as long as there are also significant constraints against pushback. Should this change, however, the opportunity-related strategies will become more impactful.

In conclusion, similar to what has been said for the strategies to increase the acceptance of the court's authority, strategies of the court to avoid and manage pushback can have the desired impact. The court is thus to some extent the master of its own destiny. However, it must be stressed that the court is not able to influence all the relevant MOC factors for pushback. Its influence is limited to begin with. And when it addresses a factor that is, given the interplay of the MOC elements, not determining for the behaviour of a group of actors, such strategies are not effective.

III. MOC IN THE CONTEXT OF REGIONAL INTEGRATION LITIGATION

After having analysed the MOC setting for human rights litigation before the court, I now turn to the regional integration context. Here again I outline the MOC factors for (potential) applicants (III.A) and for (potential) respondents (III.B). I then link these findings to the strategies of the court, showing where the court has influenced the MOC factors and whether the court has indeed tackled the determining factor that will direct the behaviour of the relevant actors (III.C).

A. MOC Factors for (Potential) Applicants

In this section, I explore the factors that shape motivation (III.A.i), opportunity (III.A.ii) and constraints (III.A.iii) for (potential) applicants before the court in regional integration matters. This overview then allows us to assess the relationship between these factors and to expose the determining factors for the various groups of potential applicants (III.A.iv).

i. Motivation

Values

As to values as motivational factors, what has been said for applicants in the human rights context regarding procedural values such as judicial independence and the rule of law applies in the ECOWAS regional integration law context as well. That is to say that for some groups of potential applicants such as private actors, value-correspondence as to these procedural values is high. Private actors from member states with rather low independence of the domestic judiciary are likely to be motivated by the independence of the ECOWAS Court in disputes against state actors. For other applicants, such as governmental actors, the level of value-correspondence diverges depending, inter alia, on the current regimes in place (see Table 4.1). The motivating impact of procedural values is thus ambivalent.

Interests

The substantive value that can motivate potential applicants to engage with the court is regional integration. Yet, this value is more likely to be important for applicants such as state governments and ECOWAS institutions than for private actors and domestic courts. For the latter groups of actors, there is little evidence that regional integration as a value is a driving force behind engaging with the ECOWAS Court. But for the ECOWAS institutions and for (various) member states, regional integration has indeed been an important value when creating the court. As Alter, Helfer and McAllister observe:

> The decision to create the ECOWAS Court was part of the broader recommitment to regional integration in the early 1990s ... The renewed governmental support for a court in the early 1990s reflected a growing sense that deeper regional integration required a judicial body to resolve disputes and interpret legal rules.[300]

This normative commitment to regional integration has not been complemented by an interest-based motivation to engage with the court. Despite the legal framework establishing a common market in the ECOWAS region, an effective common market does not yet exist in practice. In particular, the trade among member states has only intensified to a relatively small extent.[301] In fact, 'little has been seen in terms

[300] Alter, Helfer and McAllister (n 4) 746.

[301] See also ECOWAS VISION 2050 'ECOWAS of the Peoples: Peace and Prosperity for All', June 2022, para 58: ecowas.int/special_post/vision-2050/.

of volume of interstate trade and harmonisation of the rules among the Member States'.[302] To the contrary, 'West African governments benefit from maintaining barriers to intraregional trade and … these benefits, at least in the current political and economic climate, outweigh the advantages of achieving a functioning common market'.[303] As a consequence, member states have not shown an interest in enforcing regional integration law relating to economic integration before the ECOWAS Court. And due to the low level of cross-border trade, many private economic actors have little perceived interest in trade litigation involving regional integration law. Yet for those economic actors who do in fact engage in cross-border trade, the interests in addressing the ECOWAS Court are substantial: as 'tariffs, customs regulations, nontariff barriers, and roadblocks hinder cross-border economic transactions',[304] actors interested in cross-border trade would have many issues to legally challenge before the court.

As to effectiveness considerations as motivational factors, potential applicants are likely to focus much more than in the human rights context on practical outcome rather than on strategic political interests. As a consequence, non-compliance issues affect the expected effectiveness of actors' behaviour more in the regional integration law context than in the human rights context. Although there are to date only few cases decided by the court in regional integration law matters, the moderate compliance rate in other cases is also likely to shape actors' expectations concerning compliance in potential regional integration law cases. An additional effectiveness consideration concerns the specific context of free movement of persons, goods and services for which a jurisprudence of the court exists (see also below). Here, the court has adopted a rather strict standard of proof, especially with regard to the causal link between the violation of the obligation to guarantee this free movement and the damage claimed by the applicant.[305] This can further limit the expected effectiveness of free movement-related claims before the court.

A further – and rather novel – issue area for which an interest in implementing regionally integrated rules can be a motivational factor for applicants before the court is investment law. The ECOWAS Supplementary Act on Investments that entered into force in 2009 provides regional rules on investment protection. This is in line with further developments towards integrated investment rules such as in the context of the Pan-African Investment Code (2017). Observers have noted 'an appetite both to develop and to harmonize investment law in the continent'.[306] However, certain aspects limit the motivation of potential applicants to engage with the court in the investment context. First, the court is likely to be perceived as having only limited expertise in investment matters. The ECOWAS Court is not set up primarily as an investment court; its judges are not required to have experience or expertise in investment law;

[302] J Ukaigwe, *ECOWAS Law* (Springer 2016) 302.

[303] Alter, Helfer and McAllister (n 4) 773–74.

[304] ibid 738. See also LR Helfer, 'Subregional courts in Africa: Litigating the hybrid right to free movement of persons' (2018) 18 *International Journal of Constitutional Law* 235, 237. In terms of tariffs, ECOWAS has focused on the external dimension with the entry into force of the Common External Tariff in 2015. A unitary currency is envisioned but not realised yet.

[305] eg, *Sunday Charles Ugwuaba v Senegal*, 28 June 2019, ECW/CCJ/JUD/25/19, 24–26.

[306] Happold (n 27) 513.

and the court does not have an established jurisprudential body in investment law. Second, recognition and enforcement are not ensured because the decisions of the ECOWAS Court do not fall within the scope of the New York Convention on the Recognition and Enforcement of Foreign Arbitral Awards.[307]

Domestic courts can engage with the ECOWAS Court via preliminary references. They can be motivated to do so by the following aspects. First, domestic courts could be interested in shaping the interpretation of regional integration law by suggesting *their* reading of a regional integration law provision when phrasing preliminary references, hoping for this reading to be adopted by the ECOWAS Court. However, the limited role of ECOWAS regional integration law in practice makes it less likely that domestic courts perceive this potential influence as a benefit. Second, domestic courts could have a strategic interest in outmanoeuvring their own domestic apex courts based on regional integration law arguments that they bring to the ECOWAS Court via preliminary reference. While this motivation has been observed in the EU law context,[308] domestic courts in the ECOWAS region seem not to have discovered this potential benefit of the preliminary reference procedure yet. So far, the motivation of these courts is thus still low.

In contrast, the Commission as an ECOWAS institution which represents the interests of the Community (rather than of the individual member states) has an intrinsic motivation in regional integration and in regional integration law being guarded effectively by the court. Article 19(4) of the ECOWAS Treaty as amended by Supplementary Protocol A/SP.1/06/06 stipulates that the Commission 'shall exercise its powers to ensure the smooth functioning of the Community and protect the overall interest of the Community'. The Commission is the 'Principal Officer of the Community and the Chief Executive Officer of the Commission' (Article 19(1)).

Despite this functional motivation for regional integration, the specific motivation of the Commission to bring cases to the court is however limited by various aspects. These include the relatively weaker institutional position of the Commission in relation to the Authority of Heads of State and Government which is the main ECOWAS institution. As an illustration, until recently, the website of the Commission stated that 'the ECOWAS Commission defers to the authority of the Heads of State and Government whose decisions are supremely binding'. Due to this power structure and the fact that the Commission depends on cooperation with this institution, the Commission might consider it counterproductive for its overall work to risk alienating member states by bringing cases against them to the court. What is more, there are substantial challenges to the implementation of a common market that, as the Commission might consider, require addressing on a political level before involving the court. The motivational setting is, therefore, at the current stage of regional integration, rather low, however with the potential to increase if the factual situation as to economic integration improves.

[307] Pointing to this issue, Happold and Radovic (n 10) 114.

[308] eg JHH Weiler, 'The Transformation of Europe' (1991) 100 *Yale Law Journal* 2403, 2426; JA Mayoral, 'Judicial Empowerment Expanded: Political Determinants of National Courts' Cooperation with the CJEU' (2019) 25 *European Law Journal* 374.

ii. Opportunity

Jurisdiction

The jurisdiction conferred to the court by the ECOWAS legal framework provides a broad opportunity for potential applicants to engage with the court in regional integration law matters. According to Article 9 of the Protocol as amended in 2005, the court has jurisdiction for the 'interpretation and application' of the Treaty, Conventions and Protocols of the community as well as any legal acts adopted by ECOWAS (paras (a) and (b)); over the legality of legal instruments adopted by ECOWAS (c); and over infringements of the member states of the Treaty, Conventions and Protocols as well as legal instruments adopted by ECOWAS (d). This is a wide-ranging jurisdiction over regional integration matters. In particular, compared with the less explicit wording of the 1991 Protocol which merely used the terms 'interpretation and application', the court's competence to decide on the legality of acts and violations by member states is clearly stated.

What the court has not been given explicitly by the Protocol is jurisdiction over investment disputes based on the ECOWAS Supplementary Act on Investments. However, Article 9(6) of the Protocol confers jurisdiction on the court in 'any matter provided for in an agreement where the parties provide that the Court shall settle disputes arising from the agreement'. This provision arguably constitutes a basis for the court's jurisdiction in investment disputes under the Supplementary Act on Investments.[309]

Access to the Court

The access rules of the 1991 Protocol only allowed member states and the ECOWAS Authority to bring regional integration law-related matters to the court. Such matters included disputes 'between the Member States or between one or more Member States and the Institutions of the Community on the interpretation or application of the provisions of the Treaty'. This access opportunity for states and institutions has been somewhat broadened by the 2005 Protocol. Under this framework, member states have access to the court according to Article 10(a) and (b) in actions 'brought for failure of a Member state to fulfil an obligation' and in 'proceedings for the determination of the legality of an action in relation to any community text'. Both for infringement and annulment procedures, member states have access without further requirements (in contrast to individuals and corporate bodies – see below). Article 10(a) and (b) also stipulate that certain ECOWAS institutions can bring infringement and annulment procedures to the court: the Commission (former Executive Secretary) for both procedures and the Council of Ministers for the annulment procedure.

For domestic courts, the opportunity structure to engage with the ECOWAS Court in regional integration law matters is ambivalent. On the one hand, Article 10(f) of the Protocol creates the opportunity for them to engage with the ECOWAS Court via

[309] Happold and Radovic (n 10) 105 et seq.

preliminary references. This provision allows a court to refer 'on its own or at the request of any of the parties to the action' a question of interpretation of regional integration law to the ECOWAS Court. On the other hand, the very limited direct applicability of regional integration law in domestic legal orders undermines this opportunity. While the ECOWAS Treaty did initially not address this question, the Protocol A/SP.1/06/06 explicitly provided in the amended Article 9(3) and (4) of the Treaty that two kinds of legal acts of the community – supplementary acts and regulations – are directly applicable in the member states. But the Supplementary Act A/SA.3/01/10 revised this Article again, deleting the reference to direct applicability for supplementary acts so that, according to the wording of Article 9, only regulations among the various regional integration law acts (which include supplementary acts, regulations, directives, decisions, recommendations and opinions – Article 9(1) of the Treaty) are considered by the Treaty to be directly applicable. The direct applicability of the Treaty and the Protocols is not addressed. Therefore, only regulations can be applied by domestic courts and give rise to interpretive questions that might result in preliminary references.[310] And, although the ECOWAS Court has in the *Pinheiro* decision of 2012 addressed direct applicability in an obiter dictum (see also section III.C), it has not established direct applicability as a principle of ECOWAS law.[311] Moreover, the domestic law perspective on direct applicability is, for many member states, still more restrictive. As noted above, many member states that take a dualist approach to the relationship between regional integration law and domestic law have not given legal effect to regional integration law in their legal systems.[312] From the perspective of domestic law, regional integration law thus does not have the status of applicable law under domestic (constitutional) standards. This makes it unlikely that domestic courts would consider regional integration law as relevant for the cases that come before them, which in turn reduces the opportunity for addressing the ECOWAS Court via preliminary reference. In fact, domestic courts have not used preliminary references as a way to engage with the ECOWAS Court.[313]

For private actors, there is limited opportunity to engage with the court which has however somewhat broadened over time. Under the 1991 Protocol, private actors had no direct access to the court at all. The only possibility would have been for them to have a member state instituting proceedings on their behalf according to Article 9 of the 1991 Protocol. The court also did not create any access by way of interpretation when an occasion arose in the *Afolabi* case of 2004. Its decision confirmed that indirect access via member states was the only way for claims of individuals to reach the court.[314] Under the 2005 amended Protocol, private actors still cannot file cases for

[310] The issue of direct applicability is not convincingly presented in much of the ECOWAS literature which does not take the consecutive amendments of Article 9 of the Treaty into account, see eg, P Obiri-Korang, 'ECOWAS Law-making Regime: Translating Community Acts into National Laws of Member States' (2021) 11 *Legon Journal of International Affairs and Diplomacy* 1; ES Nwauche, 'Enforcing ECOWAS Law in West African National Courts' (2011) 55 *Journal of African Law* 181; Ukaigwe (n 302) 211 et seq.

[311] *Kemi Pinheiro v Ghana*, 6 July 2012, ECW/CCJ/JUD/11112, para 50.

[312] Ukaigwe (n 302) 214 et seq.

[313] ibid 224.

[314] *Olajide Afolabi v Nigeria*, 27 April 2004, ECW/CCJ/JUD/01/04.

infringement or annulment under Article 10(a) and (b). They have not been attributed a role in the general enforcement of regional integration law.

However, according to Article 10(c) of the Protocol, both individuals and corporate bodies can sue *the ECOWAS institutions* for a violation of their rights. The court has shaped this access rule in two ways. On the one hand, it has interpreted this provision broadly, allowing these applicants to instigate annulment procedures. Although the wording of Article 10(c) only speaks about the 'determination' of whether a community act violates the rights of an individual or corporate body, the court seems to allow these actors to request not only a declaration of such a violation but an annulment by the court.[315] On the other hand, the court has adopted the *Plaumann* jurisprudence of the CJEU,[316] restricting the standing to situations in which applicants can demonstrate that the contested act concerns them 'directly and personally'.[317] The court demands that the 'individual holder of such right, in the sense required by [Article 10 (c)], is the person whose interest is directly and immediately affected by the act or inaction that is being contested'.[318] This approach contains a more restrictive requirement than the one for which the wording of Article 10(c) of the Protocol provides.[319]

As regards claims *against states*, the legal framework does not provide direct access of individuals or corporations to the ECOWAS Court. When individual applicants attempted to bring regional integration law claims against member states, the court stated that

> contrary to other situations in which individuals are allowed direct access to the Court ... the Protocol on the Court does not empower individuals with the locus standi to sue a Member State for violation of its obligations enshrined in Community texts. According to Article 10(a), only a Member State or the ECOWAS Commission has access to the Court to compel a Member State to fulfill an obligation.[320]

However, private actors can address the ECOWAS Court in an indirect manner. They can, at least de jure, file cases before the domestic judiciary and submit to these courts that they should request a preliminary ruling at the ECOWAS Court. However, so far, actors have not taken this path. The limited direct applicability of regional integration law (see above) is relevant here as well.

Private actors have at least for some claims against member states obtained access to the court. The court has enabled this access by considering the free movement of goods and services under its human rights jurisdiction. In its case *Ugwuaba v Senegal* of 2019, the court interpreted the right to free movement, which most

[315] *Odafe Oserada v ECOWAS Council of Ministers*, 16 May 2008, ECW/CCJ/JUD/01/08, para 29; *Oluwatosin Rinu Adewale v ECOWAS Council of Ministers and Others*, 16 May 2012, ECW/CCJ/JUD/07/12, para 45.

[316] CJEU, Case 25-62, *Plaumann v Commission*, 15 July 1963, ECLI:EU:C:1963:17.

[317] *Odafe Oserada v ECOWAS Council of Ministers*, 16 May 2008, ECW/CCJ/JUD/01/08, para 34; *Oluwatosin Rinu Adewale v ECOWAS Council of Ministers and Others*, 16 May 2012, ECW/CCJ/JUD/07/12, para 45.

[318] *Oluwatosin Rinu Adewale v ECOWAS Council of Ministers and Others*, 16 May 2012, ECW/CCJ/JUD/07/12, para 45.

[319] See also Wiater (n 106) 324 et seq.

[320] *Kemi Pinheiro v Ghana*, 6 July 2012, ECW/CCJ/JUD/11112, para 48.

human rights courts and bodies understand as movement of persons only, in a broad manner, including not only the free movement of persons but also of goods and services.[321] The economic freedom 'free movement of goods and services' is thus attributed a human rights character in the ECOWAS context. In addition, the court addresses the – so constructed – human rights dimension of this freedom together with the regional integration law legal basis such as Articles 3 and 59 of the ECOWAS Revised Treaty as well as the Protocol A/P.1/5/79 on Free Movement of Persons, Residence and Establishment.[322] These provisions include the abolition of customs and non-tariff barriers among member states and they stipulate that 'Citizens of the Community shall have the right of entry, residence and establishment' in the member states. Through the gateway of the constructed human rights nature of a case, the court thus creates access for private actors to argue regional integration law claims.

This is an approach that the court did not take in its earlier jurisprudence. In its case *Pinheiro v Ghana* of 2012, the court distinguished between human rights and other individual rights granted to community citizens in the regional integration context.[323] The latter included, according to this jurisprudence, for example the right under Article 1 of the Protocol on Free Movement of Persons, Residence and Establishment, that is

> the right granted to a citizen who is national of the Member State to settle or establish in another Member State other than his State of origin, and to have access to economic activities, and in particular companies, under the same conditions as defined by the legislation of the host Member State for its own nationals.

The court stated that under the rules governing access of private actors to the court, these community rights which are not human rights cannot be invoked.

Given the overlap between the human right to free movement and the internal market right to free movement under the Protocol, the *Pinheiro* jurisprudence had created a situation in which access to the court 'depends on whether private litigants frame their complaints as human rights violations rather than breaches of subregional free movement rules – even if the facts underlying those complaints are identical'.[324] Accordingly, other free movement cases have been decided on a human rights basis only.[325] It may be added that this differentiation does not only matter for the access to the court but also for the legal assessment in substance as only free movement as a human right would subject restrictions to a necessity and proportionality test – while the common market rules on free movement are less restrictive for member states.[326]

[321] *Sunday Charles Ugwuaba v Senegal*, 28 June 2019, ECW/CCJ/JUD/25/19.
[322] ibid 21.
[323] eg, *Kemi Pinheiro v Ghana*, 6 July 2012, ECW/CCJ/JUD/11/12.
[324] Helfer (n 304) 251.
[325] eg, *Falana and Another v Benin and Others*, 24 January 2012, ECW/CCJ/JUD/02/12; *Baldé and Others v Senegal*, 22 February 2013, ECW/CCJ/JUG/04/13.
[326] On this issue, Helfer (n 304) 242.

Social Opportunity Structure

Especially for applicants that perceive themselves as a group such as member states and domestic courts regarding preliminary reference procedures, the social opportunity structure in the ECOWAS context is unfavourable. The tendency to conform with the behaviour of the (majority of) other group members is a factor that plays out against engaging with the court as applicants.[327] When domestic judges observe that their colleagues within their own member state as well as in other member states do not engage with the court via preliminary reference, this makes it likely that they perceive this as the social norm that in turn triggers behavioural conformity. As a result, the perceived social norm created by the behaviour of group members rather limits the opportunity for domestic courts. The same can be said about the behaviour of member states as applicants: the fact that the group members do not bring cases to the court creates a (perceived) social norm that also makes it less likely that a member state deviates from this norm. Group effects thus create an unfavourable opportunity structure for these actors to engage with the court as applicants.

iii. Constraints

A lack of knowledge among potential applicants about regional integration law and the ways to engage with the ECOWAS Court is a major constraint for actors in regional integration law matters. This concerns both potential private applicants and domestic courts with regard to preliminary references. While the awareness of the human rights jurisdiction of the court has been increasing due to a growing number of human rights cases which are also publicised in the media, this is not the case for the regional integration law jurisdiction. Cases in this area are still rare and so is the media attention. A lack of knowledge thus remains a considerable constraint.

Furthermore, financial constraints are relevant for individuals as potential applicants, similarly to what has been said on such constraints in the human rights context. This is also the case because the court seems to be less applicant-friendly in its costs decisions for certain regional integration law matters in which it ordered the unsuccessful applicant to bear the costs (rather than each party bearing their own costs as the court mostly decides for unsuccessful human rights claims).[328]

As to using *indirect* access via domestic courts as a way to engage with the ECOWAS Court, private actors face a further constraint: the perceived competing direct access to the ECOWAS Court based on its competence in human rights matters. Private actors prefer to construct their legal claims as human rights issues to be able to access the ECOWAS Court directly rather than using the indirect way. In this regard, the different jurisdictions of the ECOWAS Court create competing authority relationships. Given that different procedural frameworks apply to the regional integration law jurisdiction and the human rights jurisdiction, actors will

[327] On conformity as group effect, see ch 2.

[328] eg, *Sunday Charles Ugwuaba v Senegal*, 28 June 2019, ECW/CCJ/JUD/25/19, 26; *Odafe Oserada v ECOWAS Council of Ministers*, 16 May 2008, ECW/CCJ/JUD/01/08.

be constrained by the more favourable framework to the detriment of the less favourable one. Various aspects make the indirect access less attractive, including the longer duration of proceedings and the lack of trust of private actors in the domestic judicial system: 'national courts in West Africa are perceived (rightly or wrongly) as relatively weaker arms of government'.[329] The fact that to access the ECOWAS Court indirectly via preliminary references, applicants would need to engage with, and rely on, domestic courts, thus presents a major disadvantage as compared with the direct access based on the court's human rights jurisdiction.

In contrast to private actors and domestic courts, member states and ECOWAS institutions as potential applicants do not face the above intrinsic and extrinsic constraints. Their ability to engage with the court is thus broad.

iv. Assessment of MOC Factors

For member states, motivation is at the lowest level among the MOC factors which makes it the determining factor (see Figure 4.8). Both opportunity and unconstrained ability are rather high. States face virtually no constraints, and they have broad access in infringement and annulment procedures, yet their overall opportunity can be reduced to some extent by unfavourable group effects. In contrast, their motivation is moderate to low. Their potential motivation stems from procedural and substantive values while state interests in regional integration matters are low.

For private actors, motivation is limited to those actors who actually engage in cross-border activities. Given the existing deficits in realising the internal market, there are far fewer such actors as a further implemented regional integration would provide for. Yet for the private actors concerned, the many trade barriers provide ample grounds to bring regional integration law cases to the court – a motivation that is however reduced by effectiveness considerations. The motivation for the specific area of investment law is further lowered by the court's lack of expertise in investment law and the low effectiveness expectation with regard to enforcing such decisions domestically. Further, the opportunity for private actors is moderate. While they do not have general access to infringement and annulment procedures, they can bring claims for violations of their rights by ECOWAS institutions – and if successful, the decision will have an effect akin to the annulment procedure. In contrast, private actors only have indirect access to the court for claims against member states, with the exception of freedom of movement cases for which the court has constructed an accessory direct access. Finally, constraints for private actors are high. This includes a lack of awareness of the regional integration law jurisdiction of the court and financial considerations as well as, with regard to the indirect access via domestic courts, the competing direct access in human rights matters. In sum and compared with the moderate motivation and opportunity, the low ability to engage with the court that results from these constraints makes the lack of ability the determining MOC factor for the behaviour of private actors (see Figure 4.8).

[329] Ebobrah, 'Dual Mandate' (n 45) 101.

For the relevant ECOWAS institutions that could bring cases to the court, the motivation is, at the current stage of economic integration and given the institutional power relations within ECOWAS, rather low. Considering their inherent interest in regional integration, the motivation might however increase in the future if either the economic or institutional setting changes. In contrast, their opportunity to access the court is broad as they can instigate both infringement and annulment procedures. Constraints are virtually non-existent so that their ability to engage with the court is high. This makes motivation the determining factor for whether ECOWAS institutions bring cases to the court in regional integration law matters (see Figure 4.8).

For domestic courts, the motivation to address the court via preliminary references is low. Domestic courts would however have a broad opportunity under procedural regional integration law to engage with the court in preliminary references. But this opportunity is reduced by the issue of direct applicability of regional integration law which, from a regional integration law perspective, is limited to one kind of legal act, ie, regulations, and under domestic law, because of the restrictive stance that many domestic legal orders take on direct applicability of regional integration law in a dualist setting. Moreover, unfavourable group effects reduce the opportunity for these courts for preliminary references. Although domestic courts face no noteworthy constraints, both their motivation and opportunity are low, making it unlikely that they will bring cases to the court (see Figure 4.8).

Figure 4.8 Comparison of the MOC setting for applicants before the ECOWAS Court in relation to the regional integration jurisdiction

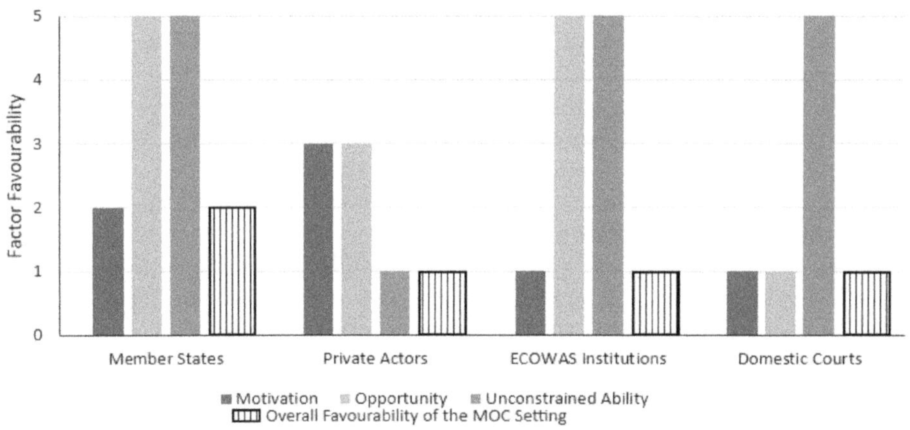

B. MOC Factors for Respondents

This section first analyses the MOC factors for the acceptance of the authority of the ECOWAS Court in regional integration law matters (III.B.i) before turning to the MOC factors for state actors' pushback against the court (III.B.ii).

i. MOC Factors for Acceptance of the Court's Authority

a. Motivation

For governmental actors, the value-correspondence regarding procedural values such as judicial independence and the rule of law and substantive values of regional integration has already been alluded to in the previous section. Accordingly, the motivating potential of value-correspondence for these actors is moderate. Further, the interest-based motivation is weaker than in the human rights context. As mentioned above, governmental actors only have a limited interest in implementing an internal market in the ECOWAS region. And they are not likely to be considerably motivated by reputational interests and dispute resolution. At least for disputes with individual private actors, the visibility of such disputes in public discourse is limited so that neither the reputational stakes for the state nor the interest in resolving this dispute is very high. In addition, regional integration law matters have only little relevance for the self-image of the state, a fact that also reduces the reputational stakes.

In contrast, the motivation of governmental actors can be boosted by a certain 'spill-over effect' from the human rights context on the behavioural level. The inertia and status quo bias that foster, over time, the acceptance of the court's authority in the growing number of human rights cases (see section II.B) can lead governmental actors to accepting the authority of the court in general, including in regional integration law cases. In addition, these actors' interest in consistent behaviour can constitute a motivational factor. If they accept the court's authority in human rights cases, it is consistent behaviour to also do so in regional integration cases.

For domestic courts as respondent actors, general rule of law considerations can be expected to have a motivational impact. While domestic courts are not likely to hold strong values or interests relating to regional integration, they have some interest in upholding a general culture of compliance with judicial decisions. As they wish for their own decisions to be implemented, hindering the implementation of decisions by the ECOWAS Court would potentially undermine the rule of law perception in their respective state. This consideration can motivate them to accept the authority of the court in the regional integration context.

For ECOWAS institutions in the role of respondents, the motivation to accept the authority of the court stems from the rationale of their functions. These institutions have been put in place to construct the legal framework for regional integration. Implementing the decisions of the court relating to regional integration law speaks to this rationale. Yet, at the same time, it is possible for ECOWAS institutions to consider themselves as interpreter and guardian of regional integration law, which would lead them to competing with the court in this respect. So far, there are, however, no indications that the motivation of the ECOWAS institutions is significantly affected by such a perception.[330]

[330] It however occurred in a recent case that the Commission did not appear in a procedure before the ECOWAS Court, yet in a case relating to the conflict with Mali – *Zadi Philipe v Authority of Heads of State and Government and Another*, 14 February 2025, ECW/CCJ/JUD/05/25.

b. Opportunity

The opportunity for ECOWAS institutions as respondents to accept the authority in regional integration law cases is broad de jure but narrow de facto. According to the legal framework of the Protocol, ECOWAS institutions can be respondents in these cases. Article 9(1) of the Protocol stipulates that the court has jurisdiction over the community and its officials and matters relating to the interpretation, application and legality of the legal instruments adopted by ECOWAS such as regulations, directives and decisions. In addition, Article 10(c) of the Protocol stipulates that an 'act or inaction of a Community official' can be the object of cases that private actors bring to the court. All forms of legal regulations by ECOWAS institutions as well as other acts or inactions if they violate a right of a private actor can be the object of proceedings before the court. De jure, the opportunity for ECOWAS institutions to accept the authority of the court is thus broad. However, de facto, the low number of cases that have reached the court in regional integration law matters reduces the de jure opportunity for institutional actors.

For state actors, the above caveat as to the rather narrow de facto opportunity applies as well. Few cases create little opportunity to accept the court's authority. But already de jure, state actors face only a moderate opportunity structure. A favourable element is the broad jurisdiction and formal standing as respondent. Articles 9(1)(d) and 10(a) provide that member states can be respondents before the court in cases relating to the failure to fulfil an obligation under the treaty, conventions and protocols, regulations, directives or decisions of ECOWAS. However, the opportunity for executive and judicial actors is reduced because of the limited direct applicability of ECOWAS law (see above). The lack of an enforcement framework according to Article 24 of the Protocol has, until recently, further limited the de jure opportunity.

c. Constraints

As in the human rights context, there are virtually no intrinsic constraints for governmental actors. They do not lack awareness of the court or its decisions. So far, there have also not been any financial constraints, in particular because state respondents were not ordered to pay excessively high damages. In addition, and in contrast to the human rights context, there are no extrinsic constraints for governmental actors due to competing authority relationships with other courts. Similarly, ECOWAS institutions do not encounter such intrinsic or extrinsic constraints. In contrast, there can be extrinsic constraints for domestic courts in some of the member states. As in the human rights context, there is a risk that governments in member states with lower rule of law standards exercise pressure on domestic courts that hinders them from implementing ECOWAS Court decisions.

d. Assessment

For governmental actors as respondents, the ability to accept the authority of the ECOWAS Court in regional integration law matters is high, given the low constraints. In contrast, motivation and opportunity are only at a moderate level, which makes them the determining factors (see Figure 4.9). In particular, their interest in an effective regional integration is not very pronounced. But their motivation can be augmented by spill-over effects from the human rights context, based on the interest in consistent behaviour as well as behavioural effects such as inertia. Opportunity is primarily limited by the lack of direct applicability of ECOWAS law and, until recently, the lack of an enforcement structure for ECOWAS Court decisions. Strategies to improve the MOC setting for governmental actors would thus need to address both motivation and opportunity factors.

Similarly, for ECOWAS institutions as respondents, the opportunity (de jure) to accept the authority of the court is rather broad, despite the de facto caveats, as is the unconstraint ability. In contrast to state actors, the motivation is likely to be higher, so that the overall MOC setting for these respondents is favourable (see Figure 4.9). Institutional actors are thus likely to accept the authority of the court to a considerable extent.

As to domestic courts, the MOC assessment is less favourable (see Figure 4.9). For many of these courts, the opportunity is, given the lack of applicability of regional integration law within the domestic legal orders, moderate at best. The motivation for these actors is moderate. There are also some potential constraints. For domestic courts, all MOC factors are thus on a comparable level so that no single determining factor exists.

Figure 4.9 Comparison of the MOC setting for respondents before the ECOWAS Court in relation to the regional integration jurisdiction

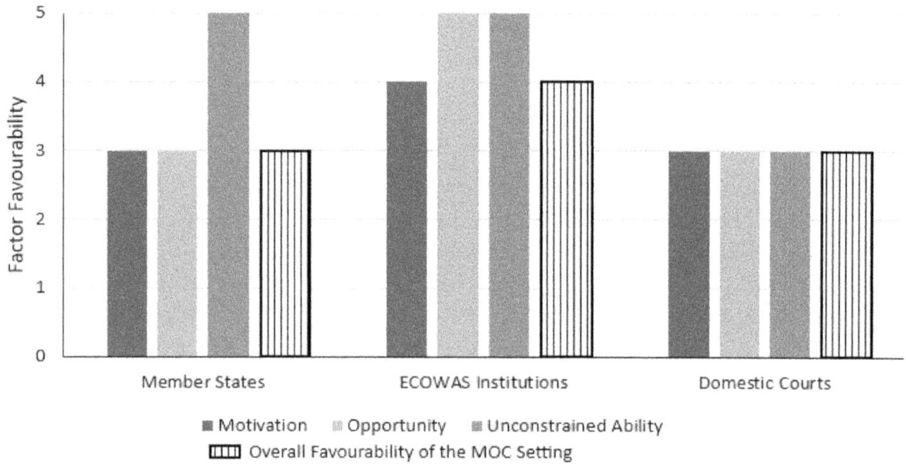

ii. MOC Factors for Pushback

After having analysed the MOC setting that determines whether respondents accept the authority of the ECOWAS Court in the first place, I turn, in this section, to the MOC factors for pushback. Unlike in the human rights context, there have been no instances of pushback specifically against the authority of the court in relation to regional integration law. I thus outline below the factors that play a role in whether actors might push back against the court in the future.

a. Motivation for Pushback

As in the human rights context, state actors with low value-correspondence regarding rule of law values are more likely to be motivated for pushback against the ECOWAS Court than other state actors (see section II.B). The value-based motivation for pushback is thus moderate for some state actors and low for others. Further, the impact of interest-based motivational factors for states to push back is less prominent than in the human rights context. To start with, unlike in the human rights context, in which the broad individual access has motivated various forms of pushback, the access rules for applicants in regional integration law cases do not constitute such a motivational factor. An exception to that is the court's recent freedom of movement jurisprudence in the *Ugwuaba* case which broadens the individual access. This jurisprudence could potentially provide motivation for pushback. Not only does it enable individuals to bring regional integration law against states to the court, a possibility not envisaged by the Protocol, but it is also based on an at the least unusual if not legally questionable understanding of the free movement of goods and services as a human right.

A further aspect that influences the motivation for pushback is whether states expect pushback to be effective behaviour. Although there have not been any pushback attempts directed specifically at the regional integration law jurisdiction of the court, the unsuccessful pushback attempts in the human rights context might lower the expected effectiveness of pushback regarding regional integration law. Given that states have witnessed the failure of the 2009 structural resistance as well as the norm contestation regarding the non-exhaustion of domestic remedies, they are likely to consider this experience when assessing future pushback attempts in the regional integration law context. However, for pushback in the form of non-compliance, states will presume such behaviour to be effective as it is currently the case in human rights cases.

b. Opportunity for Pushback

For pushback in the form of non-compliance, what has been said for non-compliance with human rights decisions of the court is relevant here as well. In particular, an opportunity not to implement the court's decisions results from the requirement under Article 24 of the Protocol to establish an enforcement structure and designate a competent authority. The fact that most member states had, for a long time, not done so affected the implementation of regional integration law decisions in these member states. And, again parallel to the human rights context, the only limited direct applicability of ECOWAS law provides an opportunity for the non-implementation of ECOWAS Court decisions.

As to other forms of pushback, the social opportunity structure creates less opportunity for pushback than in the human rights context. As there have been no occurrences of structural resistance or norm contestation in regional integration law cases before the court, states cannot model their behaviour according to a specific content of prior pushback. However, there can be a 'cross-jurisdictional' effect that influences the opportunity structure. States can perceive the pushback in the human rights context as inspiration for potential pushback in the regional integration law context. And the existence of pushback against the human rights jurisdiction also means that the conformity pull in the regional integration context is less strong than if there had been no pushback at all.

Further, the low number of cases that the court has decided so far in regional integration law matters reduces the opportunity for pushback that relates to acts of the court such as the interpretation of a potentially contestable norm or decisions with which state actors could not comply. It also reduces the de facto opportunity for pushback on a procedural level such as non-appearance before the court or preliminary objections.

c. Constraints against Pushback

As to constraints that reduce the ability of states to push back against the court in regional integration law matters, one aspect merits particular highlighting. Compared with the human rights context, in which the failed pushback attempts have shown how much supporting actors can constrain the behaviour of resisting states, the number of supporting actors is likely to be much smaller in the regional integration law context. The NGOs that supported the court in the 2009 structural resistance, are not likely to embrace the same role if a state were to attack the regional integration law jurisdiction of the court. The aims and values that these NGOs pursue do not concern this jurisdiction directly. Similarly, one would expect much less support from international actors. Regional integration among ECOWAS states is not of as much (if at all) interest to them as is the level of human rights protection.

Consequently, if the court were to face structural resistance or even backlash in the regional integration law context, the group of potential supporting actors would consist mainly of the ECOWAS institutions and other member states. For the former, regional integration is their raison d'être so that the support from this side would likely be considerable. In sum however, the constraints against pushback are, due to the less diverse group of supporting actors, more moderate than in the human rights context.

d. Assessment

Among the MOC factors for pushback, motivation seems to be the determining factor in the regional integration law context (see Figure 4.10). For most state actors, motivation for pushback is rather low, with the exception perhaps of states with low value-correspondence as to judicial independence and rule of law. In contrast, the opportunity for pushback is at least on a moderate level for pushback in the form of non-compliance. For other forms of pushback, the opportunity is less pronounced, also due to the low number of regional integration law cases before the court. Constraints against pushback are low to moderate, leading to a moderate to high ability for actors to engage in such behaviour. So far, low motivation appears as the factor that has kept actors from pushing back against the regional integration law jurisdiction and jurisprudence of the court. In the future, if the motivation increases, specifically if the court expends its *Ugwuaba* jurisprudence on free movement of goods and services, the determining factor might however change.

Figure 4.10 MOC setting for pushback against the ECOWAS Court in relation to the regional integration jurisdiction

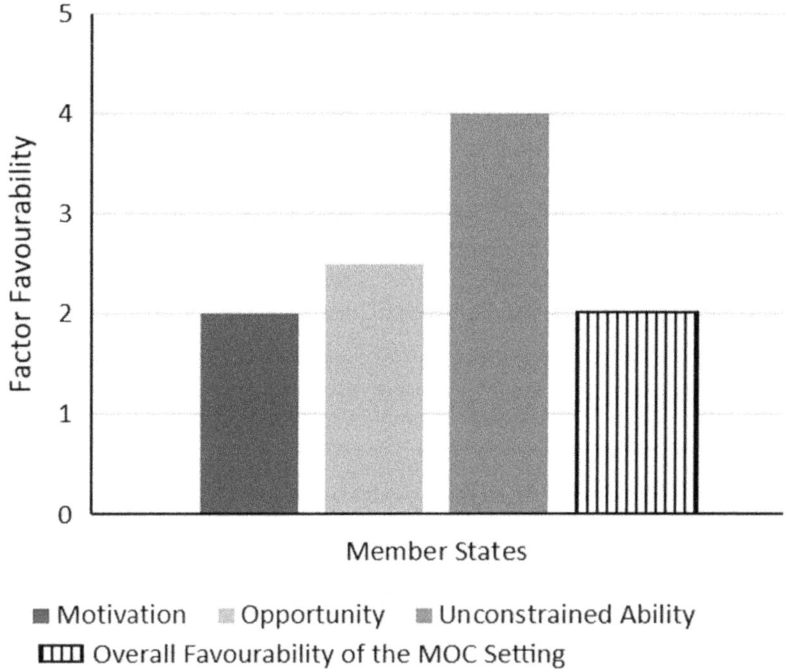

C. Assessing the Court's Strategies to Influence MOC

Due to the few cases relating to regional integration law, the court has had considerably fewer possibilities than in the human rights context to shape the MOC setting of (potential) applicants and respondents through judicial techniques. What is more, the limited engagement of potential applicants with the court in regional integration law cases led the court to focus its strategies on improving the MOC factors for applicants while strategies relating to respondents are rarer.

i. Influencing the MOC Factors for the Acceptance of the Court's Authority

a. Enhancing Motivation to Accept Authority

As a strategy to enhance the value-based motivation of actors to accept its authority, the court has emphasised the values underlying the regional integration dimension of

ECOWAS. Stressing the importance of free movement for regional integration, the court stated that

> one of the fundamental ideas of ECOWAS … is that of 'a borderless ECOWAS', wherefore the management of immigration and borders is deeply rooted in the overall raison d'être of the Community. The ECOWAS, anchored in the 1975 Treaty, [has] the aim of progressively strengthening cooperation between Member States through the free movement of goods, capital and people.[331]

With such statements, the court reminds its audiences of the value of regional integration and especially the common market freedoms. It addresses both aspects of value-correspondence. On the one hand, this statement communicates to potential applicants that the court is there to implement this value and on the other, actors – in particular member states – are reminded that they support this value in principle and should act accordingly.

Regarding domestic courts in their applicant role, the court has encouraged these actors to use the preliminary reference procedure. It has done so, inter alia, by stressing regional integration as a value. In a decision that engaged with the relationship between domestic courts and the ECOWAS Court, it stated:

> For clarification on the interpretation of the content and norms required for application of the community texts, National Courts may refer the matter to the Court of Justice … It is in this relationship between the Community Court of Justice and National Courts that the Regional integration law will strive and be appropriated by the entire Community.[332]

With respect to further value-related strategies of the court, the court's techniques to enhance value-correspondence regarding judicial independence are relevant here as well. As outlined in section II, the court does not only stress its own independence but also aims at enhancing, through its decision-making, the independence of the domestic judiciary in the member states. For private actors as potential applicants as well as for domestic courts in the context of potential preliminary references, stressing and enhancing this value-correspondence can motivate these actors to engage with the court.

In a similar manner, the strategies outlined in section II that aim at reducing the compliance deficit impact the effectiveness expectation of potential applicants. Although these strategies tackle compliance with human rights decisions, they can be beneficial for the compliance expectation regarding ECOWAS Court decisions in general. If successful, these strategies induce actors to also expect decisions in regional integration law matters to be regularly implemented. Bringing such cases to the court then would appear as effective behaviour.

b. Enhancing Opportunity to Accept Authority

Regarding the opportunity for private actors to bring regional integration law cases to the court, the court has adopted a cautious approach, akin to the one initially

[331] *Sunday Charles Ugwuaba v Senegal*, 28 June 2019, ECW/CCJ/JUD/25/19, 18.
[332] *Kemi Pinheiro v Ghana*, 6 July 2012, ECW/CCJ/JUD/11112, paras 50–52.

taken in the human rights context. To start with, in the *Afolabi* case in which the individual applicant invoked a violation of the regional integration law rules on the free movement of persons and goods, the court refrained from creating an individual access in regional integration law matters by way of jurisprudential development. As outlined, the court kept its interpretation close to the 'ordinary meaning' of Article 9 of the 1991 Protocol which it considered to be 'clear'[333] and rejected the suggestion to adopt an 'activist' interpretation.[334] In this instance, the court thus did not broaden the opportunity for private applicants by judicial means. However, the court made, on a policy level, a strong statement as to the regional integration law dimension of the case. It noted that the wording leads to this interpretation even though 'the Applicant from his application is raising a serious claim touching on free movement and free movement of goods and his rights to challenge an infringement upon his person'.[335]

In its subsequent jurisprudence, the court continued to engage with the access issue on a policy level. It gave guidance to applicants as to how to go about cases in which such direct access does not exist. In an obiter dictum, the court stated:

> [T]he Community citizen who has been a victim of an alleged violation of a right enshrined in the Community Protocol by a Member State is provided with only two alternatives: a) To ask his own State to take on the defence of his interest and file an action before the Community Court of Justice against the defaulting Member State, pursuant to Article 10(a); Or b) To decide to file an action against the defaulting Member State, addressing the domestic jurisdiction of the State where the alleged violation of his rights has occurred.[336]

Instead of broadening the access opportunity, the court pointed the relevant actors towards alternative ways of enforcing regional integration law claims.

In its more recent jurisprudence regarding freedom of movement, the court takes a more activist approach. By allowing regional integration law claims to be brought before the court in combination with human rights claims, using the human rights jurisdiction as a gateway for private-actor access in regional integration law cases (see the *Ugwuaba* case discussed above), the court broadens the opportunity for these actors to engage with the court in a key area of common market law.

Further, the court has provided a basis for increasing the opportunity structure for domestic courts in relation to the direct applicability of regional integration law. In the *Pinheiro* decision of 2012, it makes a statement in which it seems to assume that the entire body of regional integration law is directly applicable in the domestic legal orders. It states that 'national courts are also Community courts as they have competence to apply the Regional integration law which forms part of the internal order'.[337] The court does not expand on this claim and does not refer to, or engage with, Article 9 of the Treaty that only attributes direct applicability to regulations but not to other acts of secondary law or to the Treaty itself.[338] It also does not

[333] *Olajide Afolabi v Nigeria*, 27 April 2004, ECW/CCJ/JUD/01/04, paras 49, 54.
[334] ibid.
[335] ibid para 55.
[336] *Kemi Pinheiro v Ghana*, 6 July 2012, ECW/CCJ/JUD/11112, para 49.
[337] ibid para 50.
[338] Article 9 of the Treaty as amended by Protocol A/SP.1/06/06 and Supplementary Act A/SA.3/01/10.

frame direct applicability as a fundamental principle or refer to this approach in the subsequent jurisprudence. However, this statement could serve as a basis for future jurisprudence of the ECOWAS Court on the matter. And this statement creates an opportunity for any domestic court that would be inclined to take an activist stance and to apply directly other ECOWAS legal acts in their respective legal order as well. It would enable domestic courts to apply regional integration law independently of whether their respective member state has formally incorporated ECOWAS law into its legal order. For private actors, such direct applicability would broaden the opportunity for indirect access to the court via preliminary reference.

c. Limiting Constraints

In view of the existing constraints, the court's strategies to enhance knowledge about the court among its potential audiences are relevant here as well. When enhancing this awareness in the human rights context, the court flags its existence as a judicial forum in the ECOWAS region to potential applicants in all its jurisdictional areas. This can be seen as a first step to overcoming knowledge-related constraints for potential applicants in regional integration law cases. However, the court would also need to aim at enhancing knowledge about regional integration law jurisdiction, and potentially about the content of regional integration law in the first place. This seems to be at least a part of the court's 'sensitisation mission', for example when it engages with chambers of commerce or other trading associations.[339]

Moreover, it also bears mentioning here again that, in contrast to the human rights context, the court has not adopted a specific strategy to reduce financial constraints for private applicants. Its costs decisions are less applicant-friendly than for human rights applicants. Nonetheless, measures such as temporary seats which are closer to the applicants or online hearings (see above) can also reduce financial constraints for applicants in regional integration law matters.

Finally, the court has adopted, in its *Ugwuaba* jurisprudence, a strategy to address the competing authority relationships resulting from the parallel human rights and regional integration law jurisdictions in cases relating to free movement within the common market. It has de facto combined both strands of jurisdiction, removing the competition between these jurisdictions for this context. Based on this approach, private applicants can combine human rights and regional integration law claims.

d. Assessing the Court's Strategies

With its strategies to improve the MOC setting for member states and private actors, the court indeed targets the respective factors that, according to the MOC framework, determine the behaviour of these actors. For member states, motivation is at the lowest level so that the attempts of the court to stress value-correspondence and thus to increase a value-based motivation to engage with the court are well oriented.

[339] eg, 2009–2011 Annual Report of the ECOWAS Court, 66: courtecowas.org/media-and-publications/publications/annual-reports/.

For private actors, the most impactful factors differ. First, regarding these actors' claims against ECOWAS institutions, their ability is, due to significant constraints, at the lowest level among the MOC factors. The court's strategies to reduce constraints relating to a lack of awareness of the court and its jurisdiction thus target the right factors in this regard. Second, for claims of private actors against member states, the opportunity is however at the lowest level, so that these ability-related strategies alone cannot increase the likelihood of private actors addressing the court with such claims. Here, the opportunity-related strategy of the court in the *Ugwuaba* jurisprudence targets the decisive factor. Third, regarding indirect access of private actors via preliminary references by domestic courts, opportunity is at the lowest level among the MOC factors. Where the court has addressed the direct applicability issue, this opportunity-related strategy is well oriented.

In contrast, the ECOWAS Court's strategies are not expected to visibly influence the behaviour of domestic judicial actors relating to preliminary references. Although the attempt to argue for direct applicability and thus to enhance the opportunity of these courts for preliminary references addresses one of the determining factors for the courts' behaviour in this regard, increasing the opportunity is not sufficient to yield behavioural results. The courts' motivation for preliminary references is on an equally low level which means that both these factors – opportunity and motivation – would need to be targeted.

Concerning the MOC setting for ECOWAS institutions, the court does not seem to adopt any strategies to enhance the motivation of these actors, although motivation is for them the determining factor. In particular, the court has not attempted to forge an alliance with the Commission, akin to what the CJEU has done in relation to the EU Commission.[340] Yet, unlike in the EU context, such alliances that primarily seek to enhance the expected effectiveness when the Commission brings cases to the court, would arguably not be as impactful in the ECOWAS context. Rather than effectiveness concerns, the aspects that reduce the motivation of the Commission are linked to power relations among institutions and the incomplete stage of economic integration. These issues are difficult for the court to address in its strategies.

ii. Influencing the MOC Factors for Pushback

As there have been no instances of pushback specifically targeted at the regional integration law jurisdiction of the court, the (potential) court strategies aim at avoiding pushback rather than having to manage it. The strategies of the court focus on reducing motivation for pushback.

To start with, as outlined above, the court did not adopt any activist judicial strategy to broaden the access of individuals in the *Afolabi* case. Instead, it adopted its discursive strategy that avoided motivation for pushback – a pushback that would have concerned both the human rights and the regional integration law jurisdiction of the court. Similarly, the court has been very cautious as to adopting – or rather

[340] On this strategic partnership, T Björnsson and Y Shany, 'The Court of Justice of the European Union' in Shany (ed), *Assessing the Effectiveness of International Courts* (n 8) 277, 289.

not adopting – an activist stance regarding direct applicability. Although the court claimed in the *Pinheiro* case that regional integration law is directly applicable, it did not phrase this as a fundamental principle or stress the implications of such an approach in the subsequent jurisprudence. Given that the court has, in its *Afolabi* decision explicitly distanced itself from taking an activist approach, it is very likely that, here again, the court's reluctance as to making a strong claim for direct applicability (or even further principles of supranational law) is such a strategy to avoid pushback.

Further, the court's jurisprudential techniques include other pushback-reducing strategies that are present in its human rights jurisprudence. The incremental approach that the court took when expanding its approach to certain procedural questions in human rights cases is also characteristic of how the court developed its approach to individual access in freedom of movement cases. Incrementally broadening individual access, the more restrictive approach of the *Pinheiro* case is followed by a more expansive approach in the *Ugwuaba* case. What is more, the court also balanced out the broader approach in *Ugwuaba* with its strict take on the standard of proof in this case. This strategy limits the motivation for pushback because it decreases the perceived risk for member states that the freedom of movement jurisprudence will noticeably impact them.

As to deference techniques such as using notions like margin of appreciation or subsidiarity, the court has not referred to these notions in its regional integration law jurisprudence. However, after having recently started to adopt deference framing in its human rights jurisprudence, it is likely that there will be a spill-over effect from the human rights context. This would aim to keep the motivation for pushback at a low level. Similarly, the monitoring mechanism that the court has recently created by including the reporting obligations of member states can potentially be applied to the regional integration law context as well. This would contribute to reducing motivation for non-compliance in these cases. Finally, the above-mentioned policy strategy of the court to address the issue relating to Article 24 of the Protocol reduced opportunity for non-compliance in regional integration law cases.

In conclusion, the strategies of the court to avoid pushback are predominantly aimed at the decisive MOC factor. As the low motivation of member states has kept actors from pushing back against the regional integration law jurisdiction of the court, keeping this motivation low is an effective strategy. However, as there is only little motivation to begin with, the court would have some leeway. Here, the challenge for the court might be to determine how best to balance pushback avoidance on the one hand and advancing its jurisprudence on the other.

5

The European Court of Human Rights

I. INTRODUCTION TO THE EUROPEAN COURT OF HUMAN RIGHTS

The European Court of Human Rights (ECtHR) is the judicial body of the Council of Europe, a regional organisation established in 1949 with the aim 'to achieve a greater unity between its members for the purpose of safeguarding and realising the ideals and principles which are their common heritage and facilitating their economic and social progress' (Article 1 Statute Council of Europe). These ideals and principles consist of human rights protection, democracy and the rule of law. At the time of the creation of the Council of Europe, the member states were Belgium, Denmark, France, Ireland, Italy, Luxembourg, the Netherlands, Norway, Sweden and the United Kingdom; Greece and Türkiye joined in 1949; Germany, Iceland and Austria in the 1960s; Cyprus, Switzerland and Malta in the 1970s; Portugal, Spain and Liechtenstein in the 1970s; and San Marino and Finland in the 1980s. After the end of the Cold War, the enlargement towards Eastern Europe included: Hungary, Poland, Bulgaria, Estonia, Lithuania, Slovenia, the Czech Republic, Slovakia, Romania, Andorra, Latvia, Albania, Moldova, Ukraine, 'the former Yugoslav Republic of Macedonia', Croatia, Georgia in the 1990s; Armenia and Azerbaijan, Bosnia and Herzegovina, Serbia, Monaco and Montenegro in the 2000s; Russia joined in 1998 and its membership ended in 2022.

The ECtHR was established in 1959 to ensure the observance of the European Convention on Human Rights (ECHR) adopted in 1950. The Convention allows for two types of applications: individual applications from 'any person, non-governmental organisation or group of individuals' (Article 25 ECHR 1950; Article 34 ECHR) and interstate complaints by member states (Article 24 ECHR 1950; Article 33 ECHR). The present chapter accordingly distinguishes between these two groups of applicants. In addition to the court's contentious jurisdiction, the court can give advisory opinions since this competence was created by Protocol No 2 in 1970 and broadened by Protocol No 16. However, the present chapter will only refer to the contentious jurisdiction of the court.

The court was originally designed as part of a two-tier structure composed of the European Commission of Human Rights (Commission) and the ECtHR which were both mandated with ensuring the observance of the Convention (Article 19 ECHR 1950). Applications were primarily addressed by the Commission and could, as a second step, be referred to the court. The court was non-permanent in nature, and the number of judges has been equal to that of the Council of Europe member states (Article 38 ECHR 1950). The jurisdiction of the court was optional and required a declaration by member states as to the acceptance of this jurisdiction (Article 46 ECHR 1950).

The two-tier structure and the Commission were abolished by Protocol No 11 to the Convention that entered into force in 1998. Since then, the ECtHR is, as a permanent court with compulsory jurisdiction, solely responsible for the judicial human rights review within the Council of Europe. The Convention has established a monitoring system in which the Committee of Ministers is in charge of supervising the execution of the court's judgments (Article 64 ECHR 1950; Article 46(2) ECHR).

The court had delivered around 27,000 judgments on the merits by the end of 2024.[1] This output is however not evenly distributed over time. In its entire pre-Protocol No 11 period until 31 October 1998, the court had delivered 837 judgments. After an initial phase in the 1960s and 1970s when cases rarely reached the court, the number of yearly cases have increased continuously since the late 1970s. From 1975 to 1979, the court delivered 17 judgments on the merits: 40 from 1980 to 1985; 292 from 1990 to 1994; and 530 from 1995 to 1998.[2] In the post-Protocol No 11 period, the number of applications, and so to some extent also judgments, increased exponentially. After a peak in 2009 with 1,625 judgments, the average number of judgments for 2020 to 2024 was about 1,000 judgments per year.[3] Most of the ECtHR's decisions concern individual complaints. However, interstate complaints do exist – and their numbers have been increasing during the last two decades. Since the establishment of the Strasbourg system, there have been over 30 interstate complaints.[4] The distribution of cases among respondent states is also diverse. For the period from 1959 until 2020, around 40 per cent of the judgments concerned three member states: Türkiye, Russia and Italy. In recent years, Ukraine and Romania have joined the ranks of these 'high-count' states.[5]

The court has gone through various phases of development during its almost seven decades of existence.[6] The authority relationship between the court and the relevant actors has changed during these phases. The court's membership has grown from a moderately big group of member states and their respective state and non-state actors to a group of currently 46 member states that is large for a regional court. The court's reach among level 1 and level 2 actors is thus broad. The court's jurisdiction relates to the Convention and the protocols. The subject matter of this jurisdiction has been stable over time and expanded only marginally, unlike some other regional courts whose jurisdiction has increased significantly. Further, as the following sections highlight in more detail, certain actors such as domestic courts were initially reluctant to engage in discursive references and implement the jurisprudence of the court. In later years, these actors' acceptance of the ECtHR's authority has become broader. In contrast, while the compliance rates of the ECtHR are rather high, observers have

[1] See the court's statistics: www.echr.coe.int/annual-reports#.

[2] For these statistics, see E Bates, *The Evolution of the European Convention on Human Rights: From Its Inception to the Creation of a Permanent Court of Human Rights* (OUP 2010) 142.

[3] See court statistics:www.echr.coe.int/annual-reports#.

[4] A list of these complaints is available at: www.echr.coe.int/inter-state-applications.

[5] See, eg, the statistics for 2021: www.echr.coe.int/annual-reports.

[6] See for an overview of these phases, Bates, *Evolution* (n 2); A Nussberger, *The European Court of Human Rights* (OUP 2020) 1–37.

pointed to more frequent instances of partial compliance in recent years among governmental and legislative actors (see below).[7] This indicates a certain decrease in the authority relationship with these actors. In sum however, the authority relationship between the court and the relevant level 1 and level 2 actors has expanded over time. And despite some pushback during the last two decades, the court's authority has been robust. The following sections map out this development of the authority relationship in more detail.

As chapter four has done for the ECOWAS Court, the present chapter analyses both the MOC factors determining whether and to what extent level 1 and level 2 actors accept the authority of the court and the MOC factors determining the actual and potential pushback. Section II engages with the MOC factors for (potential) applicants before section III turns to the respondents and the factors for their initial acceptance of the court's authority (III.A) as well as the factors for pushback (III.B). To provide a comparison over time, the present chapter outlines how the MOC factors have changed during the court's existence. In light of this analysis, section IV assesses the strategies that the ECtHR has adopted to improve the MOC factor for the acceptance of its authority and for avoiding and managing pushback.

II. MOC FACTORS FOR (POTENTIAL) APPLICANTS

This section outlines the MOC factors that influence the behaviour of (potential) applicants before the court: motivation (II.A), opportunity (II.B) and constraints (II.C). The section addresses the MOC factors for different groups of (potential) applicants including individual applicants and NGOs as well as governmental actors in their role as applicant in inter-state complaints. Based on this assessment, I analyse which of the factors primarily determines whether (potential) applicants accept the authority of the ECtHR (II.D).

A. Motivation

Values

At the outset, human rights protection as a *substantive value* can motivate applicants to accept the authority of the court. It has motivated both individuals and NGOs to engage with the ECtHR as formal applicants and, for the latter, also via amicus curiae briefs. For NGOs, this value is a predominant motivating factor because substantive values are particularly important motivational factors for actors that are not individually affected by human rights violations. This includes NGOs with a general human rights agenda and those with an issue-specific purpose. Value-correspondence between these NGOs and the court has generally

[7] On this increasing trend, see also Report of the High-Level Reflection Group of the Council of Europe, October 2022, para 20: rm.coe.int/report-of-the-high-level-reflection-group-of-the-council-of-europe-/1680a85cf1.

been high due to the shared human rights mandate. Among the many NGOs that have addressed the court in third-party interventions, a large number of them have a general human rights mandate such as Human Rights Watch or Amnesty International. A second important intervening group of NGOs has a mandate that concerns the rights of specific individuals such as migrants, LGBT+ persons, Roma, children, prisoners and persons with disabilities.[8] Other NGOs focus on specific rights or regions of the Council of Europe space.[9]

Substantive values have also constituted a motivating factor in interstate complaints. In the early practice of state applicants, certain member states have been strongly motivated by human rights and democracy as values in the European region. They have filed interstate complaints that involved human rights violations in other member states and in which they were not directly affected. Denmark, Norway, Sweden and the Netherlands brought a case against Greece in relation to human rights violations that occurred in the context of the military coup in Greece in 1967.[10] Similarly, France, Norway, Denmark, Sweden and the Netherlands did so against Türkiye in relation to the Turkish military coup in 1980.[11] These cases were however decided by the Commission, the court was not involved. Yet these cases illustrate that states wished to uphold a common value standard, even if their immediate interests were not at stake. This has also been described as a public interest or collective enforcement role of interstate complaints,[12] or as states exercising a 'policing' function.[13] The Commission even saw this role and the related motivation as a necessary element of an interstate complaint, asserting that interstate applications should 'not be regarded as exercising a right of action for the purpose of enforcing its own rights, but rather as bringing before the Commission an alleged violation of the public order of Europe'.[14] Several interstate complaints, although not exclusively value-driven, combined the motivation to uphold values with the specific interests of the applicant. For example, in *Denmark v Turkey* introduced in 1997, the Danish government addressed both the treatment of a Danish citizen by the Turkish authorities and a 'widespread practice' in this country that was claimed to amount to torture or inhumane treatment.[15]

[8] Examples of such cases include the European Roma Rights Centre: *D.H. and Others v The Czech Republic*, 13 November 2007, App no 57325/00; the Mental Disability Advocacy Center – *Stanev v Bulgaria*, 17 January 2012, App no 36760/06. On this aspect also Nussberger, *The European Court of Human Rights* (n 6) 70.

[9] For an overview of these categories, see L Van den Eynde, 'An Empirical Look at the Amicus Curiae Practice of Human Rights NGOs before the European Court of Human Rights' (2013) 31 *Netherlands Quarterly of Human Rights* 271, 284.

[10] *Denmark, Norway, Sweden & the Netherlands v Greece (I)*, App nos 3321/67 to 3323/67 and 3344/67. See also *Denmark, Norway, Sweden & the Netherlands v Greece (II)*, App no 4448/70.

[11] *Denmark, France, Norway, Sweden & the Netherlands v Turkey*, App nos 9940/82 to 9944/82.

[12] On the collective enforcement function, I Risini, *The Inter-state Application under the European Convention on Human Rights: Between Collective Enforcement of Human Rights and International Dispute Settlement* (Brill Nijhoff 2018).

[13] Using this term, R Spano, in 'Inter-State Cases Under The European Convention On Human Rights – Experiences And Current Challenges', Proceedings of the Conference organised under the aegis of the German Presidency of the Committee of Ministers (Berlin, 12–13 April 2021) 14: rm.coe.int/interstate-cases-under-the-echr/1680a5e82c.

[14] *Austria v Italy*, 11 January 1961, App no 788/60.

[15] *Denmark v Turkey*, Friendly Settlement Judgment, 5 April 2000.

In terms of *procedural values*, judicial independence is an important motivating value. Value-correspondence between individual applicants and NGOs and the ECtHR regarding judicial independence is rather high, despite some caveats.[16] The independence of the court is in general well developed. To start with, judges do not function as state representatives but 'sit on the court in their individual capacity' (Article 21(3) ECHR). This provision signals to applicants that the court is not designed as a state-biased institution. In its self-representation, the court stresses this aspect, stating that judges are independent of their country of origin and that they do not represent the state in respect of which they are elected.[17] And, enhancing the independence in relation not only to states but also other actors, judges are not allowed to engage with activities that would be incompatible with their independence and impartiality (Article 21(4) ECHR).[18] Moreover, the rules regarding the tenure of judges are currently rather favourable for judicial independence. Judges are elected for a nine-year non-renewable term (Article 23(1) ECHR) – a setting that reduces the incentives for states to influence judges while they are in office; and for judges to be influenced. In addition, judges are well protected against dismissal by member states as the possibility of dismissal lies exclusively in the hands of the other judges (Article 23(3) ECHR). Judges also enjoy immunities during the exercise of their functions (Article 51 ECHR in connection with Article 40 Statute Council of Europe).

However, there have been certain caveats to the de jure and de facto independence of the court. In the first place, the tenure of judges has changed several times from a nine-year renewable term in the pre-Protocol No 11 period[19] to a renewable six-year term introduced by Protocol No 11 which Protocol No 14 has again replaced with a non-renewable nine-year term. The shorter and/or renewable terms have been less conducive to independent behaviour than the longer non-renewable ones.[20] Further, it can be problematic with regard to de facto judicial independence that the selection procedure for judges before the ECtHR reflects a perceived state representation where each member state picks 'their' judge.[21] At the outset, this selection procedure allows state governments 'to select line-toeing and loyal rather than critical candidates'.[22]

[16] Generally on judicial independence regarding the ECtHR, A Follesdal, 'Independent yet accountable: Stress test lessons for the European Court of Human Rights' (2017) 24 *Maastricht Journal of European and Comparative Law* 484; E Voeten, 'The Impartiality of International Judges: Evidence from the European Court of Human Rights' (2008) 102 *American Political Science Review* 417; J Luther, 'Judicial Independence and Accountability in the Council of Europe and the European Court of Human Rights' (2019) 1 *European Yearbook of Constitutional Law* 197; D Zimmermann, *The Independence of International Court* (Nomos 2014) 425–511.

[17] See, eg, the information material provided by the court 'The ECHR in 50 questions' and 'Questions and Answers': www.echr.coe.int/documents/d/echr/50questions_eng; www.echr.coe.int/documents/d/echr/questions_answers_eng.

[18] Rule 4 of the Rules of Court specifies that judges must not 'engage in any political or administrative activity or any professional activity which is incompatible with their independence or impartiality'.

[19] Article 40(1) ECHR 1950 (with special rules for the initial group of judges).

[20] Ø Stiansen, '(Non)renewable Terms and Judicial Independence in the European Court of Human Rights' (2022) 84 *Journal of Politics* 992.

[21] Generally on the selection procedure of ECtHR judges and judicial independence, A Torres Pérez, 'Can Judicial Selection Secure Judicial Independence? Constraining State Governments in Selecting International Judges' in M Bobek (ed), *Selecting Europe's Judges: A Critical Review of the Appointment Procedures to the European Courts* (OUP 2015) 181.

[22] Nussberger, *The European Court of Human Rights* (n 6) 40.

To counterbalance the governments' political influence on the selection of judges, the selection procedure has been enriched in recent years by various 'safeguards',[23] thus enhancing the preconditions for impartial judicial decision-making. These safeguards include open calls for candidates, advisory expert panels and a stronger role for the Parliamentary Assembly of the Council of Europe.

When it comes to the judges' relationship with their nominating state, there is evidence of a national bias in favour of this state.[24] In this regard, the so-called national judge rule is impactful. Under Article 26(4) ECHR, judges are automatically part of all Chamber and Grand Chamber cases against their 'own' member state. Here, it has often been difficult for judges in this role to remain impartial, especially in highly political cases,[25] and empirical analysis has shown that these judges are more likely to vote for their governments than non-national judges.[26] Furthermore, the national judge sits both in the Chamber and in the Grand Chamber, thus reviewing their own decision (Article 26(5) ECHR). This constitutes an impartiality issue and a deviation from the principle of *nemo judex in causa sua*.[27]

Value-correspondence regarding judicial independence has a diverging motivational effect depending on the applicants. The motivational effect of this value is higher for applicants in member states with a deficient rule of law practice than for applicants in other member states. In states with a low judicial independence rating – currently Ukraine, Türkiye, Moldova, Bosnia and Herzegovina, Azerbaijan and Armenia (see Table 5.2) – the domestic judiciary is often 'of little use' to applicants in human rights cases.[28] Applicants from such member states are thus likely to use the ECtHR as an independent adjudicative forum.

In addition to judicial independence, other aspects of procedural fairness can motivate applicants to engage with the court to a lesser or greater extent. In particular, applicants can legitimately expect that fair trial standards that constitute a key aspect of the court's jurisprudence are also fulfilled in proceedings before the ECtHR. However, procedural fairness has not always been guaranteed to the best possible extent. A major issue in this regard is the length of proceedings before the ECtHR. Procedural fairness is concerned when, due to the court's strategy adopted since 2009 to prioritise 'the most important, serious and urgent cases',[29] the length of proceedings can differ significantly among cases. Applicants who do not agree with the prioritisation strategy are likely to perceive this practice as unfair.

[23] ibid 40.

[24] Voeten, 'The Impartiality of International Judges' (n 16).

[25] eg, Dissenting Opinion of the Russian Judge Anatoly Kovler in *Ilaşcu and Others v Moldova and Russia*, 8 July 2004, App no 48787/99: 'This case provides an example of a situation in which "human rights become a policy"'.

[26] Voeten, 'The Impartiality of International Judges' (n 16) 428.

[27] See on this issue also D Shelton, 'Performance of Regional Human Rights Courts' in T Squatrito, OR Young, A Føllesdal and G Ulfstein (eds), *The Performance of International Courts and Tribunals* (CUP 2018) 114, 123.

[28] I Cameron, 'The Court and the member states: procedural aspects' in A Føllesdal, B Peters and G Ulfstein (eds), *Constituting Europe: The European Court of Human Rights in a National, European and Global Context* (CUP 2013) 25, 40.

[29] The Court's Priority Policy: www.echr.coe.int/documents/priority_policy_eng.pdf. On this strategy, see also section IV.A.i.

Further, the measures undertaken by the court to manage the caseload and the backlog impact certain procedural fairness aspects. This includes the single-judge procedure introduced by Protocol No 14 in 2010 and the fact that the court was able to declare cases inadmissible without providing reasons to the applicants. In fact, between 2010 and 2017, applicants in a single-judge procedure did not receive any reasons when their case was dismissed. After applicants and NGOs criticised this practice, the court adjusted it somewhat but, still, only summary reasons are provided in this procedure.[30] Further, the pilot judgment procedure that the court created in its *Broniowski* decision of 2004 (see also below) affects the procedural fairness for applicants.[31] While the applicant in the actual pilot case has full access to the court including hearings and decision, the applicants in the other cases do not. Their cases are not heard before the court nor decided on an individual bases but rather transferred directly, if the pilot case was successful, for compliance monitoring to the Committee of Ministers. This procedure thus reflects the increasing dilemma between effectiveness and procedural fairness, between individual justice and targeting structural and severe human rights violations.[32] It reduces the value-correspondence as to procedural values between applicants and the court. In fact, this motivation-limiting effect can be significant, given that procedural justice is a strong motivational factor.[33]

Interests

Individual applicants before the ECtHR are first and foremost motivated by an interest in dispute resolution. The extent to which the envisaged dispute resolution motivates them to have the court settle their dispute is dependent on whether they expect such an application to be effective. In fact, effectiveness considerations have had a diverging motivational impact over time. When the court was established, the very restrictive practice of the Commission lowered the expected effectiveness of bringing cases to the court. In the 1950s and 1960s, the Commission declared the vast majority of cases inadmissible.[34] And the few admissible cases were rarely ever referred to the court. As a result, the initial motivation to use the Convention system was low: 'lawyers and activists generally saw little use in going to Strasbourg'.[35] The expected effectiveness only increased in the 1970s when the Commission changed its

[30] ECtHR Press Release of 1 June 2017, ECHR 180 (2017), 'Launch of new system for single judge decisions with more detailed reasoning': hudoc.echr.coe.int/app/conversion/pdf?library=ECHR&id=003-5735020-7285664&filename=Launch%20of%20new%20system%20for%20single%20judge%20decisions%20with%20more%20detailed%20reasoning.pdf.

[31] *Broniowski v Poland*, 22 June 2004, App no 31443/96.

[32] This tension already shaped the discussions leading up to Protocol No 14, see Bates, *Evolution* (n 2) 499.

[33] See ch 2 and the literature cited there on procedural justice and authority.

[34] As to the statistics, see eg, MR Madsen, 'The European Court of Human Rights – From the Cold War to the Brighton Declaration and Backlash' in KJ Alter, LR Helfer and MR Madsen (eds), *International Court Authority* (OUP 2018) 243, 249: 'Of the 713 individual complaints received by the Commission from July of 1955 to March of 1960, 710 were rejected. During the next decade only fifty-four cases were declared admissible out of some 3,600 applications'.

[35] Madsen, 'The European Court of Human Rights' (n 34) 250.

practice. At this time, the Commission did not only declare more cases admissible but also started to refer cases to the court more frequently.[36]

In the 1990s, the increasing length of procedures before the Commission and court began again to reduce the expected effectiveness for applicants. The Commission was overburdened by the amount of applications as the number of admissible cases had increased ten-to-twenty-fold in comparison to the 1970s.[37] In 1994, there was a backlog of 2,672 pending cases before the Commission.[38] This led to an overall length of proceedings before obtaining a court judgment of five years on average.[39] As a reaction to this issue, the institutional reform brought about by Protocol No 11 aimed at making the Convention system more effective and 'shorten the length of Strasbourg proceedings'.[40]

In the post-Protocol No 11 period, expected effectiveness has also not been a stable factor. On the one hand, the fact that individuals obtained direct access to the court and the gatekeeping effect of the Commission disappeared, the expected effectiveness initially increased as to the pre-Protocol No 11 situation. On the other hand, the extreme increase in applications and the resulting backlog at the court leading to lengthy proceedings reduced the effectiveness expectation again. During the peak of the backlog around 2010, more than 150,000 cases were pending, and procedures took at times more than 10 years.[41]

After the backlog peak, the effectiveness expectation has increased somewhat due to certain case managing measures undertaken by the court (see also section IV). This includes, first, a case prioritisation policy the court has adopted since 2009. The court classifies cases into seven categories according to their urgency, their importance as to questions of general interest, and their seriousness.[42] According to the nature of their case, applicants thus can expect the court to render a decision more or less speedily. Second, the pilot judgment procedure created in the *Broniowski* decision of 2004 had increased the expected effectiveness for cases that are caused by structural deficiencies in the respondent state and that are part of a large number of similar cases related to these deficiencies.[43] When the court uses this procedure, it suggests general measures for the respondent state to take and thus to remedy the structural malfunctioning for all individuals concerned.[44] Further, Protocol No 14 has increased the efficiency of the court and thus the effectiveness expectation of

[36] Bates, *Evolution* (n 2) 284.

[37] ibid 453.

[38] Explanatory Report to Protocol No 11, para 21: rm.coe.int/16800cb5e9.

[39] Bates, *Evolution* (n 2) 453.

[40] Explanatory Report to Protocol No 11, para 23: rm.coe.int/16800cb5e9.

[41] A Nussberger, 'From High Hopes to Scepticism? Human Rights Protection and Rule of Law in Europe in an Ever More Hostile Environment' in H Krieger, G Nolte and A Zimmermann (eds), *The International Rule of Law: Rise or Decline?* (OUP 2019) 150, 167.

[42] See priority policy overview document: www.echr.coe.int/documents/priority_policy_eng.pdf. For the amended strategy, see press release ECHR 092 (2021), 17/03/2021.

[43] *Broniowski v Poland*, 22 June 2004, App no 31443/96. Subsequent pilot judgments include, eg: *Hutten-Czapska v Poland*, 19 June 2006, App no 35014/97; *Rumpf v Germany*, 2 September 2010, App no 46344/06; *Vassilios Athanasiou and Others v Greece*, 21 December 2010, App no 50973/08; *Dimitrov and Hamanov v Bulgaria*, 10 May 2011, App nos 48059/06 and 2708/09.

[44] On this procedure, see M Fyrnys, 'Expanding Competences by Judicial Lawmaking: The Pilot Judgment Procedure of the European Court of Human Rights' (2011) 12 *German Law Journal* 1231.

applicants. In particular, novel features such as the single judge procedure have enhanced the court's efficiency.[45]

It should be noted that the effectiveness diverges depending on whether the application is directed against a 'high-count' member state or other member state.[46] In the former case, the expected length of procedure is greater. In addition, the court has occasionally struck out all applications relating to a 'high-count' state regarding a structural issue that, according to the court, requires a political solution. For example, in *Burmych v Ukraine* – a follow-up complaint concerning a pilot judgment obliging the state to create a domestic remedy against non-execution of judgments – the court decided not to engage in substance with the more than 12,000 repetitive cases on this issue and to refer the matter to the Committee of Ministers instead.[47] When no political solution is found to such a structural problem, this means for applicants that approaching the court remains ineffective.

In the post-Protocol No 11 period, effectiveness expectations regarding admissibility were rather low. Although *in*admissibility rates varied considerably among member states, the overall rate was about 90 per cent.[48] When Protocol No 14 introduced the single judge procedure, this opened the door for the court to increase inadmissibility rates even more.[49]

In contrast, once a case has passed the admissibility threshold, effectiveness expectations have been mostly high. After an initial phase in the 1960s in which the court took a conservative approach, the success rates increased with the landmark judgments of the 1970s. In this period, the court developed several of its key lines of jurisprudence such as the living instrument doctrine and the notion of effectiveness, requiring human rights protection not to be 'theoretical and illusory, but practical and effective'.[50] This indicated to potential applicants that the court was a forum in which human rights litigation had good chances of success. Currently, the court finds at least one violation in between 80 and 90 per cent of cases decided in substance per year. For the entire period from 1959 to 2022, the overall average was around 85 per cent.[51] Success rates differ however depending on the respondent state. Comparatively low rates have been recorded, for example, for Denmark with 34 per cent or Sweden with 39 per cent as compared with mid-range states such as Germany with 56 per cent or the United Kingdom with 58 per cent and top-range states such as Ukraine with 98 per cent or Azerbaijan with 96 per cent.[52]

A further aspect that determines whether applicants expect addressing the court to be effective behaviour concerns compliance with ECtHR judgments. In this regard, expected effectiveness is generally high. Most observers evaluate compliance as

[45] On the procedural reforms of Protocol No 14, Cameron (n 28).
[46] Nussberger, 'From High Hopes to Scepticism?' (n 41) 167.
[47] *Urmych and Others v Ukraine*, 12 October 2017, App nos 46852/13 et al.
[48] Cameron (n 28) 37.
[49] ibid.
[50] *Tyrer v United Kingdom*, 25 April 1978, App no 5856/72; Airey v Ireland, 9 October 1979, App no 6289/73, para 24.
[51] See the ECtHR statistics for 1959–2022: www.echr.coe.int/Documents/Stats_violation_1959_2022_ENG.pdf.
[52] ibid.

high,[53] also in comparison to other international courts, although it is difficult to assess this rate in a detailed manner.[54] Applicants who base their expectations on past compliance rates are thus likely to evaluate positively the effectiveness of litigating admissible cases before the court.

In addition to past compliance rates, the effectiveness expectation is influenced by the compliance monitoring structure. ECtHR decisions benefit from one of the most effective monitoring structures of regional and other international courts.[55] The Committee of Ministers is explicitly charged, under Article 46(2) ECHR, with supervising the implementation of the court's decisions. The Committee of Ministers has both political tools and formal sanctions at its disposal to enforce court decisions. According to Article 8 of the Statute of the Council of Europe, sanctions could go as far as excluding the non-compliant member states from the Council of Europe. However, in practice, the Committee of Ministers rarely applies intrusive sanctions and rather puts more emphasis on political solutions.[56]

To complement the role of the Committee of Ministers, the group of monitoring agents has been extended in recent years. First, the court itself is part of the monitoring structure. According to Article 46(3) and (4) ECHR as amended by Protocol No 11, the Committee of Ministers can refer to the court questions of interpretations that might arise during the implementation process; and it can refer the question whether a respondent state has violated its obligation under Article 46(1) ECHR by refusing to abide by a final judgment. The latter procedure was used for the first time in 2017 (and decided in 2019) in *Mammadov v Azerbaijan* regarding the imprisonment of a political actor.[57] In addition, applicants can approach the court with follow-up applications when they consider that the respondent state has not taken the initial decision of the ECHR into account.[58] Second, various NGOs and other (domestic) human rights actors contribute to the compliance monitoring. They provide reports about the human rights situation in the respondent states. Further, the actors 'can criticize the action plan, the lack of interim measures to give effect to the judgment, and the delay in implementation; they can even provide recommendations for legislation and guidelines to meet the terms of the judgment'.[59]

A further aspect that influences the expected effectiveness is the burden and standard of proof applied by the court. The court considers the burden of proof to

[53] eg, S Dotan, *Reputation and Judicial Tactics: A Theory of National and International Courts* (CUP 2014) 214; Nussberger, *The European Court of Human Rights* (n 6) 181; Bates, *Evolution* (n 2) 493; D Harris, M O'Boyle and C Warbrick, *Law of the European Convention on Human Rights*, 2nd edn (OUP, 2009) 878.

[54] On the difficulty of assessing the compliance rate, Dotan (n 53) 218 (fn 9). For a possible evaluation framework, see eg, D Anagnostou and A Mungiu-Pippidi, 'Domestic Implementation of Human Rights Judgments in Europe: Legal Infrastructure and Government Effectiveness Matter' (2014) 25 *European Journal of International Law* 205.

[55] Nussberger, 'From High Hopes to Scepticism?' (n 41) 169.

[56] ibid.

[57] *Ilgar Mammadov v Azerbaijan (Art 46 (4))*, 29 May 2019, App no 15172/13.

[58] eg, *Bochan v Ukraine (No 2)*, 5 February 2015, App no 22251/08; *Verein gegen Tierfabriken Schweiz (VgT) v Switzerland (No 2)*, 30 June 2009, App no 32772/02.

[59] Nussberger, *The European Court of Human Rights* (n 6) 158.

lie, at least in general, with the party that makes a factual allegation. However, the court acknowledges that the specificity and power imbalance of various human rights situations requires for it to adjust this rule. Often, only the respondent state but not the applicant has access to relevant information and documents to corroborate the applicant's allegation. In such cases, the court has decided that

> where the events in issue lie within the exclusive knowledge of the authorities, as in the case of persons under their control in custody, strong presumptions of fact will arise in respect of injuries and death occurring during that detention. The burden of proof in such a case may be regarded as resting on the authorities to provide a satisfactory and convincing explanation.[60]

More generally, the court has recognised an obligation on the respondent state to 'furnish all necessary facilities to make possible a proper and effective examination of applications'.[61] This obligation is now enshrined in Article 38 ECHR. If the respondent state does not submit the necessary information, this may 'give rise to the drawing of inferences as to the well-foundedness of the applicant's allegations'.[62]

Finally, the remedies that applicants can obtain by addressing the court are an important factor for the expected effectiveness of such proceedings. In its early jurisprudence, the court took a restrictive approach. Although it granted damages for pecuniary losses, it limited itself, beyond such damages, to declaratory decisions as to the substantive violation. In particular, the court interpreted the possibility to 'afford just satisfaction to the injured party' (Article 50 ECHR 1950, now Article 41 ECHR) narrowly and mostly considered the declaratory judgment to be sufficient in this regard. The court decided that it 'will not make consequential orders or declaratory statements' as to the means whereby a member state has to comply with a judgment.[63] It thus did not indicate specific measures to be taken by the respondent state to remedy a violation. For example, it considered that 'the sanctions available to [the court] do not include the power to direct one of those States to institute criminal or disciplinary proceedings in accordance with its domestic law'.[64] This restrictive approach to remedies limited the expected effectiveness for applicants considerably.[65]

More recently, the court has however broadened its approach to remedies.[66] It indicates to respondent states the specific measures to take in order to remedy the violation of the applicant's rights. This can include, inter alia, reopening criminal

[60] *El-Masri v the Former Yugoslav Republic of Macedonia*, 13 December 2012, App no 39630/09, para 152. See also *Merabishvili v Georgia*, 28 November 2017, App no 72508/13, para 311.

[61] *Tanrikulu v Turkey*, 8 July 1999, App no 23763/94, para 70; *Bazorkina v Russia*, 27 July 2006, App no 69481/01, para 170.

[62] *Bazorkina v Russia*, 27 July 2006, App no 69481/01, para 171.

[63] *Selçuk and Asker v Turkey*, 24 April 1998, App no 12/1997/796/998–999, para 125.

[64] *Ireland v United Kingdom*, 18 January 1978, App no 5310/71, para 187.

[65] See also the critique of this older jurisprudence by Judge Bonello, Partly Dissenting Opinion of Judge Bonello joined by Judge Maruste, *Nikolova v Bulgaria*, 25 March 1999, App no 31195/96.

[66] For an overview of the development, see P Leach, 'No longer offering fine mantras to a parched child? The European Court's developing approach to remedies' in Føllesdal, Peters and Ulfstein (eds), *Constituting Europe* (n 28) 142.

proceedings[67] or investigations to be undertaken by the respondent state.[68] Regarding the latter, the court has expanded this obligation to investigate so that it now includes not only criminal acts committed by state actors but also acts committed by private actors that touch upon the right to life.[69] Further, the court indicates general measures with which member states can remedy systemic human rights deficiencies in their domestic systems. Even before introducing the pilot judgment procedure, the court recommended to respondent states to solve a recurring issue before the court by adjusting its legislation. For example, in *Bottazzi v Italy*, one of the first cases with such an (at least implicit) recommendation, the court stressed that litigants have no domestic remedy against lengthy judicial proceedings and considers this to be part of a 'practice that is incompatible with the Convention'.[70] Beyond *recommending* specific or general measures, the court at times also *orders* the respondent state to remedy the violation in a prescribed manner. For example, it has ordered respondents to restitute property[71] and, after having initially only recommended the reopening of criminal proceedings, it has later also ordered such a reopening.[72]

Beyond dispute resolution, a further interest motivating individual applicants to bring cases to the court are strategic political interests. In the early years of the court, several cases had already related to politically sensitive contexts and court proceedings provided a forum for political actors. As an example, the first case before the court, the *Lawless* case of 1960/61, concerned the conflict in Northern Ireland. In this case, the respondent government feared that the case would 'give an individual the opportunity of using the proceedings as a means of propaganda against his own Government'.[73] This argument illustrates how such cases can be used by applicants in the domestic political discourse.

Further, for both individual applicants and NGOs, the strategic interest in fostering social change is a motivational interest. Bringing cases to the ECtHR is 'attractive to those who wish to see new rights recognized, or to raise standards of protection for established rights'.[74] In this context, the court is seen as a forum that is 'activated – systematically – by individuals seeking to change domestic law'.[75] This form of strategic litigation has always been a prominent part of the practice before the court. For example, among the landmark cases of the 1970s, the applicant in the *Airey* case concerning access to justice in matrimonial matters[76] did not only seek a remedy for

[67] eg, *Somogyi v Italy*, 18 May 2004, App no 67972/01, para 86; *Öcalan v Turkey*, 12 May 2005, App no 46221/99, para 210; *Popov v Russia*, 13 July 2006, App no 26853/04, para 263; *Pishchalnikov v Russia*, 24 September 2009, App no 7025/04, para 99.

[68] eg, *McCann and Others v The United Kingdom*, 27 September 1995, App no 18984/91, para 161.

[69] eg, *Anna Todorova v Bulgaria*, 24 May 2011, App no 23302/03, para 72.

[70] *Bottazzi v Italy*, 28 July 1999, App no 34884/97, para 22.

[71] eg, *Papamichalopoulos and Others v Greece*, 31 October 1995, App no 14556/89; *Dacia SRL v Moldova*, decision of 24 February 2009, App no 3052/04.

[72] *Maksimov v Azerbaijan*, 8 October 2009, App no 38228/05.

[73] *Lawless v Ireland (No 1)*, 14 November 1960, App no 332/57.

[74] H Keller and A Stone Sweet, 'Assessing the Impact of the ECHR on National Legal Systems' in H Keller and A Stone Sweet (eds), *A Europe of Rights: The Impact of the ECHR on National Legal Systems* (OUP 2008) 677, 707.

[75] H Keller and A Stone Sweet, 'The Reception of the ECHR in National Legal Orders' in Keller and Stone Sweet (eds), *A Europe of Rights* (n 74) 3, 13.

[76] *Airey v Ireland*, 9 October 1979, App no 6289/73.

her personal situation but had a broader agenda, arguing for an obligation on the respondent 'to protect her and other Irish citizens like her'.[77] Further, for NGOs, the interest in bringing about social change motivates them to submit amicus curiae briefs. In fact, NGOs intervene more frequently in Grand Chamber cases than in other cases.[78] This demonstrates the motivation of these actors to influence human rights protection on a wider scale.

A motivational factor that has been important, especially since the 1990s, is the interests of applicants in transitional justice.[79] This includes issues originating in the Second World War that applicants brought to the court after the end of the Cold War as well as more recent issues such as in the context of the dissolution of the former Yugoslavia.[80] As to the former, a prominent case is *Broniowski v Poland* in which the court was faced with a structural issue of transitional justice: thousands of persons were affected by expropriations in the context of the changed Polish border after the Second World War.[81] Of these persons, 20,000 filed an application before the ECtHR. A further large-scale case, the *Kurić v Slovenia* case, concerned transitional justice interests regarding the citizenship status of persons of the former Yugoslavia.[82] Due to being native from other parts of the former Yugoslavia other than Slovenia, more than 18,000 so-called 'erased' persons had lost their status as permanent residents after the dissolution of the former Yugoslavia and were treated as aliens with unregulated status in Slovenia. Other transitional justice cases operated at a smaller scale. For example, the applicant in *Kononov v Latvia* alleged 'that his conviction for war crimes as a result of his participation in a military expedition' during the Second World War violated Article 7 ECHR.[83] Moreover, the Chechnya conflict is an example that demonstrates that transitional justice considerations also motivate NGOs to bring such issues to the court.[84] In fact, there is a higher rate of NGO involvement in conflict and post-conflict situations with structural human rights violations as compared with other cases.[85] However, not all transitional justice matters that applicants brought to the court have been addressed by the latter in substance, thus limiting the expected effectiveness of such applications. This includes issues such as 'the Communist nationalizations of property in Czechoslovakia, Slovakia and Eastern Germany and the question of whether the Czech Republic after the fall of the

[77] Submission by applicant as quoted by Bates, *Evolution* (n 2) 342.

[78] Van den Eynde, 'An Empirical Look' (n 9) 280.

[79] See generally, A Buyse and M Hamilton (eds), *Transitional Jurisprudence and the European Convention on Human Rights: Justice, Politics and Rights* (CUP 2011); I Motoc and I Ziemele (eds), *The Impact of the ECHR on Democratic Change in Central and Eastern Europe* (CUP 2016).

[80] On transitional justice in the Yugoslavian context, CK Lamont, 'Confronting the consequences of authoritarianism and conflict: the ECHR and transition' in Buyse and Hamilton (eds), *Transitional Jurisprudence and the European Convention on Human Rights* (n 79) 81.

[81] *Broniowski v Poland*, 22 June 2004, App no 31443/96.

[82] *Kurić and Others v Slovenia*, 26 June 2012, App no 26828/06.

[83] *Kononov v Latvia*, 17 May 2010, App no 36376/04, para 3.

[84] F van der Vet, 'Transitional Justice in Chechnya: NGO Political Advocacy for Implementing Chechen Judgments of the European Court of Human Rights' (2013) 38 *Review of Central and East European Law* 363.

[85] HN Haddad, *The Hidden Hands of Justice: NGOs, Human Rights, and International Courts* (CUP 2018) 65–66.

Iron Curtain could restrict the restitution of nationalized goods to Czech nationals', which the court declared inadmissible.[86]

Finally, the interest in effective behaviour is an important motivational factor for NGOs in the context of third-party interventions. NGOs that have already intervened before the court, especially when it was in a way that they perceived as impactful, are more likely to consider such behaviour to be effective in a subsequent case as well. Indeed, most amicus curiae briefs by NGOs before the court stem from 'repeat players'.[87]

Turning to *interstate complaints*, there are several interests that motivate member states to file such complaints. To start with, judicial dispute resolution of interstate conflicts is an important interest. There is a trend towards states being motivated more prominently by their interest in dispute resolution than by substantive values as in earlier cases.[88] In recent years, state applicants have been motivated to file interstate complaints due to the rising number of more fundamental conflicts between certain member states.[89] Indeed, most interstate complaints currently pending before the court concern conflicts between Azerbaijan and Armenia, between Russia and Ukraine, and between Russia and Georgia.[90] These are conflicts that go beyond isolated human rights violations but are of a more far-reaching nature. In the past, several cases concerning similar broader conflicts include the Cyprus/Türkiye conflict as well as the Ireland/United Kingdom conflict.[91]

The expected effectiveness of interstate complaints is limited. To begin with, interstate procedures are very lengthy and are not prone to prompt adjudicative responses. The long procedures make it less likely that the court's decisions in such cases can contribute to finding an immediate solution for such conflicts. The impact of such cases on dispute resolution will often be only of an indirect nature: the fact that conflicts are translated into legal language and legal claims might at times contribute to mitigating a conflict. Further, fact-finding is often very complex in interstate cases, and the ECtHR is not equipped for that. In *Georgia v Russia (II)*, the court pointed to this issue stating that

> it is particularly difficult to establish the facts in the context of an inter-State case such as the present one, which concerns an armed conflict and its consequences, involving thousands of people and taking place over a significant period of time across a vast geographical area.[92]

A further aspect that limits the expected effectiveness of interstate complaints is the territorial nature of many of these disputes. Cases relating to territorial disputes and

[86] L Wildhaber, 'The European Court of Human Rights: The Past, The Present, The Future' (2007) 22 *American University International Law Review* 521, 528, referring, inter alia, to *Jan Malhous v Czech Republic* (decision as to the admissibility), 13 December 2000, App no 33071/96; *Peter Gratzinger and Eva Gratzingerova v Czech Republic*, 10 July 2002, App no 39794/98.

[87] In a study on NGO amicus curiae briefs from 1986 to 2013, 82% were filed by repeat players. See Van den Eynde, 'An Empirical Look' (n 9) 285.

[88] On this trend, Risini (n 12) 169.

[89] Nussberger, *The European Court of Human Rights* (n 6) 51.

[90] A list of cases is available at: www.echr.coe.int/inter-state-applications.

[91] eg, *Ireland v United Kingdom*, 18 January 1978, App no 5310/71; *Cyprus v Turkey*, 10 May 2001, App no 25781/94. See further on territorial disputes section III.B.

[92] *Georgia v Russia (II)*, 21 January 2021, App no 38263/08, para 61.

even more so those that involve warfare are outside the immediate expertise of the court.

In addition to dispute resolution, states are also motivated to bring matters before the ECtHR because doing so generates international attention.[93] This motivation is comparable to strategic interests of political actors as individual applicants that go beyond an interest in the outcome of the concrete judicial decision (see chapter four). For states, such proceedings can generate both media attention and the attention of governmental actors in other states that they hope might support their cause politically. Further, initiating legal proceedings can aim at legitimising the (legal and political) claims of the applicant state and stress the rule of law-abiding attitude of the applicant. A prominent example is the 'lawfare' strategy of Ukraine in its military conflict with Russia since 2014, a strategy that has led Ukraine to bring several cases to the ECtHR, in parallel with proceedings before other international courts. For applicants that are motivated by such strategic political interests, the expected effectiveness is higher than when they are merely interested in dispute resolution.

Further, interstate complaints have been regarded as especially effective for structural or widespread human rights violations.[94] This was even more important at times in which the court had not turned yet to broaden its initially restrictive approach to remedies in the context of individual complaints. In interstate cases, the court could be expected to grant more general remedies.

Finally, it bears mentioning that for interstate complaints, state applicants can expect the effectiveness regarding the admissibility of the complaint to be high. Almost all interstate complaints have been declared admissible by the court.[95] This is due to the less restrictive admissibility criteria for interstate complaints (see section II.B).

In sum, for applicants in both individual and interstate complaints, the motivation has been at a moderate to high level, with some fluctuations. For individual applicants, the value-related motivational factors have been rather stable, except for certain fair trial values (given issues relating to length of proceedings, right to be heard and reasoned judgments) for which the value-correspondence has decreased in the last two decades. The interest-based motivation has been diverse in substance, including not only dispute resolution but also strategic political interests, an interest in social change and transitional justice-related interests. The motivational basis for individual applicants is thus broad. However, the expected effectiveness as to these aspects diverges both among aspects and among different time periods. This fluctuation is most pronounced with regard to dispute resolution for which the level of expected effectiveness started out at a rather low level in the 1960s, mainly because of low admissibility and referral rates to the court. It increased during the 1970s

[93] A Mondré in 'Inter-State Cases Under The European Convention On Human Rights – Experiences And Current Challenges', Proceedings of the Conference organised under the aegis of the German Presidency of the Committee of Ministers (Berlin, 12–13 April 2021): 48, rm.coe.int/interstate-cases-under-the-echr/1680a5e82c.

[94] On this 'comparative advantage', see the statement by the Secretary General of the Council of Europe, European Ministerial Conference on Human Rights, Rome (3–4 November 2000), CM(2000)172: rm.coe.int/16805e2eec.

[95] Risini (n 12) 49.

and 1980s when applicants faced higher admissibility and referral rates as well as high compliance rates, yet still the court's restrictive approach to remedies. It decreased in the 1990s and 2000s mainly due to the backlog of cases and fewer comprehensive compliance expectations, and despite the fact that the court started to take a broader approach to remedies. It has increased again somewhat since the mid-2010s in light of the reduced but still significant backlog and the now more comprehensive set of remedies. Finally, for NGOs, the motivation to engage with the court via third-party intervention is rather high. This motivation results, in particular, from the high value-correspondence, and the interests of these actors in social change and transitional justice.

The motivation for applicants in interstate complaints has been moderate in the first decades of the court's practice. The key motivational factor was value-related while dispute resolution did not have the motivating effect it has had in the more recent period. Yet for actors who aimed at enforcing human rights values, the expected effectiveness was high, due to, inter alia, a high admissibility rate and expected substantive outcomes that include general remedies. In later years and especially since the 2000s, the motivational basis has diversified. Applicants are also motivated by strategic interests as well as, more frequently than before, by dispute resolution. Although the expected effectiveness diverges for both these aims, being higher for the former than the latter, this wider range of motivational aspects leads to a motivational setting that can be qualified as moderate to high.

B. Opportunity

The opportunity for applicants to engage with the ECtHR is shaped by the court's jurisdiction, the rules on access to the court as well as social and practical opportunity elements.

Jurisdiction

Under Article 32 ECHR, the court has jurisdiction over 'all matters concerning the interpretation and application of the Convention and the Protocols thereto'.[96] Unlike in the ECOWAS context, applicants thus cannot bring cases relating to other regional or universal human rights instruments. While the original jurisdiction of the court was limited to the rights enshrined in the Convention, several protocols have extended the scope of protection and thus of the court's jurisdiction. This includes Protocol No 1 on property, education and election; Protocol No 4 on imprisonment for debt, free movement and expulsion; Protocols No 6 and 13 on the death penalty; Protocol No 7 on fair trial and appeal as well as equality between spouses; and Protocol No 12 on non-discrimination. These protocols have thus broadened the opportunity for applicants to bring human rights cases to the court. That said, not all member

[96] See also Article 45 ECHR 1950.

states have ratified all of the above protocols so that the opportunity structure differs depending on the envisaged respondent state. Further, Protocol No 14 has extended the jurisdiction of the court to enforcement matters. Upon request by the Committee of Ministers, the court can decide, in particular, on whether a respondent state has violated its obligation under Article 46(1) ECHR by failing to implement a judgment of the court (Article 46(4)).

In addition to instances in which the jurisdiction of the court has been expanded by protocol, the court has also adopted a broad interpretation of existing rules that define its jurisdiction. A prominent and recent example is the court's jurisprudence on extra-territorial jurisdiction.[97] In principle, the court considers the jurisdiction under Article 1 ECHR to be an 'essentially territorial notion'.[98] However, in decisions such as *Al Skeini v UK*, the court decided that a state has to comply with the Convention in extra-territorial situations 'whenever the State, through its agents, exercises control and authority over an individual' and when 'a Contracting State exercises effective control of an area outside that national territory'.[99] This approach has been further refined and broadened in the subsequent jurisprudence.[100] The court has however declined to broaden it further in the climate change context.[101] Other cases in which the court understood its jurisdiction in a broad manner include the jurisprudence on the validity of reservations made by member states to the Convention. Here, the court considered itself competent in a matter of general international law and in a manner that went beyond the existing rules (see also section III).[102]

In contrast to the ECOWAS Court, the ECtHR has not acknowledged any retroactive application of the Convention, so that the access opportunity only exists regarding situations since the entry into force of the Convention or the relevant protocol in respect of the envisaged respondent state.[103] For states that, before the entry into force of Protocol No 11, had made a declaration to accept the jurisdiction of the court at a later date than the entry into force of the Convention, the jurisdiction of the court accordingly only started to take effect with this declaration.[104] However, despite formal non-retroactivity, facts prior to ratification can become relevant in an indirect manner. If they have led to post-ratification facts that are 'extensions' of the already existing pre-ratification situation, the court exercises

[97] For an overview of how this jurisprudence has developed, see 'The Place of the European Convention on Human Rights in the European and International Legal Order: Report of the Steering Committee for Human Rights (CDDH) Adopted at its 92nd Meeting (26–29 November 2019)' 40–60.

[98] *Banković and Others v Belgium and Others*, 12 December 2001, App no 52207/99, para 61.

[99] *Al Skeini and Others v UK*, 7 July 2011, App no 55721/07, paras 137, 138.

[100] eg, *Hirsi Jamaa and Others v Italy*, 23 February 2012, App no 27765/09; *Hassan v the United Kingdom*, 16 September 2014, App no 29750/09; *Jaloud v the Netherlands*, 20 November 2014, App no 47708/08.

[101] *Duarte Agostinho and Others v Portugal and 32 others*, 9 April 2024, App no 39371/20, paras 181–214.

[102] *Belilos v Switzerland*, 29 April 1988, App no 10328/83; *Loizidou v Turkey* (Preliminary Objections), 23 March 1995, App no 15318/89; *Grande Stevens v Italy*, 4 March 2014, App no 18640/10.

[103] *Blečić v Croatia*, 8 March 2006, App no 59532/00, para 70; *Varnava and Others v Turkey*, 18 September 2009, App nos 16064/90 et al, para 130.

[104] *Šilih v Slovenia*, 9 April 2009, App no 71463/01, para 140.

its jurisdiction.[105] In particular, this has made it possible for applicants to bring (some of the) transitional justice cases to the court. Moreover, this rationale also applies to 'continuing violations' which originated prior to the critical date and continues beyond that date.[106]

A further aspect shapes the opportunity structure relating to the court's jurisdiction: the nature of member state actions that applicants can challenge before the court. In the early years of the Convention system, the Commission clarified that the scope of the review comprised not only a review of acts of the executive branch of government but also of the legislative branch. In *de Becker v Belgium*, the Commission stated that member states are obliged 'to ensure that their domestic legislation is compatible with the Convention and, if need be, to make any necessary adjustments to this end, since the Convention is binding on all the authorities of the Contracting Parties, including the legislative authority'.[107] Although the court did not decide this case on the merits because the respondent state had amended its legislation during the proceedings, it did however stress that it had jurisdiction on the matter, thus not contradicting the Commission's stance on legislative review.[108] Since then, the court has consistently upheld this view and has routinely issued judgments concerning domestic legal provisions (see also section III.A.ii). Similarly, the court has reviewed domestic judicial decisions as to their conformity with Convention rights (see section III.A.ii).

Access Rules

In contrast to the relatively stable jurisdiction of the court, the access opportunity for *individual applicants* has significantly changed over time. Initially, these applicants had a very limited access opportunity. It was optional for states who had ratified the Convention to accept individual petitions according to Article 25 ECHR 1950 and the jurisdiction of the court according to Article 46 ECHR 1950. For the court to exercise its jurisdiction, eight member states had to accept its jurisdiction. This was achieved in 1958 when Ireland, Denmark, the Netherlands, the Federal Republic of Germany, Belgium, Austria, Luxembourg and Iceland had made their respective declarations. In contrast, important member states such as France, Italy and the United Kingdom only accepted the court's jurisdiction at a later stage (see Table 5.1). Moreover, not all member states that had made declarations under Article 46 also made declarations under Article 25 regarding individual complaints – and vice versa (see Table 5.1). These optional clauses thus acted as a double hurdle to individual access to the court. Until 1990, this legal framework significantly limited the access opportunity for individuals.

[105] *Hutten-Czapska v Poland*, 19 June 2006, App no 35014/97, paras 147–53; *Kurić and Others v Slovenia*, 26 June 2012, App no 26828/06, paras 240–41. See also *Šilih v Slovenia*, 9 April 2009, App no 71463/01, paras 140–47.

[106] eg, *Almeida Garrett, Mascarenhas Falcão and Others v Portugal*, 11 January 2000, App nos 29813/96 and 30229/96, para 43.

[107] *Commission, de Becker v Belgium*, 9 June 1958, App no 214/56 (original in French; English translation as cited by Bates, *Evolution* (n 2) 208).

[108] *Becker v Belgium*, 27 March 1962, App no 214/56.

Table 5.1 Overview of declarations under Article 25 and 46 ECHR 1950[109]

Member State	Ratification/ Accession ECHR	Article 25 Declaration	Article 46 Declaration
Albania	1996	1996	1996
Austria	1958	1958	1958
Belgium	1955	1955	1955
Bulgaria	1992	1992	1992
Croatia	1997	1997	1997
Cyprus	1962	1989	1980
Czech Republic	1992 (1993)	1992 (1993)	1992 (1993)
Denmark	1953	1953	1953
Estonia	1996	1996	1996
Finland	1990	1990	1990
France	1974	1981	1974
Germany	1952	1955	1955
Greece	1953–1970, since 1974	1985	1979
Hungary	1992	1992	1992
Iceland	1953	1955	1958
Ireland	1953	1953	1953
Italy	1955	1973	1973
Latvia	1997	1997	1997
Liechtenstein	1982	1982	1982
Lithuania	1995	1995	1995
Luxembourg	1953	1958	1958
Macedonia. Former Yugoslav Republic of	1997	1997	1997
Malta	1967	1987	1987
Moldova	1997	1997	1997
Netherlands	1954	1960	1954
Norway	1952	1955	1964
Poland	1993	1993	1993
Portugal	1978	1978	1978
Romania	1994	1994	1994
Russia	1998	1998	1998

(continued)

[109] Dates according to Bates, *Evolution* (n 2) 136, 138, 447. The year in brackets is the year in which the Czech Republic and Slovakia emerged from the former Czechoslovakia that initially acceded to the Convention.

Table 5.1 *(Continued)*

Member State	Ratification/ Accession ECHR	Article 25 Declaration	Article 46 Declaration
San Marino	1989	1989	1989
Slovakia	1992 (1993)	1992 (1993)	1992 (1993)
Slovenia	1994	1994	1994
Spain	1979	1981	1979
Sweden	1952	1952	1966
Switzerland	1974	1974	1974
Turkey	1954	1987	1990
Ukraine	1997	1997	1997
United Kingdom	1951	1966	1966

In contrast to the first decades of the court's existence, the above-mentioned double hurdle had lost its practical effect by the 1990s. Although the two optional clauses were still part of the legal framework, the optional nature of jurisdiction and individual petition did not have any limiting effect on the access opportunity any further. By then, all earlier member states had made the declarations and the new member states that joined during this period made the declarations at the time when they ratified the Convention.[110]

However, even when states had made both these optional declarations, the access opportunity for individuals was still only of an indirect nature. According to Article 44 ECHR 1950, only the member states and the Commission could bring cases before the court. Under Article 25(1) ECHR 1950, individuals only could bring petitions to the Commission. If these petitions did not resolve the issue (Article 47 ECHR 1950), the Commission could decide to refer the matter to the court. The Commission thus acted as a gatekeeper to the court. It filtered applications both with regard to admissibility and merits. This limited the access opportunity for individual applicants considerably. In the 1960s and 1970s, less than 60 out of more than 4,000 applicants were declared admissible by the Commission.[111] And only in a small percentage of those cases did the Commission conclude that human rights violations occurred.[112] Further, Article 48(d) ECHR 1950 also allowed the respondent state to refer a case to the court. However, this provision had a similar gatekeeping effect for applicants. States often preferred political dispute resolution before the Committee of Ministers to judicial dispute resolution before the court.[113] In the 1960s, cases such as *Nielsen v Denmark* and the 'Austrian Criminal Procedure cases' could have been referred to the court but were resolved by the political institution.[114] The fact that state actors preferred political dispute resolution limited the opportunity for individual applicants for judicial dispute resolution before the court.

[110] However not always on the exact same date, see Bates, *Evolution* (n 2) 447.
[111] See Madsen, 'The European Court of Human Rights' (n 34) 249.
[112] ibid.
[113] Bates, *Evolution* (n 2) 194.
[114] ibid.

The participatory dimension of this indirect access opportunity was broadened somewhat by the court. In the *Lawless* case, it decided that despite individuals not having a formal applicant status before the court, they were 'directly concerned' and were thus granted an informal status within the proceedings.[115] This allowed them, inter alia, to have access to the submissions made by the formal parties to the dispute. This approach is comparable to the indirect status that the Inter-American Court of Human Rights (IACtHR) has recognised for the individuals concerned.[116]

Protocol No 11 has considerably increased the access opportunity for individuals and NGOs. Since 1998, the jurisdiction of the court as well as individual access are no longer optional. Being a member state to the Convention now means being subjected to the mandatory jurisdiction of the court. And individuals and NGOs have been given direct access to the court according to Article 34 ECHR. This access opportunity also exists for legal persons if they do not exercise 'public functions'.[117] Corporate entities thus have access to the court.[118]

Several procedural features limit the access opportunity for individuals and NGOs. To start with, applicants must exhaust domestic remedies before they can bring their case to the ECtHR (Article 35(1) ECHR). This is a provision that the court considers to be a 'basic principle' and an expression of the subsidiary nature of the Convention system.[119] In general, it therefore applies it in a rather restrictive manner. However, the court has also acknowledged that there is 'a need for a certain flexibility in the application of the rule'.[120] It has established certain exceptions to the exhaustion requirement. Most importantly, the court has decided that the respondent government must demonstrate that a remedy was 'effective [and] available in theory and in practice at the relevant time, that is to say, that it was accessible, was one which was capable of providing redress in respect of the applicant's complaints and offered reasonable prospects of success'.[121] As a result, the court can declare an application admissible even if domestic remedies have not been exhausted when the applicant can demonstrate that no such remedies exist or that existing remedies would not be effective. In particular, structural issues caused by the respondent state can also make the exhaustion requirement inapplicable. This is the case 'where an administrative practice consisting of a repetition of acts incompatible with the Convention and official tolerance by the State authorities has been shown to exist, and is of such a nature as to make proceedings futile or ineffective'.[122]

[115] *Lawless v Ireland (No 1)*, 14 November 1960, App no 332/57.

[116] Article 25 Rules of Procedure IACtHR.

[117] *Radio France and Others v France*, 23/09/2003, App no 53984/00, para 26.

[118] On corporations as applicants before the ECtHR see eg, M Emberland, 'The Corporate Veil in the Case Law of the European Court of Human Rights' (2003) 63 *Heidelberg Journal of International Law* 945.

[119] *Demopoulos and Others v Turkey* (decision on admissibility), 1 March 2010, App nos 46113/99, 3843/02, 13751/02, 13466/03, 10200/04, 14163/04, 19993/04, 21819/04, para 97; *Selmouni v France*, 28 July 1999, App no 25803/94, para 74.

[120] *Ringeisen v Austria*, 16 July 1971, App no 2614/65, para 89.

[121] *Akdivar and Others v Turkey*, 16 September 1996, App no 21893/93, para 68; *Sejdovic v Italy*, 1 March 2006, App no 56581/00, para 46.

[122] *Akdivar and Others v Turkey*, 16 September 1996, App no 21893/93, para 67.

The requirement to exhaust domestic remedies can particularly reduce the access opportunity in situations of structural rule of law issues in a member state. For example, the court rejected the admissibility of applications by persons dismissed, arrested or imprisoned in the context of the Turkish coup d'état attempt in 2016.[123] It requested that domestic remedies must be exhausted prior to addressing the court and rejected, inter alia, the applicants' argument that the domestic judiciary is no longer independent and would thus not constitute an effective remedy. This insistence on this requirement becomes problematic for the applicants involved in situations in which it is doubtful whether the domestic judiciary of the respondent state can still provide effective and independent adjudication.

Another procedural feature that limits the access opportunity is the fact that individuals can only address the court if they have been the victim of a human rights violation by a member state (Article 34 ECHR). Unlike before some other regional courts,[124] the admissibility of individual applications thus requires a victim status. The court has consistently held that

> the Convention does not provide for the institution of an actio popularis and that its task is not normally to review the relevant law and practice in abstracto, but to determine whether the manner in which they were applied to, or affected, the applicant gave rise to a violation of the Convention.[125]

Applicants have victim status when they are a direct victim of the alleged violation. This includes persons directly concerned by specific provisions of domestic legislation even if there has been no additional administrative act in application of this legislation.[126] In some circumstances, potential victims are also attributed victim status, for example when it would not be possible for the victim to have knowledge of a concrete measure that is enabled by domestic legislation but secret in nature.[127] Moreover, the court also recognises a victim status for 'any indirect victims to whom the violation would cause harm or who would have a valid and personal interest in seeing it brought to an end'.[128] The court has thus interpreted the rule in a way that created an access opportunity in particular for family members of direct victims in case of death or disappearance of the latter.

The victim requirement also applies to NGOs – and has significantly limited the access opportunity for these actors. The court has repeatedly held that NGOs cannot bring a case before the court when their interests are not at stake. For that, the fact

[123] eg, *Akif Zihni v Turkey*, 29 November 2016, App no 59061/16; *Zeynep Mercan v Turkey*, 8 November 2016, App no 56511/16; *Gökhan Köksal v Turkey*, 6 June 2017, App no 70478/16; *Kadriye Çatal v Turkey*, 7 March 2017, App no 2873/17.

[124] See eg, EACJ, *Prof. Peter Anyang' Nyong'o and Others v Attorney General of Kenya and Others*, 30 March 2007, reference no 1/2006.

[125] eg, *Roman Zakharov v Russia*, 4 December 2015, App no 47143/06, para 164 (with further references). For an early decision rejecting actio popularis, see *Klass and Others v Germany*, 6 September 1978, App no 5029/71, para 33.

[126] *Marckx v Belgium*, 13 June 1979, App no 6833/74, para 27.

[127] *Klass and Others v Germany*, 6 September 1978, App no 5029/71. Similarly, *Roman Zakharov v Russia*, 4 December 2015, App no 47143/06, paras 174–78. For a different constellation, in which the court also applies this rationale, see eg, *Dudgeon v the United Kingdom*, 22 October 1981, App no 7525/76, para 41 (legislation punishing homosexual acts).

[128] *Vallianatos and Others v Greece*, 7 November 2013, App nos 29381/09 and 32684/09, para 47.

that the interests of their members might be at stake or that the purpose for which the NGO has been created is to defend the interests of certain groups of persons who are victims of alleged violations is not sufficient.[129] In general, NGOs cannot engage in public interest litigation – such cases brought by NGOs in which they were not the immediate victims have been rejected by the court.[130] The access opportunity for NGOs is thus narrow in general, perpetuating a 'long history of NGO exclusion'.[131] This limited access opportunity for NGOs stands out in comparison to other international courts,[132] including the ECOWAS Court. However, in its recent jurisprudence the court has introduced an exception to this restrictive stance for the climate change context. In its *Klimaseniorinnen* decision of 2024, the court created a broad possibility for NGOs to bring climate cases to the court, de facto creating an *actio popularis* for climate change cases.[133] In addition, in exceptional circumstances, the court has allowed for an NGO to act as a representative of a deceased person.[134]

The victim requirement also limits the access opportunity for corporate actors, especially for shareholders of companies. The court strictly distinguishes between the corporate legal personality and the legal personality of the shareholders and the victim status of both. This can restrict the access opportunity of shareholders in circumstances in which the impugned act of the respondent state is addressed at the company and only indirectly affects the shareholders.[135] The shareholders' rights are not necessarily concerned when the company's interests and rights are at stake.

Moreover, the access opportunity for applicants is restricted by a time limit. Until 2022, this time limit was six months 'from the date on which the final decision was taken' on the domestic level (former Article 35(1) ECHR as well as Article 26 ECHR 1950). The court has somewhat broadened this access opportunity. It has developed the 'continuing situation' doctrine to adjust the time limit to long-lasting human rights violations. When there is no or no effective remedy available to the applicant and the applicant is affected by a 'continuing situation' that potentially violates Convention rights, the time limit only starts to run if and when this situation ceases.[136] However, the access opportunity regarding the time limit has become less favourable in recent years due to pushback on this matter from member states. In the context of the Brighton Declaration of 2012 (see also section III.B), the court announced that it was going to apply the time limit more restrictively than before.[137]

[129] *Nencheva and Others v Bulgaria*, 18 June 2013, App no 48609/06, para 90 (with further references); *Kalfagiannis and Pospert v Greece*, 2 July 2020, App no 74435/14, para 50.

[130] eg, *Jan Conka and Others v Belgium*, 13 March 2001, App no 51564/99; *Asselbourg and Others v Luxembourg*, 29 June 1999, App no 29121/95. See also RA Cichowski, 'Civil Society and the European Court of Human Rights' in J Christoffersen and MR Madsen (eds), *The European Court of Human Rights between Law and Politics* (OUP 2011) 77, 85.

[131] Haddad (n 85) 50.

[132] ibid 49.

[133] *Verein Klimaseniorinnen Schweiz and Others v Switzerland*, 9 April 2024, App no 53600/20.

[134] *Centre For Legal Resources On Behalf of Valentin Câmpeanu v Romania*, 17 July 2014, App no 47848/08.

[135] On this issue, Emberland (n 118). Establishing this restrictive approach: ECtHR, *Agrotexim and Others v Greece*, 24 October 1995, App no 14807/89, para 66.

[136] *Varnava and Others v Turkey*, 18 September 2009, App nos 16064/90 et al, para 159; *Sabri Güneş v Turkey*, 29 June 2012, App no 27396/06, para 54.

[137] Brighton Declaration of 19 and 20 April 2012, para 15(b).

Further, the six-month time limit has been reduced to four months by Protocol No 15 as of 1 February 2022. Both in terms of legal provisions and their jurisprudential application, the access opportunity has thus been reduced.

The interplay between the requirements to exhaust domestic remedies and the six/four-month-rule can at times have an additional limiting effect on the applicants' access opportunity. This is the case due to the court's jurisprudence that applicants do not have to exhaust remedies that are not effective. While this jurisprudence is favourable for applicants in the exhaustion context, it can be detrimental to the access opportunity in the time limit context. When an applicant pursues remedies that the ECtHR considers ineffective, these remedies will not be taken into account when calculating the starting point for the running of the time limit.[138] Assessing the effectiveness of available remedies and pursuing them is thus at the applicant's own risk. If the potential applicant chooses to pursue an ineffective remedy, this will, in general, lead to the expiration of the time limit so that the application will be inadmissible.

Moreover, Protocol No 14 has limited the access opportunity further by introducing a new ground for inadmissibility.[139] Article 35(3)(b) stipulates that the court shall declare an application inadmissible if 'the applicant has not suffered a significant disadvantage, unless respect for human rights as defined in the Convention and the Protocols thereto requires an examination of the application on the merits'.

A further element of the – indirect – opportunity structure for applicants is the invocability of the Convention before domestic courts. In the court's initial phase, only few member states had incorporated the Convention so that litigants before domestic courts could not refer to it as applicable law. This limited the opportunity for litigants to shape their claims in a way that would make their link to the Convention visible. As domestic judicial cases did not have this framing, it was less likely that litigants would bring them to the ECtHR after exhausting domestic remedies. In contrast, since member states embedded the Convention into their domestic legal orders – a trend that gathered significant speed in the 1990s – the indirect opportunity structure for applicants became more favourable. This effect has been described as follows:

> That domestic courts could apply the Convention almost immediately produced a significant growth in domestic suits that invoked Convention rights and freedoms, which in turn prompted more petitions to be filed with the Court … Countries with few or hardly any cases through the late 1980s started having a more steady flow of cases to the Court.[140]

Especially for NGOs, an important access opportunity relates to amicus curiae briefs. A possibility for such third-party interventions has however not always existed. Initially, the court only allowed third-party interventions by states. In the *Tyrer* case of 1978,[141] when the court received its first request for such an intervention by the

[138] *Prystavska v Ukraine*, 17 December 2002, App no 21287/02; *Jeronovičs v Latvia*, 5 July 2016, App no 44898/10, para 75 (with further references).

[139] Critically on this access limitation, D Shelton, 'Significantly Disadvantaged? Shrinking Access to the European Court of Human Rights' (2016) 16 *Human Rights Law Review* 303.

[140] Madsen, 'The European Court of Human Rights' (n 34) 264.

[141] *Tyrer v United Kingdom*, 25 April 1978, App no 5856/72.

National Council for Civil Liberties, it refused the intervention.[142] But it was soon after, with its 1982 Rules of Procedure, that the court had formally created this access opportunity in Rule 37(2).[143] One of the first cases in which this rule was used to grant amicus curiae status to a civil society organisation was *Malone v United Kingdom* decided in 1984.[144] Protocol No 11 introduced the current rule on third-party interventions. Under the present Article 36(2) ECHR, the court can invite, inter alia, 'any person concerned who is not the applicant to submit written comments or take part in hearings'. Although such an invitation by the court is rather rare, a prospective amicus curiae can also take the initiative to provide a brief to the court. Whether the court grants the possibility to submit a brief is at the discretion of the President of the Court.[145] The possibility for amicus curiae briefs is an opportunity to influence the court not only by legal arguments but also by providing information on legal and social facts. In particular, when the court refers to the European consensus doctrine, amicus curiae briefs are an impactful opportunity for NGOs to provide information on comparative law that can shape the court's assessment of whether such a consensus exists.[146]

Turning to *state applicants*, the access opportunity structure has always been broader than for individual applicants and NGOs. Under the ECHR 1950, state applicants already had access to the court as formal applicants (Articles 44 and 48). This access existed when the respective states had made the optional declaration under Article 46 ECHR 1950. As compared with individual applicants, only one optional clause constituted a hurdle to bringing an interstate case to the court. However, as was the case for individuals, the two-tier structure of the Strasbourg system limited this access. States had to address the Commission first. Only if it did find a violation, could the applicant state refer the matter to the court (Article 48(c) ECHR 1950). States thus also had to go through a two-step process to access the court. In contrast to individual applicants, state applicants could however refer the case to the court themselves and were not depending on a referral by the Commission. When Protocol No 11 entered into force in 1998, this gatekeeping effect disappeared for state applicants. Interstate complaints can now be addressed immediately to the court according to Article 33 ECHR.

Further, the admissibility requirements for interstate applicants are lower than for individual applicants. In particular, as Article 35(2)(b) is not applicable, interstate complaints do not become inadmissible when the applicant state instigates parallel proceedings before another regional or international body. This makes it possible for

[142] See D Shelton, 'The Participation of Nongovernmental Organizations in International Judicial Proceedings' (1994) 88 *American Journal of International Law* 611, 630.

[143] Before creating this rule, the court had accepted a third-party intervention by the British Trade Union Congress in the case of *Young, James and Webster v the United Kingdom*, 13 August 1981, App nos 7601/76 and 7806/77, para 8.

[144] *Malone v The United Kingdom*, 2 August 1984, App no 8691/79, para 8 (Post Office Engineering Union).

[145] Article 36(2) ECHR.

[146] See L Van den Eynde, 'The Consensus Argument in NGOs' Amicus Curiae Briefs Defending Minorities through a Creatively Used Majoritarian Argument' in P Kapotas and VP Tzevelekos (eds), *Building Consensus on European Consensus: Judicial Interpretation of Human Rights in Europe and Beyond* (CUP 2019) 96.

states, especially in territorial and other large-scale conflicts, to pursue a strategy of addressing various international judicial bodies simultaneously.[147] The substantive requirements of Article 35(3) – not 'manifestly ill-founded' and 'significant disadvantage' – also do not restrict state applications. Further, in view of Article 33, any member state can file an interstate complaint even if it is not directly concerned with an alleged human rights violation. A victim status of the state or its citizens is not necessary.

However, as a particularity of the Convention system in comparison to other international courts, the requirement to exhaust domestic remedies (Article 35(1)) is applicable to state applicants as well.[148] This is the case 'when the applicant State does no more than denounce a violation or violations allegedly suffered by "individuals" whose place, as it were, is taken by the State'.[149] The exhaustion requirement is the only major admissibility hurdle that can limit the access opportunity for state applicants. However, this requirement is inapplicable when there is an 'administrative practice' of the respondent state of which the applicant complains.[150] An administrative practice exists when there is 'a repetition of acts incompatible with the Convention, and official tolerance by the State'.[151] This exception has been very relevant in several interstate cases.[152]

Social Opportunity Elements

In addition to the legal opportunity structure, the social opportunity structure also constitutes a factor for whether potential applicants engage with the ECtHR. Social networks among applicants or related actors are an important aspect in this regard. For individual applicants, such networks have been especially important in the earlier phases after a state had joined the Convention system. Domestic legal actors such as lawyers, NGOs and other societal actors can create a setting in which the access of potential applicants to the court becomes easier. For example, during the 1970s and 1980s, one could observe in the United Kingdom how a strong legal field relating to human rights developed on the domestic level. The political context of many of the early cases before the court which concerned, to a considerable part, the United Kingdom, attracted the relevant actors' attention. In this country, the 'development of specialized human rights lawyers' created 'a unique situation in Europe at the

[147] eg, *Georgia v Russia (I)*, 3 July 2014, App no 13255/07 – and ICJ, *Case Concerning Application of the International Convention on the Elimination of All Forms of Racial Discrimination (Georgia v Russian Federation)*, judgment of 1 April 2011; *Ukraine v Russia (X)*, App no 11055/22; ICJ, *Allegations of Genocide under the Convention on the Prevention and Punishment of the Crime of Genocide (Ukraine v Russian Federation)*.

[148] For the parallel provision of Article 26 ECHR 1950, *Ireland v United Kingdom*, 18 January 1978, App no 5310/71, para 159. On the exhaustion requirement in the inter-state context, see Risini (n 12) 53 et seq.

[149] *Ireland v United Kingdom*, 18 January 1978, App no 5310/71, para 159.

[150] ibid.

[151] *Cyprus v Turkey*, 10 May 2001, App no 25781/94, para 99; *Georgia v Russia (I)*, 3 July 2014, App no 13255/07, para 125.

[152] eg, *Ireland v United Kingdom*, 18 January 1978, App no 5310/71; *Cyprus v Turkey*, 10 May 2001, App no 25781/94; *Georgia v Russia (I)*, 3 July 2014, App no 13255/07; *Ukraine v Russia (Re Crimea)*, 16 December 2020, App nos 20958/14 and 38334/18; *Georgia v Russia (II)*, 21 January 2021, App no 38263/08.

time'.[153] This provided the opportunity for applicants from this country to bring cases to the court.

Another way in which social opportunity elements can influence the behaviour of applicants concerns group effects among certain categories of applicants. Among member states as applicants in interstate complaints, patterns have emerged that indicate how a novel behaviour of one of the group members can be copied by other group members, thus initiating a self-enhancing development. For example, after Georgia had brought cases regarding territorial and military disputes with Russia to the court, other states such as Ukraine (against Russia) and Armenia (against Azerbaijan) have – repeatedly – brought similar cases as well. Another group of actors in which social opportunity elements play a role are NGOs. As before many other regional courts, one could also observe in the ECtHR context an increasing number of NGOs that engaged with the court, in particular by filing amicus curiae briefs. While there are certain prominent NGOs that act as 'repeat players' before the court, many smaller and very specialised NGOs have also started to adopt this behaviour.

Group effects also exist for individual applicants. When there are structural issues in a member state and applicants start to challenge these issues before the ECtHR, other potential applicants become aware of the possibility to address the court on the matter. For example, when the court started to decide cases regarding the structural deficiencies in the Italian judicial system, more and more applicants filed similar complaints. This led to a situation in which 'the ECtHR judgments arguably generated more cases than it resolved'.[154] Furthermore, applicants can become aware, as result of the behaviour of other group members, of the possibility of attacking domestic institutional actors before the ECtHR. For example, when the ECtHR found Convention violations in relation to French high courts, other applicants became aware of the possibility to challenge 'the particularities of the French justice system as incompatible with the Convention', leading to the 'ECtHR virtually [becoming] an appeals court to the supreme French courts'.[155]

Practical Opportunity Elements

The practical opportunity for applicants to engage with the court is shaped by the amount of cases that the court can handle based on its personal and financial capacities. For applicants before the ECtHR, this practical opportunity has changed over time. In the initial Convention system, the court was not of a permanent nature, and judges did not hold office on a full-time basis. This setting limited the practical opportunity structure when the court started to receive an increasing number of cases. With the Protocol No 11 reform, this feature has been adjusted with the creation of a permanent court. Further, the budget of the court is important for the practical opportunity structure. In comparison to many other regional courts, the ECtHR is in general well financed and does not face any major budgetary challenges.

[153] Madsen, 'The European Court of Human Rights' (n 34) 256.
[154] ibid 261.
[155] ibid 263.

The current annual budget is more than €88 million.[156] However, despite this comparatively high amount, the court has at times faced some issues. It has been 'confronted with a shrinking budget due to political squabbles and the Member States' general unwillingness to enhance financial support'.[157] But so far, the practical opportunity structure for applicants has been only modestly reduced by these aspects.

In conclusion, for applicants in individual complaints, the opportunity to engage with the court developed from a rather low level in the initial phase of the court to a moderate level in later years. While the subject-matter jurisdiction of the court provided a rather broad and even increasing opportunity over time, the low to moderate access opportunity has significantly limited the overall opportunity for individual applicants. The optional and indirect access for individuals in the first decades as well as the restrictive admissibility criteria have led to the initially low-access opportunity. Although this opportunity increased in the 1980s and 1990s and especially after Protocol No 11 entered into force, the restrictive admissibility criteria continue to limit access – and even more so in recent years – which leads to an only moderately favourable opportunity structure. For NGOs, the access opportunity was initially very low as there was no possibility of third-party intervention, and the victim requirement limited the access as formal applicants significantly. Access has somewhat increased since the 1980s when third-party interventions became possible yet remained low to moderate given that the victim requirement is still in place, except for the climate change context. For applicants in interstate complaints, the opportunity structure has been more favourable than for individual applicants. State applicants benefit from the same broad subject-matter jurisdiction as individual applicants, and the access opportunity has already initially been at least moderate due to the direct access and the less restrictive admissibility criteria. It became rather broad in the post-Protocol No 11 period when the two-tier structure of the Convention system was abolished.

C. Constraints

Intrinsic Constraints

Unlike in the context of other regional courts such as the ECOWAS Court, applicants in individual complaint cases were never highly constrained by a lack of knowledge of the court. As Madsen observes for the early years of the court's practice:

> Considering both the number of applications as well as the diversity of applicants from states to individuals during this early period, there is little doubt that relevant legal constituencies were aware of both the Court and the Commission.[158]

However, this statement was certainly only true for a section of the potential applicants. The awareness among applicants is likely to have been significantly divergent among applicants from different member states, and among different societal groups.

[156] The budget for 2025 is €88,500,000.
[157] Nussberger, *The European Court of Human Rights* (n 6) 48.
[158] Madsen, 'The European Court of Human Rights' (n 34) 250.

The fact that even legal actors within the member states such as domestic judges had a limited awareness of the court in its early period (see section III.A) indicates that among legal practitioners, let alone individuals of the general public, the awareness of the court was not widespread. It has however increased over time. Several factors have contributed to the by now high visibility of the court. To start with, the general awareness of the court has increased with the many high-politics and/or socially controversial decisions that it took over the decades. Especially in the concerned member states, media coverage has created a broad visibility of the court as an institution. For example, due to the various high-profile cases decided by the ECtHR involving the United Kingdom as respondent state, the court gained visibility among the potential UK applicants early in its existence.[159] By the 1980s, this had become a more widespread setting: the rising number of applications was made possible by 'a better informed legal profession, greater media coverage of successful cases and, most of all, an awareness by litigants and lawyers that, in matters touching on constitutional rights, the Court is the final arbiter in Europe'.[160] Moreover, especially for newer member states, the information offices established by the court in certain member states have contributed to making potential applicants more aware of the court. These offices also enhance the more specific knowledge about the procedure before the court, 'providing … potential applicants with information on admissibility issues'.[161]

Regarding financial constraints, the situation is more favourable for potential applicants to the ECtHR than for applicants before the ECOWAS Court. Most member states of the Council of Europe are high-income countries according to the World Bank categorisation.[162] Around a quarter of the member states are classified as upper-middle-income countries.[163] Further, the costs for individual complaints only constitute low to moderate constraints. At the ECtHR itself, applicants do not face any court fees. And in case the court does not find in their favour, applicants also do not have to bear the costs of respondent states. However, the admissibility criteria for individual complaints contribute to creating financial constraints. Applicants must first exhaust domestic remedies, a process that can be very cost-intensive. This constraining effect will of course vary among member states, given that legal procedures entail different costs in different legal orders. For member states which provide a system of legal aid, the financially constraining effect of the requirement to exhaust domestic remedies is reduced for certain groups of applicants. In addition, on the level of the ECtHR, the court can grant costs to successful applicants as part of just satisfaction under Article 41 ECHR, and it can even grant legal aid to applicants who otherwise would not have sufficient means (see also section IV.A.iii). In sum, financial constraints exist, they are however only low to moderate.

[159] ibid 265.

[160] M O'Boyle, 'The Reconstruction of the Strasbourg Human Rights System' (1992) 14 *Dublin University Law Journal* 41, 46.

[161] Keller and Stone Sweet, 'Assessing the Impact of the ECHR on National Legal Systems' (n 74) 707.

[162] Data for 2024. See: datatopics.worldbank.org/world-development-indicators/the-world-by-income-and-region.html.

[163] ibid. This includes Türkiye, Georgia, Armenia, Azerbaijan, Serbia, Bosnia and Herzegovina, Montenegro, Albania, Northmacedonia, Moldova and Ukraine.

In contrast, state applicants are neither constrained by a lack of awareness of the court nor by financial considerations.

Extrinsic Constraints

For private applicants and NGOs, extrinsic constraints can stem from state actors that try to discourage or prevent them addressing the ECtHR. There have indeed been instances in which, for example in Azerbaijan, state authorities have criminally persecuted lawyers who represented applicants before the ECtHR against this state.[164] In Russia, there have also been instances in which 'Russian authorities went as far as to intimidate victims and their lawyers'.[165] Further, certain states have targeted NGOs that were active in human rights matters and before the court. This includes the Russian anti-NGO legislation of 2012.[166] Although such extrinsic constraints are not generalisable for all potential applicants before the ECtHR, they are however a factor for some applicants in some member states.

Further extrinsic constraints come in the form of competing authority relationships. In the European legal space and especially due to its dense and multilayered human rights architecture, applicants indeed find themselves in (potential) authority relationships with a range of judicial actors. These include domestic courts, international human rights bodies such as the UN Human Rights Committee and other specialised treaty bodies as well as the Court of Justice of the European Union (CJEU) with its growing fundamental rights and rule of law jurisprudence. Regarding the UN Human Rights Committee, the competing authority relationship has had, for a long time, a low constraining effect on applicants. The coexistence of the ECtHR and the Committee is characterised, in general, by 'a "two-speed" human rights protection system' with a 'robust regional system' and a 'weaker global system'.[167] However, in the last few years the Committee has adopted a number of decisions that are more far-reaching than the jurisprudence of the ECtHR on the same subject matter. This includes, inter alia, a decision in 2018 on the French Burka ban[168] and decisions in 2016 and 2017 on the Irish abortion ban.[169] For these subject matters, applicants can perceive the Committee as a more promising forum, which would in

[164] See *Aliyev v Azerbaijan*, 20 September 2018, App nos 68762/14 and 71200/14; *Annagi Hajibeyli v Azerbaijan*, 22 October 2015, App no 2204/11.

[165] A Matta and A Mazmanyan, 'Russia: In Quest for A European Identity' in P Popelier, S Lambrecht and K Lemmens (eds), *Criticism of the European Court of Human Rights, Shifting the Convention System: Counter-Dynamics at the National and EU Level* (Intersentia 2016) 481, 487.

[166] Russian Federal Law No 121-FZ 'On Amendments to Legislative Acts of the Russian Federation regarding the Regulation of the Activities of Non-profit Organisations Performing the Functions of a Foreign Agent'.

[167] Y Shany, 'Can Strasbourg be replicated at a global level? A view from Geneva' in HP Aust and E Demir-Gürsel, *The European Court of Human Rights: Current Challenges in Historical Perspective* (Edward Elgar 2021) 71, 78.

[168] Human Rights Committee, Yaker v France, Communication no 2747/2016, Views of 17 July 2018, UN Doc CCPR/C/123/D/2747/2016 – as compared with ECtHR, *S.A.S. v France*, 1 July 2014, App no 43835/11.

[169] Human Rights Committee, Amanda Mellet v Ireland, Communication no 2324/2013, Views of 31 March 2016, UN Doc CCPR/C/116/D/2324/2013; and Siobhán Whelan v Ireland, Communication no 2425/2014, Views of 17 March 2017, UN Doc CCPR/C/119/D/2425/2014 – as compared with ECtHR, *A, B and C v Ireland*, 16 December 2010, App no 25579/05.

turn constrain their authority relationship to the ECtHR. In contrast, regarding the CJEU, the competing authority relationship for applicants is not very pronounced considering that individual applicants do not have a generalised direct access to this court. Moreover, it is possible for applicants to first invoke the European Union (EU) Fundamental Rights Charter potentially arguing for a preliminary reference to the CJEU and later bring the case to the ECtHR. A constraining effect thus is more likely to result from international judicial bodies rather than from the CJEU. The same is true for domestic courts which, due to the requirement to exhaust domestic remedies, do not constitute a competing authority for applicants in the way it is the case for applicants in the ECOWAS context.

Finally, for state applicants, competing authority relationships with other courts also do not create a strong constraining factor. Under Article 35 ECHR, it is possible for applicants in interstate complaints to instigate cases before different international bodies at the same time. Applicants thus do not have to choose between different forums but can pursue cases before different courts at the same time.

In conclusion, only individual applicants face constraints that would hinder them from engaging with the court. State applicants in interstate complaints are neither intrinsically nor extrinsically constrained. For individual applicants, intrinsic constraints have been significant but have decreased over time. While the low to moderate financial constraints remained rather stable, the initially rather high knowledge-related constraints became moderate until the period around the 1980s and are rather low in recent decades. However, extrinsic constraints have increased at least for certain applicants who might face pressure from governmental actors or, depending on the subject matter of their case, competing authority relationships.

D. Assessment of MOC Factors

For individuals, the MOC setting to engage with the court has significantly changed over time. In the first decades of the court's practice, one could observe the classical 'bottleneck' situation described by the MOA framework (see chapter two). Motivation was at a moderate to high level while opportunity and unconstrained ability were low. Motivational factors included substantive and procedural values as well as a broad range of interests such as dispute resolution, strategic political interests, and an interest in social change and transitional justice – each however with varying effectiveness expectations. The only rather low opportunity was, despite broad subject-matter jurisdiction of the court, mainly due to the limited access opportunity. The low ability at this time primarily resulted from knowledge-related constraints. In this MOC setting, potential applicants could thus not engage with the court to the extent indicated by their motivational factors alone because this behaviour was hindered by a lack of opportunity and ability. In this setting, opportunity and unconstrained ability were the factors that, according to the MOC framework, determined the behaviour of the potential applicants because they were at the lowest level among the MOC factors. This means that an increase in motivation would not have led to a significantly different behaviour. Regarding the strategies that the court undertook during this period to improve the MOC setting, impactful strategies thus would have had to be directed to opportunity and unconstrained ability, while strategies aiming at increasing motivation would not have been fruitful in terms of behaviour change.

However, this MOC setting became more favourable in later years, which also led to a shift as to the determining factor. Figure 5.1 illustrates this development. While motivation remained roughly at the same moderate to high level with some fluctuations that were mostly due to changing expected effectiveness, opportunity and unconstrained ability increased. In particular due to lower intrinsic constraints, the ability has developed to a moderate to high level, thus roughly catching up with the level of motivation. In contrast, while the opportunity structure also became more favourable, there are still many aspects, mainly relating to the restrictive admissibility criteria, that keep opportunity at a merely moderate level. Compared with motivation and unconstrained ability, opportunity can thus be qualified as being at the lowest level. As a result, based on the MOC framework, opportunity has become the determining factor that predominantly shapes the behaviour of potential applicants. Any strategies to improve the MOC setting for individual applicants would thus need to address the elements of the opportunity structure.

Figure 5.1 Development over time of the MOC setting for individual applicants before the ECtHR[170]

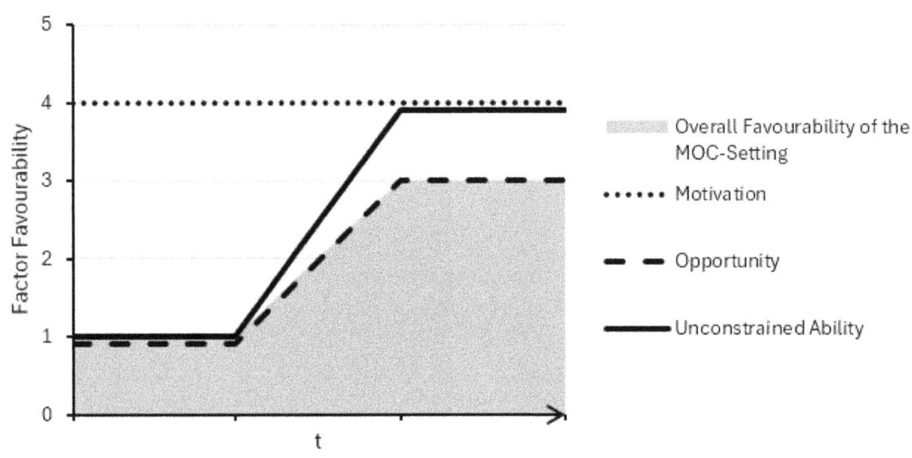

For NGOs, opportunity has been – despite some developments in the MOC setting – the determining factor during the court's entire existence (see Figure 5.2). These actors have a rather high level of motivation to engage with the court considering the high value-correspondence and their interest in social change and transitional justice. Similarly, the unconstrained ability of NGOs has been rather high. Only for NGOs in some member states with deficient rule of law standards, have extrinsic constraints led in the last decades to a reduced level of ability. In contrast, opportunity has stood out and continues to stand out as to its rather low level. Initially, opportunity was very

[170] The illustrations in this chapter translate the quantification used for the assessment in this book – low, moderate to low, moderate, moderate to high, high – into a scale of 0 to 5.

low both regarding a formal applicant status of NGOs and third-party interventions. Although the latter became possible in the 1980s and the applicant status has recently been facilitated for climate change cases, the overall opportunity setting remains only low to moderate. As a result, opportunity continues to be the MOC factor that is at the lowest level compared to motivation and ability. Opportunity thus determines the behaviour of these actors. Strategies of the court to improve the MOC setting would need to primarily address this factor.

Figure 5.2 Development over time of the MOC setting for NGOs as applicants before the ECtHR

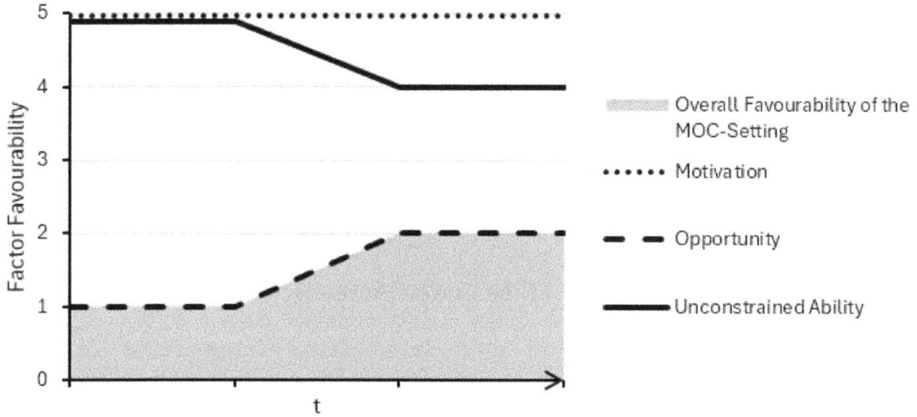

For state applicants in interstate complaints, the MOC setting differs – compared with applicants in individual complaints – both as to the overall favourability of this setting and to the determining factor. In the first decades, opportunity and unconstrained ability were considerably more favourable than in the context of individual complaints. As there were virtually no constraints, the ability to engage with the court was very high. Opportunity was also rather favourable. The broad subject-matter jurisdiction and the at least moderate access opportunity with direct access and less restrictive admissibility criteria than applicable to individual applicants, led to a moderate to high level of the overall opportunity factor. In comparison, motivation was at the lowest level of these factors, with only a moderate level during the first decades, as dispute resolution did not yet have a strong motivating effect. In this setting, motivation was thus the determining factor for the potential applicants' behaviour. Despite high ability and moderate to high opportunity, the only moderate motivation was, according to the MOC framework, predominantly decisive for whether potential state applicants engaged with the court. In later years, motivation and opportunity increased (see Figure 5.3). Following the Protocol No 11 reform and the end of the two-tier structure of the Strasbourg system, the opportunity for state applicants to access the court has become broad. These applicants have also become more strongly motivated by dispute resolution so that the motivational level can be qualified as moderate to high. Although the MOC setting is thus very favourable, motivation remains slightly less pronounced than the other factors so that it continues to be the determining factor according to the MOC framework.

Figure 5.3 Development over time of the MOC setting for state applicants before the ECtHR

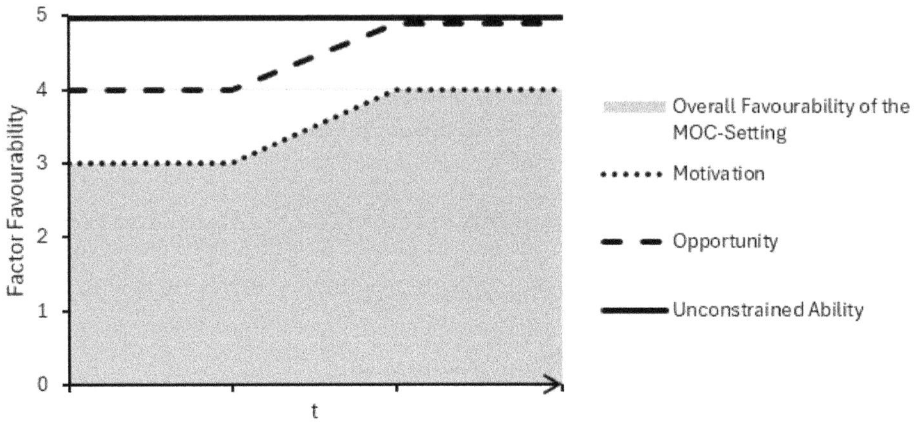

III. MOC FACTORS FOR RESPONDENTS

A. MOC Factors for Acceptance of the Court's Authority

i. Motivation

Values

As part of the Council of Europe regime, the ECtHR is a strongly value-based institution. Human rights, democracy and the rule of law are the values that the Convention enshrines and that the Council of Europe advocates. In its 2023 Reykjavík Declaration aptly titled 'United around our values', the member states have recently reaffirmed this common value-basis.[171]

In the initial phase of the court, the values that motivated member states to create the court and to accept its authority were significantly influenced by the experience of the Second Word War as well as the unfolding Cold War. One set of values thus related to 'liberal democratic ideals' that states wished to solidify and to 'lock … into the Western European form of government'.[172] In this vein, the court was intended to 'constitute a collective insurance policy against the relapse of democracies into dictatorships'.[173] Member states wanted to ensure that human rights values persisted as guiding values for their own political systems as well as in the political systems of the other member states. The Convention system was considered to be 'a sort of "insurance" against the danger of an undemocratic take-over of power'.[174]

[171] Declaration of the Reykjavík Summit, 4th Summit of Heads of State and Government of the Council of Europe, 16–17 May 2023.
[172] Madsen, 'The European Court of Human Rights' (n 34) 246.
[173] Wildhaber, 'The European Court of Human Rights' (n 86) 523. See in detail Bates, *Evolution* (n 2) 44–76.
[174] Nussberger, *The European Court of Human Rights* (n 6) 12.

This was a motivating factor for most member states, although some states such as France were only motivated by upholding these values in other member states rather than within their own jurisdiction, seeing themselves as having 'no lessons to learn from anyone'.[175] At the same time, the Convention system was perceived as a tool 'for providing liberal democracies with a moral high ground, from which non-democratic regimes could be criticized'.[176] Later, democratic values also motivated the reforms that member states undertook via the various protocols to the Convention. With these reforms, they considered an international human rights review to be a 'means … of strengthening and developing a healthy, dynamic democratic society'.[177]

Further, member states wished to emphasise and strengthen the unity and common values among them. The Preamble of the Convention declares that member states have 'a common heritage of political traditions, ideals, freedom and the rule of law' and that they pursue 'greater unity' between them. This motivation persisted during the following decades. As the former ECtHR judge Rudolf Bernhardt observed:

> The member states of the Council of Europe and the parties to the Convention have recognized that the interpretation and the application of the European Convention can contribute to uniform European standards … [T]here is a feeling among the member states that there exists a common European standard and that this standard should be further developed.[178]

Until the end of the 1980s, the de facto value-correspondence between member states and the court was high. Both the original member states and those that successively joined until the late 1980s were rule of law-based democracies.[179] Although some member states such as Portugal and Spain joined the Council of Europe and accepted the court's jurisdiction at a stage when they were newly established democracies that still had to improve and consolidate their rule of law and human rights practice, the aspirational value basis was present in these states as well. Overall, the basic values mentioned in the Preamble were thus widely shared among member states. In particular, the fact that member states up until the enlargement of the 1990s had a robust rule of law culture and high appreciation for rule of law values has been an important motivational factor for high compliance rates despite member states often criticising ECtHR decisions.[180]

However, although both aspirational and de facto value-correspondence as to human rights protection was high in general, certain aspects were less pronounced. First, there was a certain disagreement among member states as to the meaning of human rights. In the court's initial phase, 'the very notion of human rights law was

[175] See Bates, *Evolution* (n 2) 177 with further references.

[176] Shany (n 167) 76.

[177] P Mahoney, 'Parting thoughts of an outgoing Registrar of the European Court of Human Rights' (2005) 26 *Human Rights Law Journal* 345, 345.

[178] R Bernhardt, 'Commentary: The European system' (1986–1987) 2 *Connecticut Journal of International Law* 299, 299–300.

[179] Greece only accepted the jurisdiction of the court in 1979, thus after the time of its military regime. And Turkey, although a party to the Convention since 1954, only accepted the court's jurisdiction in 1990.

[180] M O'Boyle, 'Reflections on the Effectiveness of the European System for the Protection of Human Rights' in A Bayefsky (ed), *The UN Human Rights System in the 21st Century* (Kluwer 2000) 169, 178.

ambiguous and was more often associated with politics than law'.[181] Second, and maybe even more importantly for the ECtHR, many member states did not have a long-standing tradition of human rights jurisprudence within their domestic legal orders. Initially, member states 'were not used to "doing" human rights' and only gradually adopted an understanding of human rights adjudication that was influenced by the US model as well as some constitutional courts in Europe such as the German Constitutional Court.[182] This affected the value-correspondence as to the institutional role of courts in safeguarding human rights.[183] In particular, many member states were not used to the idea of courts exercising a constitutional review of legislative acts. Posing a challenge to the acceptance of such a review by the ECtHR, 'the constitutional law and separation of powers doctrines of most European states either strictly limited, or prohibited altogether, the judicial review of statutes by most or all domestic courts'.[184] Further, not all member states considered it to be the role of courts to undertake a proportionality assessment. Initially, 'proportionality analysis was native only to the legal systems of Germany and Switzerland', but not to other member states.[185] However, for many member states the domestic adjudicative systems developed and 'matured' at the same time as the ECtHR, in conjunction with the Commission, built up the European human rights review – a parallel that has 'facilitated the court's efforts to build its own political legitimacy'.[186] The judicial review of legislative acts as well as the use of a proportionality assessment have by now become part of the judicial practice in most member states (with one prominent exception being the United Kingdom – see section III.B).

The value-correspondence during the 1990s has been partly inversed compared with the court's earlier years. The aspirational value-correspondence was very high while the de facto value-correspondence decreased significantly. As to the former, it was a period in which human rights values were very prominently promoted on the international level, including by regional organisations. There was 'a zeitgeist not only favourable, but enthusiastic about human rights protection'.[187] This particularly high motivating effect led member states to amend the institutional structure of the ECtHR via Protocol No 11, creating a permanent court with mandatory jurisdiction and direct access for individual applicants.[188] And the initial caveats to value-correspondence as to the content of human rights and the role of the court especially in reviewing legislative acts only persisted for a few member states.

Further, for many states that ratified the Convention in the 1990s, the value of democracy was a strong motivational factor for accepting the authority of the court. In these states, 'democracy and rights protection were strongly equated' so that 'the convention offered an established, "external", and therefore legitimate, normative

[181] Madsen, 'The European Court of Human Rights' (n 34) 250–51.
[182] Nussberger, *The European Court of Human Rights* (n 6) 13.
[183] See also Madsen, 'The European Court of Human Rights' (n 34) 251.
[184] A Stone Sweet, W Sandholtz, M Andenas, 'The Failure to Destroy the Authority of the European Court of Human Rights: 2010–2018', University of Hong Kong Faculty of Law Research Paper No 2022/12: papers.ssrn.com/sol3/papers.cfm?abstract_id=4055713.
[185] Keller and Stone Sweet, 'The Reception of the ECHR in National Legal Orders' (n 75) 11.
[186] Keller and Stone Sweet, 'Assessing the Impact of the ECHR on National Legal Systems' (n 74) 678.
[187] Nussberger, *The European Court of Human Rights* (n 6) 27.
[188] ibid.

standard for the transition to constitutional democracy'.[189] Value-correspondence regarding democracy as a value that is at least also protected by the court was thus high at this stage and within this group of state actors. As a result, this value shaped the attitude of the central and East European states towards the court: 'the desire to break with the totalitarian past as a matter of principle made the attitudes towards the Court and its case law generally very positive'.[190]

However, de facto value-correspondence has become less pronounced with the 1990s enlargement. The Council of Europe had lowered the standard for accession (Articles 3 and 4 of its Statute) since the 1990s in order to facilitate the enlargement.[191] When countries such as Romania, Croatia and Russia were admitted, this demonstrated how, in a step-by-step process, the required standards have been relaxed more and more.[192] The Russian accession was especially controversial, in particular due to the structural human rights violations in the Chechnya context prior and post-accession.[193] By 1994, the then Secretary General of the Council of Europe had already pointed to the greater heterogeneity and the aspirational purpose of accession:

> [T]he Council is no longer concerned simply with helping its members to remain pluralistic democracies showing respect for human rights; it is often concerned with helping its members (as well as applicant States) to become democracies in that full sense of the term ... By comparison with the period 1949–89, the Europe of the Council of Europe is thus less homogeneous and more unstable.[194]

This assessment still remains valid today, however to a different extent as compared with the 1990s. On the one hand, several states still have a medium to low rule of law standard. Among the currently 46 member states, 10 are only 'partly free' and two are 'not free' according to the Freedom House rating of 2025 (see Table 5.2). Moreover, during the last two decades, the value-correspondence as to certain member states has decreased because of political shifts in these countries. A comparison of the rule of law index ratings from 1996 and 2023 (Worldwide Governance Indicators) shows that, among the member states that accepted the jurisdiction of the court in the 1990s, the rule of law standard has become lower in some member states. This includes most prominently Hungary, Poland and Türkiye. The rule of law standard has also decreased significantly for some older member states including Greece, Italy, Spain and Cyprus. On the other hand, the trend for the other member states that joined in the 1990s is positive. The majority have substantially increased their rule of law standard. Thus, although there is still heterogeneity among the member states, this heterogeneity is less structured around an East/West divide. Overall, the value-correspondence has increased for some member states and decreased for others.

[189] Keller and Stone Sweet, 'Assessing the Impact of the ECHR on National Legal Systems' (n 74) 679.

[190] I Ziemele, 'Conclusions' in Motoc and Ziemele (eds), *The Impact of the ECHR on Democratic Change in Central and Eastern Europe* (n 79) 491, 496.

[191] Bates, *Evolution* (n 2) 447–48.

[192] ibid 448.

[193] See generally on the accession, B Bowring, 'Russia's accession to the Council of Europe and human rights: Four years on' (2000) *Helsinki Monitor* 53.

[194] Discussion paper by the Secretary General of the Council of Europe 'The Council of Europe in the new Europe', 27 April 1994, CM(94)78, 2–3: rm.coe.int/0900001680523515.

Table 5.2 Standards of the rule of law as well as political rights and civil liberties in Council of Europe Member States

Member State	Freedom House Report 2025: overall score and rating	Freedom House Report 2025: judicial independence	WJP Rule of Law Index 2024 *Overall score and global rank [among 140 assessed states]*	Worldwide Governance Indicators: rule of law *[for 2023]* *Estimate of Governance (−2.5 to +2.5) and Percentile rank among countries*	Worldwide Governance Indicators: rule of law *[for 1996]* *Estimate of Governance (−2.5 to +2.5) and Percentile rank among countries*
Albania	68 Partly Free	3/4	0.8–89	−0.16–45.75	−0.68–28.64
Andorra	93 Free	4/4	n/a	1.48–91.51	1.16–86.43
Armenia	54 Partly Free	1/4	n/a	−0.12–49.06	−0.47–37.69
Austria	93 Free	4/4	0.79–13	1.75–97.17	1.81–97.49
Azerbaijan	7 Not Free	0/4	n/a	−0.57–29.25	−1.20–13.07
Belgium	96 Free	4/4	0.78–17	1.30–88.21	1.37–89.95
Bosnia and Herzegovina	52 Partly Free	1/4	0.52–71	−0.35–39.62	−0.24–43.22
Bulgaria	77 Free	3/4	0.56–59	−0.01–53.77	−0.34–39.70
Croatia	82 Free	3/4	0.61–45	0.36–59.43	−0.63–31.16
Cyprus	91 Free	4/4	0.67–31	0.63–71.70	0.86–78.39
Czech Republic	95 Free	4/4	0.74–20	1.14–84.43	0.92–79.90
Denmark	97 Free	4/4	0.90–1	1.91–99.53	1.82–97.99
Estonia	96 Free	4/4	0.82–10	1.43–89.62	0.57–66.33
Finland	100 Free	4/4	0.87–3	1.97–100.00	1.91–98.99
France	89 Free	4/4	0.72–22	1.18–84.91	1.48–91.96
Georgia	55 Partly Free	2/4	0.60–49	0.18–55.19	−1.26–11.06
Germany	95 Free	4/4	0.83–5	1.55–92.92	1.61–93.97
Greece	85 Free	3/4	0.60–47	0.21–57.08	1.05–83.42
Hungary	65 Partly Free	2/4	0.51–73	0.13–63.21	0.91–79.40
Iceland	95 Free	4/4	n/a	1.72–96.70	1.60–93.47
Ireland	97 Free	4/4	0.82–9	1.63–93.87	1.50–92.96
Italy	89 Free	4/4	0.66–32	0.39–60.85	1.06–84.42
Latvia	89 Free	3/4	0.73–21	1.04–83.02	0.13–56.78
Liechtenstein	90 Free	3/4	n/a	1.71–96.23	1.47–91.46

(continued)

Table 5.2 *(Continued)*

Member State	Freedom House Report 2025: overall score and rating	Freedom House Report 2025: judicial independence	WJP Rule of Law Index 2024 *Overall score and global rank [among 140 assessed states]*	Worldwide Governance Indicators: rule of law *[for 2023]* *Estimate of Governance (−2.5 to +2.5) and Percentile rank among countries*	Worldwide Governance Indicators: rule of law *[for 1996]* *Estimate of Governance (−2.5 to +2.5) and Percentile rank among countries*
Lithuania	89 Free	3/4	0.77–18	1.27–86.79	0.45–63.32
Luxembourg	97 Free	4/4	0.83–7	1.75–97.64	1.71–95.98
Malta	87 Free	4/4	0.67–30	0.70–75.47	1.05–83.92
Moldova	60 Partly Free	1/4	0.54–64	−0.15–47.17	−0.12–47.74
Monaco	82 Free	3/4	n/a	1.48–91.51	0.81–76.88
Montenegro	69 Partly Free	2/4	n/a	−0.01–52.36	n/a
Netherlands	97 Free	4/4	0.83–8	1.61–94.34	1.70–95.48
North Macedonia	67 Partly Free	2/4	0.53–67	−0.17–45.28	−0.31–40.70
Norway	100 Free	4/4	0.89–2	1.83–99.06	1.92–99.50
Poland	82 Free	2/4	0.66–33	0.46–65.09	0.77–70.85
Portugal	96 Free	4/4	0.68–28	1.07–83.49	1.29–88.94
Romania	82 Free	3/4	0.62–41	0.44–64.15	−0.02–50.25
San Marino	97 Free	4/4	n/a	1.18–91.51	0.81–76.88
Serbia	56 Partly Free	2/4	0.47–94	−0.07–51.42	−1.26–10.55
Slovak Republic	89 Free	3/4	0.66–34	0.60–68.87	0.16–57.29
Slovenia	96 Free	4/4	0.69–27	1.04–82.55	1.07–84.92
Spain	90 Free	3/4	0.71–25	0.82–78.30	1.44–90.45
Sweden	99 Free	4/4	0.86–4	1.60–93.40	1.80–96.98
Switzerland	96 Free	4/4	n/a	1.76–98.58	1.93–100.00
Türkiye	33 Not Free	1/4	0.42–117	−0.51–32.55	−0.14–47.24
Ukraine	51 Partly Free	1/4	0.49–88	−0.89–19.81	−0.82–22.61
United Kingdom	92 Free	4/4	0.78–15	1.40–89.15	1.63–94.47
[former MS: Russia]	12 Not Free	1/4	0.43–113	−1.19–12.26	−0.79–24.62

Interests

A range of interests can motivate member states to accept the authority of the ECtHR. First, reputational interests are a motivational factor for member states that joined the Convention system and accepted the jurisdiction of the court after a period of autocratic, military or otherwise undemocratic regime.[195] Over the decades, this concerned different groups of member states such as Germany, Italy and Austria after their 1940s regimes, Spain, Portugal and Greece after their regime changes in the 1970s and the post-communist states in the 1990s.[196] This motivational interest is particularly high when the other member states within the group have a high human rights reputation. The general interest in a positive human rights reputation is, in this case, intensified by an interest in group membership. Especially for states 'whose human rights records was tainted', accession to the Convention and accepting the authority of the court was seen as 'a signal to the outside world that a State is "member of the club" and upholds the same standards as others'.[197] For example, regarding the member states that joined in the 1990s, accession and acceptance of the authority of the court was seen as a way 'to certify their membership in the circle of good European countries'.[198]

Relatedly, many member states that joined in the 1990s and later were motivated by their (potential) future membership of the EU. New member states had (and have) to fulfil the so-called 'Copenhagen criteria' which require democracy, the rule of law and human rights. Joining the Council of Europe was a first step to becoming members of the EU.[199] Similarly, states also saw joining the Council of Europe as a stepping-stone for potentially joining NATO.[200]

A further interest that can motivate respondents to accept the authority of the court is dispute resolution. Regarding interstate complaints, what has been said on this motivation in section II.A is applicable to state respondents as well. In contrast, in the context of individual complaints, dispute resolution is a motivational factor that is less generalisable and that varies depending on the type of case and applicant. As mentioned in the previous chapter, especially when applicants with high visibility and a broad reach (such as political actors or NGOs) bring a case to the court,

[195] See also generally on the wish to demonstrate a commitment to human rights as a factor for compliance, C Hillebrecht, *Domestic Politics and International Human Rights Tribunals: The Problem of Compliance* (CUP 2014) 25.

[196] On the motivation of Spain and Portugal to 'demonstrat[e] their intention of burying their recent fascist pasts', Bates, *Evolution* (n 2) 284. On Russia's motivation to accede in order to demonstrate that, after the communist regime, Russia had embraced human rights and the rule of law, I Busygina and J Kahn, 'Russia, the Council of Europe, and "Ruxit", or Why Non-Democratic Illiberal Regimes Join International Organizations' (2020) 67 *Problems of Post-Communism* 64, 68.

[197] Nussberger, *The European Court of Human Rights* (n 6) 12.

[198] Keller and Stone Sweet, 'Assessing the Impact of the ECHR on National Legal Systems' (n 74) 679. On whether the reputational interest in signing a human rights treaty also comes with a motivation to comply with its norms, M Burstein, 'The Will to Enforce: An Examination of the Political Constraints Upon a Regional Court of Human Rights' (2006) 24 *Berkeley Journal of International Law* 423, 434.

[199] See also Nussberger, *The European Court of Human Rights* (n 6) 25.

[200] On this aspect, MR Madsen, 'From boom to backlash? The European Court of Human Rights and the transformation of Europe' in Aust and Demir-Gürsel, *The European Court of Human Rights: Current Challenges in Historical Perspective* (n 167) 21, 27.

government actors have an interest in this dispute being resolved so that it no longer shapes the public discourse.

For member states who accepted the jurisdiction of the court in the early period of the court's existence, there were certain specific motivational factors. During this period, states assessed their interests and potential costs without foreseeing the upcoming developments. They 'seriously underestimated the degree to which the ECHR would impact on their domestic legal systems'.[201] This was due, in part, to the restrictive approach that the court took in its early years: 'more and more governments accepted the Court and the individual petition because they simply did not fear the Court's influence'.[202] For example, when the United Kingdom accepted the court's jurisdiction in 1966, politicians expected this step to have very little impact given that the domestic human rights protection was thought to go beyond what the Convention required.[203]

Relatedly, for many early member states, accepting the authority of the court was a multi-step process that made the costs of joining the Strasbourg system appear relatively low.[204] Considering that both the jurisdiction of the court and the individual access were optional features of the original system, it was possible for member states to ratify the Convention first without accepting these optional features. Such a ratification however presented a first step that, according to the 'foot-in-the-door' effect,[205] would have made it easier for member states to accept the second and third steps as well. Although this initially optional system seems, at its face, to have slowed down the process of states accepting the authority of the court,[206] it is in fact likely that it has contributed to lowering the bar for states to accept the jurisdiction of the court. The practice of several member states in the early years to accept the jurisdiction of the court only for a specific period of time has had a similar effect. Member states such as Norway, Sweden, Belgium, the United Kingdom and Italy made declarations regarding the court's jurisdiction or the individual complaint mechanism only for two to five years with the possibility of renewal.[207] This would have enhanced the motivation to accept the jurisdiction as the stakes were perceived as less high.

Further, the two-tier system of the Commission and the court created an additional interest in accepting the authority of the court. In the first 20 years of its existence, the Commission had gained a reputation among member states of being somewhat activist in their human rights review. This motivated respondent states to refer cases to the court, hoping that a more conservative court would come to more state-friendly conclusions than the Commission. For example, the United Kingdom

[201] Keller and Stone Sweet, 'Assessing the Impact of the ECHR on National Legal Systems' (n 74) 678.

[202] Madsen, 'The European Court of Human Rights' (n 34) 251.

[203] Bates, *Evolution* (n 2) 189–91.

[204] Madsen, 'The European Court of Human Rights' (n 34) 246.

[205] See ch 2, and JL Freedman and SC Fraser, 'Compliance without pressure: the foot-in-the-door technique' (1966) 4 *Journal of Personality and Social Psychology* 195.

[206] For this reading, see Madsen, 'The European Court of Human Rights' (n 34) 246.

[207] Bates, *Evolution* (n 2) 176, 279; M Breuer, 'Principled resistance to the European Court of Human Rights and its case law: a comparative assessment' in Aust and Demir-Gürsel, *The European Court of Human Rights: Current Challenges in Historical Perspective* (n 167) 43, 46.

referred the *Golder* case to the court in 1973 with the aim to 'clip the wings of the overenthusiastic Commission'.[208]

A motivational factor that becomes more relevant the longer a state is a member of the Convention system, and the more it has accepted the court's authority in the past, is the state's interest in consistent behaviour. When a member state has engaged with the ECtHR and accepted its authority in several cases, state actors will perceive this behaviour as reflecting a normative preference. As actors tend to opt for consistent behaviour, their past behaviour leads to an interest in upholding this preference.[209] The longer the behaviour is perpetuated, the more actors perceive their interest in consistent decision-making as a predominant motivational factor. Moreover, the behavioural factors of inertia and status quo bias (see chapter two) become relevant the longer the authority relationship between the state actors and the ECtHR lasts. When repeatedly engaging with the ECtHR, state actors will question less and less whether to accept the authority of the court in the case at hand but, as an expression of inertia, perpetuate the behaviour adopted on earlier occasions. In addition, the status quo bias is likely to enhance the value that actors attribute to the preferences expressed by previous behaviour. When weighing options, it is thus more likely that they decide to adopt the behavioural choice reflective of the status quo and thus continue to accept the authority of the ECtHR. For member states in the ECtHR context, it was therefore not beneficial for the development of these motivational factors that there have been only a few or no judgments against some states during the earlier decades of the court's practice. For example, the court did not find against Denmark for more than 30 years (1953–88).[210] In contrast, and due to the developing practice of the court, the later a member state joined the Convention system the more likely it was that it would engage with the court as a respondent soon after, and in a frequently recurring manner. For those member states, the interest in consistent behaviour as well as inertia and the status quo bias have become relevant motivational factors more rapidly.

Among the motivational interests specifically regarding compliance, the monitoring mechanism by the Committee of Ministers (and to a lesser extent by the court itself) provides an important incentive. As mentioned in the previous chapters, monitoring has a motivational effect because it makes it more likely that other actors become aware of non-compliance which can lead to reputational disadvantages or even formal sanctions – consequences that the respective actor aims to avoid.[211] The monitoring mechanism includes 'hard' sanctions that go as far as a member state being 'suspended from its rights of representation and requested by the Committee of Ministers to withdraw' (Article 8 Statute of the Council of Europe). However, as the Committee of Ministers has not used these sanctions as a general enforcement tool, their practical motivating effect is limited. Rather, the Committee of Ministers enforcement strategy focuses on reputational costs. It

[208] Bates, *Evolution* (n 2) 290.
[209] See ch 2 and RB Cialdini, *Influence: Science and Practice*, 5th edn (Pearson Education 2009) 51 et seq.
[210] Madsen, 'The European Court of Human Rights' (n 34) 255.
[211] DT Welsh and LD Ordóñez, 'Conscience without Cognition: The Effects of Subconscious Priming on Ethical Behavior' (2014) 57 *Academy of Management Journal* 723.

mainly works with 'diplomatic sanctions such as the (repeated) adoption of resolutions'.[212] Such resolutions keep the compliance obligation and the compliance deficit salient for the respondent and for the other member states that are the reference points for reputational costs. This reputational interest is reinforced further when the Committee of Ministers involves the court according to Article 46(4) ECtHR. And, as mentioned above, other actors such as NGOs contribute to the compliance monitoring by providing reports about the human rights situation in the respondent states. Moreover, litigants can return to the court in follow-up proceedings on non-compliance. The monitoring function is thus diversified. It mobilises both institutional actors (Committee of Ministers) and private actors (NGOs and litigants) to increase salience and reputational costs for respondent states that fail to comply with ECtHR decisions.

However, there have been some concerns since the late 1990s regarding the effectiveness of monitoring by the Committee of Ministers. The Committee started to struggle with the number of decisions for which it had to monitor implementation, leading to lengthy monitoring procedures.[213] In addition, since the court has created the pilot judgment procedure, the Committee has had to face increasingly complex judgments and a diverse range of domestic actors involved in the implementation.[214] This reduces the motivational effect of the compliance monitoring. Despite these issues, the monitoring system is still qualified as effective, especially as it is only in a small number of cases that member states have refused to comply with judgments (see section III.B).

For *domestic courts*, one can observe specific motivational factors. To start with, most domestic courts have a strategic interest in accepting the authority of the ECtHR. Implementing the Convention and the court's jurisprudence empowers them in their relation to domestic governmental and legislative actors. As Keller and Stone Sweet observe:

> [I]n most States, the incorporation of the EcHR has enhanced the overall authority of the ordinary courts vis-à-vis all other non-judicial officials … In Europe today, judicial authority includes the competence to review the legal validity of all Government acts under the convention.[215]

An exception to this rationale is constitutional courts. In member states with a formal constitutional court, these actors have already, in accordance with the nature of their institution, the above powers vis-a-vis governmental and legislative actors. For constitutional courts, instead of an empowerment, accepting the authority of the ECtHR means accepting a competing human rights authority. Strategic interest thus rather runs counter to accepting the authority of the court than motivating it (see also section III.B).

As a factor in specific circumstances, an alliance of domestic courts with the ECtHR against governmental actors can be a motivating factor in member states

[212] Nussberger, 'From High Hopes to Scepticism?' (n 41) 169 (fn 91).
[213] Bates, *Evolution* (n 2) 493–94.
[214] ibid 494.
[215] Keller and Stone Sweet, 'Assessing the Impact of the ECHR on National Legal Systems' (n 74) 687–88.

with low judicial independence standards and declining human rights standards. For example, the ECtHR has been an external ally for the Hungarian Constitutional Court in light of the eroding rule of law and constitutional protection in post-2010 Hungary.[216] Establishing the ECHR as a minimum standard, it stated that 'the legal protection offered by the Constitutional Court may not be lower than the level of protection guaranteed internationally (particularly as elaborated by the Strasbourg Court of Human Rights)'.[217]

In addition, the relationship among domestic courts also constitutes an important motivational factor. When defining their stance as to the ECHR and the ECtHR, domestic courts often act strategically with the aim of strengthening their power position vis-a-vis their respective supreme or constitutional courts. This has been observed as a common approach in states such as Austria, Belgium, the Czech Republic, Italy and Türkiye.[218] However, this strategic interest has been limited by the reaction of some of the targeted constitutional courts. For example, the Italian Constitutional Court integrated the Convention rights into its constitutional review to reassert its predominant role in human rights interpretation and to make sure that domestic courts refer preliminary references to the Constitutional Court when Convention rights are at stake.[219] Moreover, it bears mentioning that internal power struggles are not a motivating factor for domestic courts in all member states. For example, in Poland, lower courts have perceived the ECtHR 'as an "interfering superior" rather than as an ally'.[220]

A further motivational factor has shaped the behaviour of domestic courts in states without a full-scale constitutional review and in states in which constitutional courts were newly created. Here, domestic courts were interested in referring to the ECHR and the jurisprudence of the ECtHR to fill gaps in the domestic legal framework or to use this jurisprudence as a guideline. Such a motivation has been described for courts in the Netherlands, Switzerland, Belgium, Poland and the Czech Republic.[221] References to the ECtHR thus fulfil a practical function but are also seen by domestic courts in this context as a 'tool of empowerment' and of legitimation.[222]

As for governmental actors, the interest of domestic courts in consistent behaviour is likely to contribute to the courts' motivation to engage with the jurisprudence of the ECtHR. In member states in which courts have started to refer to this jurisprudence, such referencing has generally increased over time. States in which domestic

[216] E Polgári, 'Hungary: "Gains And Losses" Changing the Relationship with the European Court of Human Rights' in Popelier, Lambrecht and Lemmens (eds), *Criticism of the European Court of Human Rights, Shifting the Convention System* (n 165) 295, 316.

[217] Hungarian Constitutional Court, decision no 61/2011 (VII. 13.) V.2.2.

[218] S Lambrecht, 'Assessing the Existence of Criticism of the European Court of Human Rights' in Popelier, Lambrecht and Lemmens (eds), *Criticism of the European Court of Human Rights, Shifting the Convention System* (n 165) 505, 538.

[219] Italian Constitutional Court, decision nos 348 and 349/2007 of 22 October 2007. On this jurisprudence as part of the position of the Italian judiciary towards the ECHR, G Martinico, 'Italy: Between Constitutional Openness and Resistance' in Popelier, Lambrecht and Lemmens (eds), *Criticism of the European Court of Human Rights, Shifting the Convention System* (n 165) 177, 182 et seq.

[220] K Kowalik-Bańczyk, 'Poland: The Taming of the Shrew' in Popelier, Lambrecht and Lemmens (eds), *Criticism of the European Court of Human Rights, Shifting the Convention System* (n 165) 199, 233.

[221] Lambrecht (n 218) 550.

[222] ibid.

courts – and especially also constitutional and apex courts – have referred to the ECtHR frequently include, inter alia, Austria, Belgium, Norway, Poland and the United Kingdom.[223]

Finally, an interest in accepting the authority of the court results from the effect of the Strasbourg system itself. Certain domestic courts that had, for a time, a conflictual relationship with the ECtHR such as French and British courts eventually wanted 'to reduce their vulnerability to findings of violation'.[224] This led them to incorporate the jurisprudence of the ECtHR more readily.

In sum, member states, in particular governmental actors, have been strongly motivated by values and only to some extent by interests. There has been, both in the pre-Protocol No 11 and post-Protocol No 11 periods, a high level of aspirational value-correspondence regarding human rights and democratic values as protected by the ECtHR. It peaked at the two points in time that were crucial for the court's development: when the Convention was adopted and first set into practice; and during the 1990s when Protocol No 11 was adopted and the enlargement took place. An initially weaker value-correspondence as to the role of courts has strengthened over time in almost all member states. The de facto value-correspondence as to human rights protection and the rule of law was initially high, thus corroborating an overall high value-correspondence. With the enlargement, this de facto value-correspondence decreased and has since morphed into an altering heterogeneity among member states. This means that the level of value-correspondence changed for some member states while remaining stable for others.

Moreover, the interests that motivate governmental actors to accept the authority of the court have also changed over time. Among the rather stable interests are dispute resolution and interests relating to the monitoring system of the Convention. Reputational considerations play a role throughout the decades, yet not to the same extent for all actors as they have been especially important for member states after regime changes. The interest in consistent behaviour adds to that, increasing over time. Given that member states have joined the jurisdiction of the court at different periods, this interest gained importance in an asynchronous manner. Low expected costs and the possibility to outplay the Commission were motivating effects mostly in the early phase.

Regarding domestic courts, the motivation to accept the authority of the court is mostly interest-driven. These interests were rather low in the early phase of the court's practice. Only gradually, consistent behaviour started to have a motivating effect. Further, different from the ECOWAS context, strategic interests have come to play a significant role as well. This includes both an empowerment towards governmental and legislative actors as well as towards other domestic courts. Yet this motivational effect only materialised rather slowly so that it has contributed to the overall motivation of judicial actors more prominently in later decades.

ii. Opportunity

The legal opportunity structure for respondents is first and foremost shaped by Articles 33 and 34 ECHR (Articles 24 and 25 ECHR 1950). These provisions stipulate

[223] ibid 536.
[224] Keller and Stone Sweet, 'Assessing the Impact of the ECHR on National Legal Systems' (n 74) 705–06.

that only member states can assume the role of formal respondent. Neither Council of Europe institutions nor international organisations or private actors within member states can become respondents before the court under the human rights jurisdiction. Although applicants have tried to broaden the scope of potential applicants, the court has confirmed that only claims against member states are admissible.[225]

The respondent status of member states translates to actors from the executive, legislative and judicial branches of government. For *executive actors* within the member states, the legal opportunity structure is shaped by the fact that the Convention and the ECtHR jurisprudence do not enjoy direct effect within the domestic legal orders. When the Convention was drafted, states did not consider it necessary to include a provision on its relationship towards domestic law. The prevailing opinion was 'that the States were already fully protecting all Convention rights in their domestic law'.[226] Moreover, domestic law only slowly gave effect to the Convention. For many decades, many member states had not incorporated it into their legal orders. For example, until the 1980s,

> the French position was that the convention had virtually no legal status in the internal order. In that State's view, a High contracting Party, faced with a violation of the convention, entirely discharged its responsibilities merely by compensating the affected applicant.[227]

Over the decades and especially in the 1990s, member states have changed their stance on this matter. All member states have incorporated the Convention so that it is applicable in their domestic legal orders. In many member states, the status of the Convention is explicitly defined by domestic constitutional or statutory provisions. This can include the internal legal effect of the Convention, the rank within the domestic hierarchy of norms and the effect of decisions of the ECtHR. As to the two latter points, the approaches vary widely among legal orders.[228]

Further, the de facto opportunity for executive actors has broadened over time. In the 1960s and early 1970s, only very few cases reached the court and were decided on the merits.[229] For member states, this meant that in practice the opportunity to accept the authority of the court was limited. From the mid-1970s onwards, this opportunity broadened steadily until it reached the broad de facto opportunity of the 1990s and post-Protocol No 11 period. Moreover, the de facto opportunity varies strongly among member states. For some member states, only a few cases reached the court and/or the court found very few violations so that the respective governmental actors had little opportunity to accept the authority of the court by implementing its decisions. As already mentioned, the court did not find against Denmark for more than 30 years (1953–88).[230] In contrast, executive actors in member states with high

[225] *Kyriakoula Stephens v Cyprus, Turkey and the United Nations*, 11 December 2008, App no 45267/06; *Commission, X v the United Kingdom*, 10 December 1976, App no 6956/75 (with further references).

[226] Bates, *Evolution* (n 2) 158.

[227] Keller and Stone Sweet, 'Assessing the Impact of the ECHR on National Legal Systems' (n 74) 682–83.

[228] See for an overview, H Keller and Alec Stone Sweet (eds), *A Europe of Rights: The Impact of the ECHR on National Legal Systems* (OUP 2008).

[229] The court had decided only 9 cases on the merits by 1974, leading to this period being termed the 'sleeping beauty' years of the courts. See J Frowein, 'European Integration through Fundamental Rights' (1984) 18 *Michigan Journal of Law Reform* 5, 8; Bates, *Evolution* (n 2) 257.

[230] Madsen, 'The European Court of Human Rights' (n 34) 255.

application rates such as Türkiye, Russia (until the end of its Council of Europe membership), Romania, Italy, Ukraine and Moldova have broad opportunity to accept the authority of the court as these countries have faced a consistently high number of cases and violation findings over time.

Regarding the content of decisions addressing domestic executive actors, the opportunity for these actors to accept the authority of the court has broadened over time along with the court's changing approach to remedies. Initially, these actors were required to compensate applicants financially when the court granted such compensation, a rather narrow opportunity for acceptance. More recently, as the court has turned to more demanding remedies, executive actors also have an opportunity to adjust their behaviour to more far-reaching orders. For example, when the court requires a respondent to conduct investigations regarding the killings of human beings, this obligation creates a broad opportunity for executive actors to accept the authority of the court.[231]

Concerning *legislative actors*, the opportunity has never been narrow as was initially the case in the ECOWAS context. Rather, the opportunity started out at a moderate level and broadened over time. As already mentioned, the Commission had established as early as 1958 that member states are obliged 'to ensure that their domestic legislation is compatible with the Convention and, if need be, to make any necessary adjustments'.[232] In the jurisprudence of the court, requirements for legislative actors are most closely related to the notion of positive obligations of member states as developed in the *Marckx* decision of 1979.[233] The court has recognised a general obligation for a respondent state to amend its legislation if the human rights violation has been caused by this legislation and can only be remedied by a legislative amendment.[234] As a result, the court has reviewed domestic legislation as to their compatibility with the Convention. This created an opportunity for legislative actors to accept the authority of the court. However, until the 1990s, the court did not issue specific recommendations or even orders as to how the legislator of the respondent state should adjust their domestic law. The legal opportunity for the legislator to accept the authority was thus only moderate.

In the late 1990s, the court started to recommend and later even to order legislative amendments. It has done so especially in situations in which it has detected structural human rights issues in member states. The court's more demanding approach thus goes hand in hand with a growing number of structural human rights violations and the creation of the pilot judgment procedure. For example, the court has obliged respondents to create novel procedural tools or to change criminal law provisions or procedural rules.[235] Further, the court has been at times quite

[231] eg, *McCann and Others v The United Kingdom*, 27 September 1995, App no 18984/91, para 161; *Ergi v Turkey*, 28 July 1998, App no 66/1997/850/1057, paras 82, 98.

[232] *Commission, de Becker v Belgium*, 9 June 1958, App no 214/56 (original in French; English translation as cited by Bates, *Evolution* (n 2) 208).

[233] *Marckx v Belgium*, 13 June 1979, App no 6833/74, para 31.

[234] ibid para 31: requiring 'the existence in domestic law of legal safeguards'. This has been further spelled out in the later jurisprudence, see eg, *Maestri v Italy*, 17 February 2004, App no 39748/98, para 47.

[235] eg, *Rumpf v Germany*, 2 September 2010, App no 46344/06; *Dimitrov and Hamanov v Bulgaria*, 10 May 2011, App nos 48059/06 and 2708/09.

demanding as to the time frame to implement legislative remedies.[236] For example, in *L v Lithuania*, the court ordered the respondent to 'pass the required subsidiary legislation … within three months of the present judgment becoming final'.[237] This novel and more demanding approach has created a broad opportunity for legislative actors to accept the authority of the court by implementing specific recommendations or orders.

For *domestic courts*, as for executive and legislative actors, the opportunity structure has also expanded over time. From the outset, this opportunity has been at least moderate. Unlike in the ECOWAS context, the fact that the court can review domestic judicial decisions has not been contested. The court confirmed early in its practice that the 'European supervision [that it exercises …] covers not only the basic legislation but also the decision applying it, even one given by an independent court'.[238] However, the court has emphasised that 'it is not its function to deal with errors of fact or law allegedly committed by a national court unless and in so far as they may have infringed rights and freedoms protected by the Convention'.[239] In particular with regard to Article 6 ECHR, the court clarified that it 'should not act as a fourth-instance body and will therefore not question … the national courts' assessment, unless their findings can be regarded as arbitrary or manifestly unreasonable'.[240]

Further, the legal opportunity structure for domestic courts to accept the authority of the ECtHR is shaped by domestic law. What has been said above about the relationship between the Convention and domestic law is relevant here as well. Especially when the domestic legislators transposed the Convention into domestic law, this broadened the opportunity for domestic courts. In addition, the relationship between the jurisprudence of the ECtHR and that of the domestic judiciary has been shaped by domestic constitutional and apex courts.[241] Constitutional and apex courts were reluctant to give direct effect to the Convention and the decisions of the ECtHR in earlier decades, with many however shifting their approach during the 1990s and 2000s.[242] For lower courts, this jurisprudential framework largely determines the legal opportunity structure for accepting the authority of the ECtHR.

In the last three decades, the legal opportunity structure has been specified further as to whether, when and how domestic courts can and should take judgments of the ECtHR into account. In many member states, constitutional or apex courts have established an obligation under constitutional law to implement the decisions of the

[236] eg, the court gave a time limit of one year to respondents in *Rumpf v Germany*, 2 September 2010, App no 46344/06; *Vassilios Athanasiou and Others v Greece*, 21 December 2010, App no 50973/08; *Dimitrov and Hamanov v Bulgaria*, 10 May 2011, App nos 48059/06 and 2708/09.

[237] *L v Lithuania*, 11 September 2007, App no 27527/03.

[238] *Handyside v The United Kingdom*, 7 December 1976, App no 5493/72, para 49. For a further example of the earlier case reviewing juridical acts, see *Sunday Times v The United Kingdom*, 26 April 1979, App no 6538/74.

[239] *García Ruiz v Spain*, 21 January 1999, App no 30544/96, para 28; *De Tommaso v Italy*, 23 February 2017, App no 43395/09, para 170.

[240] *De Tommaso v Italy*, 23 February 2017, App no 43395/09, para 170.

[241] For an overview, Keller and Stone Sweet, 'Assessing the Impact of the ECHR on National Legal Systems' (n 74) 705.

[242] On the initial reluctance, see Bates, *Evolution* (n 2) 162.

ECtHR. Such an obligation exists, for example, in Spain, Poland, Slovakia, Germany and Italy.[243] In other member states, an obligation for domestic courts to take into account the jurisprudence of the ECtHR has been created by the legislator. In the United Kingdom, the Human Rights Act of 1998 stipulates in section 2 (1)(a) that domestic courts must do so when 'determining a question which has arisen in connection with a Convention right'. Indeed, after this provision came into force, there has been an upsurge in references from domestic courts to the ECtHR.[244] A similar increase could be observed when the Norwegian Human Rights Act was enacted in 1999.[245] This Act and a related landmark case of the Supreme Court establishing that domestic courts must apply the method of interpretation adopted by the ECtHR have created this opportunity for domestic courts to reference the ECtHR's jurisprudence.[246] These developments further underline that the opportunity for domestic courts to accept the authority is rather broad.

The opportunity structure for respondent actors is also characterised by several *social opportunity elements*. In the first place, a group effect could be observed regarding the acceptance of the two optional clauses (jurisdiction and direct access) that characterised the initial Strasbourg system (see section II.B). Initially, the practice among states that had ratified the Convention was heterogenous. Up until the 1960s and 1970s, important member states such as Italy, France and the United Kingdom had not made Article 25 and/or 46 declarations. As a result, the group practice did not yet exercise a strong conformity pull towards accepting the authority of the ECtHR. For example, the Italian government referred explicitly to this group practice, stating that it 'thought it best not to adhere to certain more specifically binding clauses of the Convention until these have been accepted by almost all the member States'.[247] And as Bates observes, 'there was little political embarrassment in not making' these declarations.[248] However, as more and more member states accepted these clauses, '[w]hat had been originally understood as real as well as legal options became perceived in Europe as politically non-optional'.[249] The social norm within the group was so clear and dominant, that it had become 'difficult' for group members not to conform and 'to stay behind'.[250] At the latest by 1990, the clauses were de facto mandatory and all member states that joined in this period made both declarations at the time of ratification (see Table 5.1).

[243] See the respective chapters on these states in Keller and Stone Sweet, *A Europe of Rights* (n 228).

[244] R Masterman, 'The United Kingdom: From Strasbourg Surrogacy Towards A British Bill Of Rights?' in Popelier, Labrecht and Lemmens (eds), *Criticism of the European Court of Human Rights, Shifting the Convention System* (n 165) 449, 455 (fn 32), citing Kier Starmer: 'Between October 2000 and April 2002, the ECHR was substantively considered in 431 cases in the High Court or above [... while] in the 21 years from July 1975 to July 1996, the ECHR was substantively considered in 316 cases in the High Court or above'.

[245] M Reiertsen, 'Norway: New Constitutionalism, New Counter-Dynamics?' in Popelier, Lambrecht and Lemmens (eds), *Criticism of the European Court of Human Rights, Shifting the Convention System* (n 165) 361, 365: 'Between 1950 to 1990 the ECHR was a theme in 22 cases before the Norwegian Supreme Court, between 1990 to 2000 in 316 cases and between 2000 to 2015 in 1045 cases'.

[246] Reiertsen (n 245) 364.

[247] See Bates, *Evolution* (n 2) 178 with further references.

[248] ibid 177.

[249] Nussberger, *The European Court of Human Rights* (n 6) 156.

[250] ibid.

Further, in several member states the acceptance of the ECtHR's authority by domestic courts has been facilitated by group effects. This plays out most visibly among courts of the same hierarchical position. In France, it was first the Cour de cassation that, in an initial period, accepted the authority of the ECtHR, referring to its jurisprudence and implementing its decisions.[251] This indicated to other high courts within the French judicial system, such as the Conseil d'État, that the practice of an important group member is in favour of accepting the authority of the ECtHR. Eventually, the French courts aligned their approach to the Convention-friendly position of the Court de cassation.[252] Further, group effects can contribute to very consistent behaviour from group members. In states such as the Netherlands, all courts, that is both lower and higher courts, refer to the ECtHR jurisprudence very consistently.[253] The social norm triggering conforming behaviour is thus strong. In addition, such an explicit and visible practice of high courts in one member state can also be perceived by domestic courts in other member states as being part of group practice. The closer and more visible the networks between domestic courts of different member states have become, the more likely it is that the behaviour of courts in other member states is perceived as the behaviour of a group member.

In conclusion, the opportunity structure for all state actors – executive, legislative and judicial – has broadened over time. For the latter two, the developing opportunity started off at a moderate level before developing to a broad level. For legislative actors, the opportunity broadened with the court's more demanding approach as to remedies that require legislative amendments. And for domestic courts, the opportunity increased in the 1990s and 2000s especially when domestic law and/or jurisprudence gave internal effect to the ECHR and ECtHR decisions in many member states and when the social opportunity structure became more favourable. The opportunity structure for executive actors also benefited from these developments (remedies, internal effect and social opportunity). It has thus reached a high level during the past decades, while being moderate to low in the court's earlier period.

iii. Constraints

For governmental actors, the constraining factors are low to moderate. First, as to intrinsic factors, financial constraints have for a long time only played a minor role. Initially, the ECtHR was rather reluctant to grant financial compensation so that the overall burden for member states was very manageable. However, especially since the court has used the pilot judgment procedure, the number of applicants for which a state must pay compensation can become more substantial. Further, the ECtHR does not generally award amounts that would significantly challenge the budget of member states. An exception to the general practice was the damages awarded by the

[251] On this practice, Madsen, 'The European Court of Human Rights' (n 34) 262; K Blay-Grabarczyk and C Maubernard, 'France: "Je T'aime, Moi Non Plus"' in Popelier, Lambrecht and Lemmens (eds), *Criticism of the European Court of Human Rights, Shifting the Convention System* (n 165) 269, 286 et seq.

[252] ibid.

[253] J Gerards, 'The Netherlands: Political Dynamics, Institutional Robustness' in Popelier, Lambrecht and Lemmens (eds), *Criticism of the European Court of Human Rights, Shifting the Convention System* (n 165) 327, 348–49.

court in the *Yukos* case, a sum of €1.8 billion that Russia however did not pay.[254] In the context of non-financial remedies, financial constraints can be more significant. Particularly regarding structural violations, member states would often need significant funds to fully remedy the underlying issues. For example, to reduce the length of judicial proceedings, a state would need to employ more judges; and to improve prison conditions, investments in infrastructure are necessary. As a result, when the court turned to broadening the scope of remedies ordered, this increased the financial constraints for member states.

In some member states, a further intrinsic constraint regarding compliance both by governmental and legislative actors can be the 'legal infrastructure capacity and government effectiveness' within a state.[255] In states with insufficient resources allocated to governmental and legislative actors as well as a lack of expertise, it is less likely that ECtHR judgments will be implemented speedily or at all.[256] Such constraints have, for example, been observed for the implementation process in Greece and Romania.[257] This constraint became more important when the member states became more heterogeneous as to their governance practices from the 1990s onwards.

As to extrinsic constraints, governmental actors can be constrained by competing authority relationships with other regional or international courts or bodies. This includes the CJEU in relation to its growing human rights and rule of law jurisprudence. Diverging decisions are however not very likely, considering that the CJEU takes into account the jurisprudence of the court, especially in view of Article 52(3) of the EU Fundamental Rights Charter. For further harmonisation, the ECtHR at times also takes the jurisprudence of the CJEU into account.[258] In contrast, regarding UN human rights treaty bodies, diverging human rights interpretations have, as already mentioned, been more frequent in recent years.[259] In this regard, a certain constraining effect of the competing authority relationships for governmental actors exists.

For legislative actors, a specific constraint are the time limits that the ECtHR has set for legislative amendments (see above). Such time limits can become a real challenge in complex legislative systems. However, this factor of course only hinders timely compliance, but it does not stop legislative actors from implementing the required amendment at a later stage.

As regards domestic courts, the (limited) knowledge about the ECtHR and its jurisprudence has had a constraining effect. This concerns the knowledge about human rights law in general as well as of the court's case law.[260] These aspects are especially important when it comes to engaging with the ECtHR's jurisprudence on a

[254] *Oao Neftyanaya Kompaniya Yukos v Russia*, 31 July 2014, App no 14902/04 (just satisfaction).

[255] Anagnostou and Mungiu-Pippidi (n 54) 225.

[256] ibid 221, 223.

[257] ibid.

[258] For a recent example, see *Guðmundur Andri Ástráðsson v Iceland*, 1 December 2020, App no 26374/18.

[259] See for a direct conflict, eg, Human Rights Committee, Hebbadj v France, Communication no 2807/2016, Views of 17 July 2018, UN Doc CCPR/C/123/D/2807/2016 and Human Rights Committee, Yaker v France, Communication no 2747/2016, Views of 17 July 2018, UN Doc CCPR/C/123/D/2747/2016 – as compared with ECtHR, *S.A.S. v France*, 1 July 2014, App no 43835/11.

[260] Keller and Stone Sweet, 'Assessing the Impact of the ECHR on National Legal Systems' (n 74) 706.

discursive level and to taking its case law into account in future cases.[261] This intrinsic constraint has been more prevalent in the earlier decades of the ECtHR's existence as compared with the current stage. The longer a state is subject to the jurisdiction of the court, the more visible the court is to the relevant domestic actors. Here, applicants have also had a role in increasing the awareness of domestic courts by introducing legal arguments relating to the Convention and the jurisprudence of the ECtHR into domestic judicial proceedings.

Further, the accessibility of the court's case law is a factor that also changed over time. While the decisions of the court were rather difficult to access in the earlier decades of the ECtHR's practice and often required domestic judges to have access to specialised libraries, digitalisation has greatly reduced this constraint. Digital accessibility of court decisions via HUDOC is, in principle, possible for domestic courts in all member states and at all levels. However, it is of course true that today the sheer quantity of decisions presents a challenge to accessibility of the case law. Against this backdrop, the fact sheets that the court provides on its website in relation to individual rights as well as the Knowledge Sharing platform (ECHR–KS) are important elements to keep the knowledge-related intrinsic constraints for domestic courts at a moderate level or lower.

Domestic courts also face extrinsic constraints – most prominently, by governmental actors. Keller and Stone Sweet note that 'the more national judges seek to increase the effectiveness of convention rights in the domestic order, the more likely it is that they will face resistance on the part of other government actors'.[262] Governmental actors are also more likely to exercise pressure on domestic judges when the rule of law standard in the respective member state (and especially the aspect of separation of powers and judicial independence) is deficient. For example, in the case of Türkiye, Akbulut observed in the mid-2010s that

> the current political atmosphere in Turkey creates a certain level of fear within the judiciary that even the most liberal members of the judiciary may not apply international human rights law especially in cases having links with the members of the government or their close environment.[263]

In particular, the Turkish Constitutional Court has been attacked by the government which threatened the court's existence in reaction to judgments favourable to rights such as freedom of expression.[264] As a result, the constraints for domestic courts vary greatly among member states. While until the enlargement of the 1990s domestic courts mostly faced intrinsic rather than extrinsic constraints, extrinsic constraints have since then become more predominant for a larger section of domestic courts.

[261] eg, pointing to the limited knowledge about the Convention among the Russian judiciary, A Burkov, 'How to improve the results of a reluctant player: The case of Russia and the European Convention on Human Rights' in S Flogaitis, T Zwart and J Fraser (eds), *The European Court of Human Rights and its Discontents: Turning Criticism into Strength* (Edward Elgar 2013) 147, 153 et seq.

[262] Keller and Stone Sweet, 'Assessing the Impact of the ECHR on National Legal Systems' (n 74) 706.

[263] O Akbulut, 'Turkey: The European Convention On Human Rights As A Tool For Modernisation' in Popelier, Lambrecht and Lemmens (eds), *Criticism of the European Court of Human Rights, Shifting the Convention System* (n 165) 413, 443.

[264] eg, the media report about such threats in 2016: *Independent* (12 March 2016), 'Turkish President Erdogan threatens court's 'existence' after it releases two journalists': www.independent.co.uk/news/world/europe/erdogan-threatens-court-s-existence-after-it-releases-two-journalists-a6927421.html.

Moreover, domestic courts can face competing authority relationships. To start with, lower domestic courts can consider themselves to be hindered from considering the jurisprudence of the ECtHR when their domestic apex court has decided differently. The lower court then must decide whom to follow, ie, which authority relationship to prioritise. For example, when domestic apex courts in France in the 1980s refused to follow the ECtHR, this also constrained lower courts from accepting the authority of the ECtHR.[265] A similar competing authority relationship can occur when domestic courts are faced with diverging decisions by other international bodies, such as in the case of the above-mentioned contradictions with UN treaty bodies. However, the domestic legal orders of member states diverge as to the effect of these pronouncements and the meaning for domestic judicial decision-making, often only attributing limiting legal value to them.[266] The constraining effect thus seems lower in this respect for domestic courts as compared with governmental actors.

In conclusion, the constraints for respondent actors have changed over time. For executive and legislative actors, constraints were rather low in the earlier decades and have increased especially due to the court's more demanding approach to remedies. In contrast, for domestic courts at least in certain groups of member states, the constraints have decreased. While the intrinsic constraints as to the knowledge about the court and its jurisprudence were rather high to begin with, this has much less been the case in recent decades. However, for domestic courts in some member states, extrinsic constraints especially by governmental actors add to these lower intrinsic constraints so that the overall level remains moderate. In addition, the constraining effect of competing authority relationships is in general rather low, while being higher for some domestic courts depending on their approach to the internal effect of competing decisions by international human rights bodies.

iv. Assessment of MOC Factors

Based on the above analysis, the following can be said about the MOC setting for the respective state actors. First, for governmental and legislative actors, the MOC setting is nearly identical. For these actors, the MOC setting has changed over time, including as to the determining factor. This development is illustrated in Figure 5.4. In the court's initial phase, opportunity has been the determining factor for whether governmental and legislative actors have accepted the authority of the court. During this phase, the opportunity was moderate to low, while motivation and unconstrained ability were rather high. As the opportunity factor was thus at the lowest level, it most prominently shaped the behaviour of these actors according to the MOC framework (see chapter two). The motivation was rather high due to the high – both aspirational and de facto – value-correspondence regarding human rights, democratic and rule of law values, in combination with certain interests that were particularly pronounced during this period. This includes the low expected costs of membership as compared

[265] See generally, Blay-Grabarczyk and Maubernard (n 251).

[266] As an example, Spanish courts have considered such treaty body decisions as binding (Supreme Court, Judgment 1263/2018, 17 July 2018) while German courts have rejected such binding effect (eg, German Constitutional Court, 29 January 2019, 2 BvC 62/14).

with the gains for reputational interests and group membership. Only weak value-correspondence as to the institutional role of courts constituted a caveat to this overall high level of motivation. Similarly high was the ability to accept the authority of the court as the constraints for governmental and legislative actors to do so were low. The moderate to low opportunity thus determined the behaviour in light of the court's restrictive approach to remedies and the – for many member states – lack of internal effect of the Convention and the court's decisions.

In later periods, especially during the 1990s, the MOC setting changed. Opportunity has become broad and was thus not the determining factor any longer. During this decade, the constraints were still rather low so that the ability to accept the authority of the court remained high. As to the motivational setting, the 1990s came with a change in substance which however did not yet translate into a strong change regarding the overall level of motivation. Aspirational value correspondence as well as the reputational interests and interests relating to group membership were particularly high during the 1990s and thus led, despite the lower de facto value-correspondence, to a generally still rather high level of motivation. During this period, motivation, opportunity and unconstrained ability were thus high, creating a nearly ideal MOC setting. It was this comprehensive setting that determined the actors' behaviour during this time rather than one single factor.

Since the 2000s, the MOC setting has changed again. The overall motivational level has decreased, as the interest-based factors are less pronounced and cannot counterbalance the heterogeneous de facto value-correspondence to the same extent as during the 1990s. Considering the variety among member states' motivation during this period, motivation for the purposes of the MOC assessment can be qualified as moderate. While the opportunity is broad, there are more prominent constraints and therefore only a moderate ability to accept the authority of the court. Such constraints include financial constraints and competing authority relationships. According to the MOC framework, this means that motivation and constraints which are both at a moderate level determine conjointly the behaviour of governmental and legislative actors.

Figure 5.4 Development over time of the MOC setting for executive and legislative actors as respondents before the ECtHR

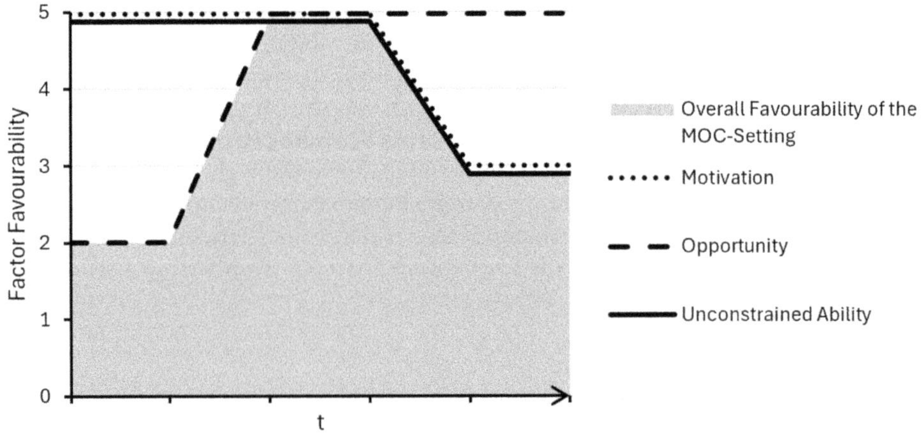

For domestic courts, one can also observe a development in the MOC setting. In earlier years, motivation was at the lowest level among the MOC factors and thus determined the behaviour of judicial actors according to the MOC framework. While opportunity and unconstrained ability were at a moderate level, the motivation for judicial actors to accept the authority of the ECtHR was low. Over the decades, all three factors however became more favourable, while the interrelation of the MOC factors however remained identical for most judicial actors. Motivation has become moderate to high for domestic courts (other than constitutional courts for which it has remained rather low) due to their strategic interests to use ECtHR decisions in their relationships with other domestic courts as well as due to an interest in consistent behaviour favouring the authority relationship with the ECtHR. Further, the opportunity for these actors became broad when most domestic laws enabled the internal applicability of the Convention and ECtHR decisions. An increasingly favourable opportunity structure adds to these legal opportunity elements. And the unconstrained ability decreased when the knowledge-related intrinsic constraints became less high. For most domestic courts, this means that in light of a broad opportunity and high ability, the moderate to high motivation remains the determining factor (see Figure 5.5). An exception are courts in member states with a low rule of law practice. Here the constraints resulting from actual or feared pressure by governmental actors is a significant constraint that leads to a rather low ability. For courts in these member states, this low ability is the determining factor.

Figure 5.5 Development over time of the MOC setting for domestic courts as respondents before the ECtHR

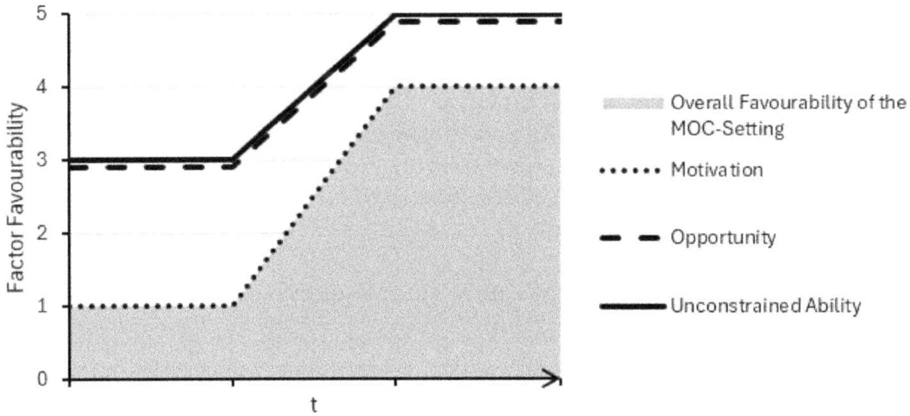

As a result of these diverse MOC settings for the different actors and the respective time periods, there have been different factors that the ECtHR would have had to address in their strategies to make the MOC setting for respondents more favourable. At times, the determining factor was opportunity, at times motivation, at times constraints – and at times two factors in conjunction. In section IV, I assess to what extent the ECtHR has addressed the relevant factor for each situation and whether it has contributed to increasing the favourability of the MOC setting.

B. MOC Factors for Pushback against the Court's Authority

This section turns from the MOC factors shaping the initial acceptance of the ECtHR's authority by respondents to the factors that determine whether respondents push back against the court.

The forms of pushback that the ECtHR has witnessed over the decades range from instances of structural resistance and backlash by state governments and domestic courts to (partial) non-compliance by different state actors.[267] To start with, member states have withdrawn or attempted to withdraw twice in the court's history. In 1969, Greece under its military regime withdrew from the Council of Europe. This was however at a time when Greece had not yet accepted the authority of the court. This pushback was thus directed at the Convention system as such rather than at the court as an institution. Later pushback attempts included, or even directly targeted the court. Russia threatened to withdraw from the Council of Europe in the context of the Crimea conflict, also withholding contributions to the Council budget.[268] And in 2022, Russia attempted to withdraw before the Council of Europe decided to revoke its membership. Both these instances of pushback were not exclusively targeted at the court, but the court was part of the affected institutions. In explicit reaction to decisions of the court, other states such as the United Kingdom have considered withdrawing but have so far not done so.[269] Further, the Brighton and Copenhagen conferences of 2012 and 2018 were used by several member states for an attempt to structurally resist the court. The rather far-reaching draft declarations proposed and supported by certain member states are a clear expression of pushback.[270] In contrast, whether the final outcome of these conferences – in particular Protocol No 15 – can be qualified as pushback, is debatable.[271] The 'ambiguous nature' of the changes introduced by Protocol No 15 including the reference to subsidiarity and the margin of appreciation into the Convention text makes it possible to interpret these changes either as marginal or as substantive.[272] Further, there have been instances in which member states have, as a form of pushback, hindered institutional reforms. This was the case for Russia that refused to ratify Protocol No 14 for several years due to its opposition to the single judge procedure introduced by this Protocol.[273]

[267] See generally on forms of pushback against the ECtHR, P Popelier, S Lambrecht and K Lemmens (eds), *Criticism of the European Court of Human Rights, Shifting the Convention System: Counter-Dynamics at the National and EU Level* (Intersentia 2016); on pushback and alternative concepts for structural resistance, M Breuer, 'The Concept of "Principled Resistance" to ECtHR Judgments: A Useful Tool to Analyse Implementation Deficits?' (2021) 12 *Journal of International Dispute Settlement* 250; M Breuer (ed), *Principled Resistance to ECtHR Judgments: A New Paradigm?* (Springer 2019).

[268] See, on this conflict, Busygina and Kahn (n 196) 73.

[269] The government of the United Kingdom has, for example, considered withdrawing as a reaction to the 1995 McCann case. See Lambrecht (n 218) 525.

[270] See LR Glas, 'From Interlaken to Copenhagen: What Has Become of the Proposals Aiming to Reform the Functioning of the European Court of Human Rights?' (2020) 20 *Human Rights Law Review* 121.

[271] Diverging stances on this question take, eg, Madsen, 'The European Court of Human Rights' (n 34); LR Helfer and E Voeten, 'Walking Back Human Rights in Europe?' (2020) 31 *European Journal of International Law* 797; Stone Sweet, Sandholtz and Andenas (n 184).

[272] Lambrecht (n 218) 523.

[273] See on this issue, B Bowring, 'The Russian Federation, Protocol No 14 (and 14bis), and the Battle for the Soul of the ECHR' (2010) 2 *Göttingen Journal of International Law* 589.

Non-compliance has (so far) not been considered, for most member states, a major form of pushback in the ECtHR context. Until the entry into force of Protocol No 11, the compliance rate has been described as 'generally recognised to be exemplary'.[274] Apart from occasional delayed implementations, there had been until then only two instances in which respondent states – Greece and Türkiye – openly refused to implement a judgment.[275] However, regarding Türkiye, partial non-compliance had already been an issue in the pre-Protocol No 11 period. In this state, non-compliance has indeed been persistent and structural, thus reflecting pushback against the court.[276]

After Protocol No 11 entered into force, non-compliance became more frequent. A general trend towards more partial compliance or even non-compliance, has been observed, including by member states from both Eastern and Western Europe.[277] Partial compliance is especially prominent with regard to decisions that concern structural issues on the domestic level. For example, in the Italian cases concerning the length of judicial proceedings, 'the Italian government generally paid the damages awarded by the ECtHR [but] the root of the problem – the archaic legal proceedings – was not sufficiently reformed'.[278] Yet such partial non-compliance often appears incidental, rather than necessarily expressing a critical stance by state actors. In contrast, other instances of non-compliance are an explicit expression of pushback. Most prominently, state actors in the United Kingdom and Russia have used non-compliance as a tool for pushback.[279] In the prisoners' voting rights cases, both states have refused to (fully) implement these decisions in 'open defiance and opposition' to the court.[280] However, Russia subsequently went further and turned its issue-specific pushback to structural resistance. It adopted legislation that allowed Russian state actors not to implement an ECtHR decision when it conflicted with the Russian Constitution.[281] In particular, the legislator empowered the Russian Constitutional Court to declare ECtHR decisions 'non-executable' when conflicting with the domestic constitution.[282]

Finally, an important set of actors that have pushed back against the ECtHR are domestic courts. In several member states, constitutional or supreme courts have refused to implement ECtHR judgments under certain conditions. To begin with, the

[274] D Harris, M O'Boyle and C Warbrick, *Law of the European Convention on Human Rights*, 1st edn (OUP 1995) 702.

[275] See Bates, *Evolution* (n 2) 420. The cases were Loizidou v Turkey [Art 50], 28 July 1998, no. 40/1993/435/514; Stran Greek Refineries and Stratis Andreadis v Greece, 9 December 1994, App no 13427/87.

[276] Madsen, 'The European Court of Human Rights' (n 34) 262.

[277] ibid 269 (with statistics).

[278] ibid 261.

[279] On Russia's 'politics of partial compliance', Hillebrecht (n 195).

[280] Nussberger, 'From High Hopes to Scepticism?' (n 41) 164.

[281] Federal Law of the Russian Federation No 7 FKZ of 14 December 2015 'Amending the Law on the Russian Constitutional Court: Federal Constitutional Law'. See also RM Fleig-Goldstein, 'The Russian Constitutional Court versus the European Court of Human Rights: How the Strasbourg Court Should Respond to Russia's Refusal to Execute ECtHR Judgments' (2017) 56 *Columbia Journal of Transnational Law* 172.

[282] Federal Law of the Russian Federation No 7-FKZ of 14 December 2015 'Amendments to the Federal Constitutional Law on the Constitutional Court of the Russian Federation'; see on this law Venice Commission, Opinion No 832/2015, 20 January 2016, CDL-REF(2016)006.

French courts have denied, for a long time, any binding value of ECtHR decisions.[283] In the 1980s especially they used 'a strategy of "bypassing", particularly by neutralising the impact of European rulings' before gradually changing their position.[284] Another line of critical jurisprudence has been initiated by the Austrian Constitutional Court. It stressed, in the *Miltner* case of 1987, that it considered it possible to disregard ECtHR jurisprudence if doing otherwise would violate constitutional provisions – and, on this basis, refused to implement the ECtHR's decision on the matter.[285] Similarly, the German Constitutional Court in its *Görgülü* decision of 2004 decided that there was no obligation for domestic courts to implement ECtHR judgments 'in a schematic way'.[286] Rather, such an implementation, if it violates 'prior-ranking law', would 'violate fundamental rights in conjunction with the principle of the rule of law'.[287] And the Supreme Court of the United Kingdom decided in 2010 that it 'is not bound to follow every decision of the EurCtHR' but that it would do so only under certain conditions.[288] For this court, the conditions are that 'there is a clear and constant line of decisions whose effect is not inconsistent with some fundamental substantive or procedural aspect of [domestic] law, and whose reasoning does not appear to overlook or misunderstand some argument or point of principle'.[289] Finally, for the Italian Constitutional Court in its jurisprudence of 2015, the implementation of ECtHR judgments is equally conditioned on the ECtHR's case law being consolidated,[290] except for pilot judgments of which the court accepts implementation.[291] A more aggressive version of the above line of jurisprudence has been adopted by the Russian Constitutional Court. In a series of decisions, in particular since 2015, the court was strongly critical of the ECtHR's jurisprudence, demanded that the ECtHR should respect 'the national constitutional identity' and decided that an ECtHR judgment cannot be implemented when it violates the Russian Constitution.[292] The court stated that

> a decision of an authorized inter-state body, including a judgment of the European Court of Human Rights, cannot be executed by the Russian Federation … if interpretation of the norm of an international treaty, which this decision is based on, violates respective provisions of the Constitution of the Russian Federation.[293]

[283] Blay-Grabarczyk and Maubernard (n 251) 286.

[284] ibid.

[285] Austrian Constitutional Court, Miltner, VfSlg 11500/1987. See on this decision and its 'rebellious' character, A Gamper, 'Austria: Endorsing The Convention System, Endorsing The Constitution' in Popelier, Lambrecht and Lemmens (eds), *Criticism of the European Court of Human Rights, Shifting the Convention System* (n 165) 75, 77–80.

[286] German Constitutional Court, 14 October 2004, 2 BvR 1481/04, para 47.

[287] ibid.

[288] *Manchester City Council v Pinnock* [2010] UKSC 45 (3 November 2010) para 48.

[289] ibid.

[290] Italian Constitutional Court, decision of 14 January 2015, no 49/2015, 16 (of the English translation): 'It is thus only "consolidated law" resulting from the case law of the European Court on which the national courts are required to base their interpretation, whilst there is no obligation to do so in cases involving rulings that do not express a position that has not become final'.

[291] ibid 17.

[292] Russian Constitutional Court, 14 July 2015, no 21-P/2015; 19 April 2016, no 12-P/2016; 19 January 2017, no 1-II/2017. See also Venice Commission, CDL-AD(2020)009.

[293] Russian Constitutional Court, 14 July 2015, no 21-P/2015, cited according to Venice Commission, CDL-AD(2016)005, 5.

This jurisprudence was a model for the above-mentioned Russian legislation explicitly allowing non-implementation in cases of conflict with the Constitution. A similarly aggressive stance has been taken by the Polish Constitutional Tribunal in its recent jurisprudence on Article 6 ECHR. In a decision of 2021, the Tribunal declared that this article and the related jurisprudence of the ECtHR is incompatible with the Polish Constitution in as far as the interpretation of the term 'court' in this provision is also meant to include the Constitutional Tribunal, and in as far as the ECtHR considers itself competent to review the election of judges to this court.[294] This decision was a reaction to the *Xero Flor* decision of the ECtHR in which the court declared the Polish Constitutional Tribunal to be unlawfully constituted due to judges in this court having been elected in a process with 'grave irregularities'.[295] The Tribunal declared this ECtHR decision to be ultra vires and without effect. And by declaring Article 6 ECHR in part incompatible with the Constitution, it even goes beyond declaring an individual judgment of the ECtHR inapplicable.[296] In a subsequent decision in 2022, the court broadened its declaration of incompatibility. It declared unconstitutional any review competence of the ECtHR as to the organisational structure of the Polish judicial system and any application of Article 6 ECHR that would give the ECtHR the power to 'independently create norms, by interpreting the Convention, pertaining to the procedure for appointing national court judges'.[297]

In this section, I assess the MOC framework for these instances of pushback in more detail and outline further potential for pushback. I refer to structural resistance and backlash as well as to less intensive forms of pushback such as (partial) non-compliance and critical discourse. In terms of actors, I analyse the MOC factors for governmental and judicial actors, as both of these groups have pushed back against the court during different periods of the court's practice.

i. Motivation for Pushback

For *governmental actors*, the motivation for pushback is quite varied. To start with, high-politics, including geopolitics, and even territorial and military conflicts between member states have motivated the withdrawal (attempt) by Greece and Russia. The Greek case (that only reached the Commission but not the court) concerned the military coup in Greece in 1967 which resulted in widespread human rights violations including torture.[298] The Greek government accused the Commission of being biased and withdrew from the Convention before the Committee of Ministers could suspend Greek membership.[299] In the case of Russia, its war against Ukraine and the ensuing decision of the Committee of Ministers to launch the procedure under Article 8 of the

[294] Polish Constitutional Tribunal, 24 November 2021, case ref K 6/21.

[295] *Xero Flor w Polsce sp. z o.o. v Poland*, 7 May 2021, App no 4907/18.

[296] On this point, A Ploszka, 'It Never Rains but it Pours. The Polish Constitutional Tribunal Declares the European Convention on Human Rights Unconstitutional' (2022) *Hague Journal on the Rule of Law*: doi.org/10.1007/s40803-022-00174-w.

[297] Polish Constitutional Tribunal, 10 March 2022, case ref K 7/21.

[298] *Denmark, Norway, Sweden and the Netherlands v Greece (I)*, App nos 3321/67 to 3323/67 and 3344/67.

[299] Bates, *Evolution* (n 2) 267–68.

Statute to suspend Russia from its rights of representation in the Council of Europe[300] motivated Russia to declare its withdrawal from the Council. In its declaration of withdrawal, Russia stated that it withdrew as a reaction to 'those who deliberately escalated tensions and turned the Organisation [i.e. the Council of Europe] into an instrument for achieving their geopolitical goals'.[301] In both cases, the backlash was however directed against the overall system of the Council of Europe, without specifically targeting the ECtHR. This shows that aspects that motivate general pushback against the Council of Europe are relevant for the relationship between the court and the member states as well. This said, the court was involved in the above dispute with Russia, deciding both individual and state complaints against Russia regarding territorial and military conflicts. The court has thus played a role in shaping the dispute between this (former) member state and the Council of Europe. This includes not only the cases on the Russia/Ukraine conflict but also other military activities such as the judgments on Chechnya, finding violations of Articles 2 and 3 ECHR. This matter was addressed in *Yusupova and Bazayeva v Russia* against which Russia had already pushed back.[302] Further, the court's jurisprudence on the Russian military presence in the Transnistrian region was perceived as controversial as well.[303] The Russian representative on the Committee of Ministers said that the court's decision on this matter was 'inconsistent, controversial, subjective, politically and legally wrong'.[304]

The involvement of the court in territorial and military conflicts as well as state security concerns has also motivated pushback at a lesser scale than withdrawal from the Convention system. For example, the Turkish government 'completely rejected the findings and the judgment of the ECtHR' in the Cyprus cases concerning the territory of Northern Cyprus, a territory that Türkiye brought under military control in the 1970s.[305] Türkiye's reaction was thus open non-compliance, without however going further in its pushback. In the case of the United Kingdom, the conflict about Northern Ireland has been brought to the court on several occasions. High-profile cases include *Ireland v United Kingdom* that the court decided in 1978, a case concerning the ill-treatment of individuals by British authorities in the context of terrorism and civil disorder.[306] The United Kingdom reacted to this case first by obstructing the investigations undertaken by the Commission.[307] It then however accepted the decision of the court, which in fact was notably more deferential to the respondent than the Commission had been.[308] A later case touching upon this conflict was the *McCann* case of 1995 concerning the so-called Gibraltar shootings involving the

[300] Committee of Ministers, 25 February 2022, CM/Del/Dec(2022)1426ter/2.3.

[301] Declaration by the Minister of Foreign Affairs of the Russian Federation of 15 March 2022 (unofficial translation), part of CoE document Secretariat of the Committee of Ministers DD(2022)101.

[302] *Isayeva, Yusupova and Bazayeva v Russia*, 24 February 2005, App nos 57947/00, 57948/00 and 57949/00.

[303] *Ilaşcu and Others v Moldova and Russia*, 8 July 2004, App no 48787/99.

[304] Press Release, European Court of Human Rights, Grand Chamber Judgment in the Case of Ilascu and Others v Moldova and Russia (8 July 2004), cited as quoted by Wildhaber, 'The European Court of Human Rights' (n 86) 532.

[305] Akbulut (n 263) 424.

[306] *Ireland v United Kingdom*, 18 January 1978, App no 5310/71.

[307] Bates, *Evolution* (n 2) 272.

[308] This concerned the interpretation of the notion of torture as well as the application of Article 15 of the Convention. See on the criticisms of this case, Bates, *Evolution* (n 2) 273 et seq.

IRA.[309] As a reaction, 'withdrawal of the right of individual petition … was debated at Cabinet level'.[310] Although such a withdrawal did not occur, the governmental actors tried to create a transnational momentum for pushback. In 1996, it circulated a position paper to other member states which – somewhat foreshadowing the Brighton initiative – was aimed at pushing the court to refer more frequently to the margin of appreciation doctrine to the benefit of respondent states.[311]

Since the enlargement in the 1990s and beyond, territorial conflicts have played a considerable role in the jurisprudence of the court. They tend to trigger huge numbers of individual applications, a fact that gives even more prominence to the sensitive issues at stake in such cases. Important territorial conflicts that lead to cases before the court include cases against Moldova and Russia regarding Transnistria,[312] Georgia concerning South Ossetia,[313] and Russia regarding Chechnya and Ukraine.[314]

Further, the court decided cases relating to the 'War on Terror' by the United Kingdom, preventing the deportation of individuals who were qualified by the United Kingdom as terrorists. This triggered critical reactions not only in British public opinion but also from state actors. For example, David Cameron, then Prime Minister of the United Kingdom, is reported commenting on the *Abu Qatada* decision of 2012,[315] that it would undermine the fight against terror and, as interpreted by the court, '[h]uman rights laws put lives at risk'.[316] For the then Home Secretary, Theresa May, the decision was a 'crazy interpretation of our human rights laws' and she contemplated withdrawal from the Convention.[317]

Related issues that have motivated pushback concern in particular member states with authoritarian tendencies. Decisions in favour of the political opposition or that aim at strengthening opposition rights and media plurality more generally are likely to motivate pushback at least in the form of non-compliance. As such decisions undermine the authoritarian rationale, governmental actors in these member states are likely to feel threatened in their personal power positions. For example, although the ECtHR has repeatedly decided that the provision of Turkish criminal law penalising 'insulting the president' violates Convention rights,[318] Türkiye has not complied

[309] *McCann and Others v The United Kingdom*, 27 September 1995, App no 18984/91.
[310] Bates, *Evolution* (n 2) 434.
[311] ibid 437–38.
[312] *Ilaşcu and Others v Moldova and Russia*, 8 July 2004, App no 48787/99.
[313] ECtHR, press release, 10 October 2008: 'As of 9 October 2008 the European Court of Human Rights had received some 2,729 applications from South Ossetians'.
[314] eg, *Isayeva, Yusupova and Bazayeva v Russia*, 24 February 2005, App nos 57947/00, 57948/00 and 57949/00; Ukraine v Russian Federation (re Crimea), App no 20958/14; *Ukraine v Russia (X)*, App no 11055/22; *Oliynichenko v Russia and Ukraine*, App no 31258/22.
[315] *Othman (Abu Qatada) v the United Kingdom*, 17 January 2012, App no 8139/09.
[316] '"Human rights laws put lives at risk": Cameron tells Euro court it harms fight against terror' *Mail Online* (26 January 2012) – as cited by A Donald, J Gordon and P Leach, *Equality and Human Rights Commission Research report 83 – The UK and the European Court of Human Rights* (2012) 154 (fn 469): www.equalityhumanrights.com/sites/default/files/83._european_court_of_human_rights.pdf.
[317] 'Theresa May criticises human rights convention after Abu Qatada affair' *Guardian* (8 July 2013): www.theguardian.com/world/2013/jul/08/theresa-may-human-rights-abu-qatada.
[318] A recent case on this issue in which the court demands a legislative amendment to remedy the violation is *Vedat Şorli v Turkey*, App no 42048/19, 19 October 2021, para 54 (with further references).

with these decisions and continued to detain journalists based on this provision.[319] Similarly, the jurisprudence of the ECtHR that addresses the authoritarian tendencies initiated by the rule of law downslide in Poland has been met both with harsh criticism by governmental actors as well as by a strategy to avoid compliance. The latter has been to initiate proceedings before the Constitutional Tribunal with the aim 'to obtain a judgment that will serve as a pretext not to enforce the Xero Flor judgment',[320] a strategy that led to the above-mentioned Constitutional Tribunal decision of 2021.

Regarding the subject matter of the court's jurisprudence, cases relating to controversially perceived social values have been a motivational factor for pushback. This includes, for example, cases relating to migration. In the context of the Brighton and Copenhagen pushback attempts, the Danish pushback was influenced by debates around refugee and migrant rights fuelled by domestic right-wing parties.[321] This was related to cases concerning the expulsion of non-Danish individuals that the ECtHR's jurisprudence on Article 8 ECHR had hindered and that Danish politicians including the Prime Minister and the Minister of Justice had criticised harshly.[322] Migration has been, and continues to be, a topic that motivates pushback in other member states as well. In various contexts, the 'increased salience of immigration politics … fuelled the campaigns for restoring national control over human rights'.[323] Recently, in a declaration in May 2025, a group of states comprising Denmark, Italy, Austria, Estonia, Belgium, the Czech Republic, Poland, Latvia and Lithuania urged the ECtHR to adjust its jurisprudence and give states more leeway in relation to measures relating to 'criminal foreign nationals'.[324]

A further example of socially and politically sensitive subject-matters that can motivate pushback are judgments concerning LGBT+ rights. This subject matter is particularly prone to motivate pushback because the court has, through the development of its jurisprudence, increased the obligations for member states in this regard.[325] For example, regarding transsexual rights, the court expanded the relevant obligations in its *Goodwin* decision of 2002 as compared to the prior *Rees* case of 1986.[326] For state actors that promote so-called traditional family values, such decisions can provide a significant motivation for pushback. This motivational potential has also been reflected in the reaction of dissenting judges at the court. For example, the judges from the Czech Republic and Poland expressed their criticism against the majority decision in *Orlandi and Others v Italy* concerning same-sex marriages, arguing that the traditional concept of marriage is 'part of the common

[319] On this issue, Council of Europe report DGI(2022)2, 'Freedom of Expression in 2021', 5–6: rm.coe.int/freedom-of-expression-2021-en/1680a6525e.
[320] Ploszka (n 296).
[321] Stone Sweet, Sandholtz and Andenas (n 184).
[322] See Madsen, 'From boom to backlash? (n 200) 39.
[323] ibid.
[324] Statement of 22 May 2025: www.governo.it/sites/governo.it/files/Lettera_aperta_22052025.pdf.
[325] eg, LR Helfer and E Voeten, 'International Courts as Agents of Legal Change: Evidence from LGBT Rights in Europe' (2014) 68 *International Organization* 77, 88; Dotan (n 53) 228.
[326] *Rees v The United Kingdom*, 17 October 1986, App no 9532/81; *Christine Goodwin v The United Kingdom*, 11 July 2002, App no 28957/95.

legal heritage'.[327] Such pronouncements reflect discursive pushback that can also be linked to the positions of the respective governmental actors.

Another socially sensitive issue which has motivated case-specific pushback are religious matters. In *Lautsi v Italy*, a case that concerned crucifixes in public school classrooms, the initial decision of the court did not only cause harsh criticism by the Italian government but also from many other member states.[328] The then President, Silvio Berlusconi, declared: 'This decision is not acceptable for us Italians. It is one of those decisions that make us doubt Europe's common sense'.[329] Moreover, a large group of member states acted as third-party interveners before the court when the case was referred to the Grand Chamber, voicing criticism of the initial decision.[330] This issue also resonated shortly after the Interlaken Conference in 2010 at which the Italian representative emphasised that 'les questions qui touchent de près les sentiments et les traditions nationales doivent être réglementées au niveau national'.[331]

Further, for the United Kingdom and Russia, prisoners' voting rights have been a highly controversial subject matter. In the *Hirst* case, the court decided that the blanket ban in the United Kingdom regarding voting rights of prisoners violated the Convention.[332] This case generated broad media attention and critique, portraying the court as undemocratically overruling legislative decisions.[333] State actors followed suit. The state refused to implement the decisions for many years. In a follow-up judgment, the court addressed this non-compliance by ordering the United Kingdom to amend the respective legislation within a period of six months.[334] Illustrating the ongoing heated emotional debate in the United Kingdom surrounding this issue, the then Prime Minister David Cameron commented on this decision in a harsh tone: despite considering implementation of this decision, it would make him 'physically ill even to contemplate having to give the vote to anyone who is in prison'.[335] Even further, he threatened to pull the United Kingdom from the Convention.[336] For Russia, the *Anchugov and Gladkov* decision of the ECtHR motivated similar pushback on the topic of prisoner voting bans.[337] As in the British case, the court found a violation and

[327] *Orlandi and Others v Italy*, 14 December 2017, App nos 26431/12, 26742/12, 44057/12 and 60088/12, dissenting opinion by Pejchal and Wojtyczek JJ, para 5.

[328] *Lautsi and Others v Italy*, 3 November 2009, App no 30814/06. The Grand Chamber reversed this decision in its decision of 18 March 2011.

[329] See S Mancini, 'The Crucifix Rage: Supranational Constitutionalism Bumps against the Counter-Majoritarian Difficulty' (2010) 6 *European Constitutional Law Review* 6.

[330] The intervening member states were Armenia, Bulgaria, Cyprus, Russia, Greece, Lithuania, Malta, Monaco, Romania and San Marino.

[331] Statement by the Italian representative Alfredo Mantica, Proceedings, High Level Conference on the Future of the European Court of Human Rights, Interlaken, 18–19 February 2010, 63: rm.coe.int/proceedings-actes-high-level-conference-on-the-future-of-the-european-/1680695aae.

[332] *Hirst v United Kingdom (No 2)*, 6 October 2005, App no 74025/01.

[333] As an example of critique by political actors, see D Davis, 'Britain Must Defy the European Court of Human Rights on Prisoner Voting as Strasbourg is Exceeding its Authority' in Flogaitis, Zwart and Fraser (eds), *The European Court of Human Rights and its Discontents* (n 261) 65.

[334] *Greens and MT v The United Kingdom*, 23 November 2010, App nos 60041/08 and 60054/08.

[335] HC Deb, 3 November 2010, vol 517, col 921: publications.parliament.uk/pa/cm201011/cmhansrd/cm101103/debtext/101103-0001.htm.

[336] Madsen, 'The European Court of Human Rights' (n 34) 267.

[337] *Anchugov and Gladkov v Russia*, 4 July 2013, App nos 11157/04 and 15162/05.

triggered considerable pushback. Not only governmental actors but also the domestic judiciary opposed this decision. The Russian Constitutional Court decided that, in light of Article 32(3) of the Russian Constitution which regulates prisoners' voting, implementing the ECtHR's decision would violate domestic constitutional law.[338]

A further potential motivation for pushback is structural rather than issue specific. Member states have been motivated to push back against the court when they perceived the court encroaching on their sovereignty and engaging in judicial activism. Reproaches of judicial activism have occurred whenever the court expands the obligations for member states. During the 1970s, several of the landmark cases of this time, especially in relation to Article 6 ECHR, have led to such reactions. In the *Golder* decision of 1975, the court recognised a right to access to a court although such a right was not explicitly mentioned in the wording of the article.[339] The United Kingdom had already harshly criticised this approach before the Commission, arguing that this created a new obligation for the state to which it had not agreed when ratifying the Convention.[340] Before the court, it warned the ECtHR of the 'danger of the interpretative process crossing the legislative line'.[341] An important other example from the 1970s is the court's jurisprudence on fair trial obligations regarding the interpretation of the term 'the determination of his civil rights and obligations' according to Article 6 ECHR. Starting with *Ringeisen v Austria* and *König v Germany*, the court interpretated the term 'civil rights' extensively,[342] leading to an extended applicability of this provision, inter alia, in the context of procedures before administrative courts.[343] This jurisprudence has had a significant 'constitutional' impact on the domestic law of member states as the procedural obligations following from this provision can require states to change their procedural frameworks substantially.[344] As a result, this jurisprudence 'generated strong resistance in countries like Austria, Switzerland and Germany'.[345] A recent example in which state actors have argued that the ECtHR encroaches on the sovereignty of the member state is the Polish pushback against the court's jurisprudence on judicial independence. In reaction to the ECtHR's *Xero Flor* decision,[346] the speaker of the lower house of the Polish Parliament stated:

> Today's ruling sets a dangerous precedent and unlawful interference with the sovereignty of the Polish State. In fact, the European Court of Human Rights, i.e. a judicial body set up to protect the law, usurps the powers which it does not have.[347]

[338] Russian Constitutional Court, 19 April 2016, no 12-П/2016, translation provided by the Venice Commission, CDL-REF(2016)033: www.venice.coe.int/webforms/documents/default.aspx?pdffile=CDL-REF(2016)033-e.

[339] *Golder v The United Kingdom*, 21 February 1975, App no 4451/70.

[340] Bates, *Evolution* (n 2) 291.

[341] As quoted by Bates, *Evolution* (n 2) 294.

[342] *Ringeisen v Austria*, 16 July 1971, App no 2614/65, para 94; *König v Germany*, 28 June 1978, App no 6232/73, paras 88–90.

[343] eg, *Benthem v the Netherlands*, 23 October 1985, App no 8848/80.

[344] Generally on the constitutional impact, C Tomuschat, 'Europe – a Common Constitutional Space' in B De Witte and C Forder (eds), *The Common Law of Europe and the Future of Legal Education* (Kluwer 1992) 133; J Frowein, 'The Transformation of Constitutional Law through the European Convention on Human Rights' (2008) 41 *Israel Law Review* 489.

[345] Keller and Stone Sweet, 'Assessing the Impact of the ECHR on National Legal Systems' (n 74) 696.

[346] *Xero Flor w Polsce sp. z o.o. v Poland*, 7 May 2021, App no 4907/18.

[347] Statement by the Speaker of the Sejm [Elżbieta Witek] on the precedent ruling of the ECHR on the status of judges, 7 May 2021: www.sejm.gov.pl/sejm9.nsf/komunikat.xsp?document

As an overall tendency, the court has expanded the obligation of member states continuously as part of its 'progressive' jurisprudence, both on procedural and substantive matters.[348] ECtHR judges have acknowledged this development, stating that the court and the Commission 'have gradually extended and raised the level of protection afforded to the rights and freedoms guaranteed by the Convention'.[349] This general tendency has sparked criticism from member states for decades. It was already observed in the 1990s that there was, among member states, 'a growing dissatisfaction with and sometimes even obstruction to the consequences resulting from the judicial activism which the Court is alleged to practice' and that at least some member states thought that 'the protection emanating from the Convention is now approaching the limits of what is acceptable'.[350] In the 2000s and 2010s, this dissatisfaction translated into the pushback attempts that certain member states undertook in the context of the Brighton and Copenhagen conferences.

A cross-cutting aspect of the court's jurisprudence that state actors might qualify as 'activist' is the European consensus doctrine. The court has created this notion, inter alia, to establish new standards of protection when there is a uniform approach among member states supporting this standard.[351] It is based on a comparative assessment of the domestic law of member states as well as of international legal practice. However, over time, the court has used this doctrine broadly by constructing obligations for member states based on societal developments that take place only in some but not necessarily all or nearly all member states. For example, in *Hirst*, the court constructed its jurisprudence on prisoners' voting rights despite the fact that 13 of the then member states did not allow prisoners' voting.[352] This approach – criticised as 'majoritarian activism'[353] – has motivated pushback especially from those states in which the respective development has not taken place. Moreover, when the court has referred to international legal instruments to justify a common standard or consensus, the court did not put much value on state consent. Instead, it took international instruments as evidence for a shifting legal standard independently of whether or how many of the member states were party to these instruments. The court has made this approach explicit. In *Demir and Baykara v Turkey*, the court stated that 'it is not necessary for the respondent State to have ratified the entire collection of instruments that are applicable in respect of the precise subject matter of the case concerned'.[354]

In addition to the 'majoritarian' nature of the European consensus doctrine, this jurisprudence and the living instrument approach in general is also prone to criticism

Id=804094FBC164BFEBC12586CE005EE176. See also a similar statement by the Polish Ministry of Justice issued after the Constitutional Tribunal's decision of November 2021, Ministry of Justice Press Release of 25 November 2021: www.gov.pl/web/sprawiedliwosc/europejski-trybunal-praw-czlowieka-nie-moze-oceniac-legalnosci-wyboru-polskich-sedziow.

[348] Using the term 'progressive', Joint Dissenting Opinion by Costa, Ress, Türmen, Zupančič and Steiner JJ, *Hatton and Others v The United Kingdom*, 8 July 2003, App no 36022/97.

[349] ibid.

[350] P van Dijk and GJ van Hoof, *Theory and Practice of the European Convention on Human Rights* (Kluwer 1990) 617–18.

[351] In addition, the notion is used to justify a broad margin of appreciation for member states in the absence of a European consensus.

[352] *Hirst v United Kingdom (No 2)*, 6 October 2005, App no 74025/01, para 81.

[353] Helfer and Voeten, 'International Courts as Agents of Legal Change' (n 325) 106.

[354] *Demir And Baykara v Turkey*, 12 November 2008, App no 34503/97, para 86.

due to an often insufficient evidentiary basis. The court only very selectively provides empirical evidence of the social and legal trends that it claims and uses as the foundation for its jurisprudence.[355] In earlier decades, the judgments using the European consensus doctrine only contained 'short, pithy statements referring very opaquely to the legal situation and developments of the Member States'.[356] But even in its more recent decisions, the court is still very selective and unsystematic in its review of domestic and international legal sources that it uses to establish a consensus. While in earlier decades, this approach has not led to much criticism,[357] more recently the weak evidentiary basis has sparked disapproval.

Relatedly, the living instrument doctrine which goes back to the *Tyrer* decision of 1978 and on which the European consensus doctrine is founded has the potential of motivating pushback.[358] It reflects the self-understanding of the court as exercising a transformative function (see also below). When the court first established this doctrine, it did so without providing a legal-doctrinal explanation for this approach.[359] This in itself could have led the court's audiences to perceive this jurisprudence as activist. The court only provided legal policy arguments, if at all, for this doctrine.[360] However, there has been no major pushback against the living instrument doctrine as such, arguably also due to the strategies of the court to limit the motivation for pushback (see section IV.B). The same can be said about the recognition of positive obligations of member states, reflecting the effective protection doctrine. When the court decided in the 1970s that the Convention rights are not limited to negative obligations of the state, this was a major jurisprudential development at the time.[361] From the perspective of states, the duties and financial implications relating to positive obligations blurred the boundary between civil and political rights on the one hand and economic, social and cultural rights on the other.[362] However, member states accepted this jurisprudence without any significant pushback specifically against this doctrine.

An aspect of the court's jurisprudence that can be perceived both as activist and as reflective of a self-understanding that encroaches upon the sovereignty-related interests of member states is the use of the term 'constitutional'. Although the idea of the Convention as fulfilling a constitutional function underlay the jurisprudence of the court since the landmark decisions of the 1970s[363] and during the 1980s, the term had

[355] Critically, eg, Nussberger, *The European Court of Human Rights* (n 6) 81; LR Helfer, 'Consensus, coherence and the European Convention on Human Rights' (1993) 26 *Cornell International Law Journal* 133.

[356] E Bates, 'Consensus in the Legitimacy-Building Era of the European Court of Human Rights' in Kapotas and Tzevelekos (eds), *Building Consensus on European Consensus* (n 146) 42, 54–55.

[357] ibid 56.

[358] *Tyrer v United Kingdom*, 25 April 1978, App no 5856/72.

[359] See critically, A Mowbray, 'The Creativity of the European Court of Human Rights' (2005) 5 *Human Rights Law Review* 57.

[360] eg, *Selmouni v France*, 28 July 1999, App no 25803/94, para 101; *Stafford v The United Kingdom*, 28 May 2002, App no 46295/99, para 68.

[361] See also Bates, *Evolution* (n 2) 346.

[362] Memorial of the Government of Ireland in *Airey v Ireland*, 9 October 1979, App no 6289/73 – as cited by Bates, *Evolution* (n 2) 344: 'more closely associated with economic, social and cultural rights than fundamental human rights'.

[363] Bates, *Evolution* (n 2) 305.

explicitly been used in the court's jurisprudence since the 1990s. Already demonstrating this mindset, the then President of the Court, Rolv Ryssdal, had described the ECtHR as 'a kind of constitutional court for Europe in human rights matters'.[364] Since the *Loizidou* decision of 1995, the court speaks of the Convention as a 'constitutional instrument of European public order'.[365] Five years later, the then President of the Court, Luzius Wildhaber, argued for a more pronounced constitutional function of the court.[366] Later, he also described the court as becoming a 'European quasi-Constitutional Court'.[367] In the academic debate, authors have argued for such a constitutional function as well.[368] This constitutional self-understanding can motivate pushback for state actors who do not share the institutional value reflected in such a role for the court. More generally, it touches upon the sovereignty interests of member states when the notions of constitution and constitutional court are used to designate legal instruments and judicial bodies outside the domestic realm.

A related motivation for pushback lies in the fact that the court also reviews legislative acts. In the United Kingdom, especially, parliamentary sovereignty has been perceived as being endangered by ECtHR jurisprudence. The President of the Supreme Court of the United Kingdom pointedly expressed this sentiment, stating that the 'idea of courts overruling decisions of the UK parliament', as the ECtHR does, is 'a little short of offensive to our notions of constitutional propriety'.[369] The most prominent example in this regard is, here again, the *Hirst* case[370] which triggered both prolonged non-compliance by state actors and extensive criticism from politicians and the British media, 'portray[ing] the Court as effectively overruling legitimate democratic British political decisions and the doctrine of Parliamentary Supremacy'.[371] Although this pushback motivation is particularly strong in the context of the United Kingdom, actors in other member states such as Switzerland, Belgium, the Netherlands and Denmark have also taken up this line of argumentation.[372] As Madsen observed, '[t]his critique had in common an argumentation that emphasised the democratic legitimacy of parliamentarian decision-making over the more thin institutional legitimacy of the ECtHR to review those decisions in view of the ECHR'.[373] In Switzerland, this democratic legitimacy

[364] R Ryssdal, 'Brian Walsh and the European Court of Human Rights' in J O'Reilly (ed), *Human Rights and Constitutional Law* (Round Hall Press 1992) 5, 6.

[365] *Loizidou v Turkey* (Preliminary Objections), 23 March 1995, App no 15318/89, para 75. See also, eg, *Bosphorus Hava Yollari Turizm Ve Ticaret Anonim Şirketi v Ireland*, 30 June 2005, App no 45036/98, para 156; *Michaud v France*, 6 December 2012, App no 12323/11, para 103; *Avotiņš v Latvia*, 23 May 2016, App no 17502/07, para 112.

[366] L Wildhaber, 'A Constitutional Future for the European Court of Human Rights?' (2002) 23 *Human Rights Law Journal* 161.

[367] Wildhaber, 'The European Court of Human Rights' (n 86) 528.

[368] eg, S Greer, *The European Convention on Human Rights: Achievements, Problems and Prospects* (CUP 2006); W Sadurski, *Constitutionalism and the Enlargement of Europe* (OUP, 2012); OM Arnardóttir, 'The Brighton Aftermath and the Changing Role of the European Court of Human Rights' (2018) 9 *Journal of International Dispute Settlement* 223.

[369] David Neuberger, 'The British and Europe', Cambridge Freshfields Annual Law Lecture 2014: www.nottingham.ac.uk/hrlc/documents/specialevents/neuberger-speech-120214.pdf.

[370] *Hirst v United Kingdom (No 2)*, 6 October 2005, App no 74025/01.

[371] Madsen, 'The European Court of Human Rights' (n 34) 267.

[372] Madsen, 'From boom to backlash? (n 200) 38.

[373] ibid.

related pushback took, in particular, the form of a popular initiative of 2016 – the so-called self-determination initiative – aiming, ultimately unsuccessfully,[374] at constraining the impact of ECtHR decision-making in Switzerland to safeguard the democratic rights of the people. The supporters of this initiative saw the ECtHR as affecting a fundamental principle of this state's democratic system: in this case popular sovereignty.[375]

A further aspect of the court's jurisprudence that directly touches upon the sovereignty interests of member states and thus can motivate pushback concerns the validity of reservations or 'interpretative declarations' to the Convention and Protocols. In *Belilos v Switzerland* in 1988, the court did not only declare Switzerland's reservation invalid, it also decided – in an approach that diverges from general international law – that the state is fully bound by the treaty due to the invalidity of the reservation.[376] This approach, which the court has upheld ever since, has spurred pushback from Switzerland and other member states. During the proceedings, the Swiss government made 'veiled threats to the effect that Switzerland might decide to denounce the Convention if it did not get its way'.[377] When it did not succeed, a motion in the Council of States to denounce the Convention was initiated and it failed by only one vote.[378] Other member states such as Türkiye and Italy also had to face this jurisprudence. In the *Loizidou* case of 1995,[379] Türkiye argued that it had qualified its consent to the optional clauses in a manner that would exclude jurisdiction of the court for Northern Cyprus. But the court held that the optional clauses did not allow for territorial or substantive limitations because otherwise member states 'would be free to subscribe to separate regimes of enforcement of Convention obligations depending on the scope of their acceptances'.[380] As in *Belilos*, it came to the conclusion that Türkiye's acceptance of the optional clauses were fully effective, despite the only qualified consent. This directly touched, here again, on the sovereignty of the respondent state. Despite its critique of this approach, Türkiye did not push back by withdrawing or not renewing the declarations regarding the optional clauses. However, it did not accept the *Loizidou* decision in substance and openly refused to implement it. In contrast, Italy did not push back as much against the *Grande Stevens* decision of 2014 in which the court declared invalid an Italian reservation in respect of Article 4 of Protocol No 7.[381]

[374] The initiative was rejected in 2018.

[375] See also on this motivation for the Swiss pushback, Breuer, 'Principled resistance to the European Court of Human Rights and its case law' (n 207) 62. For an overview of the criticism of the ECtHR in Switzerland, see T Altwicker, 'Switzerland: The Substitute Constitution in Times of Popular Dissent' in Popelier, Lambrecht and Lemmens (eds), *Criticism of the European Court of Human Rights, Shifting the Convention System* (n 165) 385.

[376] *Belilos v Switzerland*, 29 April 1988, App no 10328/83, para 50 et seq. See generally on this case, I Cameron and F Horn, 'Reservations to the European Convention on Human Rights' (1990) 33 *German Yearbook of International Law* 69; S Marks, 'Reservations Unhinged: The Belilos Case before the European Court of Human Rights' (1990) 39 *International & Comparative Law Quarterly* 300.

[377] Cameron and Horn (n 376) 116.

[378] ibid 117.

[379] *Loizidou v Turkey* (Preliminary Objections), 23 March 1995, App no 15318/89.

[380] ibid para 75.

[381] *Grande Stevens v Italy*, 4 March 2014, App no 18640/10, paras 204–11.

A different aspect of the court's jurisprudence that has the potential to motivate pushback is the frequent changes in its jurisprudence.[382] Not only might states perceive their Convention obligations as unpredictable due to such changes. But this practice can also reinforce the impression of judicial activism and thus further motivate pushback related to this activism. This issue does not only arise when the court deliberately departs from a previous decision due to an evolutive interpretation. Inconsistencies also exist among the decisions of different chambers on similar matters. In fact, in the Brighton Declaration, member states explicitly criticised the lack of consistency among chambers. They thus 'invite[d] the Court to have regard to the importance of consistency where judgments relate to aspects of the same issue'.[383]

For *domestic courts*, certain particular factors can motivate pushback against the court. To start with, the most likely, and the most visible, judicial actors pushing back against the ECtHR are domestic constitutional courts. From the perspective of these courts, the ECtHR is a competing institution in charge of human rights adjudication. The (perceived) monopoly in this regard of domestic constitutional courts is challenged by the ECtHR. This is even more so since the court presents itself as a 'constitutional' court for the European region (see above). Further, the ECtHR also challenges the self-understanding of domestic courts as having the 'final say' in human rights matters. The ECtHR is thus not only a competing authoritative entity but also one that assumes competence to 'overrule' domestic constitutional courts in Convention-related human rights matters. As a result, 'all constitutional courts have taken pains to stress that it is the national constitution that ultimately regulates the relationship between the domestic legal order and the convention system'.[384] This is the conceptual basis for pushback from these courts. As outlined above, constitutional courts that prominently pushed back against the authority of the ECtHR include the Austrian, German and Italian constitutional courts as well as, with a different background, the Russian and Polish constitutional courts. As has been observed for the German Constitutional Court, its jurisprudence on the domestic impact of the ECtHR's jurisprudence reflects the 'power struggle between Karlsruhe and Strasbourg on the proper allocation of (judicial) powers'.[385] And, in the same vein, the Italian constitutional court declared that domestic courts are no 'passive receptors of an exegetic command established elsewhere in the forms of a judicial pronouncement'.[386]

Expressing concern for their own power, both constitutional and other apex courts also have, on certain occasions, opposed amendment of the Convention. This is the case regarding Protocol No 16 which introduced the possibility for domestic courts to request advisory opinions in a preliminary reference procedure. For example, Belgium

[382] eg, *Christine Goodwin v The United Kingdom*, 11 July 2002, App no 28957/95; *Demir And Baykara v Turkey*, 12 November 2008, App no 34503/97; *Sergey Zolotukhin v Russia*, 10 February 2009, App no 14939/03.

[383] Brighton Declaration of 19 and 20 April 2012, para 25.

[384] Keller and Stone Sweet, 'Assessing the Impact of the ECHR on National Legal Systems' (n 74) 688.

[385] Breuer, 'Principled resistance to the European Court of Human Rights and its case law' (n 207) 68.

[386] Italian Constitutional Court, 14 January 2015, no 49/2015, 15 (of the English translation).

did not sign this protocol and, according to media reports, this was 'because judges from the highest courts opposed the system of preliminary opinions'.[387]

Especially in judicial systems without a (fully-fledged) constitutional court, other courts also entered into a conflictual relationship with the ECtHR. This was, for example, the case for Irish, British and French courts during certain periods of their (changing) relationship with the ECtHR.[388] Here, one of the motivational factors for pushback seems to have been the mere fact of being criticised by the ECtHR. For example, after the French courts had rather enthusiastically implemented the judgments of the ECtHR in the 1980s, this changed when the ECtHR started to criticise the French judicial system.[389] This led them to push back by refusing to take the ECtHR's jurisprudence into account.[390] As Madsen describes, it was the self-perception of the French courts that was affected: 'the French highest courts were surprised – if not offended – when the ECtHR began to criticize … the functioning of French courts. Counterattacking, the Cour de Cassation launched a rebellion against the Court'.[391]

Similar patterns emerged when the ECtHR decided that judgments by domestic constitutional courts violated Convention rights. For example, in *Markin v Russia*, the ECtHR harshly criticised the reasoning of the Russian Constitutional Court.[392] While the subject matter was of a rather routine nature (parental leave for men in the Russian military), the self-image of the domestic court was affected. The result was a public statement by the president of this court in the Russian media, engaging the 'limits of obedience'.[393] He stated that 'when decisions of the Strasbourg Court are doubtful from the point of view of the essence of the European Convention itself … Russia has the right to work out a defensive mechanism against such decisions'.[394] Further, one can argue that the pushback from the German Constitutional Court in the *Görgülü* decision was motivated, at least in part, by this factor. This pushback originated in a conflict concerning *Hannover v Germany*.[395] In this case, the ECtHR weighed the conflicting rights to privacy and freedom of expression differently from what had been done by the German Constitutional Court.

In addition, several of the motivating factors that are relevant for pushback from governmental actors also motivate domestic courts to push back against the ECtHR. Sovereignty interests play a significant role in this regard. For example, in its advisory

[387] P Popelier, 'Belgium: Faithful, Obedient, and Just a Little Irritated' in Popelier, Lambrecht and Lemmens (eds), *Criticism of the European Court of Human Rights, Shifting the Convention System* (n 165) 103, 110.

[388] See the respective contributions in Popelier, Lambrecht and Lemmens (n 267).

[389] On the initially positive reaction of French courts, MR Madsen, 'Resistance to the European Court of Human Rights: The Institutional and Sociological Consequences of Principled Resistance' in Breuer (ed), *Principled Resistance to ECtHR Judgments: A New Paradigm?* (n 267) 35, 47.

[390] Blay-Grabarczyk and Maubernard (n 251).

[391] Madsen, 'The European Court of Human Rights' (n 34) 262.

[392] *Konstantin Markin v Russia*, 7 October 2010, App no 30078/06, para 57.

[393] Valery Zorkin, Rossiskaya Gazeta, 29 October 2010 – cited according to Nussberger, *The European Court of Human Rights* (n 6) 126.

[394] Cited as translated in J Kahn, 'The Relationship between the European Court of Human Rights and the Constitutional Court of the Russian Federation: Conflicting Conceptions of Sovereignty in Strasbourg and St Petersburg' (2019) 30 *European Journal of International Law* 933, 937.

[395] *Von Hannover v Germany*, 24 June 2004, App no 59320/00.

decision of 2015, the Russian Constitutional Court used sovereignty as a legal notion to justify why in cases of conflict with the Russian Constitution, it is not possible to implement ECtHR decisions.[396] It referred to 'imperative norms of customary international law (jus cogens), to which without doubts the principle of sovereign equality and respect for rights inherent in sovereignty and the principle of non-interference with internal affairs of states belong'.[397] Similarly, the Polish Constitutional Tribunal held that the ECtHR, by reviewing the election of judges in its *Xero Flor* decision, encroached upon the competences of the Polish Parliament and President.[398] Further, the aspects of the court's jurisprudence that can be perceived as activist such as the living instrument doctrine and the European consensus approach have pushback-motivating potential. For example, it has been argued that the *Görgülü* decision of the German Constitutional Court has been 'a warning vis-à-vis the [ECtHR] not to go too far with its evolutive interpretation'.[399]

Finally, domestic apex and constitutional courts in the dense European legal space with its multifaced judicial interactions can, when shaping their relationship with the ECtHR, be influenced by their stance regarding other international courts. Considerations of consistent behaviour can play a role in this regard. The fact that a domestic court has pushed back against other international courts such as the International Court of Justice (ICJ) or the CJEU can lower the threshold for potential resistance against the ECtHR. Domestic courts for which this is relevant include, for example, the Italian Constitutional Court that has pushed back, in varied intensity, against the CJEU (eg, in the context of the counter-limits jurisprudence or the *Taricco* saga)[400] and the ICJ (in the state immunity context).[401] The German Constitutional Court's critical stance with regard to the CJEU over the last decade and its push-back in its ultra vires decision of 2020 can also contribute to creating a behavioural setting in which pushback against other courts such as the ECtHR are perceived as more acceptable – although so far, such a 'spill-over effect' has not materialised in the court's jurisprudence.

In conclusion, the motivation for *governmental actors* to push back against the ECtHR is high. There is a wide range of factors that, to a large extent, have existed for decades and further increased over time. These factors have motivated push-back in the past and have the potential to do so in the future. This includes factors relating to politically sensitive or socially controversial subject matters decided by the court. And it relates to structural features of the court's jurisprudence such as its evolutive interpretation of the Convention and the 'majoritarian activism' of the European consensus doctrine, as well as the court's self-understanding as a European constitutional court. Further aspects such as the review of legislative acts and the

[396] Russian Constitutional Court, 14 July 2015, no 21-P/2015, translation provided by the Venice Commission in CDL-REF(2016)019.

[397] ibid.

[398] Polish Constitutional Tribunal, 24 November 2021, case ref K 6/21. See the summary of the judgment by Ploszka (n 296).

[399] Breuer, 'Principled resistance to the European Court of Human Rights and its case law' (n 207) 57.

[400] Italian Constitutional Court, 18 December 1973, no 183/1973 (*Frontini*); preliminary reference no 24/2017 (*Taricco II*).

[401] Italian Constitutional Court, 22 October 2014, no 238/2014.

jurisprudence on the validity of reservations can motivate certain state actors to push back as these aspects are perceived, to diverging extents, to affect the member states' sovereignty interests. Regarding *domestic courts*, the pushback motivation has been particularly high for constitutional courts. After being lower during the earlier decades, the growing de facto authority of the ECtHR in human rights matters, its evolutive interpretation as well as its constitutional self-understanding have increased the pushback motivation in particular since the 1990s. In contrast, the pushback motivation for ordinary courts was higher in earlier years and has decreased during the past decades.

ii. Opportunity for Pushback

The opportunity for pushback was initially rather broad but has decreased over time, especially since the late 1990s. To start with, pushback in the form of withdrawal from the court's jurisdiction has been easy for member states in the earlier phase of the court. When the jurisdiction of the court was optional for Council of Europe members, the possibility to make a declaration accepting this jurisdiction for only a few years at a time has created an opportunity for pushback (see also section II.B). Having to renew this declaration every few years has created an opportunity for governmental actors to retreat from the court merely through inaction. Although state actors have not taken this opportunity to fully retreat from the court, they have used it for less intensive forms of pushback. As a reaction to the '*Belgian Linguistics*' case brought to the court in 1965,[402] the Belgian government considered protesting against the approach that the Commission had taken in this case, and the fact that it had referred the case hastily to the court just before the expiry of the Article 46 declaration, by withholding the renewal of this declaration.[403] Although, in the end, it renewed this declaration, it translated its criticism into a shorter period of renewal (two instead of five years).[404] Similarly, the United Kingdom reduced the length of renewal of the optional declarations from three to two years in 1972 as a reaction to controversial cases such as the '*East African Asians*' cases before the Commission[405] which had caused concern among British officials.[406] In the 1980s, France and Germany reduced their renewal of the Article 25 declaration and, in the case of Germany, also for the Article 46 declaration from five to three years.[407] Germany had done so after it had been the respondent in several high-profile cases before the court.[408]

[402] Decided by the court in 1968: *Case 'Relating to Certain Aspects of the Laws on the Use of Languages in Education in Belgium' v Belgium*, 23 July 1968, App nos 1474/62, 1677/62, 1691/62, 1769/63, 1994/63, 2126/64.

[403] Bates, *Evolution* (n 2) 229.

[404] ibid.

[405] Commission, 31 applications of *East African Asians v United Kingdom*, 6 March 1978, App nos 4626/70 et al.

[406] Bates, *Evolution* (n 2) 286.

[407] ibid 427–28.

[408] eg, *Oztürk v Germany*, 21 February 1984, App no 8544/79; *Glasenapp v Germany*, 28 August 1986, App no 9228/80.

The possibility of periodic renewal or in fact non-renewal was acknowledged by (some) member states as an important opportunity for pushback. In the negotiations leading to Protocol No 11, the United Kingdom (supported by Türkiye) stressed that the non-renewal threat enabled a power-balance between the member states and the court, stating that

> the opportunity to review the Court's performance periodically, and make a conscious decision to renew the right of individual petition, is right and proper as a democratic safeguard, and [the United Kingdom] therefore regards maintaining the status quo in this respect as absolutely essential.[409]

Despite this argument, member states did not uphold this treaty feature in Protocol No 11, thus eliminating this pushback opportunity for the period since 1998.

In contrast to the above development, the opportunity for withdrawal from the Convention system altogether has remained stable over time. Under Article 65 ECHR 1950 and Article 58 ECHR, member states can withdraw from the Convention or cease to be a party to it when they withdraw from the Council of Europe. Currently, member states can withdraw at any time while a state could not withdraw within the first five years after accession. The legal opportunity structure for withdrawals thus did not exist during these five years but has been broad after this period.

Among the opportunity elements that have continuously existed throughout the court's practice is the legal opportunity structure for amendments to the Convention system. The Convention does not contain any specific rules on amendments so that general international law (in particular Article 40 and 41 Vienna Convention on the Law of Treaties (VCLT)) applies. In application thereof, the protocols to the Convention contain provisions as to their ratification and entry into force that define the opportunity structure in this regard. These rules indicate that member states have designed the Convention system as a multi-speed system in which protocol standards are not necessarily applicable to all member states. Many of the protocols to the Convention do not require the consent of all member states to enter into force. This amendment framework creates a broader opportunity structure for pushback than is the case in the ECOWAS context where member states can only amend treaty provisions by unanimity. It would be possible for a group of member states that wishes to push back against the court to do so by way of protocol that only requires ratification by a smaller group of member states. Only the limit set out in Article 41(b) VCLT would narrow this opportunity as to the potential content of such amendment. So far, this broad opportunity has however not been used in this manner. When Protocol No 15 was adopted as result of a pushback attempt during the Brighton Conference, member states opted for a protocol that required the ratification of all member states. As a result, the final content of this protocol was much less intrusive into the authority of the ECtHR than in the initial proposal to the Brighton Declaration. De facto, the self-imposed

[409] Declaration of the British expert as quoted by A Drzemczewski, 'A Major Overhaul of the European Human Rights Convention Mechanism: Protocol 11' (1195) 6 *Collected Course of the Academy of European Law* 121, 174–75 (fn 81).

unanimity requirement has thus limited the pushback opportunity. Yet this was an opportunity setting that was chosen at this instance and it is possible that states during future pushback attempts will opt for a different setting.

For pushback in the form of norm contestation, the procedural framework before the court provides an opportunity for respondent states to oppose certain norms or the interpretation thereof given by the court. Most prominently, states have frequently used the possibility of raising preliminary objections to push for a broad interpretation of the requirement to exhaust domestic remedies. Further, preliminary objections have been used for norm contestation regarding the interpretation of the time limit of Article 35(1) ECHR and jurisdictional questions such as the extra-territorial application of Convention rights.

Regarding pushback in the form of non-compliance, the domestic approach regarding the relationship between the Convention and domestic law has initially created a broad opportunity for state actors not to comply with ECtHR decisions. Until the 1990s, many states had not yet incorporated the Convention into their legal orders. For administrative actors and domestic courts, especially, this created an opportunity for non-compliance with ECtHR decisions. This situation has however changed since member states have given internal effect to the Convention (see section III.A.ii). The dualist approach taken by many of the member states has become irrelevant for the opportunity structure.[410] Moreover, as an international element of the opportunity structure, the monitoring system of the Council of Ministers limits the opportunity for non-compliance. It makes non-compliance salient so that there is little opportunity for respondents to disregard the court's decisions without other actors noticing it. In later years, the monitoring mechanism has been intensified by involving the court and private actors. As already mentioned, this includes the role of the court under Article 46(4) ECtHR as well as NGOs that have contributed to compliance monitoring since the Committee of Ministers changed its Rule 9.2 in 2006.[411]

The subject matter of the cases that the court decides can also create an opportunity for pushback, in addition to motivating it. As has been shown in the ECOWAS context, cases brought by opposition politicians can provide an opportunity for respondents to portray the court as a political actor and push back against it discursively and otherwise. For the ECtHR, this opportunity has been lower than is the case before the ECOWAS Court as applications from domestic political actors have been less significant before the ECtHR.

In the ECtHR context, one can also observe how *social opportunity elements* shape the opportunity for pushback. To start with, the 'true partner effect' has been relevant both for governmental and judicial actors. As outlined in chapter two, this term describes the fact that an actor is more likely to disobey an authoritative entity when another actor is doing so as well.[412] In the context of the Brighton Conference

[410] On the irrelevance of monist or dualist approaches, see also Keller and Stone Sweet, 'Assessing the Impact of the ECHR on National Legal Systems' (n 74) 683; Lambrecht (n 218) 505.

[411] On this development, Haddad (n 85) 79.

[412] See ch 2 and, eg, WN Morris and RS Miller, 'The Effects of Consensus-Breaking and Consensus-Preempting Partners on Reduction of Conformity' (1975) 11 *Journal of Experimental Social Psychology* 215.

of 2012, the first significant pushback attempt by member states, the alliance between the United Kingdom and Russia, seems to follow this pattern. What might appear 'as an odd, informal alliance' is indicative of state actors pushing back against the court in novel ways because they each had partners who were also 'outspoken critics of the Court'.[413] As a further expression of this 'partnership', the Russian government first implemented its law of 2015 creating a formal possibility not to comply with ECtHR decisions[414] in the *Anchugov and Gladkov* case – a case that mirrored the *Hirst* case against which the United Kingdom has pushed back.[415]

Moreover, 'true partner effects' can also play a role in the behaviour of domestic courts. The Russian constitutional court pointed out in its advisory opinion of 2015 in which it recognised the possibility of not complying with ECtHR decisions when they are not in conformity with the domestic constitution that '[d]eviation from judgments of the European Court of Human Rights ... takes place also in the practice of European states'.[416] It cites at length the relevant jurisprudence of the German, Austrian and Italian constitutional courts as well as the Supreme Court of the United Kingdom. This indicates that judicial actors that explicitly and intentionally push back against the ECtHR are likely to look for 'partners' that have already done so to facilitate this behaviour. Such partners can also only be perceived or self-constructed, as evidenced by the Russian Constitutional Court's reading of the German Constitutional Court's decision in *Görgülü*. Although the latter also established a constitutional law exception to the implementation of ECtHR decisions, there are considerable differences between the approaches of the two courts – a fact also highlighted and criticised by the Venice Commission.[417]

Relatedly, the critical discourses within member states have influenced each other among group members from different states. In particuar, in the years before and after the Brighton Declaration, one could observe this interstate 'diffusion of critical discourse' when 'critics from countries with comparatively few cases in Strasbourg – such as Denmark and Finland – adopt[ed] the very same discursive means as states facing more serious challenges from Strasbourg'.[418] States seem to perceive themselves as part of a group in which ECtHR jurisprudence that is seen as encroaching upon a certain state's interests also affects other members of this group. As a result of such dynamics, critical reactions against such jurisprudence in one member state influence the behaviour of actors in other member states.

Finally, an opportunity element that is specific to the states that are also EU members is the interaction between pushback directed at the EU and pushback directed at the Convention system. In some states, the criticism articulated against the

[413] Madsen, 'The European Court of Human Rights' (n 34) 267.

[414] Amendments to the Federal Constitutional Law on the Constitutional Court of the Russian Federation of 14 December 2015 – translated by the Venice Commission in CDL-REF(2016)006.

[415] Pointing to the fact that this was an explicit choice by the Russian government, Kahn (n 394) 950.

[416] Russian Constitutional Court, 14 July 2015, no 21-P/2015, translation provided by the Venice Commission in CDL-REF(2016)019.

[417] CDL-AD(2016)016-e, Russian Federation – Final Opinion on the Amendments to the Federal Constitutional Law on the Constitutional Court adopted by the Venice Commission at its 107th Plenary Session (Venice, 10–11 June 2016) paras 134–38.

[418] Madsen, 'The European Court of Human Rights' (n 34) 270.

EU by certain political parties and governmental actors has provided the opportunity to also criticise the Convention system.[419] Political pushback in such cases expands from the EU as an entity that, from the perspective of such actors, encroaches upon state sovereignty to other entities of a similar character.

In conclusion, the opportunity for pushback in the form of withdrawal from the court's jurisdiction has been very broad during the first decades of the court's practice and has decreased to a lower but still rather broad level. The opportunity for pushback in the form of treaty amendments has remained rather broad and the opportunity for norm contestation regarding procedural norms is also rather broad. The opportunity for non-compliance has been moderate to broad in the first decades of the court's practice and can be qualified since the late 1990s as moderate to low.

iii. Constraints against Pushback

The key constraining factor against pushback from member states is the extrinsic constraint provided by actors that support the court against pushback. In fact, the court has had a diverging range of supporting actors. In its early period, the other institutions within the Strasbourg system were the main supporters of the court. It was not only the court's registry but also the Commission's registry and the Human Rights Division of the Council of Europe that participated in promoting the Convention system.[420] Further, the specific pushback attempts have shown the role and importance of state actors as constraining factors for pushback. In the context of the Brighton Conference, a number of states opposed the initial proposal by the United Kingdom that aimed at cutting back the competences of the court. States such as Austria, Belgium, the Czech Republic, Germany and Poland were not willing to contribute to weakening the court and the overall Convention system.[421] Due to this support for the court, member states very much scaled back in the final Brighton Declaration the pushback still reflected in the draft Declaration. Finally, regarding non-compliance, supporting actors have contributed to put pressure on member states to comply with ECtHR decisions. This includes NGOs that have assumed a supporting role on the domestic level. They have advocated against non-compliance including in member states with a lower rule of law practice.[422] Further, the Venice Commission, established in 1990, has an indirect role not only regarding non-compliance in some matters but regarding the general relationship between state actors, including domestic courts, and the ECtHR. It has, for example, provided an analysis of, and opinions about, decisions of domestic courts such as the Russian Constitutional Court that were instances of pushback.

[419] Lambrecht (n 218) 517.

[420] S Hennette-Vauchez, 'The ECHR and the Birth of (European) Human Rights Law as an Academic Discipline' in A Vauche and B de Witte (eds), *Lawyering Europe: European Law as a Transnational Social Field* (Hart Publishing 2013) 117, 122.

[421] Lambrecht (n 218) 519.

[422] On NGOs and their impact on compliance by Russia, van der Vet (n 84).

In comparison to the ECOWAS context, it bears mentioning that the ECtHR started off with a much less diverse group of supporting actors. While for the ECOWAS Court, NGOs have accompanied the creation of the court and lobbied for it, thus establishing a close link that translated into crucial support during backlash by member states, this was not (or at least to a much lesser extent) the case for the ECtHR. The connection with NGOs only developed gradually, also influenced by the fact that NGOs have a limited procedural access opportunity before the court. As a result, for structural resistance or backlash by member states that go beyond non-compliance, the other member states have long been the key supporting actors and still have a crucial role in this regard.

An intrinsic factor that can constrain pushback from state actors directly or indirectly is knowledge related. When actors that can be potentially motivated to push back against the court have only a low awareness of the court's activities, this makes it less likely for them to push back. The ECtHR benefits from this constraint with regard to member states in which the court and its jurisprudence is not very visible. For example, in the Czech Republic, the lack of salience has the effect that the 'Court also remains invisible to Czech populist/extremist parties [so that they] do not view the Court as an enemy and therefore do not exploit and misrepresent its case law in their political agenda'.[423] Similarly, the rather low awareness of the court and the Convention system in Italy – especially as compared with the EU and the CJEU – has led to the observation that political actors do not call for reform or consider pushback against the court, unlike in the EU context.[424]

Further, a behavioural constraint against pushback is the status quo bias (see chapter two). An example is the jurisprudence of the court on the notion of 'civil rights' in Article 6 ECHR that the court interpreted broadly and thus created far-reaching procedural obligations for member states against which many of them resisted strongly (see section III.B.i). While this jurisprudence triggered pushback when the court first developed it in the 1970s, it has since been considered established case law that states consider to be the status quo of Convention obligations. The pushback-motivating potential has thus been constrained over time.

To sum up, the constraints against pushback from member states are moderate to high, mostly due to the institutional, civil society and member state support for the court. These constraining factors however developed gradually and were lower in earlier periods of the court.

iv. Assessment of MOC Factors

The above analysis has shown that the MOC setting for pushback from state actors has been very heterogeneous. For governmental actors, the MOC setting differs depending on the form of pushback and depending on the time period. For several forms of pushback, the determining MOC factor, ie, the factor that is at the lowest

[423] L Majerčík, 'Czech Republic: Strasbourg Case Law Undisputed' in Popelier, Lambrecht and Lemmens (eds), *Criticism of the European Court of Human Rights, Shifting the Convention System* (n 165) 131, 136.
[424] Martinico (n 219) 179.

level and that – according to the MOC framework – determines the respective actors' behaviour, has fluctuated over time. During the 1960s, the motivation for pushback was rather low, mainly due to the very limited role that the court played in the Convention system at the time. But both the opportunity and unconstrained ability for pushback were high, with the exception of pushback by non-compliance. For the latter, the ability was somewhat lower than for other forms of pushback because of the compliance monitoring by the Committee of Ministers. Overall, during this time, the low motivation was the determining MOC factor.

From the 1970s onwards, the motivation for pushback increased to a moderate level especially because of the landmark decisions of this decade that laid the foundation for the transformative jurisprudence of the court. During the 1970s and 1980s, this motivational setting was accompanied by a still rather broad opportunity for pushback by withdrawal, non-renewal of optional clauses, treaty amendment, norm contestation and – although to a lesser extent – non-compliance. The ability for pushback during this time was also rather high. The court did not yet benefit from the diverse group of supporting actors from which it was going to benefit in later years. And behavioural effects relating to a status quo of certain jurisprudential features had not had much time to develop yet. But due to the lower visibility of the court as compared with later decades, certain state actors were more strongly constrained by a lack of knowledge about the pushback-motivating jurisprudence of the court – a factor that to some extent mitigates the pushback-enabling effect of the lower extrinsic constraints. However, as the ability for pushback remained overall rather high, the still moderate motivation for pushback was the determining factor within the MOC setting during this period. It indeed translated into only few instances of pushback in this time.

Since the 1990s, the motivation for pushback has continued to increase while the opportunity and ability have decreased. In particular, the opportunity for non-renewal of the optional clauses disappeared with Protocol No 11 and the opportunity for non-compliance by administrative and judicial actors decreased when member states gave effect to the Convention in their domestic legal orders. In contrast, the opportunity for withdrawal and amendments has remained high. The ability for pushback decreased as the constraining effect of a growing network of supporting actors broadened. In addition, the constraining effect of the status quo bias as to major jurisprudential features had reached a significant extent by the 1990s. As a result, the moderate to low ability of state actors to push back against the court became the determining factor for forms of pushback other than non-compliance. It is the factor that is at the lowest level as compared with the rather high motivation and moderate to high opportunity for pushback. For non-compliance, opportunity and ability are both moderate to low so that these factors conjointly determine the actors' behaviour (in light of the high motivation for pushback). The fact that, despite the many factors that are pushback-motivating in nature, there have not been more instances of structural resistance and backlash as well as a rather high compliance rate can thus be attributed to the constraining factors, and regarding non-compliance also to the opportunity structure. Figure 5.6 and Figure 5.7 illustrate the different developments over time of the MOC setting for non-compliance and other forms of pushback.

Figure 5.6 Development over time of the MOC setting for pushback from governmental actors (forms of pushback other than non-compliance)

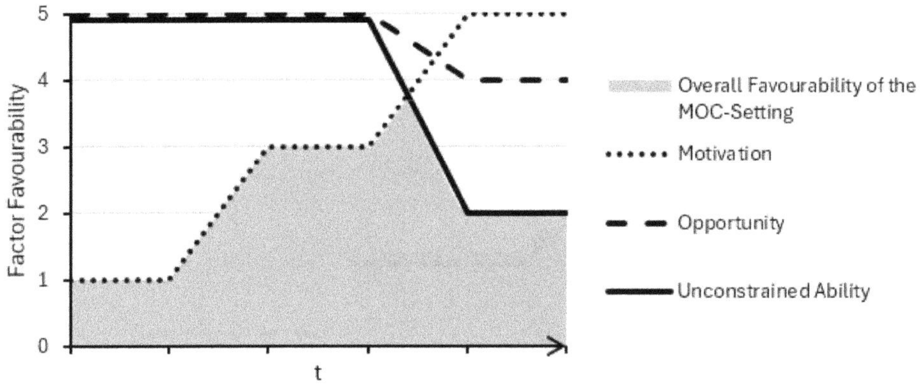

Figure 5.7 Development over time of the MOC setting for pushback from governmental actors (non-compliance)

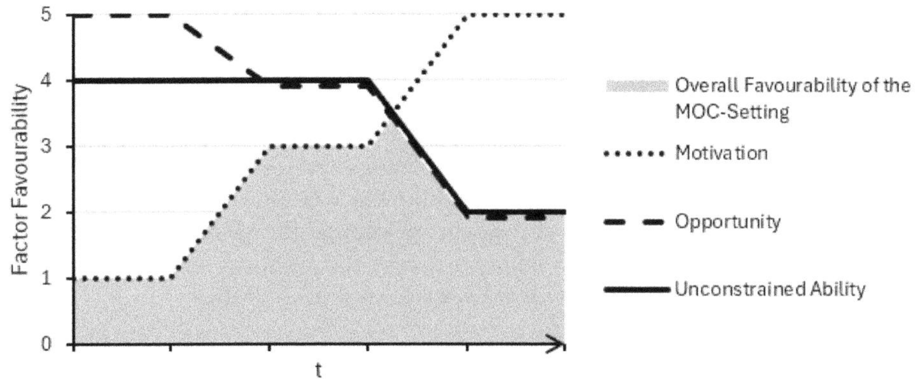

For domestic courts, the changing motivation and opportunity structure (especially for non-compliance) as well as for the unconstrained ability for pushback also leads to diverging MOC settings. For constitutional courts during the first decades of the ECtHR's practice, the rather high opportunity and ability for pushback meant that the at most moderate motivation for pushback was the determining factor according to the MOC framework. The constitutional courts' motivation thus shaped their behaviour. In contrast, the situation has been reversed in the more recent period since the 1990s. The pushback motivation for constitutional courts increased while opportunity and unconstrained ability decreased. The latter two have thus become the factors that predominantly shape the pushback behaviour of these actors (see Figure 5.8). For other domestic courts, the motivation for pushback seems to have been higher in earlier years than more recently – as has been the development for opportunity and unconstrained ability. As a result, motivation, opportunity and ability have developed in a parallel manner, so that, due to the similar level of the three factors, one cannot discern a single determining factor for the behaviour of these actors. All factors have equally shaped the behaviour of these courts.

Figure 5.8 Development over time of the MOC setting for pushback from domestic constitutional courts

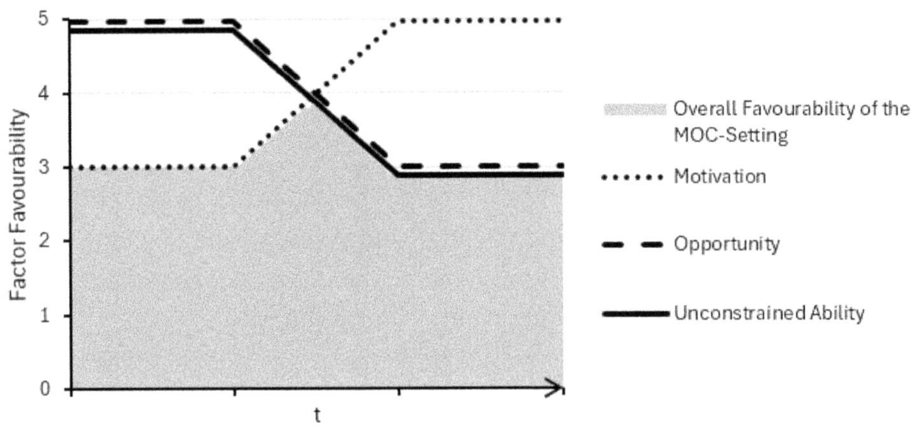

IV. ASSESSING THE COURT'S STRATEGIES TO INFLUENCE MOC

After having outlined the MOC setting for applicants and respondents in the previous sections, I now turn to analysing how the court has influenced the respective MOC factors. I first assess the strategies of the court to improve the MOC setting that determines whether applicants and respondents accept the authority of the court (IV.A) before addressing strategies to avoid and manage pushback (IV.B).

A. Increasing MOC for Accepting the Court's Authority

i. Enhancing Motivation

a. Enhancing Motivation of Respondents

The court addresses and strengthens the *values* that can contribute to motivating respondents to accept the authority of the court. To start with, human rights protection as a value is inherently addressed in all its jurisprudence. However, the court specifically targets this value when it deals with structural human rights violations in a member state. The various tools that the court has developed in view of such structural issues contribute to strengthening value-correspondence as a motivating factor. This includes, inter alia, the pilot judgment procedure, far-reaching remedies such as requiring legislative amendments, and the fact that the court prioritises cases with a 'structural or endemic situation' based on its priority policy.[425]

The court also engages with the other motivational values mentioned in section III.A.i. To begin with, this is the case for rule of law values. Although this notion is mentioned only in the preamble of the ECHR, the court has elevated this value and its legal status. Former Court President Robert Spano emphasised that 'the rule of law has been the lodestar guiding the development of the case-law of the European Court of Human Rights'.[426] The court in its *Golder* decision of 1975 found the rule of law to be 'one of the features of the common spiritual heritage of the member States of the Council of Europe'.[427] Since this case, the court has operationalised the rule of law by establishing it as a principle 'underlying the Convention'[428] and 'inherent in all the Articles of the Convention'.[429] According to Spano, this translates into the rule of law assuming various functions as an 'overarching principle' and as a more specific 'rule with quite fixed content'.[430] The multilayered normative role of this principle makes it possible for the court to link individual rights, in particular fair trial guarantees, to the rule of law. This enhances the value-related motivation of respondents to accept decisions in relation to these rights. And it makes the rule of law as a motivating value in the Convention system more visible.

Moreover, the jurisprudence of the court has significantly influenced several rule of law elements in the member states. Examples in the court's early jurisprudence, especially in the 1970s, include the fair trial and procedural law guarantees under Article 6 ECHR that the court established and expanded over time.[431] Since the 1990s, the court has influenced most prominently rule of law elements in East and Central European member states,[432] concerning fair trial aspects such as access to court, equality of arms or the right to defence.

More recently, the rule of law jurisprudence of the court has turned in particular to judicial independence in the domestic legal orders.[433] The court has stressed the 'importance of safeguarding the independence of the judiciary'.[434] It has, as an expression of de jure independence, set limits for the dismissal of judges.[435] And it has also started to adjudicate on the judicial appointment procedure, taking note of the recent jurisprudence of the CJEU on the matter.[436] It has stressed that the Convention

[425] Such cases are grouped into category II, see the court's priority policy: www.echr.coe.int/documents/priority_policy_eng.pdf.

[426] R Spano, 'The rule of law as the lodestar of the European Convention on Human Rights: The Strasbourg Court and the independence of the judiciary' (2021) 27 *European Law Journal* 211, 212.

[427] *Golder v The United Kingdom*, 21 February 1975, App no 4451/70, para 34.

[428] *Ramda v France*, 19 December 2017, App no 78477/11, para 60.

[429] *Lekić v Slovenia*, 11 December 2018, App no 36480/07, para 94. See also *Selahattin Demirtaş v Turkey (No 2)*, 22 December 2020, App no 14305/17, para 249.

[430] Spano, 'The rule of law' (n 426) 215.

[431] See section III.B.i, and eg, *Ringeisen v Austria*, 16 July 1971, App no 2614/65; *König v Germany*, 28 June 1978, App no 6232/73.

[432] Ziemele (n 190) 494.

[433] Spano, 'The rule of law' (n 426).

[434] *Baka v Hungary*, 23 June 2016, App no 20261/12, para 165.

[435] ibid; *Denisov v Ukraine*, 25 September 2018, App no 76639/11.

[436] *Guðmundur Andri Ástráðsson v Iceland*, 1 December 2020, App no 26374/18. See on the CJEU–ECtHR interaction regarding juridical independence, Spano, 'The rule of law' (n 426) 223–26.

requires not only de jure but also de facto independence. In *Agrokomplex v Ukraine*, the court stated that

> the State's respecting the authority of the courts is an indispensable precondition for public confidence in the courts and, more broadly, for the rule of law. For this to be the case, the constitutional safeguards of the independence and impartiality of the judiciary do not suffice. They must be effectively incorporated into everyday administrative attitudes and practices.[437]

In subsequent cases regarding the detention of judges by Turkish authorities, the court has further clarified the importance of de facto independence. It emphasised that

> where domestic law has granted judicial protection to members of the judiciary in order to safeguard the independent exercise of their functions, it is essential that such arrangements should be properly complied with.[438]

Further, it has stressed that even if a state has formal rules establishing de jure independence, the Convention requirements as to judicial independence and the rule of law are not fulfilled when state actors adopt a behaviour 'aimed at creating a negative atmosphere around the legal actions of the … applicant and constituting direct attempts to interfere in those proceedings'.[439] In sum, this jurisprudence aims at ensuring a high level of both aspirational and de facto value-correspondence as to judicial independence.

A further value that is addressed by the court in a way that can increase the value-related motivation to accept the authority of the court is democracy. The court has stressed that '[d]emocracy is … a fundamental feature of the European public order'.[440] The court has linked the values of democracy and the rule of law by considering the latter to be 'one of the fundamental principles of a democratic society'.[441] It also stressed 'the prominent place held in a democratic society by the right to a fair trial';[442] and regarding judicial independence, the 'confidence which the courts must inspire in a democratic society'.[443] More generally, the court decided in its *Turkish Communist Party* case that democracy is the only political system compatible with the Convention.[444] It further concretised the relationship between democracy and the rights guaranteed in the ECtHR in its subsequent

[437] *Agrokompleks v Ukraine*, 6 October 2011, App no 23465/03, para 136.
[438] *Alparslan Altan v Turkey*, 16 April 2019, App no 12778/17, para 102.
[439] *Rinau v Lithuania*, 14 January 2020, App no 10926/09, para 211.
[440] *United Communist Party of Turkey and Others v Turkey*, 30 January 1998, App no 133/1996/752/951, para 45.
[441] *Lekić v Slovenia*, 11 December 2018, App no 36480/07, para 94. See also *Uspaskich v Lithuania*, 20 December 2016, App no 14737/08, para 87.
[442] *Airey v Ireland*, 9 October 1979, App no 6289/73, para 24; *Artico v Italy*, 13 May 1980, App no 6694/74, para 33.
[443] *Sramek v Austria*, 22 October 1984, App no 8790/79, para 42. This formulation is established jurisprudence, see eg, *Ramos Nunes de Carvalho e Sá v Portugal*, 6 November 2018, App nos 55391/13, 57728/13 and 74041/13, para 149; *Sacilor Lormines v France*, 9 November 2006, App no 65411/01, para 60; *Kleyn and Others v the Netherlands*, 6 May 2003, App nos 9343/98, 39651/98, 43147/98 and 46664/99, para 191.
[444] *United Communist Party of Turkey and Others v Turkey*, 30 January 1998, App no 133/1996/752/951, para 45.

jurisprudence.[445] In particular, the jurisprudence of the court regarding media freedom and the persecution of members of the political opposition in certain member states aims at fostering the visibility of democratic values and at improving their realisation on the ground.[446] In this connection, the court has developed the framework of Article 18 ECHR as a 'measuring instrument for democracy'.[447] The court distinguishes 'between "normal" Convention violations and Convention violations showing an anti-Convention spirit of the authorities'.[448] Moreover, in the specific context of regime change, the jurisprudence of the court has, in many states concerned by democratic transition, improved the democratic practices by state actors: 'the authorities concerned through the implementation of the Strasbourg judgments have been learning how to operate democratically in concrete instances or specific domains'.[449] And in terms of concrete legal changes initiated by the court, 'new democracies have quite easily accepted all the changes that were suggested to them through the Court's case law'.[450]

Regarding the value of state actors to create 'greater unity' among member states (see section III.A.i), the court has used the European consensus doctrine to speak to this motivation.[451] Normatively, the notion of European consensus emphasises unity as a goal of the regional human rights project. By referring to this notion, the court increases the visibility of this value. Moreover, on a practical level, the court uses this notion to harmonise human rights standards based on the practice in the (majority of) member states. The use of the European consensus doctrine thus has a unifying function. It is a key element of the 'rapprochement constitutionnel' that has been observed as an impact of the ECtHR jurisprudence on member states.[452] As an additional harmonising instrument, the fact that the court uses 'autonomous concepts' aims at providing legal standards applicable to all member states.[453] The court developed this approach in its *Engel* decision of 1974.[454] Instead of applying notions stated in the Convention text as they are understood in domestic law, the court adopts an 'autonomous' interpretation of these notions. This autonomous interpretation is applicable to all member states and thus sets a unified standard. For example, the court has used this approach prominently regarding the notions of 'criminal charge'

[445] eg, *Case of Refah Partisi (The Welfare Party) and Others v Turkey*, 13 February 2003, App nos 41340/98, 41342/98, 41343/98 and 41344/98.

[446] eg, *Navalnyy v Russia*, 15 November 2018, App nos 29580/12, 36847/12, 11252/13 et al; *Selahattin Demirtaş v Turkey (No 2)*, 22 December 2020, App no 14305/17; *Ilgar Mammadov v Azerbaijan*, 22 May 2014, App no 15172/13; *Merabishvili v Georgia*, 28 November 2017, App no 72508/13; *Lutsenko v Ukraine*, 3 July 2012, App no 6492/11.

[447] Joint Concurring Opinion of Yudkivska, Tsotsoria and Vehabović JJ in *Merabishvili v Georgia*, 28 November 2017, App no 72508/13.

[448] Nussberger, *The European Court of Human Rights* (n 6) 190.

[449] Ziemele (n 190) 495.

[450] ibid 456.

[451] See also Shany (n 167) 77.

[452] Tomuschat (n 344) para 135.

[453] On autonomous concepts as one of the key principles of interpretation used by the court, P Mahoney, 'The Comparative Method in Judgments of the European Court of Human Rights: Reference back to National Law' in Swiss Institute of Comparative Law (ed), *The Role Of Comparative Law In The Emergence of European Law* (2000) 143, 145–46; Nussberger, *The European Court of Human Rights* (n 6) 104–07.

[454] *Engel and Others v the Netherlands*, 8 June 1976, App nos 5100/71, 5101/71, 5102/71, 5354/72, 5370/72.

and 'civil rights and obligations' in Article 6 ECtHR as well as 'deprived of his liberty' in Article 5 ECHR.[455]

In addition to enhancing value-correspondence, the court also aims at increasing the *interests* that can motivate respondents to accept the authority of the court. To start with, the court took into account the sovereignty-related interests of member states very prominently in its early practice – together with the Commission. As apparent especially from the interstate complaint regarding the United Kingdom/Ireland but also from the low rates of violations found in individual complaints, an approach of 'legal diplomacy' addressing the interests of respondent states was prevailing.[456] At this time, the court, much like the Commission, 'gained the image of being minimalistic and even state-friendly in their operations'.[457] This approach made it possible for the court to have states accept its authority by participating in the proceedings and thus build a basis for triggering an interest in consistent behaviour that would in turn motivate states to accept the authority of the court continuously and in a more widespread manner.

Further, given the well-developed compliance and monitoring framework, there has been less necessity for the ECtHR as compared with the ECOWAS Court to adopt far-reaching strategies regarding compliance. However, as non-compliance has become more frequent than in earlier years, the court has, especially in the last two decades, repeatedly stressed to respondents the importance of compliance with its judgments. It has stated that the monitoring mechanism by the Committee of Ministers 'demonstrates the importance of effective implementation of judgments'.[458] The court has also emphasised the 'importance of [the] effective execution [of its judgments], in good faith and in a manner compatible with the "conclusions and spirit" of those judgments'.[459] In this context, it has clarified, that under Rule 6 of the 'Rules of the Committee of Ministers for the supervision of the execution of judgments and of the terms of friendly settlements', respondent states are '*required* to provide the Committee of Ministers with detailed, up-to-date information on developments in the process of executing judgments that are binding on them'.[460] The court has therefore addressed elements of the monitoring mechanism that can motivate respondent states to comply with its judgments.

In relation to domestic courts, the ECtHR has adopted a strategy of dialogue and networking. This includes visits and meetings with judges of the supreme and constitutional courts of the member states. In particular during the enlargement of

[455] ibid; *Ringeisen v Austria*, 16 July 1971, App no 2614/65; *König v Germany*, 28 June 1978, App no 6232/73.

[456] Madsen, 'The European Court of Human Rights' (n 34) 249; MR Madsen, 'The Protracted Institutionalization of the Strasbourg Court: From Legal Diplomacy to Integrationist Jurisprudence' in J Christoffersen and MR Madsen (eds), *The European Court of Human Rights between Law and Politics* (n 130) 43.

[457] Madsen, 'The European Court of Human Rights' (n 34) 249.

[458] *Verein Gegen Tierfabriken Schweiz (VgT) v Switzerland (No 2)*, 30 June 2009, App no 32772/02, para 84; *Ilgar Mammadov v Azerbaijan (Art 46 (4))*, 29 May 2019, App no 15172/13, para 147.

[459] *Ilgar Mammadov v Azerbaijan (Art 46 (4))*, 29 May 2019, App no 15172/13, para 149; *Emre v Switzerland (No 2)*, 11 October 2011, App no 5056/10, para 75.

[460] *Ilgar Mammadov v Azerbaijan (Art 46 (4))*, 29 May 2019, App no 15172/13, para 152 (emphasis added).

the 1990s, the ECtHR adopted a specific strategy to enhance the motivation of judges in Central and Eastern European states when these states joined the Convention system. As Luzius Wildhaber recounts, he made it his 'policy to visit … the judiciary … of practically all the new ECHR members … to show that the national judiciaries were taken seriously and were considered a central part in a common enterprise'.[461] More generally, in 2015, the court established the 'Superior Courts Network' to institutionalise the informal exchanges with all domestic courts which are part of the network. One of this network's purposes is 'to enrich dialogue and the implementation of the Convention'.[462]

b. Enhancing Motivation of Potential Applicants

The applicant-related strategies of the court mainly concern applicants in the context of *individual complaints*. While the court had focused, during its first years of its practice, on strategies to enhance the acceptance by respondents, it shifted its approach in the late 1970s. It addressed the values and interests of (potential) applicants more intensely by changing its objectives to 'an independent mission of setting common standards across Europe and a quest for a real protection of human rights under the ECHR'.[463]

For a high level of value-correspondence with respect to procedural *values*, the court has adopted policy strategies concerning its independence. To begin with, the court stresses in its self-representation designed for potential applicants that judges are independent of their country of origin and that they do not represent the state in respect of which they are elected.[464] Further, on a practical level, the court has sought to maintain and increase its independence from member states. A prominent example is how the court defended its independence in the context of the Brighton Conference. In relation to the draft declaration, the court expressed its concerns that, if the declaration were to include instructions as to how the court should apply the subsidiarity principle and the margin of appreciation, this could be perceived as undermining the court's independence from member states. The then President of the Court, Sir Nicolas Bratza, voiced his concern 'that Governments can in some way dictate to the Court how its case-law should evolve or how it should carry out the judicial functions conferred on it'.[465] The member states did indeed hear this objection and agreed to introduce the formulation 'as developed in the Court's case-law'. Later, the subsequent President, Dean Spielmann, also strongly criticised the attempt of member states to be involved via consultations in changing the Rules of Court: 'I see this as a desire to exercise control over our Court which, I feel, is inconsistent with the current challenges'.[466] Moreover, the court has also 'defended jealously' its independence

[461] L Wildhaber, 'Comments on the early years and conclusions' in Motoc and Ziemele (eds), *The Impact of the ECHR on Democratic Change in Central and Eastern Europe* (n 79) 6, 11–12.

[462] See description on the SCN website: www.echr.coe.int/superior-courts-network.

[463] Madsen, 'The European Court of Human Rights' (n 34) 252.

[464] See, eg, the court's information material (n 17).

[465] Sir Nicolas Bratza, Speech at Brighton Conference, Brighton, 18–20 April 2012: www.echr.coe.int/Documents/Speech_20120420_Bratza_Brighton_ENG.pdf.

[466] Dean Spielmann, 'The successes of and challenges for the European Court, seen from the inside', Proceedings of the Oslo Conference on the Long-term Future of the European Court of Human Rights,

vis-a-vis the executive actors within the Council of Europe.[467] This concerns the operational dimension of judicial independence that includes decisions regarding staff appointments, budget and internal working methods. For example, the then Registrar of the Court, Paul Mahoney, warned repeatedly against interference by actors such as the Council of Europe Secretariat General on these matters.[468]

Another procedural value was addressed by the court in its pre-Protocol No 11 phase. When the court increased the participation rights of individual applicants despite their lack of formal status as party to the proceedings, it influenced value-correspondence as to procedural justice. As mentioned in chapter two, being able to engage in a discourse with the authoritative entity enhances the actors' perception of procedural fairness which is a motivational factor for accepting authority. For individual applicants, the jurisprudentially constructed informal participatory status has thus increased value-correspondence during this period.

Concerning the *interests* of individual applicants, the court has adopted a wide range of strategies to enhance the interest-based motivation for accepting the authority of the court. A key interest addressed by the court is the interest in social change that has motivated many applicants. Among the jurisprudential tools that the court has used since the 1970s for this purpose is the living instrument doctrine. The court developed this doctrine in an explicitly strategic manner. When the court decided in the *Tyrer* case that 'the Convention is a living instrument which ... must be interpreted in the light of present-day conditions', it reconstructed its own institutional function as a transformative function.[469] The many decisions that have referred to the living instrument doctrine since its creation re-emphasise this (self-attributed) function, motivating applicants to approach the court with a transformative agenda.[470]

But the court does not only indicate its readiness to respond to a transformative agenda when deciding in favour of the respective applicants. It often also does so when it finds in favour of the respondent. It signals to the applicant 'that it is open to revisiting the issue in the future'.[471] For example, in a case regarding the use of donors for in vitro fertilisation, the court stated:

> Even if it finds no breach of Article 8 in the present case, the Court considers that this area, in which the law appears to be continuously evolving and which is subject to a particularly dynamic development in science and law, needs to be kept under review by the Contracting States.[472]

42 (English translation as in GT-GDR-G(2014)R2 Addendum I, 16 October 2014, 2): rm.coe.int/CoERMPublicCommonSearchServices/DisplayDCTMContent?documentId=090000168047078a.

[467] Mahoney, Parting thoughts' (n 177) 348.

[468] ibid; P Mahoney, 'Separation of Powers in the Council of Europe: The Status of the European Court of Human Rights vis-à-vis the Authorities of the Council of Europe' (2003) 24 *Human Rights Law Journal* 152.

[469] *Tyrer v United Kingdom*, 25 April 1978, App no 5856/72. See also *Marckx v Belgium*, 13 June 1979, App no 6833/74, para 41.

[470] Decisions referring to the living instrument doctrine include, eg, *Soering v United Kingdom*, 7 July 1989, App no 14038/88, para 102; *Loizidou v Turkey* (Preliminary Objections), 23 March 1995, App no 15318/89, para 71; *Selmouni v France*, 28 July 1999, App no 25803/94, para 101; *Matthews v The United Kingdom*, 18 February 1999, App no 24833/94, para 39.

[471] Helfer and Voeten, 'Walking Back Human Rights in Europe?' (n 271) 802.

[472] *S.H. and Others v Austria*, 3 November 2011, App no 57813/00, para 118.

The transformative potential of the living instrument doctrine – and thus the motivational effect on applicants – has fluctuated over time, largely depending on how the court operationalised its connection to the 'European consensus'. From the 1970s to 1990s, the court limited the effect of this doctrine, in a part of its jurisprudence, by making it dependent on a clearly discernible 'common standard' or a 'generally shared approach' among member states.[473] If such a standard did not exist, the court concluded that it could not adopt an evolutive interpretation of the respective Convention right. During this time, the court was somewhat reluctant to fully embrace a strategy to foster the applicants' transformative agenda because it also wanted to give considerable weight to its strategies aiming at enhancing the respondents' motivation to accept its authority. As Angelika Nussberger, former Vice-President of the Court, summarises:

> Some wanted it to change society, others wanted it to guarantee stability. It is, however, difficult to bring about change and stability at the same time. The Court was caught in the dilemma of living up to very different expectations.[474]

In contrast, in the 2000s the court spoke much more forcefully to the transformative interests of applicants. It understood the common standard in a broader, internationally oriented manner.[475] In *Goodwin v United Kingdom*, a case concerning the legal recognition of transsexual persons, the court explicitly departed from the narrowly construed common standard approach, stating:

> The Court accordingly attaches less importance to the lack of evidence of a common European approach to the resolution of the legal and practical problems posed, than to the clear and uncontested evidence of a continuing international trend in favour not only of increased social acceptance of transsexuals but of legal recognition of the new sexual identity of post-operative transsexuals.[476]

In contrast, the court has more recently adjusted its strategy concerning its transformative approach. Certain novel aspects of its jurisprudence do not foster the transformative motivation of applicants any more. For example, the court has changed its standard for the review of domestic judicial decisions. In particular, it has given leeway to domestic courts as to the outcome of their decisions as long as they take into account the *established* jurisprudence of the ECtHR. As Çali, observes, this approach runs counter to a transformative agenda because it 'binds the ECtHR to its past case law and can hamper its dynamism. The emphasis placed on the well-established case law of the ECtHR is a move away from its transformative promise'.[477] The strategy of the court to enhance this motivational factor is thus less pronounced than in previous years.

[473] eg, *Handyside v The United Kingdom*, 7 December 1976, App no 5493/72; *Sheffield and Horsham v The United Kingdom*, 30 July 1998, App no 31–32/1997/815–816/1018–1019, paras 57, 58.

[474] Nussberger, 'From High Hopes to Scepticism?' (n 41) 159.

[475] See on this shift, G Letsas, 'The ECHR as a living instrument: its meaning and legitimacy' in Føllesdal, Peters and Ulfstein (eds), *Constituting Europe* (n 28) 106.

[476] *Christine Goodwin v The United Kingdom*, 11 July 2002, App no 28957/95, para 85.

[477] B Çalı, 'From flexible to variable standards of judicial review: the responsible domestic courts doctrine at the European Court of Human Rights' in OM Arnardóttir and A Buyse (eds) *Shifting Centres of Gravity in Human Rights Protection Rethinking relations between the ECHR, EU and national legal orders* (Routledge 2016) 144, 160.

In addition to addressing the interest in social change, the court has also enhanced the motivation for applicants who seek legal change in cases of structural human rights violations. When the court decides that the judicial remedies in a respondent state are ineffective and waives the requirement of prior exhaustion of these remedies, the court 'sends a powerful signal about the inadequacy of national rights protection and invites reform'.[478] Further, the court speaks to the interests of applicants who challenge structural issues by indicating general measures to remedy structural human rights violations. This is a practice that developed in light of the large number of repetitive cases that applicants brought against Italy concerning the excessive length of judicial proceedings (see section II.A). The court emphasised the obligation of respondent states to remedy the structural issue, stating that the finding of a violation 'imposes on the respondent State a legal obligation … to choose … the general and/or, if appropriate, individual measures to be adopted in their domestic legal order to put an end to the violation found by the Court and to redress so far as possible the effects'.[479]

Further, the pilot judgment procedure created by the court speaks to the interests of applicants in having the court address the structural dimension of human rights violations. In the context of this strategy, the court has first used policy tools, lobbying for an explicit provision on pilot judgments in Protocol No 14. In 2003 during the negotiation process, the court submitted a Position Paper that contained detailed suggestions for such a procedure.[480] When this policy strategy failed, the court shifted to a jurisprudential tool by creating this procedure itself in the *Broniowski v Poland* case. In 2011, the court formalised the procedure by including it in the Rules of the Court (Rule 61).

Regarding the interest in transitional justice of applicants in member states that have experienced regime changes, the court has not shied away from addressing transitional issues and has created a rather favourable setting for them. On a procedural level, this includes the use of the pilot judgment procedure to deal with large-scale transitional justice issues. Further, the court has, at least in some circumstances, recognised a right of victims and their families to know the truth about massive rights violations during transitional phases.[481] And it has stressed 'the importance to [the respondent state's] society of knowing the truth about the events'.[482] As a result, the court has considered it necessary for the respective state to conduct investigations into such events even beyond the statutory limitation of criminal liability. However, the court's strategy regarding truth-seeking as transitional justice interests only goes so far. In particular, the court has rejected the notion that the obligation to investigate under Article 2 ECHR would also include investigations with the (mere) aim of 'establishing a historical truth'.[483]

Further, the court has adopted various strategies to address the interests of applicants in effective behaviour. A jurisprudential tool targeting this motivational factor

[478] Keller and Stone Sweet, 'Assessing the Impact of the ECHR on National Legal Systems' (n 74) 702.
[479] *Scozzari and Giunta v Italy*, 13 July 2000, App nos 39221/98 and 41963/98, para 249.
[480] See Fyrnys (n 44) 1239.
[481] *Association '21 Décembre 1989' and Others v Romania*, 24 May 2011, App nos 33810/07 and 18817/08, para 144.
[482] ibid 194.
[483] *Janowiec and Others v Russia*, 21 October 2013, App nos 55508/07 and 29520/09, para 143.

is the effectiveness doctrine. In the landmark case on this doctrine, *Airey v Ireland* in 1979, the court coined its often-cited phrase that the 'Convention is intended to guarantee not rights that are theoretical or illusory but rights that are practical and effective'.[484] In this case, this rationale made it possible for the court to decide that access to a court in matrimonial matters requiring legal representation that the applicant could not afford was not effective due to the lack of a legal aid system. According to the court, there is a positive obligation for states to provide access to legal representation if 'such assistance proves indispensable for an effective access to court'.[485] This formulation highlights that the effectiveness doctrine is also closely related to the notion of positive obligations, a notion established in the *Marckx* judgment of the same year.[486] Both these notions make it possible for the court to decide cases in favour of applicants and thus to foster their perception that addressing the court is effective behaviour.

Moreover, an important strategy to enhance the motivation of applicants in effective behaviour has been the court's shift to providing more far-reaching remedies. As outlined in section II.A, the court has in the last two decades gone beyond its initially restrictive stance. It now provides recommendations as to the means that respondent states should use to implement its judgments and, in certain cases, even issues specific orders. It has justified this novel approach stating that if a state were not to take the prescribed measures, it would violate its 'obligation under Article 46(1) of the Convention to abide by the Court's judgment' and would prolong the violation of substantive obligation imposed by the respective Article of the Convention.[487]

Before taking this more far-reaching approach to remedies, the court has adopted a (limited) strategy to enhance the effective implementation of its decisions regarding compensation. It developed the 'just satisfaction' remedy under Article 50 ECHR 1950 (now Article 41 ECHR) in a way that was procedurally favourable to the individual.[488] For example, it did not require the applicant to exhaust domestic remedies again for this claim but saw the Article 50 procedure as part of the overall procedure before the ECtHR.[489] While being applicant-friendly as to the procedural requirements, it however took a rather restrictive approach as to the content of just satisfaction. In many cases, the court declared that it was 'not necessary to afford to the applicant any just satisfaction other than that resulting from the finding of a violation of his rights'.[490]

Finally, to reduce the backlog and make the court more efficient in order to enhance the effectiveness expectation of applicants, the court has adopted both judicial and

[484] *Airey v Ireland*, 9 October 1979, App no 6289/73, para 24.

[485] ibid para 26.

[486] In this decision, the court held with regard to Article 8 ECHR that 'in addition to [the] primarily negative [obligation], there may be positive obligations inherent in an effective "respect" for family life'. *Marckx v Belgium*, 13 June 1979, App no 6833/74, para 31.

[487] See, eg, for the order to release applicants from custody: *Ilaşcu and Others v Moldova and Russia* 8 July 2004, App no 48787/99, para 490.

[488] Bates, *Evolution* (n 2) 407.

[489] *De Wilde, Ooms and Versyp ('Vagrancy') v Belgium (Article 50)*, 10 March 1972, App nos 2832/66, 2835/66, 2899/66, para 16.

[490] eg, *Golder v The United Kingdom*, 21 February 1975, App no 4451/70, para 46.

policy strategies to enable procedural reforms. In the early 2000s when Protocol No 14 was being negotiated, the then President of the Court, Luzius Wildhaber, made detailed suggestions as to how to streamline the procedure before the court and prioritise cases to enhance effectiveness.[491] Although member states did not include all proposals into the protocol text, this lobbying strategy showed some results. Further, the court continued to follow this agenda within its direct sphere of influence. In 2009, it adopted a priority policy according to which cases are categorised into priority groups. The court amended Rule 41 of the Rules of Court to provide that it can set out criteria regarding the 'importance and urgency' of cases to streamline its processing of cases.[492] And as mentioned above, it created the pilot judgment procedure as an important tool to address the backlog caused by repetitive cases resulting from structural human rights violations.

Regarding *state applicants* in interstate cases, the court has only adopted few strategies that explicitly aim at this group of applicants. An exception is the court's approach to engage with these applicants' interest in effective dispute resolution. By initially prioritising interstate complaints and putting a lot of effort and resources into these cases, the court has aimed at fostering the interest of state applicants in dispute resolution before the court. However, more recently, the court has changed this strategy. It has removed interstate complaints from its priority policy – where they were previously grouped into category II – and decided to focus on important individual applications.[493]

ii. Enhancing Opportunity

a. Enhancing Opportunity for Applicants

To start with, the ECtHR has enhanced the *jurisdiction-related opportunity* for applicants in several ways, although not in an extensive manner. The most significant approach to broadening jurisdiction has been the court's jurisprudence on the extra-territorial application of Convention rights. As outlined above, the court has recognised in its recent case law that member states have to also abide by Convention obligations in situations outside their state territory when they exercise (through their agents) control over an individual.[494] Further, the court has broadened the jurisdictional opportunity with its jurisprudence on the (in)validity of reservations to the Convention.[495] When the court decided that a state is unconditionally bound by the Convention or a protocol, declaring a reservation invalid, the opportunity for applicants who otherwise would not be able to bring a case against the respective state becomes broader. And regarding the temporal dimension of the court's jurisdiction,

[491] See on these proposals, Bates, *Evolution* (n 2) 498–99.

[492] On this policy, Cameron (n 28) 42–43.

[493] See the court's priority policy: www.echr.coe.int/documents/priority_policy_eng.pdf.

[494] *Al Skeini and Others v UK*, 7 July 2011, App no 55721/07; *Hirsi Jamaa and Others v Italy*, 23 February 2012, App no 27765/09; *Hassan v the United Kingdom*, 16 September 2014, App no 29750/09; *Jaloud v the Netherlands*, 20 November 2014, App no 47708/08.

[495] *Belilos v Switzerland*, 29 April 1988, App no 10328/83; *Loizidou v Turkey* (Preliminary Objections), 23 March 1995, App no 15318/89; *Grande Stevens v Italy*, 4 March 2014, App no 18640/10. See on this jurisprudence also section III.B.i.

its jurisprudence on 'continuing violations' and on post-ratification facts that are 'extensions' of the already existing pre-ratification situation has broadened the opportunity for applicants.[496] Moreover, the court has somewhat expanded the legal basis for its decision-making. Although the Convention and its protocols remain at the core of the court's jurisdiction, it has found ways to refer to other international legal instruments when interpreting the Convention. It has made this strategy explicit, stating that

> the Court has never considered the provisions of the Convention as the sole framework of reference for the interpretation of the rights and freedoms enshrined therein. On the contrary, it must also take into account any relevant rules and principles of international law applicable in relations between the Contracting Parties.[497]

The court has also addressed the admissibility criteria that shape the *access opportunity*. It has focused on strategies concerning individual complaints under Article 34 ECHR. It spelled out its general strategy in the *Klass* decision of 1978:

> The procedural provisions of the Convention must, in view of the fact that the Convention and its institutions were set up to protect the individual, be applied in a manner which serves to make the system of individual applications efficacious.[498]

In the original Convention system that was composed of the Commission and the court, the court has expanded the access opportunity for applicants by creating an indirect procedural role for applicants during court proceedings. As mentioned above, the court gave applicants access to the relevant documents such as the Commission's reports and allowed them to be represented before the court.[499] The court took this step despite resistance from the respondent state who feared that applicants would use the court as a forum for political propaganda.[500] This procedural empowerment initiated by the court was fostered later when the court gave full rights of audience to the applicants in the late 1970s, a right formalised in the court's Rules of Procedure in 1982.[501]

Moreover, in the court's early years during the 1960s when the Commission had referred barely any cases to the court, the court used policy means to expand the opportunity of applicants in this regard. Judges of the court criticised that the Commission would prevent the court from fulfilling its function and denying the court its role as a judicial dispute resolution mechanism, a role that the Commission was eager to assume, but not intended to.[502] And indeed, the Commission referred more cases to the court starting from the late 1960s.[503]

As a further part of the court's judicial strategy, it enhanced the access opportunity for applicants when it recognised exceptions to the admissibility criteria set out

[496] *Hutten-Czapska v Poland*, 19 June 2006, App no 35014/97, paras 147–53; *Kurić and Others v Slovenia*, 26 June 2012, App no 26828/06, paras 240–41. See also *Šilih v Slovenia*, 9 April 2009, App no 71463/01, paras 140–47; *Almeida Garrett, Mascarenhas Falcão and Others v Portugal*, 11 January 2000, App nos 29813/96 and 30229/96, para 43.
[497] *Demir And Baykara v Turkey*, 12 November 2008, App no 34503/97, para 67 (with further references).
[498] *Klass and Others v Germany*, 6 September 1978, App no 5029/71, para 34.
[499] *Lawless v Ireland (No 1)*, 14 November 1960, App no 332/57.
[500] Bates, *Evolution* (n 2) 202.
[501] ibid 204.
[502] H Rolin, 'Has the European Court of Human Rights a future?' (1965) 11 *Howard Law Journal* 442.
[503] Bates, *Evolution* (n 2) 225.

in Articles 34 and 35 ECHR. This includes in particular the exception to the requirement to exhaust domestic remedies in cases in which doing so would be manifestly ineffective in remedying the alleged violation (see also section II.B).[504] This exception is especially impactful in broadening the opportunity structure for applicants in situations in which an 'administrative practice' exists which violates Convention rights and is tolerated by the respondent state.[505] In such situations, the access opportunity for all applicants concerned is expanded significantly. This access-enhancing strategy is also one of the few strategies that does not only address individual applicants but also state applicants in interstate cases.[506]

The court has also adopted an access-broadening approach regarding the novel admissibility criterion of Article 35(3)(b) ECHR. It has restrained the access-limiting effect by narrowing the scope of this provision. It has rejected the applicability of this provision for certain rights such as Articles 2, 3 and 5 because of the importance and fundamental nature of these rights.[507] For other rights such as Articles 9 and 10, the court has declared that 'the application of the admissibility criterion contained in Article 35 § 3 (b) of the Convention should take due account of the importance of this freedom and be subject to careful scrutiny by the Court'.[508]

The strategy of the court regarding the time limit of Article 3(1) ECHR has been ambivalent. On the one hand, it has broadened the access opportunity by creating the 'continuing violations' exception to the time limit. This makes it possible for applicants to bring cases to the court relating to human rights violations that emerged a long time before the so-constructed six/four-month period. On the other hand, the court has contributed to narrowing the access opportunity by extra-judicial means. It has, in the context of the Brighton Conference, suggested reducing the time limit to four instead of six months – a suggestion that has been implemented by Protocol No 15. Moreover, in the context of the Brighton Conference, the court has declared that it was going to apply the time limit more strictly.[509]

Similarly, the court has adopted a rather restrictive stance as to the victim status required under Article 34 ECHR. Only for a very small group of applicants such as family members of deceased victims has the court broadened the access opportunity regarding this admissibility criterion. In contrast, especially for NGOs, the restrictive interpretation of the victim requirement has significantly limited the access opportunity. The only exception to this restrictive stance is the 'de facto actio popularis' possibility recently established by the court for the climate change context (see section II.B).

[504] *Akdivar and Others v Turkey*, 16 September 1996, App no 21893/93, para 68; *Sejdovic v Italy*, 1 March 2006, App no 56581/00, para 46.

[505] *Akdivar and Others v Turkey*, 16 September 1996, App no 21893/93, para 67.

[506] See section II.B.

[507] *Zelčs v Latvia*, 20 February 2020, App no 65367/16, para 44 (with further references); *Makuchyan and Minasyan v Azerbaijan and Hungary*, 26 May 2020, App no 17247/13, paras 69–73; *Y v Latvia*, 21 October 2014, App no 61183/08, para 44.

[508] *Stavropoulos and Others v Greece*, 25 June 2020, App no 52484/18, para 29.

[509] See Brighton Declaration of 19 and 20 April 2012, para 15(b): 'The Conference … [w]elcomes the stricter application of the time limit in Article 35(1) of the Convention envisaged by the Court'.

That the court has not sought to enhance more broadly the access opportunity of NGOs as formal applicants is a reflection of the scepticism towards NGOs that was predominant at the court for a long time.[510] Even more recently, a court official has been cited stating that 'the Court does not see NGOs as representing victims, it sees them as having an interest'.[511] As a moderate step towards including NGOs, the court has however developed a strategy as to amicus curiae briefs that has become increasingly permissive over time. The court's approach has developed from not allowing such briefs in the 1970s to including them in its Rules of Court in 1982 (Rule 37(2)) but being somewhat hesitant as to their value, to a practice that accepts amicus curiae requests in most instances and even encourages such interventions.[512]

Finally, a further way in which the court has expanded the opportunity for applicants to engage with the court is Rule 39 of the court's rules of procedures. This rule makes it possible for applicants to seek interim measures from the court. This provision has been created by the court itself and has been applied in a way that has made these measures 'an effective instrument of human rights protection'.[513] In particular, this has been the case since the *Mamatkulov and Askarov v Turkey* case of 2005 in which the court clarified that interim measures are binding and that states violate Article 34 ECtHR when they do not comply with these measures.[514] However, in earlier decisions, it still had concluded that given that no Convention or protocol provision explicitly regulates interim measures, such measures are not binding on respondent states.[515]

b. Enhancing Opportunity for Respondents

In contrast to what has been said about the ECtHR's influence on the opportunity structure for applicants, the court has largely shaped and expanded the opportunity for respondents. Most importantly, the court has recognised early on that it reviews not only executive acts but also legislative acts and decisions by domestic courts (see section III.A.ii). For the domestic legislator and judiciary, this jurisprudence has created the opportunity to accept the authority of the court. Moreover, the court has expanded this opportunity for state actors over time, most prominently since the late 1990s, in relation to remedies. When the court started to order specific remedies (eg, criminal investigations) to implement positive obligations, it created the opportunity for executive actors to accept the authority of the court by active behaviour. Similarly, with regard to legislative actors, the court broadened the opportunity by recommending or even ordering specific legislative amendments to comply with Convention standards.

Regarding the limiting effect that the relationship between regional and domestic law can have for the compliance opportunity, the court has not adopted far-reaching

[510] Haddad (n 85) 55 et seq.
[511] ibid 61.
[512] Van den Eynde, 'An Empirical Look' (n 9) 281.
[513] Nussberger, *The European Court of Human Rights* (n 6) 62.
[514] *Mamatkulov and Askarov v Turkey*, 4 February 2005, App nos 46827/99 and 46951/99, para 109 et seq.
[515] *Cruz Varas and Others v Sweden*, 20 March 1991, App no 15576/89, para 102.

strategies. It has left it largely to domestic legal orders to shape the relationship between regional and domestic law. However, some of the court's other jurisprudential tools influence this relationship indirectly. A strategy in this regard is the fact that the court has started to order respondents to take general measures, as in the context of pilot judgment procedures. Such general measures make it possible to overcome the limitations of the Convention system that does not provide for a direct effect of the ECtHR's decisions in the member states.[516] While, only based on Convention law, administrative and judicial actors cannot directly apply the court's case law in their respective legal orders, they can apply domestic legal provisions that have been amended after the ECtHR has ordered such an amendment. In this way, the court creates a framework that complements the effect that the domestic legal orders attribute to the Convention.

iii. Limiting Constraints

a. Limiting Constraints for Applicants

The court has adopted a multifaceted strategy to reduce intrinsic constraints that would prevent applicants from bringing cases to the court. Most importantly, the court has been aware for a long time that it is important to reduce constraints that (potential) applicants might face as to the knowledge about the court and its case law. As outreach measures to enhance knowledge about the court, it has, as already mentioned, established information offices in certain – especially newer – member states. These offices have contributed to making applicants more aware of the court in general and provide information about the details of the procedure, and in particular the admissibility criteria before the court.

While in the pre-digital aera, there were rather selective ways in which the court could reach potential applicants directly, this has changed especially since the 2000s. The court now provides a wide range of informational materials and tools on its website. As to the general procedures, the court offers, inter alia, guides on 'how to lodge an application', 'how to make a valid application', on the 'procedure before the ECtHR' and on 'interim measures'.[517] On the substantive jurisprudence, it provides fact sheets as a summary of important jurisprudence on the respective Convention rights[518] as well as Case-law Guides by Article.[519] And of course, the court has created comprehensive access to its decisions on the HUDOC database. To complement these materials, the court has also created a 'Knowledge Sharing Platform (ECHR–KS)' on which further information on the court's case law can be accessed.[520] With regard to these informational tools, the court has also addressed the language barrier that can hinder applicants from accessing the respective information. The decisions and the informational materials are available

[516] See also Fyrnys (n 44) 1245.
[517] Available at: www.echr.coe.int/Pages/home.aspx?p=applicants&c=.
[518] Availabe at: www.echr.coe.int/factsheets.
[519] Availabe at: ks.echr.coe.int/web/echr-ks/all-case-law-guides.
[520] See: ks.echr.coe.int/.

in several languages. The court 'is active in making [its case law] available in as many languages as possible'.[521]

The court has also adopted a procedural law strategy to address knowledge-related constraints. With regard to the admissibility requirement to exhaust domestic remedies, it has held that it is not necessary that the applicant has invoked the respective Convention right explicitly during the domestic proceedings as long as the complaint has been raised 'in substance'.[522] This makes it possible for applicants to bring cases to the court even if they were not aware, at the time of the domestic proceedings, of the Convention right or the possibility of filing human rights applications before the ECtHR.

The court has also adopted strategies to reduce financial constraints for potential applicants. To begin with, applicants do not risk being burdened with the respondent's costs if their application is declared inadmissible or if they lose on the merits. The court does not issue cost orders to the disadvantage of the applicant. If, conversely, the applicant is successful, the court has outlined in the 'practical directions' that are included in its Rules of Court that, as part of just satisfaction under Article 41 ECHR,

> [t]he Court can order the reimbursement to the applicant of costs and expenses which he or she has necessarily, thus unavoidably, incurred – first at the domestic level, and subsequently in the proceedings before the Court itself … Such costs and expenses will typically include the cost of legal assistance, court registration and translation fees, postal expenses.

In addition, according to Rules 105–10 of the Rules of Court, the President of the Chamber can grant legal aid to an applicant. The court is thus able, if needed, to support applicants financially during the ongoing procedure and not only retrospectively via the cost order. Taken together, these measures make it possible for the court to reduce the financial constraints for applicants considerably.

Regarding extrinsic constraints, the court can reduce the constraining effect that might occur when applicants face competing authority relationships from other judicial bodies. A strategy in this regard is to take the jurisprudence of the UN treaty bodies into account. Convergent lines of jurisprudence make it less likely that applicants perceive these bodies as competing entities as compared with the ECtHR. Indeed, the court regularly refers to the interpretation by these bodies of the international human rights treaties when interpreting Convention provisions.[523] And in *Hassan v United Kingdom*, the court emphasised its overall approach towards other international legal sources, stating that 'the Convention … should so far as possible be interpreted in harmony with other rules of international law of which it forms part'.[524]

[521] Nussberger, *The European Court of Human Rights* (n 6) 71.
[522] *Castells v Spain*, 23 April 1992, App no 11798/85, paras 27, 32.
[523] W Sandholtz, 'Human rights courts and global constitutionalism: Coordination through judicial dialogue' (2021) 10 *Global Constitutionalism* 439, 453.
[524] *Hassan v The United Kingdom*, 16 September 2014, App no 29750/09, para 77.

b. Limiting Constraints for Respondents

Concerning the constraints for respondents to accept the authority of the ECtHR, the court has focused mostly on strategies regarding domestic courts. It has addressed intrinsic constraints that would ensue from limited knowledge by domestic courts about the ECtHR and its jurisprudence. The above-mentioned tools such as fact sheets, Case-law Guides by Article, and the HUDOC platform also contribute to lowering constraints for domestic courts. In addition, and as a tool specifically targeted at domestic courts, the ECtHR uses the Superior Courts Network to decrease knowledge-related constraints. This network's goal is 'to create a practical and useful means of exchanging relevant information on Convention case-law and related matters'.[525] In earlier periods, the court has used regular visits to the domestic judiciary to raise awareness of the Convention system and provide information. This was an important part of the court's strategy in the 1990s regarding judiciaries in the new member states from Central and Eastern Europe.[526]

In contrast, it is more difficult for the ECtHR to address extrinsic constraints that exist for state actors. Some strategies do, however, exist. When domestic courts are constrained to accept the authority of the ECtHR because governmental actors pressure them to do otherwise, the ECtHR can contribute to mitigating such constraints by its rule of law-related jurisprudence. The case law on separation of powers and judicial independence can improve the overall setting in which domestic courts and governmental actors interact, making it harder for the latter to exercise pressure on the former. Moreover, regarding extrinsic constraints resulting from competing authority relationships that state actors might face towards other international judicial bodies, the ECtHR can also adopt strategies to lower such constraints. When it takes into account the jurisprudence of these other judicial bodies, it makes it less likely that conflicting decisions arise with which state actors cannot simultaneously comply. For example, when the ECtHR refers to the jurisprudence of the CJEU on judicial independence,[527] it ensures that in cases against respondents that are also EU member states, it does not create incompatible standards. Similarly, the court avoids competing outcomes when it takes into account the jurisprudence of UN treaty bodies and other international courts as mentioned above.

iv. Assessment of Strategies

Regarding the MOC setting for applicants, the ECtHR has not transformed this setting as intensely as other regional courts have done. In particular, the opportunity structure which has been the determining factor for individual applicants – initially together with unconstrained ability and later on its own (see section II.D) – has been targeted in only a rather limited manner by the court. The court did not, in general, adopt a strategy to enhance the access opportunity. While some aspects of its admissibility jurisprudence have indeed made the opportunity structure somewhat more

[525] See the description on the SCN website: www.echr.coe.int/superior-courts-network.
[526] Wildhaber, 'Comments on the early years and conclusions' (n 461) 11.
[527] eg, in *Guðmundur Andri Ástráðsson v Iceland*, 1 December 2020, App no 26374/18.

favourable, the overall approach is ambivalent. The court has adopted in particular a rather restrictive approach to the required victim status and, in part, to the time limit of Article 35 ECHR. Significant jurisprudential enhancements of the opportunity structure are mostly limited to establishing exceptions to the requirement to exhaust domestic remedies under Article 34 ECHR and, in the pre-Protocol No 11 period, to the indirect participatory rights that the court attributed to individual applicants in lieu of their formal status as a party to the proceedings. On the one hand, the court's strategy regarding access has been influenced by policy considerations. In light of the backlog accumulated since the 1990s, broader access would have increased the issue. And since the 2010s, the fact that member states, as part of the Brighton and Copenhagen pushback attempts, urged the court to apply the admissibility criteria strictly, led the court to consider its admissibility jurisprudence as part of a strategy to manage pushback rather than to enhance the MOC setting for applicants. On the other hand, however, the court has not adopted any bold strategies regarding access even at a time where neither workload nor pushback considerations would have held it back from doing so. This demonstrates that the court's activist agenda has always focused on substantive standards rather than the procedural framework. This is true not only for the access of individuals but also for NGOs. For the latter, the court has not broadened the formal access except for the recent climate change jurisprudence and has only very gradually created an indirect access opportunity for these actors as amicus curiae. The court thus has played a crucial role in keeping the opportunity factor within the MOC setting for applicants in individual complaints at an initially low and later moderate level. It has contributed to maintaining opportunity as the determining factor for the behaviour of these actors.

In contrast, the court has developed more pronounced strategies to enhance motivation and unconstrained ability. Given that unconstrained ability was indeed one of the factors that shaped the behaviour of individual applicants in the first decades, constraints-related strategies were well targeted from the perspective of the MOC framework. A key strategy of the court in this regard addressed the lack of awareness of the court and/or knowledge about its jurisprudence. Given that, for individual applicants, this intrinsic constraint was the most prominent constraint, the court's strategy to increase this knowledge indeed targeted an important behavioural factor. Similarly, the court's strategy to reduce the financial constraints of applicants have contributed to reducing intrinsic constraints for individual applicants.

The court has also adopted a considerable number of motivation-related strategies. Since the 1970s, the court's jurisprudence has continuously had a rather high motivational effect especially regarding social change and it aimed at upholding this effect. The court even broadened the motivational basis further, including by its developing stance on remedies and its jurisprudence in transitional justice situations. And the court attempted to counter the detrimental effect that the backlog of cases had on the applicants' interest in effective behaviour. However, due to the interrelationship of the factors within the MOC framework, this strategy alone has not been able to enhance the overall MOC setting and significantly impact the behaviour of applicants. This is the case because opportunity and, in the earlier decades, also unconstrained ability, determined this behaviour. Nonetheless, the court's strategy of maintaining the moderate to high motivational level speaks to the necessary nature of motivation as an MOC factor. As outlined in chapter two, each MOC factor is a necessary even though not sufficient precondition for accepting the authority of the court. Moreover, the motivation-related strategies highlight that, even beyond situations of backlash, it can become important for a court to also aim at *maintaining* a certain level of MOC – rather than letting it decrease. In such situations, the court seeks to stabilise the authority relationship rather than improve it.

Regarding applicants in interstate cases, the court has adopted only few strategies to improve the MOC setting. As motivation has been, according to the MOC framework, the determining factor for these applicants, such strategies were only effective when they aimed at enhancing state applicants' motivation to bring cases to the court. The fact that the court has during most of its practice attributed a high priority to interstate cases has thus been a well-targeted strategy.

Turning to respondents, the court has influenced the MOC setting for the distinct groups of state actors differently. To begin with, regarding executive and legislative actors, the court has adopted only relatively few strategies to improve the MOC setting. In the first decades until the 1980s, the court did not engage with the opportunity elements that caused opportunity to be at a moderate to low level. It upheld its restrictive approach to remedies and did not address the fact that, in the legal orders of many member states, the Convention and the case law of the ECtHR did not have any internal effect. Only in later years, when it changed its stance on remedies, this jurisprudence broadened the opportunity especially for executive actors. In this way, the court contributed at least in part to the very favourable MOC setting of the 1990s. In the period since the 2000s, the court has adopted further strategies to influence the MOC setting. As motivation decreased during this time, the court has primarily aimed at maintaining and enhancing the value-correspondence between the court and the member states. Some of these strategies that addressed, inter alia, human rights, rule of law and democratic values were already adopted before the 2000s. But considering that motivation only then became a determining factor, these strategies were most significant during this time. It also bears mentioning that, regarding financial constraints, the court's jurisprudence has increased rather than decreased constraints for member states when it started to take a broader approach to remedies. The court has thus contributed to shaping the current MOC setting in which motivation and constraints are at a moderate level and thereby constitute the determining factors for the behaviour of these state actors. Overall, the influence of the court on the MOC setting for executive and legislative actors has thus been ambivalent.

Concerning domestic judicial actors, the court's strategies have influenced the MOC setting in several ways. As motivation has been the determining factor for these actors to accept the authority of the court (see section III.A.iv), the strategy to enhance this motivation via dialogue and networking has been well targeted. As to the opportunity for domestic courts, the ECtHR has not adopted any substantive strategies aimed at broadening this opportunity. It however upheld the fundamental opportunity element for domestic courts when it confirmed the Commission's approach that the acts of all state actors, including of judicial actors, can be reviewed as to their compatibility with the Convention. In this way, it ensured that some opportunity exists so that the necessary (although not sufficient) requirement of the MOC framework is satisfied. Further strategies to enhance opportunity would indeed not have been effective at a period in which motivation was at the lowest level and thus determined the behaviour of domestic courts. Finally, the court's strategies that address constraints – in particular increasing knowledge about the court and its jurisprudence – have influenced the MOC setting in a different manner. On the one hand, enhancing the unconstrained ability of judicial actors to accept the court's authority could not improve the overall MOC setting because motivation was the lowest and thus determining factor. On the other hand, there has been an indirect effect. Had ability remained at the moderate level of the early years, it would have become the lowest among the MOC factors for domestic courts because both motivation and opportunity have increased over the decades. The court's strategy to enhance knowledge about the court among the domestic judiciary has contributed to decreasing constraints and thus to not letting unconstrained ability become the determining factor within the current MOC setting.

In conclusion, the strategies of the court to increase the MOC factors for applicants and respondents for accepting the authority relationship of the court have thus been moderately effective. The court has shaped the MOC setting for these actors to some extent but not across the board of factors, actors and time periods. It even showed a specific reluctance regarding certain factors such as opportunity for applicants. And strategies for maintaining factors on a stable level rather than for improving them have played a considerable role for the ECtHR.

B. Avoiding and Managing Pushback

This section turns to the strategies that the court adopts to influence the MOC framework with the aim to avoid or to manage pushback.

i. Decreasing Motivation for Pushback

One of the main jurisprudential strategies to reduce the motivation for pushback is the 'margin of appreciation' doctrine of the court. It is a 'pragmatic device which can accommodate the sovereignty concerns of the Contracting States'.[528] It has a structural dimension concerning the reviewability of a state act – that is, the court refrains from reviewing the act due to the margin of appreciation – and a substantive dimension concerning the justifiability of such an act – that is, the court reviews the act but finds it to be justified due to the margin of appreciation.[529] This doctrine is connected to the notion of subsidiarity, a link that has been formalised by Protocol No 15. This Protocol provides that member states enjoy a margin of appreciation 'in accordance with the principle of subsidiarity'. When the court refers to the margin of

[528] R St John Macdonald, 'The Margin of Appreciation' in R St John Macdonald, F Matscher and H Petzold (eds), *The European System for the Protection of Human Rights* (Nijhoff 1993) 83, 124.

[529] See on these two dimensions, G Letsas, *A Theory of Interpretation of the European Convention on Human Rights* (OUP 2007) 80–98; Macdonald (n 528) 84–84; OM Arnardóttir, 'Rethinking the Two Margins of Appreciation' (2016) 12 *European Constitutional Law Review* 27.

appreciation, subsidiarity and sovereignty interests of member states are thus explicitly addressed.[530] As observed by Ronald Saint John Macdonald who served as judge at the ECtHR from 1980 to 1998:

> The margin of appreciation gives the flexibility needed to avoid damaging confrontations between the Court and Contracting States over their respective spheres of authority and enables the Court to balance the sovereignty of Contracting Parties with their obligations under the Convention.[531]

The subsidiarity approach has long been part of the court's strategy to decrease motivation for pushback. Even before employing the term 'margin of appreciation', the rationale was reflected in the court's jurisprudence. In the *Belgian Linguistics* case of 1968, the court emphasised that it would not 'assume the role of the competent national authorities' as this would amount to 'los[ing] sight of the subsidiary nature of the international machinery of collective enforcement established by the Convention'.[532]

The court referred explicitly to the margin of appreciation for the first time in the *Handyside v United Kingdom* decision of 1976. It observed that 'the machinery of protection established by the Convention is subsidiary to the national systems safeguarding human rights ... The domestic margin of appreciation ... goes hand in hand with a European supervision'.[533]

Two years later in *Ireland v United Kingdom*, the court employed this notion in a very deferential manner, granting a wide margin of appreciation to member states in the context of Article 15 ECHR.[534] This already indicated the high potential of this notion for accommodating the sovereignty interests of member states. In fact, the margin of appreciation doctrine is 'a counterpoint to the living-instrument doctrine' that the court also developed in the 1970s and it is 'especially relevant for sensitive moral questions'.[535] Due to its necessary openness, it is an adjustable tool for the court to tailor its jurisprudence in a way that best addresses the relevant MOC factor and the diverging sensitivity of the subject matter. In this regard, the court has held that '[i]n matters of general policy, on which opinions within a democratic society may reasonably differ widely, the role of the domestic policy-maker should be given special weight'.[536] For example, the court found it 'natural that the margin of appreciation available to the legislature in implementing social and economic policies should be a wide one'.[537] The court has also explained the different rationales of giving leeway to member states in certain contexts. An example is the decision on

[530] On subsidiarity in the jurisprudence of the court, see eg, R Spano, 'Universality or Diversity of Human Rights? Strasbourg in the Age of Subsidiarity' (2014) 14 *Human Rights Law Review* 487.

[531] Macdonald (n 528) 123.

[532] *Case 'Relating to Certain Aspects of the Laws on the Use of Languages in Education in Belgium' v Belgium*, 23 July 1968, App nos 1474/62, 1677/62, 1691/62, 1769/63, 1994/63, 2126/64, para 10.

[533] *Handyside v The United Kingdom*, 7 December 1976, App no 5493/72, paras 48–49.

[534] *Ireland v United Kingdom*, 18 January 1978, App no 5310/71.

[535] Nussberger, *The European Court of Human Rights* (n 6) 90.

[536] *Hatton and Others v The United Kingdom*, 8 July 2003, App no 36022/97, para 97; *S.A.S. v France*, 1 July 2014, App no 43835/11, para 154.

[537] *James and Others v The United Kingdom*, 21 February 1986, App no 8793/79, para 46; *Hutten-Czapska v Poland*, 19 June 2006, App no 35014/97, para 166.

the French burka ban in which the court emphasised the democratic legitimacy of the domestic decision, stating that:

> the Court has a duty to exercise a degree of restraint in its review of Convention compliance, since such review will lead it to assess a balance that has been struck by means of a democratic process within the society in question.[538]

Further, the court has adopted a strategy of differentiation to reduce the motivation for pushback from states with a high level of human rights protection. Scholars have argued for decades that the court gives a wider margin of appreciation to these states as compared with member states with a deficient human rights practice.[539] The rationale for this approach is that, as compared with member states with a deficient human rights practice, 'high-reputation states can cause great damage to the ECHR by noncompliance or criticism'.[540] This approach has also been described as a 'variable geometry' approach, differentiating between a good faith and a bad faith jurisprudence depending on the good or bad human rights practice of a respondent state.[541] The observation that the court has differentiated between these groups of states is based, inter alia, on decisions such as the *Bancovic* case and the *Loizidou* case for which the court assessed state jurisdiction and the ensuing territorial application of the Convention very differently.[542] In the former case, it took a very narrow approach which enabled it to avoid assessing a potential violation of the right to life by several 'high-reputation states' in Europe, a situation in which 'it would have had to face formidable resistance by these powerful nations'.[543] In contrast, in *Loizidou*, the court found that Türkiye was responsible for human rights violations in Northern Cyprus, which is outside its state territory, as it exercised effective control over this territory. Further, a quantitative analysis of decisions until 2016 has revealed that the outcome of the court's decisions has changed over time for certain groups of state respondents: while for 'established democracies', the court has recently found fewer violations as compared with earlier phases of its practice, this is not the case for member states that do not fall within this category.[544] For the latter, the court still finds violations at the same rate as it previously did. Although this strategy can be effective in reducing the motivation for pushback among 'high-reputation states', the flipside of this approach is however risking that member states with a lower level of human rights protection, and who thus do not benefit from the wider margin, might

[538] *S.A.S. v France*, 1 July 2014, App no 43835/11, para 154.

[539] JF Hartman, 'Derogation from Human Rights Treaties in Public Emergencies' (1981) 22 *Harvard International Law Journal* 1, 29; B Mangan, 'Protecting Human Rights in National Emergencies: Shortcomings in the European System and a Proposal for Reform' (1988) 10 *Human Rights Quarterly* 372, 383; F Ni Aolain, 'The Emergence of Diversity: Differences in Human Rights Jurisprudence' (1995) 19 *Fordham International Law Journal* 101, 114; Dotan (n 53) 244 et seq.

[540] Dotan (n 53) 235.

[541] B Çalı, 'Coping with Crisis: Whither the Variable Geometry in the Jurisprudence of the European Court of Human Rights' (2018) 35 *Wisconsin International Law Journal* 237.

[542] *Vlastimir and Borka Banković and Others v Belgium and Others* (Admissibility), 12 December 2001, App no 52207/99; *Loizidou v Turkey* (Preliminary Objections), 23 March 1995, App no 15318/89.

[543] Dotan (n 53) 248.

[544] Ø Stiansen and E Voeten, 'Backlash and Judicial Restraint: Evidence from the European Court of Human Rights' (2020) 64 *International Studies Quarterly* 770.

consider this to be unfair treatment. They might perceive this differentiating jurisprudence as a motivation for pushback.

A more recent trend in the jurisprudence of the court that can also be described as a strategy to reduce the pushback motivation by increasing deference is the proceduralisation trend. The court has been observed to increasingly frame legal issues as procedural in nature and to focus on procedural obligations rather than engaging with the substantive question of an alleged rights violation.[545] This is a tool to shift the case to a less controversial level that is less likely to motivate pushback. Moreover, focusing on procedural obligations makes it possible for the court to allow state actors to enjoy a broader leeway. While complying with procedural obligations, they can decide the substantive issue either way.

Regarding the review of domestic judicial decisions, this proceduralisation strategy is somewhat broader.[546] It includes a turn to 'more structured review standards' regarding judicial decisions, a trend that has been described as a 'responsible courts doctrine' and 'a qualified form of margin of appreciation'.[547] For example, when deciding about the amount of discretion that it gives to domestic courts, the ECtHR takes into account the quality of the domestic judicial reasoning and whether domestic courts have referred to principles established in the jurisprudence of the ECtHR. In *Hannover v Germany (2)*, the court stated:

> Where the balancing exercise has been undertaken by the national authorities in conformity with the criteria laid down in the Court's case-law, the Court would require strong reasons to substitute its view for that of the domestic courts.[548]

Under the condition that a domestic court applies the ECtHR's jurisprudence in a consistent manner, the court gives – unless there are 'strong reasons' to do otherwise – deference to the domestic judiciary as to the outcome of the decision. Observers see this strategy not only as a general strategy but also as the court's reaction to 'the backlash the Court has faced to its effective and dynamic interpretation of human rights case law from some domestic judiciaries'.[549]

A further strategy with which the court has given deference to member states to decrease the pushback motivation relates to remedies. The court has initially limited the potential pushback-motivating effect by refraining from indicating any specific measures (see section II.A). But even when the court started to indicate such measures, it tried to limit the pushback-motivating effect of this jurisprudence. It emphasised the member states' discretion as to how to implement the

[545] R Spano, 'The Future of the European Court of Human Rights – Subsidiarity, Process-based Review and Rule of Law' (2018) *Human Rights Law Review* 473; T Kleinlein, 'The Procedural Approach of the European Court of Human Rights: Between Subsidiarity and Dynamic Evolution' (2019) 68 *International & Comparative Law Quarterly* 91; P Popelier and C Van de Heyning, 'Subsidiarity Post-Brighton: Procedural Rationality as Answer?' (2017) 30 *Leiden Journal of International Law* 5.

[546] On the difference between this approach regarding domestic courts and other state actors, see also Arnardóttir, 'The Brighton Aftermath' (n 368), 228.

[547] Çalı, 'From flexible to variable standards of judicial review' (n 477).

[548] *von Hannover v Germany (No 2)*, 7 February 2012, App nos 40660/08 and 60641/08, para 107. The court has used similar words to describe this approach in subsequent decisions, eg, *Palomo Sanchez and Others v Spain*, 12 September 2011, App nos 28955/06, 28957/06, 28959/06 and 28964/06, para 57.

[549] Çalı, 'From flexible to variable standards of judicial review' (n 477) 152.

court's decisions, with few exceptions. The court summarises this approach as follows:

> [E]xceptionally … the Court will seek to indicate the type of measure that might be taken in order to put an end to a violation it has found to exist. In such circumstances, it may propose various options and leave the choice of measure and its implementation to the discretion of the State concerned … In certain cases, the nature of the violation found may be such as to leave no real choice as to the measures required to remedy it and the Court may decide to indicate a specific measure.[550]

As a further strategy, the court's jurisprudence is characterised by an incremental approach. When the court has expanded the obligations that it imposes on states by broadening the protective dimension of Convention rights, it has in general done so in an incremental manner. In particular, the court has used the doctrines of evolutive interpretation and effectiveness 'to change its doctrine gradually in a way that increasingly protects human rights in Europe'.[551] This strategy is akin to a 'foot-in-the-door' technique that uses smaller initial demands as a first step to reduce the resistance against further broader demands (see chapter two). This is exemplified by the court's jurisprudence on abortion regulation. As Gerards observes, starting from *Tysiac v Poland*,[552] the court, 'in each of the cases decided … went one step further and it clarified its stand on yet another issue, thus gradually building a system of more general standards and principles to be applied in later cases'.[553] A further example of this approach is the introduction of the pilot judgment procedure by the court. By introducing this procedure 'in several judgments that refer to each other, the ECHR was able to reduce resistance to this revolutionary move by appearing consistent'.[554] Moreover, the court expanded this tool incrementally to different groups of respondents. Only when 'this doctrine [had] matured and was generally accepted as legitimate', the court then also used it against 'established democracies'/'high-reputation states'.[555]

The pilot judgment procedure is in fact an example of how the court has used several cumulative strategies to reduce the pushback motivation against such a major jurisprudential creation. Initially, the court had lobbied for introducing such a procedure into Protocol No 14. Although this attempt failed and the court finally created the procedure by jurisprudential means, it however did so in line with the position of the Council of Ministers that had encouraged the court to address the issue of structural violations.[556] The court thus ensured political support before creating this

[550] *Oleksandr Volkov v Ukraine*, 9 January 2013, App no 21722/11, para 195.

[551] Dotan (n 53) 225.

[552] *Tysiąc v Poland*, 20 March 2007, App no 5410/03.

[553] J Gerards, 'Margin of Appreciation and Incrementalism in the Case Law of the European Court of Human Rights' (2018) 18 *Human Rights Law Review* 495, 507–08.

[554] Dotan (n 53) 236.

[555] ibid 254. See eg, *Rumpf v Germany*, 2 September 2010, App no 46344/06; *Vassilios Athanasiou and Others v Greece*, 21 December 2010, App no 50973/08.

[556] Committee of Ministers, Resolution on Judgments Revealing an Underlying Systemic Problem, Res(2004)3, 12 May 2004: 'Invites the Court: […] to identify […] what it considers to be an underlying systemic problem and the source of this problem, in particular when it is likely to give rise to numerous applications'.

procedure. Moreover, the court has, when using this procedure, carefully laid out the reasons for why it created this procedure and for why member states should accept it. It did so by directly speaking to the interests of member states and framing them in a manner that can lead to behavioural effects contributing to keeping a low pushback motivation. These interests include the interest in an effective Convention system. This is an interest that the court frames as a loss scenario ('threat'), thereby potentially making use of the loss aversion of state actors. Loss aversion is a behavioural phenomenon according to which it is likely that actors value an outcome higher when it is framed as loss scenario rather than as gain scenario (see chapter two).[557] In *Hutten-Czapska v Poland*, the court stated:

> One of the relevant factors considered by the Court in devising and applying [the pilot-judgment procedure] has been the growing threat to the Convention system resulting from large numbers of repetitive cases that derive from, among other things, the same structural or systemic problem.[558]

More generally, the court has adopted several strategies to reduce the pushback-motivating effect of changes in its jurisprudence. To start with, it thoroughly explains the rationale of such changes. The court has, for example, provided the following explanation for why it considers it at times necessary to overturn its older jurisprudence:

> While it is in the interests of legal certainty, foreseeability and equality before the law that the Court should not depart, without good reason, from precedents laid down in previous cases, a failure by the Court to maintain a dynamic and evolutive approach would risk rendering it a bar to reform or improvement.[559]

In addition to explaining the rationale for change, the court also limits the effect of overturning its jurisprudence. It refuses to hear cases anew that, based on the novel jurisprudential approach, would have been decided differently. The court clarified:

> The Court's case-law is constantly evolving and if these jurisprudential developments were to permit unsuccessful applicants to reintroduce their complaints, final judgments would continually be called into question by the lodging of fresh applications.[560]

Further, the court has limited the pushback-motivating effect of its living instrument and evolutive interpretation doctrine by refraining from using this doctrine in situations that would undermine the explicit exercise of sovereignty by member states. Taking into account the fact that member states have created a specific protocol regarding the death penalty, the court refrained from interpreting Article 3 ECHR in a way as to prohibit this penalty. Highlighting its respect for the primary rule-shaping role of member states, it stated that Protocol No 6

[557] eg, D Kahneman, J Knetsch and R Thaler, 'Anomalies: The Endowment Effect, Loss Aversion, and Status Quo Bias' (1991) 5 *Journal of Economic Perspectives* 193, 197–99; E Zamir, 'Loss Aversion and the Law' (2012) 65 *Vanderbilt Law Review* 829.

[558] *Hutten-Czapska v Poland*, 19 June 2006, App no 35014/97, para 234.

[559] *Bayatyan v Armenia*, 7 July 2011, App no 23459/03, para 98; *Vilho Eskelinen and Others v Finland*, 19 April 2007, App no 63235/00, para 56.

[560] *Phillip Harkins v The United Kingdom*, 15 June 2017, App no 71537/14, para 56.

> shows that the intention of the Contracting Parties as recently as 1983 was to adopt the normal method of amendment of the text in order to introduce a new obligation to abolish capital punishment in time of peace and, what is more, to do so by an optional instrument allowing each State to choose the moment when to undertake such an engagement. In these conditions, ... Article 3 cannot be interpreted as generally prohibiting the death penalty.[561]

The rationale here was not to 'trespas[s] upon the policy-making powers of member States', which the court would do 'if it sought to circumvent the Convention amendment process by interpreting the existing text to achieve similar developments of Convention rights and freedoms'.[562]

Using the notion of European consensus can be seen as an additional strategy to reduce the pushback motivation when the court adopts an evolutive interpretation and establishes more demanding standards. The notion defers to member states and their legal standards and aims at legitimising the interpretation adopted by the court. This is part of a 'strategy to enable the ECtHR to retain the support of the States parties to the ECHR and set increasingly higher human rights standards'.[563] What is more, European consensus and the indirect role that it gives to domestic legislation is perceived as counter-balancing the democratic legitimacy issue referred to as so-called counter-majoritarian difficulty.[564] However, this strategy might be double-edged. The above legitimacy considerations might enhance the motivation of member states to accept the authority of the court as long as they are not the respondent in cases in which the court uses the consensus doctrine. If a state is, however, singled out as an 'outlier', this 'may actually fan the flames of national sovereignty', as has been arguably the case in the United Kingdom.[565]

A further strategy that can help the court to avoid the perception that it decides in an activist and unprincipled manner is to concretise abstract notions as far as possible. An example is the court's jurisprudence on the notion of proportionality. To increase the perceived 'objectivity of its jurisprudence in specific areas the Court has elaborated lists of factors to be taken into account in the framework of the proportionality analysis'.[566] This is especially relevant in multi-polar human rights constellations in which the court must balance the rights of different right holders. For contexts such as the relationship between the right to private life on the one hand and freedom of expression on the other hand,[567] the court has developed specific guidelines that enable the court to adjudicate in a way that is more likely to be perceived as consistent, foreseeable and principled than if such guidelines did not exist.

[561] *Soering v United Kingdom*, 7 July 1989, App no 14038/88, para 103.

[562] Mowbray (n 359) 67.

[563] J Theilen, *European Consensus between Strategy and Principle: The Uses of Vertically Comparative Legal Reasoning in Regional Human Rights Adjudication* (Nomos 2021) 330.

[564] K Dzehtsiarou, *European Consensus and the Legitimacy of the European Court of Human Rights* (CUP 2015) 121–29. See also T Kleinlein, 'Constructive Consensus and Domestic Democracy' in Kapotas and Tzevelekos (eds), *Building Consensus on European Consensus* (n 146) 210.

[565] M Amos, 'Can European Consensus Encourage Acceptance of the European Convention on Human Rights in the United Kingdom?' in Kapotas and Tzevelekos (eds), *Building Consensus on European Consensus* (n 146) 258, 281.

[566] Nussberger, *The European Court of Human Rights* (n 6) 97.

[567] eg, *Axel Springer AG v Germany*, 7 February 2012, App no 39954/08; *von Hannover v Germany (No 2)*, 7 February 2012, App nos 40660/08 and 60641/08.

On a different note, the ECtHR has also sought to reduce the motivation for pushback that can result from actors perceiving the court to be under the influence of external actors. In particular, and unlike some other regional courts, it cites only rather sparsely the jurisprudence of non-European courts.[568] However, the strategy to avoid perceived external influences is not strongly pronounced. In addition to the occasional references to non-European courts, the ECtHR has also referred to non-European legal instruments and domestic legal practice to establish a 'European consensus' with the aim of adopting an evolutive interpretation of the Convention.

In addition to the many jurisprudential tools mentioned above, the court uses informal tools to decrease the motivation for pushback. It regularly meets with governmental actors to create a fruitful basis for cooperation. The member states welcomed this practice in the Copenhagen Declaration as an 'ongoing constructive dialogue'.[569] This strategy also has a value-related dimension. Such dialogue can enhance procedural fairness perceptions because it provides a participatory element for the relationship between the court and the member states.

Along with the court's general strategies to reduce the motivation for pushback, the court has adopted specific strategies to *manage ongoing pushback*. To start with, in cases in which pushback concerned specific topics within the court's jurisprudence, the court reacted to pushback by adjusting this jurisprudence. An early example is the reaction of the court when the United Kingdom criticised its effective interpretation of Article 6 ECHR in the *Golder* case of 1975 (see section III.B.i).[570] In the *Trade Unions* cases immediately after this decision, the court showed consideration for the arguments made by the United Kingdom in *Golder*. It decided in favour of the respondent by rejecting the notion that Article 11 could be interpreted broadly, based on the *Golder* rationale, as containing a 'right to consultation' or a right to a collective agreement with the state.[571] Similarly, in view of the United Kingdom's refusal to implement the *Hirst* decision, the court has attempted to manage this pushback by qualifying its approach to prisoners' voting rights. In *Scoppola v Italy*, it held that under certain conditions (in particular a non-automatic voting rights deprivation), voting bans are possible.[572] In this case, the United Kingdom had intervened forcefully, reiterating its opposition against *Hirst*.[573] The court's jurisprudential adjustment is thus a step towards the United Kingdom, yet without giving up its stance on blanket bans.

With regard to more intense forms of pushback, such as structural resistance, the court has also adopted a strategy of adjustment. Scholars have argued that the court has in recent years given a wider margin of appreciation to some of the member

[568] E Voeten, 'Borrowing and Nonborrowing among International Courts' (2010) 39 *Journal of Legal Studies* 547, 562–66; Sandholtz (n 523).

[569] Copenhagen Declaration, High Level Conference meeting in Copenhagen on 12 and 13 April 2018, para 37.

[570] *Golder v The United Kingdom*, 21 February 1975, App no 4451/70.

[571] *National Union of Belgian Police v Belgium*, 27 October 1975, App no 4464/70, para 38; *Swedish Engine Drivers' Union v Sweden*, 6 February 1976, App no 5614/72, para 39.

[572] *Scoppola v Italy (No 3)*, 22 May 2012, App no 126/05.

[573] The arguments of the United Kingdom as third-party intervener are summarised in *Scoppola v Italy (No 3)*, 22 May 2012, App no 126/05, paras 75–80.

states that have pushed back against the court in the context of the Brighton and Copenhagen conferences.[574] This includes states such as the United Kingdom and Denmark that were prominent actors in these pushback attempts. This is to say that for those states, the margin seems wider than before the pushback attempt and wider than for other member states. However, based on the differentiated approach mentioned above, the court did not manage pushback from member states such as Russia or Türkiye in the same way as it did regarding pushback from member states with a higher level of human rights protection. For example, the court has issued a high number of decisions regarding the Russian military operation in Chechnya which were harshly criticised by Russia. The court did however not change its approach to Russia and continued to apply a strict human rights standard in cases against this respondent.[575]

A possible indirect strategy to reduce the motivation for pushback relates to admissibility decisions. As Graham has argued, the court might be using the admissibility stage in a strategic manner in relation to critical member states such as the United Kingdom.[576] It has stricken out cases as 'manifestly ill-founded' by way of decision under Article 35(3)(a) ECHR with a cursory and at times unconvincing reasoning but with the result of upholding a decision of the domestic Supreme Court. According to Graham, this might be part of a broader strategy which avoids that such cases draw media attention to the court and spark novel criticism of the court as an institution. Rather than fuelling critical narratives, this strategy reassures the domestic court that 'they need not worry about being overruled' and, with regard to the wider political and general audience, this strategy 'may help to convince those sceptical of European overreach that the Court will only intervene where necessary, and that they need not worry about excessive meddling'.[577]

Finally, scholars have discussed, controversially, whether the court has, as a reaction to the attempted pushback during the Brighton Conference, reduced the substantive obligations that it imposes on member states in general. Helfer and Voeten have argued that, based on an analysis of dissenting opinions, the court might be 'walking back' on certain rights, ie, taking an approach that is less protective of these rights in favour of greater deference to states.[578] Madsen finds an 'increase in the percentage of cases that refer to either the margin of appreciation or subsidiarity' which however seems to have already started at the time of the Interlaken Conference.[579] Arnardóttir argues that, since the Brighton declaration, the court has given a wider margin under the condition that these actors duly take the Convention rights and the jurisprudence of the ECtHR into account.[580] This is akin to the general observation

[574] Madsen, 'The European Court of Human Rights' (n 34) 268.
[575] Dotan (n 53) 255.
[576] L Graham, 'Strategic Admissibility Decisions in the European Court of Human Rights' (2020) 69 *International & Comparative Law Quarterly* 79.
[577] ibid 96.
[578] Helfer and Voeten, 'Walking Back Human Rights in Europe?' (n 271).
[579] MR Madsen, 'Rebalancing European Human Rights: Has the Brighton Declaration Engendered a New Deal on Human Rights in Europe?' (2018) 9 *Journal of International Dispute Settlement* 199, 210.
[580] Arnardóttir, 'The Brighton Aftermath' (n 368). See also JP Rui, 'The Interlaken, Izmir and Brighton Declarations: Towards a Paradigm Shift in the Strasbourg Court's Interpretation of the European Convention of Human Rights?' (2013) 31 *Nordic Journal of Human Rights* 28.

that there is a certain procedural turn observable in the jurisprudence of the court.[581] On the other side of the spectrum, Stone Sweet, Sandholtz and Andenas have argued that the 'walking back' observation made by Helfer and Voeten based on dissenting opinions does not reflect the actual trend in the jurisprudence of the court.[582] According to them, the court does not take a rights-restrictive approach. Similarly, Gerards has argued that the court often uses the margin of appreciation as an 'empty rhetorical device' and that a substantive assessment of decisions does not point to a less protective trend.[583]

ii. Decreasing Opportunity for Pushback

Among its strategies to avoid and manage pushback, the court has focused mostly on reducing the motivation. There are only few aspects of the court's jurisprudence that address the opportunity for pushback.

Regarding pushback in the form of non-compliance, the court's approach to remedies has influenced the opportunity structure. During the – comparatively long – period in which the court took a very restrictive approach as to remedies and limited itself to issuing declaratory decisions, it reduced the opportunity for non-compliance as compared with its later, more demanding approach. Declaratory decisions do not necessitate implementation and thus do not pose any compliance issues. Moreover, the discretion that the court later gave to respondents as to the measures with which the respondent would implement the court's judgment reduced the opportunity for non-compliance. When state actors have a range of options that would all qualify as complying with the ECtHR decision, the opportunity for non-compliance is less pronounced as compared with a single compliance option. In contrast, when the court started to indicate or order more far-reaching measures, it increased the opportunity for non-compliance.

It bears mentioning that the court has not adopted – much like the ECOWAS Court but unlike, for example, the CJEU, the EACJ or the IACtHR – any substantive strategy to reduce the opportunity for non-compliance resulting from the fact that member states were reluctant to transpose the Convention into domestic law or to otherwise give internal effect to the Convention and the decisions of the court. Only after member states had addressed this element of the opportunity structure themselves, the court used – rather incidentally than intentionally – general measures as ordered in particular in pilot judgments to somewhat compensate the lack of direct effect (see section III.B).

[581] On this trend, see Spano, 'The Future of the European Court of Human Rights' (n 545); Kleinlein, 'The Procedural Approach of the European Court of Human Rights' (n 545); Popelier and Van de Heyning (n 545).

[582] Stone Sweet, Sandholtz and Andenas (n 184). Even Helfer and Voeten, 'Walking Back Human Rights in Europe?' (n 271) 804, acknowledge that 'our review of all Grand Chamber judgments reveals that the ECtHR has never expressly overturned a prior ruling in a rights-restrictive direction. Nor are we aware of any majority judgment that cites the living instrument, European consensus or other legal doctrine to justify narrowing a right that the Court had previously expanded'.

[583] Gerards, 'Margin of Appreciation' (n 553) 500 et seq.

Similarly, the ECtHR has not adopted any strategy to reduce the opportunity for amendments that could be used for pushback against the court. It has not created any conditions or limitations to such amendments. And during the pre-Protocol No 11 period, the court also did not influence the opportunity structure for periodic renewals that member states have indeed used repeatedly to push back against the court (see section III.B)

iii. Increasing Constraints against Pushback

Strategies to increase constraints against pushback focus on supporting actors. The ECtHR has only late in its existence and, in part, somewhat reluctantly started to engage with (potential) supporting actors that could constrain member states in pushback attempts. In particular, the ECtHR has been very hesitant to attribute any role to NGOs, be it as formal applicants or as third-party interveners (see above). This however meant that the court has had, for a long time, only little possibility to create such alliances. Only recently, the court has engaged more closely with NGOs in the context of amicus curiae briefs and concerning the new role of NGOs as actors in the monitoring framework.

The court has mostly focused on state actors as supporting actors against pushback. A strategy in this regard is the variable geometry approach outlined above according to which the court aims at maintaining the support of certain groups of member states, and in particular high-reputation states. With this strategy, the court can contribute to creating power dynamics among member states that enable supportive states to constrain other states. As states were indeed the key constraining factor in the Brighton and Copenhagen context, the court seems to aim at upholding this setting.

Moreover, certain strategies of the court can also contribute to fostering alliances with domestic actors that would be able to constrain other actors within their own member state. For example, the Superior Court Network created by the ECtHR can be a tool to strengthen alliances with judicial actors that can support the ECtHR if their respective governmental or legislative actors try to push back against the ECtHR. In addition, this network might also promote interrelations among judicial actors of different member states. This can strengthen human rights adjudication as a transnational legal field which then might in turn create a self-understanding of judicial actors that would lead them, together as a group, to support the ECtHR against future pushback.

Finally, the court can also increase pushback constraints that can result from behavioural effects such as the status quo bias (see chapter two). A jurisprudential tool that speaks to this bias is the European consensus doctrine. By making the claim inherent in this notion that a certain legal standard is already the consensus among member states, the court presents this legal standard as the status quo in the Council of Europe space. The standard is framed as pre-existing rather than a novel approach taken by the ECtHR. With this framing, the court contributes to activating the status quo bias which is likely to make states perceive this (alleged) status quo more positively than the framing as a novel standard would be.

iv. Assessment of Strategies

This section has shown that the court's strategy to reduce the MOC factors for pushback has, for a long time, focused on decreasing pushback motivation. Only more recently has the court substantially expanded its strategies to enhancing constraints as well. From the perspective of the MOC framework, to concentrate on motivation made sense for the court when motivation was the determining factor for pushback. This was the case until the 1990s for executive and legislative actors as well as for domestic constitutional courts. During this period, motivation was at the lowest level among the MOC factors for pushback and thus shaped the pushback behaviour. Keeping this motivation as low as possible was the most effective strategy. As opportunity and unconstrained ability were at higher levels than motivation, decreasing these factors would not have affected the pushback behaviour as long as motivation remained at the lowest level among these factors.

In contrast, when the motivation for pushback increased, strategies to reduce opportunity and ability became more important. The court chose to address only the ability for pushback and specifically to strengthen the constraints stemming from supporting actors. Unlike some other factors that contribute to the MOC framework, this is a factor that the court can influence substantially. Its strategies to strengthen its alliances with certain governmental actors but also NGOs and domestic courts have contributed to increasing the constraints against pushback as compared with earlier periods. However, the court has turned more explicitly to supporting state actors than non-state actors, so that it has not yet exhausted the scope of possible strategies regarding the latter.

As to the content of the motivation-related strategies, the court has used many jurisprudential and some non-judicial tools such as policy suggestions as well as regular dialogue with state actors. Most of the jurisprudential tools have been used for many decades. Although some strategies have taken varying forms or extents, they have been rather consistent in substance. What stands out as an exception is the proceduralisation strategy that the court has developed only in the more recent period. This is a novel tool to implement the subsidiarity principle and to decrease the pushback motivation especially of domestic courts. The tendency to predominantly using existing tools can be observed both for the general strategy of the court to reduce pushback motivation and for the specific context of managing ongoing pushback. In the latter situations, the court has also drawn on its well-established tools, yet by adjusting them to the respective situations. The way in which the court has applied the margin of appreciation doctrine over the years, including in its variable geometry manifestation, prominently reflects this approach. The broad range of existing tools as well as their flexibility makes it possible for the court to significantly shift the level of deference reflected in its jurisprudence for managing pushback.

Finally, the above assessment has also illustrated the ways in which court strategies can influence different MOC factors at once. For example, the court's strategy to take, for many decades, a restrictive approach to remedies has affected both pushback motivation and pushback opportunity. Although it is likely that the court has primarily targeted the pushback motivation, it has, with the same tool, also reduced the opportunity for non-compliance. In this example, one tool has positively affected two MOC factors for the same group of actors ('intra-actor' effect, see chapter three). In contrast, multifaceted effects can also be opposed in nature. As mentioned for variable geometry jurisprudence, giving broader deference to high reputation states aims at reducing the pushback motivation of these states while at the same time risking increasing the pushback motivation of other states. And of course, strategies that reduce the pushback motivation for state actors can negatively affect the motivation for applicants to engage with the court (as an expression of an 'inter-actors' effect). The court has taken this latter interrelation into account by paring activist elements of its jurisprudence that speak to the interests of applicants but are likely to motivate pushback, with deferential tools that indicate to member states that the court also takes into account their interests. In this regard, the court balances its multifaceted strategies in a way that is common in the jurisprudence of other regional courts as well.

6

Comparative and Concluding Insights on the Authority of International Courts

THIS CONCLUDING CHAPTER connects the case studies from chapters four and five and links these findings back to the general questions raised in the first part of this book about the factors that shape the authority relationship between international courts and their audiences. First, I provide a comparative analysis regarding the MOC settings in the courts assessed in Part II of this book: the Court of Justice of the Economic Community of West African States (ECOWAS Court) and the European Court of Human Rights (ECtHR) (section I). Second, I address a specific category of factors: psychological factors in the narrow sense. I outline how these factors have influenced the MOC setting in the two courts and how these courts have engaged with these factors (section II). Third, I address, based on the findings of this book, certain issues that have, in part, been controversially discussed in the legal and political science scholarship on international courts, including the impact of legal factors on the one hand and of political factors on the other, as well as the development of the authority of international courts over time (section III). To conclude the chapter and the book, I end with some reflections on how to go forward when assessing the MOC setting for other international courts (section IV).

I. COMPARATIVE INSIGHTS FROM THE MOC ANALYSIS

In this section, I summarise and compare the findings for the courts assessed in this book. I first compare the MOC settings for the courts and their respective audiences, pointing to the determining factors for the different groups of actors (I.A). I then turn to assessing the agency for such changes, showing how state actors, non-state actors and the regional courts themselves have influenced the MOC settings (I.B).

A. Comparison of the MOC Settings for the ECOWAS Court and ECtHR

i. Human Rights Context

The MOC settings for selected groups of *applicants* in human rights cases before the ECOWAS Court and the ECtHR are represented by Figure 6.1 (initial setting) and Figure 6.2 (current setting).[1] In the initial setting, both individual applicants and NGOs before the ECtHR and the ECOWAS Court faced a very unfavourable opportunity structure. This resulted in low overall favourability of the MOC setting. Opportunity was at the lowest level among the MOC factors and thus determined the behaviour of these groups of applicants. Although particularly for NGOs, motivation and ability were high in the context of both the ECtHR and the ECOWAS Court, the lack of opportunity significantly limited the extent to which these actors could engage with the court.

In the current setting, the overall favourability of the MOC settings is moderate, with some variations. The ECtHR provides a more favourable MOC setting for individuals than the ECOWAS Court. Yet for NGOs, the MOC setting is more favourable before the ECOWAS Court. For NGOs, opportunity is the determining factor for the authority relationship towards both courts. In the ECOWAS context, opportunity shares this position with the factor of 'unconstrained ability'. The legal framework of jurisdiction and access opportunity thus influences most prominently whether and to what extent NGOs accept the authority of the court. In contrast, for individual applicants, there is no common determining factor that would stand out. For individual applicants before the ECOWAS Court, constraints are the determining factor; for individual applicants before the ECtHR, the determining factor is opportunity.

Figure 6.1 Comparison of the initial MOC setting for selected applicants before the ECOWAS Court and the ECtHR in the human rights context

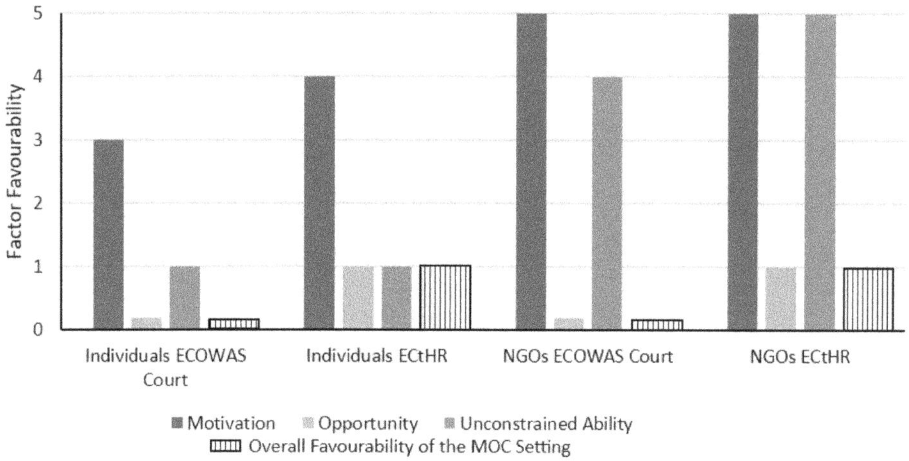

[1] See chs 4 and 5 for the other groups of applicants.

Figure 6.2 Comparison of the current MOC setting for selected applicants before the ECOWAS Court and the ECtHR in the human rights context

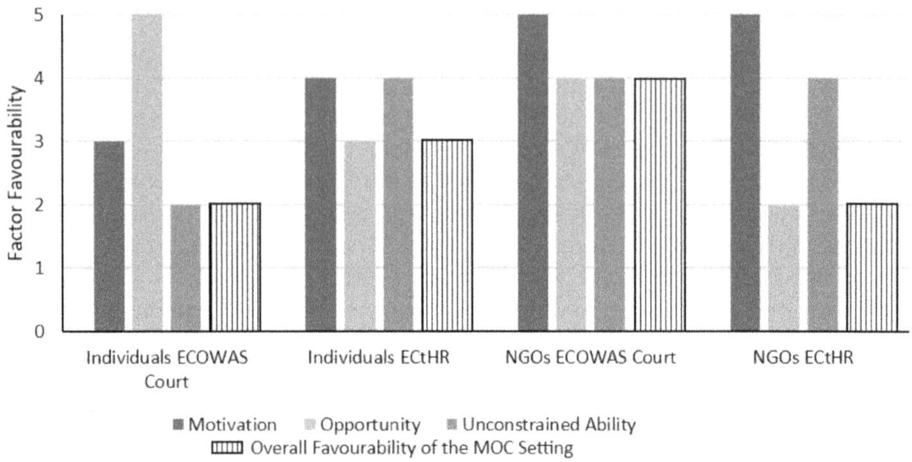

Turning to the MOC setting for *respondents* in human rights cases, the determining factors are diverse across time and courts (see Figure 6.3. for the initial setting and Figure 6.4. for the current setting). In the initial setting, motivation and opportunity was determining for executive actors in the ECOWAS context, while for the ECtHR, opportunity was the sole determining factor. In the current setting, motivation is determining in the ECOWAS setting, as compared with motivation and constraints in the ECtHR context. For both courts, there has thus been a shift from opportunity to motivation as a crucial factor for the authority relationship with executive actors. In contrast, for domestic courts as respondent actors, opportunity was the determining factor in the initial ECOWAS setting as compared with motivation in the initial ECtHR setting. In the current setting, motivation is the determining factor both in the ECOWAS and ECtHR context. While the overall MOC setting was more favourable for executive actors than for domestic courts in the initial setting of both the ECOWAS Court and the ECtHR, this remains the case only for the ECOWAS Court. In relation to the ECtHR, domestic courts are currently in a more favourable MOC setting than executive actors. Moreover, for domestic courts, the MOC setting is currently much more favourable in the ECtHR context as compared with the ECOWAS context, while for executive actors, the overall favourability is similar. For both courts and both sets of actors, there has been a trend towards broadening the opportunity structure.

Figure 6.3 Comparison of the initial MOC setting for selected respondents before the ECOWAS Court and the ECtHR in the human rights context

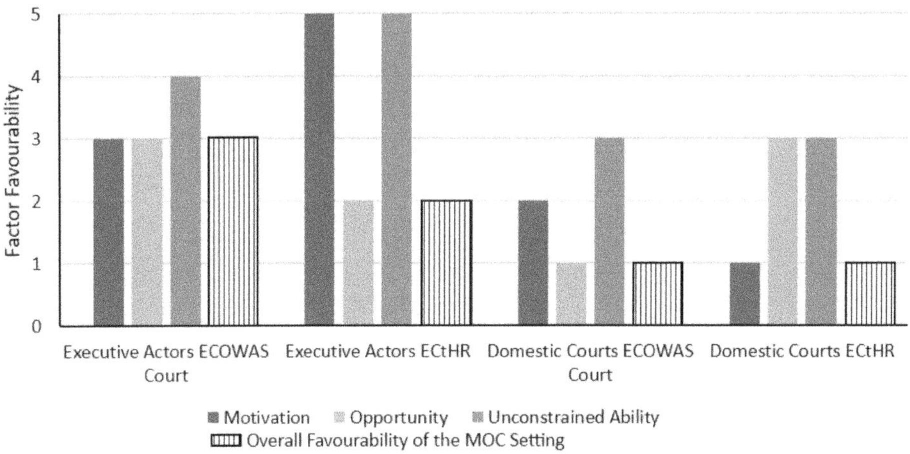

Figure 6.4 Comparison of the current MOC setting for selected respondents before the ECOWAS Court and the ECtHR in the human rights context

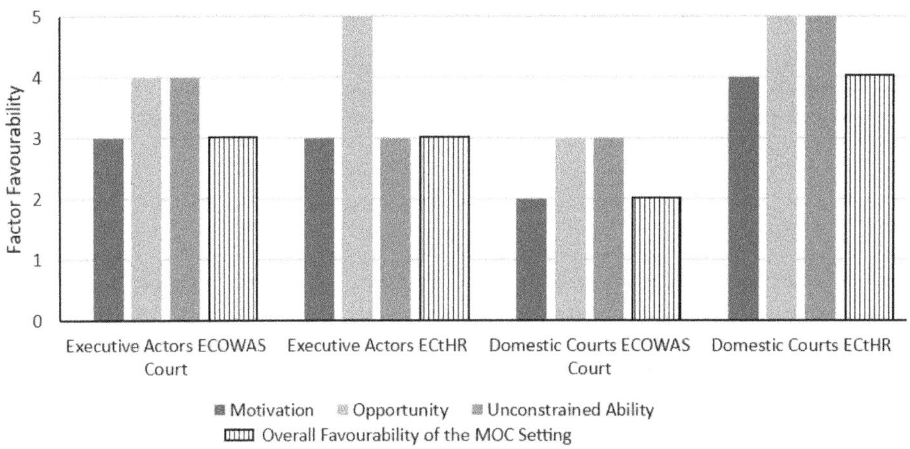

ii. Comparison with the Regional Integration Context

A comparison of the MOC settings for the regional integration context and the human rights context before the ECOWAS Court shows that these settings differ significantly.

With regard to *applicants*, the favourability of the MOC settings for private applicants diverge (see Figure 6.5). It is the most favourable for corporate applicants in the human rights context and the least favourable for private actors in the regional integration context. For the latter, constraints are the determining factor, as is the case for individual applicants in the human rights context. For corporate actors in the human rights context, motivation and opportunity are however the determining factors. In contrast, for all public applicants, ie, member states, ECOWAS institutions, as well as domestic courts regarding preliminary references, the low or low to moderate motivation is the determining factor.

Figure 6.5 Comparison of the MOC setting for selected applicants before the ECOWAS Court

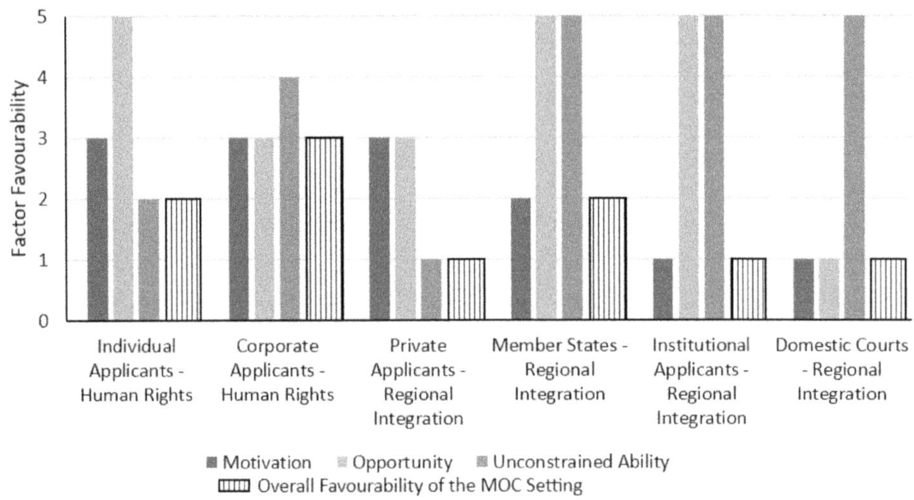

As to *respondents* before the ECOWAS Court, for governmental actors, the unconstrained ability is high in the regional integration context, but motivation and opportunity are on a moderate level so that they conjointly determine the behaviour of these actors (see Figure 6.6). In comparison, the overall favourability of the MOC setting is equally moderate for the human rights context. Yet here, motivation is the sole determining factor. Opportunity and unconstrained ability diverge among the two contexts. For domestic courts, the MOC factors in the regional integration context are on a similar moderate level with no single determining factor. In contrast, motivation is lower in the human rights context, which leads to a less favourable overall MOC setting than in the regional integration context.

Figure 6.6 Comparison of the MOC setting for selected respondents before the ECOWAS Court

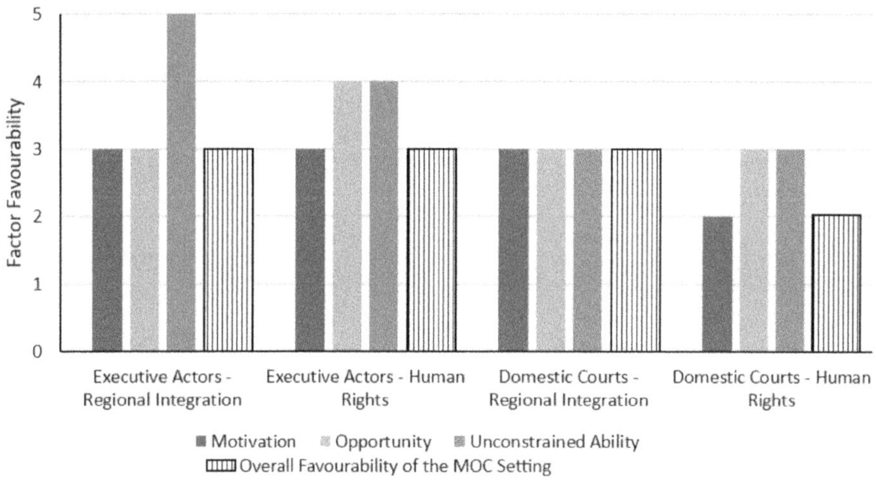

iii. MOC Setting for Pushback

When comparing, for both courts, pushback by governmental actors in the human rights context, the MOC setting differs across courts, across types of pushback and to some extent, across time periods. For non-compliance by ECOWAS member states, the low to moderate ability is the determining factor due to the moderate to high constraints (see Figure 6.7). For non-compliance in the ECtHR context, motivation was determined during the early period of the ECtHR, while, in the current setting, opportunity and ability conjointly shape non-compliant behaviour. Concerning the other forms of pushback such as norm contestation and structural resistance by treaty amendment, the motivation and opportunity are higher in the ECtHR context than in relation to the ECOWAS Court. Yet for both courts, the rather low level of unconstrained ability is the determining factor. In sum, despite the above differences, the favourability of the current MOC setting for all forms of pushback at both courts is at the same – moderate to low – level.

As to the changes in the MOC factors, two aspects merit highlighting. While, for pushback against the ECOWAS Court, constraints were moderate to high from the beginning, the constraints regarding pushback against the ECtHR only gradually developed to a higher level. The main constraining factors are supporting actors which can include private actors such as NGOs and other civil society groups but also other member states; and time-related behavioural factors such as the status quo bias. Further, specifically with regard to pushback by domestic courts, one can observe both decreasing and increasing motivation for pushback. While pushback motivation decreased for ordinary domestic courts in their relationship towards the ECtHR, it increased for constitutional courts vis-a-vis the ECtHR. The pushback motivation of domestic courts is also set up to increase in the ECOWAS context because of the competitive setting between the ECOWAS Court and domestic courts where parallel proceedings are possible.

In comparison to the human rights context, the MOC setting in the regional integration context is less favourable for pushback against the ECOWAS Court. The low to moderate motivation for pushback is the determining factor here, as compared with constraints being the determining factor for the human rights context. Motivation and opportunity are lower in the regional integration context than in the human rights context. Yet the unconstrained ability for pushback is higher which is primarily due to the fact that there are fewer supporting actors that would be able to constrain pushback. The role of non-state actors such as NGOs is much less pronounced here than in the human rights context.

Figure 6.7 Comparison of the current MOC setting for pushback by governmental actors against the ECOWAS Court and the ECtHR in the human rights context

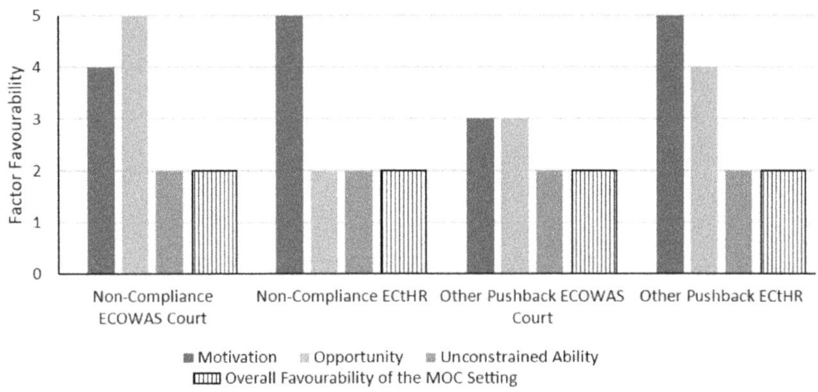

iv. Development Over Time

The assessment in chapters four and five has shown that shifts in the MOC factors are frequent and have occurred across the board. Such developments can be linked to changes in the law, in the political setting or in the practical circumstances. Legal changes include formal amendments to the relevant treaty provisions, changes in the jurisprudence by the respective regional court and changes in the domestic legal framework. Changes in the political setting can occur, for example, when the human rights, rule of law and/or governance practice within certain member states changes, when the membership of the regional organisation diversifies or when geopolitical parameters change. Practical circumstances include, inter alia, the knowledge of the relevant actors about the regional court and the capacity of the regional court to manage its case load in light of the budget and staff conditions.

Shifts in the MOC settings have been both positive in the sense of making the MOC factors more favourable for certain groups of actors, and negative in the sense of a less favourable MOC setting. The illustrations of the development over time regarding the relevant MOC factors that are provided by the figures above as well as by the figures included in chapters four and five show these positive and negative shifts. For applicants, there has been a trend from an initially lower to a higher level of motivation, opportunity and unconstrained ability. This is most noticeable for the opportunity factor. Examples include the pre-2005 ECOWAS

Court which provided no jurisdictional or access opportunity for applicants in human rights cases before such an opportunity was created by the 2005 Protocol and, similarly, the narrow opportunity of individual applicants before the ECtHR in the pre-Protocol No 11 period which broadened with the institutional changes brought about by this protocol. Before the ECtHR, the opportunity also broadened over time for other applicants such as NGOs and state applicants. With regard to constraints, there are also certain patterns that point to a reduction at least in the intrinsic constraints. Knowledge-related constraints for applicants have reduced over time for both courts, however to divergent extents. Financial constraints have also decreased somewhat. Further, the motivation of applicants has increased for various reasons. For example, the motivation of state applicants before the ECtHR increased when these actors developed a stronger interest in dispute resolution by the ECtHR of interstate conflicts. And, when the expected effectiveness of bringing cases to the court increased as has been the case for the ECOWAS Court as well as, for a certain period, for the ECtHR, the motivation for applicants has increased as well.

For respondents, certain MOC features have also become more favourable. Before both courts, the opportunity for legislative and judicial actors but also for executive actors has broadened. This occurred when courts broadened the range of acts included in their review and when they expanded the range of remedies to more demanding orders. Regarding motivation as an MOC factor, there have been fewer instances in which this factor has become more favourable. An example is the motivation of ordinary domestic courts to accept the authority of the ECtHR. This motivation started off at a rather low level and increased over time. This was due to a developing interest of domestic courts to use the ECtHR authority relationship as a tool in their relationship towards other domestic courts as well as to an interest in consistent behaviour. Regarding the last MOC factor, unconstrained ability, the knowledge-related constraints for domestic courts also decreased over time.

However, the MOC factors do not always become more favourable. Rather, certain factors have deteriorated over time whereas for others, one can observe a development akin to a 'wave movement'. Such a movement occurs when a factor has first become more favourable than it started out but eventually developed in a negative direction again. For example, the opportunity for individual applicants before the ECtHR first broadened with Protocol No 11 and later narrowed somewhat when additional admissibility criteria were introduced and the court has further limited access in its admissibility jurisprudence. Before the ECOWAS Court, the access opportunity for NGOs was first broadly shaped by the court before the court reduced it somewhat again. Further, motivation has also decreased in some instances. This has been the case for the motivation of governmental and legislative actors in their role as respondents before the ECtHR. While the motivation was rather high during the first decades of the court's practice, it decreased to a moderate level in the post-2000 period. Finally, constraints can increase – which leads to a decrease in the ability to accept the courts' authority. Extrinsic constraints are more likely to do so, as has been the case for governmental pressure on applicants before the regional courts. In contrast, before the ECOWAS Court, one could observe a decrease as well as a 'wave movement' concerning the competing authority relationship of applicants and respondents towards the African Court on Human and Peoples' Rights (ACtHPR) that existed for certain member states only for a certain time.

When looking at the MOC setting for pushback, one can also perceive certain developments over time. As to the motivation for pushback, there have been fluctuations in both directions. Some factors have decreased such as the initial doubts about the ECOWAS Court's expertise in human rights matters and the pushback motivating effect of certain lines of jurisprudence. The latter is mitigated by habituation as, for example, in the case of the ECtHR's jurisprudence on procedural rights that initially had a strong pushback-motivating effect. In contrast, other aspects of the courts' jurisprudence have increased pushback motivation. Regarding governmental actors in the ECtHR context, there was an increase in the pushback motivation from a low level during the 1960s to a moderate level from the 1970s onwards due to the far-reaching landmark decisions during this time, until the rather high level that has existed since the 1990s when the court was restructured. A similar development has taken place for the relationship between domestic constitutional courts and the ECtHR in light of a perceived institutional competition from the perspective of the former. Before the ECOWAS Court, a competitive relationship between domestic courts and the regional court is inherent in the legal framework so that the pushback motivation is likely to increase further the more cases reach the ECOWAS Court.

Regarding the opportunity for pushback, one can also observe instances both of increase and decrease over time. The opportunity for pushback against the ECtHR by governmental actors has become narrower. This was in particular the case with the Protocol No 11 amendment when the opportunity for pushback by non-renewal of the optional clauses as to jurisdiction and individual access disappeared, and when member states gave effect to the Convention in their domestic legal orders, thus reducing the opportunity for non-compliance. Similarly, the opportunity for domestic courts to push back against the ECtHR has decreased over time. Further, the opportunity for pushback in the form of norm contestation and structural resistance against the ECOWAS Court has also become narrower over time. However, an increase in the opportunity for non-compliance has, for example, occurred when the court changed its approach to remedies from issuing only declaratory judgments to also including orders.

The shifts in the level of unconstrained ability to push back against the regional courts have so far only been one-directional. This ability decreased when the group of supporting actors broadened, as in the case of the ECtHR. It also did so when, over time, the status quo bias increasingly became an obstacle against the contestation of certain norms.

B. Influencing MOC: Who can Change the MOC Factors and How?

The second general observation that one can make based on the assessment undertaken in this book relates to the agency for change. Which actors can influence the MOC factors, and by which means?

To start with, the actors that might appear as having the primary agency are *state actors*. These actors have a particular influence on the opportunity structure both for applicants and respondents. Member states can shape the legal framework which primarily determines the opportunity to accept the authority of the respective court. They can do so in two ways. First, governmental actors and, in terms of ratification, also legislative actors create the international legal norms, that is the treaty or convention that constitutes the jurisdiction of the court, the norms that regulate the access for applicants and the status of actors as potential respondents. Second, legislative actors as well as domestic courts shape the domestic legal framework that provides important elements for the opportunity structure both for applicants and respondents. This concerns in particular the domestic applicability of the respective international law norms and of the decisions of the international court. It can also concern the enforcement regime of these decisions.

In addition, state actors including domestic courts can influence the non-legal elements of the opportunity structure. For example, their compliance or non-compliance with the decisions of their respective regional court or their enforcement of these decisions contribute to the social opportunity structure that influences the behaviour of state actors in other member states by creating group practice. This is the case when the ensuing social norms within the respective group exercise a conformity pull (see also section II). This can have an opportunity-limiting effect as in the case of the domestic courts' decision not to enforce ECOWAS Court judgments domestically, or when domestic courts do not engage with their respective regional court via preliminary references. But it can also have a positive effect, for example, when domestic courts have given effect to ECtHR decisions within their respective legal orders, establishing a group practice incentivising other domestic courts to also do so.

In contrast to the opportunity structure, motivational and constraining factors for applicants are rarely targeted by state actors explicitly with the aim of creating a favourable MOC setting. State actors can however influence the motivation and constraints in a negative manner. This is the case when governmental actors put pressure on applicants, including on domestic courts as potential initiators of preliminary references, to restrict any acceptance of the international court's authority. Further, the behaviour of state actors has a de facto influence on the motivation of applicants. Whether or not state actors comply with decisions of their respective regional court influences whether applicants consider it to be effective behaviour to bring cases to the court. Moreover, the level of rule of law and judicial independence within the member states can, if deficient, contribute to motivating applicants to bring cases to the regional court instead of addressing domestic courts, especially when no exhaustion of domestic remedies is required.

State actors also influence the motivation and constraints for respondents, both concerning acceptance and pushback. In view of acceptance, member states can influence the motivation of other state actors. For example, they can create group incentives that would motivate states to accept the jurisdiction of a court, as has been the case when the member states of the European Union (EU) made the ratification of the European Convention on Human Rights (ECHR) one of the preconditions for EU accession of new member states. Further, state actors can function as supporting actors against pushback by other state actors. This was observable in the context of structural resistance against the ECOWAS Court and the ECtHR. Supporting member states have prevented member states from amending the respective treaties as an act of pushback, which would otherwise have curtailed the authority of their respective regional court.

For *non-state actors*, the direct influence on the MOC factors is more limited. First, they can indirectly push for changes in the legal infrastructure that shapes the opportunity factor. NGOs have lobbied for certain features of the courts' jurisprudence and access opportunity and successfully impacted the MOC setting. For the ECOWAS Court, NGOs were already intensely involved in the process of creating the courts in the first place. And they have lobbied for a further broadening of the opportunity structure by formally amending the treaty framework such as in the case of the 2005 Protocol in the ECOWAS context that created the human rights jurisdiction and individual access. During the reforms of the ECtHR procedure, NGOs were also part of the actors that contributed reform proposals. Moreover, non-state actors can bring about change to the legal framework by inviting the respective regional court to change this framework jurisprudentially, as applicants tried before the ECOWAS Court in the *Afolabi* case.

In addition to changing the legal framework that shapes the opportunity structure, non-state actors can also influence the constraints, especially for applicants. NGOs have contributed to limiting knowledge-related constraints by raising awareness about the courts. Even individual applicants can, at least de facto, reduce these constraints when they bring cases to the courts that attract media coverage and public attention. As to financial constraints, NGOs have aimed at reducing these constraints by providing funding or legal support for potential applicants and by representing groups of individuals before the courts that otherwise would not have been able to bring their case to this forum. The latter is a particularly impactful tool for NGOs before the ECOWAS Court that allows not only for representation but also for genuine *actio popularis* cases. But even before courts with a more restrictive access opportunity for NGOs such as the ECtHR, NGOs have decreased the constraints for vulnerable groups such as migrants, Roma, children, prisoners and persons with disabilities.

The *regional courts* themselves can considerably shape MOC factors. As the assessment in this book has demonstrated, these courts can influence all three elements of the MOC framework – both by making it more favourable and by making it less favourable.

As for member states, courts have the most direct influence on *opportunity* (both for applicants and respondents) because this is the factor that is most directly shaped by legal norms. For applicants, this concerns both jurisdictional and access elements of the opportunity structure. For example, the ECtHR has broadened the jurisdictional opportunity by expanding its jurisdiction territorially and substantively. And both courts have expanded the access opportunity for applicants by creating exceptions to the time limit (eg, continuing violations). They have also done so when creating access for applicants such as NGOs that were not explicitly mentioned by the relevant rules. In contrast, they have reduced it when establishing restrictive requirements for access. For example, after initially taking a broader approach, the ECOWAS Court has reduced the opportunities for NGOs to bring *actio popularis* claims to the court. Similarly, the ECtHR has reduced the opportunity for individual applicants by applying admissibility criteria more strictly than before. Overall, both courts have been reluctant to enhance the access opportunity for certain applicants.

This is the case for individuals before the ECtHR as well as for corporate actors before the ECOWAS Court.

For respondents, the courts have had a major impact on the range of state actors that are addressed by their decisions. Both courts have established the opportunity for legislative and judicial actors when they started to review legislative and judicial acts. And they have broadened the opportunity for governmental and other state actors when they expanded their approach to remedies. This includes going beyond declaratory decisions by ordering financial compensation, but also by granting more far-reaching remedies such as, inter alia, ordering retrials, investigations, the release of prisoners, providing information to victims, and legislative amendments.

The courts' impact on the *motivation* of applicants and respondents is also extensive. Regarding the motivation of applicants, the courts have increased, maintained and at times even decreased this motivation. They have increased it by strengthening the value-related motivation and they have addressed the various interests of applicants. For example, concerning the interest in effective dispute resolution, both courts have adopted strategies such as countering backlog-related effectiveness issues and increasing compliance with their decisions. Courts have also addressed the interests that go beyond dispute resolution. This includes providing a forum for political actors and their interests in legitimation and mobilisation, as has prominently been the case before the ECOWAS Court, addressing transitional justice interests, and providing a means of bringing about social change as most extensively undertaken by the ECtHR. Although the courts have aimed at enhancing motivation in many ways, this has not always been the case in all situations. The ECtHR has also adopted strategies to maintain the existing level of motivation rather than trying to increase it further.

Regarding the motivation of respondents, the courts have aimed at increasing both value-correspondence and interests in accepting their authority. Both courts have specifically emphasised rule of law values to increase the motivation of governmental actors and influenced, in terms of de facto value-correspondence, rule of law elements such as judicial independence in the member states. They have also strengthened, depending on the context, values such as human rights protection, democracy and regional integration. Further, the ECOWAS Court has adopted strategies to increase the interests of governmental actors in dispute resolution and compliance, inter alia, by establishing or strengthening a monitoring mechanism. Moreover, elements or periods of deference in the courts' jurisprudence have affected both the motivation to accept the authority of the court and the motivation to push back against them. Finally, regarding domestic courts, motivation-related strategies focus on enhancing value-correspondence and, for the ECtHR, also include tools such as dialogue and networking with domestic judicial actors.

With regard to *constraints*, it is more difficult for courts to influence the relevant factors, although courts have realised their importance. Both courts have primarily targeted intrinsic constraints for applicants. To reduce knowledge-related constraints, they provide information on their websites (although to a varying extent), entertain networks with actors such as NGOs and bar associations to spread knowledge about the court among individual applicants and domestic courts, visit actors in their member states, open information offices and hold court sessions at temporary seats. To reduce financial constraints, their strategies include refraining from issuing cost orders to the detriment of applicants and providing legal aid and getting geographically closer to the applicants by using temporary seats. Regarding extrinsic constraints, courts have also taken some measures. This includes limiting competing authority relationships such as those created by a dual jurisdiction of the court or by other adjudicative bodies.

In contrast, courts did not aim as much at reducing constraints for respondents. This is primarily due to the fact that constraints for respondents are structurally rather low to begin with. One of the exceptions concerns domestic courts. When regional courts aim at improving the rule of law and governance standards in their member states, this can contribute to reducing extrinsic constraints for domestic courts stemming from governmental pressure. Further, the above strategies that enhance awareness of the regional courts' jurisprudence also benefit domestic courts as respondent actors. It enables them to discursively engage with the jurisprudence of their respective regional court. Finally, courts can influence extrinsic constraints by lowering the constraining effect of competing authority relationships with other international judicative bodies and domestic courts.

Turning to the MOC setting for *pushback*, both courts have influenced all three MOC factors. As to the motivation for pushback, depending on the existing MOC setting, the courts have adopted strategies to reduce a rather high motivation for pushback as well as strategies to maintain a rather low level thereof. In both situations, they mainly targeted the sovereignty-related interests of state actors. Courts have avoided jurisprudential developments that could be perceived as activist and used deference tools such as the margin of appreciation, a variable geometry approach or the proceduralisation strategy adopted by the ECtHR. Further, when courts include activist elements into their jurisprudence, they mitigate the pushback-motivating effect by using an incremental approach. Moreover, discursive tools play a role both for managing ongoing pushback and for avoiding it. The former is exemplified by the continuous discursive engagement by the ECOWAS Court with state actors that persistently contest the rule that applicants do not have to exhaust domestic remedies. An example of the latter is the ECtHR's dialogue with state actors in non-judicial settings.

Concerning the opportunity for pushback, the courts have focused mostly on reducing the opportunity for non-compliance. This includes limiting remedies to declaratory decisions so that the relevant state actors have less opportunity for non-compliance. In addition, the ECOWAS Court has used a policy strategy to lobby for the creation of the domestic legal framework required by Article 24 of the Protocol to the ECOWAS Treaty regarding the execution of ECOWAS Court judgments.

As to the constraints against pushback, both courts have adopted strategies relating to supporting actors that, in case of pushback, can restrain the relevant state actors. The ECOWAS Court has focused on alliances with non-state actors such as NGOs and bar associations. While the ECtHR has in its more recent practice also strengthened its relationship with these actors, it however puts more emphasis on its relationship towards those state actors that can constrain pushback by other state actors.

Finally, in terms of the tools that the courts use to influence the MOC setting, one can observe that both courts use jurisprudential and non-judicial means.[2] The former are generally more immediate and far-reaching. As outlined above, they address mainly motivation and opportunity for applicants and respondents and can both enhance and reduce these factors significantly. In contrast, non-judicial means only aim at enhancing the MOC setting for applicants and respondents. Such means include, inter alia, lobbying for treaty amendments, networking strategies, providing information and holding court sessions in regions other than that of the permanent seat. Moreover, it bears mentioning that courts use non-judicial means both in addition and instead of jurisprudential tools to bring about change in the MOC setting. They use them when a particular factor cannot be addressed by judicial means, such as regarding knowledge-related constraints for applicants. And they use them in situations in which they could have addressed a factor by jurisprudential means as well. For example, the ECOWAS Court had refused to do so in the *Afolabi* case and instead lobbied successfully for the treaty amendment brought about by the 2005 Protocol. The court has used non-judicial means as a less far-reaching alternative to jurisprudential means in terms of activism. Yet by doing so, it has impacted the opportunity structure in a more impactful manner because the change is likely to be more robust and less prone to trigger pushback.

II. INSIGHTS ON PSYCHOLOGICAL FACTORS FOR THE AUTHORITY RELATIONSHIP

After this general assessment of the MOC settings in the two courts analysed in this book, I turn to a specific category of factors for authority relationships: a selection of psychological factors in the narrow sense. I compare the findings on this matter for the two courts (II.A) and outline how these factors have influenced the MOC setting (II.B). I then give an overview of how these courts and other actors can influence, and have influenced, these factors (II.C).

A. Comparative Assessment

When comparing the factors for the authority relationships of the ECOWAS Court and the ECtHR, one can make several observations. To start with, psychological factors play a role for both courts. The factors that have been relevant throughout are the effects relating to the actors' social group as well as those relating to the continuing character of the authority relationship, such as inertia and the status quo bias.

Effects relating to the actors' social group have influenced the authority relationships in various ways. In the first place, both for applicants and respondents, opportunity as an MOC factor is shaped by social opportunity elements such as

[2] On the differentiation between judicial and extra-judicial techniques, S Caserta and P Cebulak, 'Resilience Techniques of International Courts in Times of Resistance to International Law' (2021) 70 *International & Comparative Law Quarterly* 737.

the conformity pull that a homogenous behaviour of group members and the ensuing social norm generate (see chapter two). Regarding applicants, however, such conformity pull does not occur for all groups of applicants. Applicant groups for which this is pertinent are NGOs, domestic courts in their role as potential initiators of preliminary references, and member states as applicants. For NGOs in the ECOWAS context, positive group dynamics are pronounced because, in this group, the practice to engage with the ECOWAS Court is well developed. In contrast, regarding preliminary references by domestic courts, the group practice is unfavourable in regional integration cases before the ECOWAS Court. As the (majority of the) group does not initiate preliminary references, individual courts are likely to conform with this norm. A negative effect of group practice can occur for member states as applicants before a court. When member states observe that other member states do not bring cases to their regional court, it is likely that they conform to this behaviour. In relation to the ECOWAS Court, the behaviour of member states is very homogenous in this regard, thus exercising a conformity pull against state applications. Before the ECtHR, the group practice is more diverse, with an increasing number of interstate complaints, so that there is at least no unfavourable conformity pull.

Turning to respondents, such group effects play a role for governmental actors as well as domestic courts. Regarding the former, the ECtHR and its pre-Protocol No 11 regime has shown this effect. In the earlier period, the practice of member states as to whether they accepted the two optional clauses concerning jurisdiction and individual access was very heterogenous so that a conformity pull could not develop from this group practice. This was however different in later years when, during the 1980s, the broad majority of member states had made both declarations. During this period, the conformity pull to accept the authority of the court in this way was high. Moreover, group effects among domestic courts as respondent actors have been relevant before both regional courts. Before the ECOWAS Court, the group practice among domestic courts regarding the enforcement of ECOWAS Court decisions has been homogenous, yet unfavourable for the authority relationship. When domestic courts refused to enforce the decisions, it created an unfavourable social norm for domestic courts in other member states as well. In the ECtHR context, domestic courts have also been exposed to intra-state conformity pulls. Chapter five has addressed the very homogenous practice among Dutch courts to refer to ECtHR jurisprudence as well as the acceptance of the ECtHR's authority by French courts that increasingly showed a favourable group practice until all courts conformed to this practice. In addition, as the courts in most member states have accepted the ECtHR's authority, there is also a conformity pull across member states.

The inverse effect of the conformity pull that group behaviour and the ensuing social norm can generate is the 'true partner effect' relevant in pushback situations (see chapter two). This phenomenon was in line with certain instances of pushback against the ECtHR. As outlined in chapter five, the 'alliance' between the United Kingdom and Russia in the context of the Brighton Conference of 2012 as well as the parallel non-compliance approaches of these states in the prisoners' voting cases exemplifies such pushback partnerships between member states. Further, 'true partner effects' are likely to have influenced the pushback against the ECtHR by domestic courts. In particular when domestic constitutional courts engaged in such pushback, they explicitly referred to the critical approaches and doctrinal constructions used by courts of other member states.

Similar patterns akin to a 'true partner effect' are also observable for other international courts. Examples of pushback in 'true partner' constellations by governmental actors are the backlash against the International Criminal Court when three African states (Burundi, South Africa and the Gambia) made withdrawal declarations from this court in October and November of 2016 (which however were not all effective);[3] and the clustered withdrawals of the optional declaration by Tanzania, Côte d'Ivoire and Benin regarding individual access to the ACtHPR.[4] Regarding such patterns among domestic courts, a further example is the pushback against the Court of Justice of the European Union (CJEU) by constitutional courts based on their respective constitutional identity and ultra vires jurisprudence.[5]

In contrast, when structural resistance and backlash occurred in the ECOWAS context, the relevant actor did not have a 'true partner'. The Gambia pushed back against the ECOWAS Court as a single actor, without being able to convince the other member states to curtail the authority of the court.

A further psychological effect that has played a role for the courts assessed in this book is the 'foot-in-the-door' technique (see chapter two). This technique has become relevant both as part of the treaty structure and as an element of the courts' jurisprudence. The former was the case in the ECtHR's initial Convention system in which the court's jurisdiction and individual access were optional features and where states could make the optional declarations for short periods and renew them recurrently. This made it possible for states to join the Convention system in several steps. During this process, accepting the first step was akin to a 'foot-in-the-door' that made it more likely that states would subsequently accept the full authority relationship.

Moreover, the courts have used a 'foot-in-the-door' technique as part of their jurisprudence. It is a strategy to reduce pushback against jurisprudence that is more demanding on member states. When they used an incremental approach to expand either jurisdictional and procedural rules or substantive obligations, doing so step by step facilitates, after states have accepted the lesser demands, the acceptance of more far-reaching obligations. Jurisdictional expansion through a 'foot-in-the-door' technique has been used by the ECOWAS Court. From reviewing only executive acts, it has expanded its review to legislative and judicial acts and, with regard to the latter, has also done so in an incremental manner. The ECtHR has used the 'foot-in-the-door' technique both for procedural and for substantive expansions. The jurisprudentially constructed pilot judgment procedure is an example of a procedural expansion that happened in an incremental manner. And substantive obligations have been expanded incrementally in many fields, including the jurisprudence on abortion

[3] Burundi made its declaration on 27 October 2016, South Africa on 21 October 2016 and the Gambia on 10 November 2016.

[4] Tanzania withdrew its declaration under Article 34 AChHPR on 14 November 2019, Benin on 24 March 2020 and Côte d'Ivoire on 28 April 2020.

[5] eg, German Constitutional Court, 30 June 2009, 2 BvE 2/08 and 5 May 2020, 2 BvR 859/15; Polish Constitutional Court, 11 May 2005, K 18/04 and 24 November 2010, K 32/09, section 3.3; Czech Constitutional Court, 26 November 2008, Pl. US. 19/08, paras 120, 139, 216; Danish Supreme Court, 6 April 1998, I 361/1997; Hungarian Constitutional Court, 30 November 2016, 22/2016 (XII. 5.) AB.

regulation mentioned in chapter five. These examples and the overall success of incremental approaches by courts also demonstrate that the 'foot-in-the-door' technique is applicable to a range of state actors. The underlying psychological mechanism such as the self-perception of actors and their interest in consistent behaviour can influence the behaviour of actors other than individuals.[6]

Another psychological factor that has influenced the authority relationships of both courts are the time-related effects of inertia and the status quo bias. For respondents, inertia and the status quo bias (see chapter two) can influence both the MOC setting for the acceptance of the court's authority and for pushback. This is possible because respondent actors are in continuing authority relationships with their respective regional courts in which they face repeatedly similar situations.

For these effects to occur, the number of cases brought against the respective member states is important. This has become especially apparent when comparing the earlier decades of the ECtHR with its 1990s enlargement period. As outlined in chapter five, there were very few cases against some member states during the first decades, so that respondent actors from these member states barely had any opportunity, if at all, to engage with the court. For these actors, repetitive situations were sparse so that inertia and the status quo bias in favour of accepting the court's authority could not develop significantly for a long time. In contrast, for newer member states that joined in particular during the 1990s enlargement, the situation was different. Here, respondent actors were faced early after their state's accession with repetitive situations in which they engaged with the court and its jurisprudence. Inertia and a status quo bias in favour of the court's authority could thus develop much faster.

For the ECOWAS Court, inertia and the status quo bias are becoming relevant in the human rights context. The increasing number of human rights cases in recent years has made these effects more impactful across member states. In contrast, these effects could not yet develop substantially in the regional integration context due to the low number of cases on this matter. However, due to the dual jurisdiction of this court, positive 'spill-over effects' might occur. This means that inertia and a status quo bias developed in the human rights context can motivate respondents to also accept the authority in the regional integration context.

Inertia and the status quo bias are also elements that constrain pushback by state actors. Before the two courts, such effects seem to have influenced pushback against both procedural rules and substantive norms. Regarding pushback against procedural rules, the constraining effect of such psychological factors has been the most visible before the ECOWAS Court. Here, state actors had initially contested the access rule that applicants can bring cases to the court without exhaustion of domestic remedies. Over time, there has been a significant decrease in preliminary objections against this rule, a development that is likely influenced by the above effects. An example regarding pushback against substantive norms is the ECtHR's extensive interpretation of Article 6 ECHR. While state actors initially pushed back against the broad interpretation of terms such as 'civil rights' in the 1970s when the court adopted this

[6] See on the psychological process contributing to this effect, ch 3 and JM Burger, 'The Foot-in-the-Door Compliance Procedure: A Multiple-Process Analysis and Review' (1999) 3 *Personality and Social Psychology Review* 27.

approach, it is now considered part of the established case law. Pushback against this jurisprudence is strongly constrained by inertia and the status quo bias.

B. Psychological Factors and MOC

The assessment in this book has highlighted that the above psychological effects are relevant for all three MOC factors, ie, motivation, opportunity and constraints. For each factor, there is at least one psychological effect that can influence the factor. Most prominently, effects relating to group behaviour are an important part of the opportunity structure for respondents and for some applicants. This psychological effect seems to be the most impactful among the above-mentioned effects in comparison to the other elements of this MOC factor. Yet, this effect can be both favourable and unfavourable for the authority relationship between the respective court and its audiences. Further, inertia and the status quo bias can be relevant both for the motivation to accept authority and for constraints against pushback. And the 'foot-in-the-door' technique has facilitated the acceptance of the court's authority by increasing the motivation of member states and has been used by courts to reduce the pushback motivation. This also shows that the psychological effects concern both the MOC setting for the acceptance of the international court's authority and the MOC setting for pushback.

Several psychological factors are particularly important for perpetuating existing authority relationships, as compared with the initial acceptance of an international court's authority. This is the case for inertia and the status quo bias. For these effects to be beneficial for an authority relationship, this relationship must have already existed for a certain time. Further, group effects are often also more pronounced at a later stage of an international court's existence rather than during the initial phase. When many actors within a group were already able to engage in a behaviour that reflects the acceptance of the court's authority, it is more likely that a homogenous group practice and thus a (perceived) social norm developed which in turn generates a conformity pull. However, group effects can also be relevant at the initial stage of an authority relationship when there is an occasion for such behaviour, and this behaviour is very visible to the respective actors.

C. Influencing Psychological Factors

International courts can, within limits, influence the psychological factors that shape their authority relationships. In the first place, courts can relate to some of the above psychological effects as a strategy to improve the MOC setting for respondents. Most prominently, the 'foot-in-the-door' technique is an important and fully-fledged tool in this regard. With this tool, courts can directly trigger the respective psychological effect. Other jurisprudential tools also address psychological effects, yet more indirectly. They primarily do so by framing certain notions in a way that can lead to psychological effects. Such a tool that deserves highlighting here again is the ECtHR's European consensus doctrine that can contribute to increasing constraints against pushback. With this framing as a pre-existing standard, the court contributes to activating the status quo bias which is likely to make states perceive this (alleged) status quo more positively than framing as a novel standard would be.

Courts are not the only actors that can frame legal notions or arguments in a way that can trigger psychological effects relevant for the MOC setting. For example, state actors can cause such effects by designing the legal framework accordingly. The above-mentioned design of the initial Strasbourg system in which states could accept the authority of the ECtHR in a step-by-step process akin to a 'foot-in-the-door' setting illustrates how the states' agency over treaty design can shape psychological factors. Moreover, state actors and some non-state actors such as NGOs have at least a de facto role in shaping the practice among their respective groups of actors (see also section I.B). They thus contribute to creating a social norm which in turn generates a conformity pull for other actors.

III. INSIGHTS FOR THE LAW AND POLITICAL SCIENCE DISCOURSE

In this section, I return to a range of questions that characterise the discourse about international courts from a legal and a political science perspective and that have been discussed controversially in the literature (see chapters one and three). I outline the insights that the MOC assessment employed in this book provides for these questions. The first set of questions relates to the impact of the legal factors on the one hand (III.A) and the political factors on the other (III.B). I then address the development of courts over time (III.C.) as well as the relationship between certain MOC factors (III.D).

A. Impact of the Legal Framework on the Authority of International Courts

The assessment undertaken in this book has highlighted in what way and in which situations the legal framework influences whether actors accept the authority of international courts. It has shown that law primary shapes the opportunity structure for applicants and respondents but also influences – directly or indirectly – motivation and constraints.

For opportunity, jurisdiction and access are directly determined by law. They are the key opportunity elements for applicants and respondents. Non-legal aspects such as the social opportunity structure created by the behaviour of other group members as well as the practical opportunity elements relating to budget, staffing and other aspects that affect the capacity of the court to decide cases influence opportunity less strongly than the legal factors – at least for the two courts assessed in this book.

As to motivation, the relevant legal factors closely interact with non-legal factors. For example, law significantly shapes the value-correspondence between the court and its audiences in view of procedural values. The way in which the court and the procedures are designed as to judicial independence and fair trial guarantees shapes value-correspondence in this regard. This is also an aspect that speaks to the institutionalist perspective on international courts which emphasises the institutional design as a relevant feature for authority relationships.[7] Further, the jurisprudence of the respective court influences whether applicants see their interests realised when approaching the court. The courts' case law is thus an important legal element for the motivation of these actors. Inversely, this jurisprudence significantly shapes the motivation for pushback by state actors.

Concerning constraints, financial constraints are indirectly influenced by the respective legal norms on costs, fees and damages, yet in an interplay with non-legal factors such as the economic development of the member state and the resulting financial resources of actors. Moreover, constraints stemming from competing authority relationships with domestic or international judicial bodies are also shaped by law, both by the norms regulating the procedure before the international court and by the norms regulating the competing judicial bodies.

The assessment also highlights how legal sources from different legal spaces influence the MOC setting, creating a cross-border infrastructure.[8] Relevant legal sources are, on the one hand, international in nature such as the respective treaties, conventions and protocols relevant for the court's jurisdiction. On the other hand, domestic law also plays a role in shaping the MOC setting. In some contexts, a further legal source can indirectly influence the MOC setting, in particular extrinsic constraints: the legal framework of other international judicial bodies regarding which actors can be in a competing authority relationship.

In terms of development over time, the assessment of the two regional courts selected for this book has shown that both the international and domestic legal elements and both the formal rules as well as the related jurisprudence can change, thus altering the MOC setting. For both courts, states have amended the formal legal framework by protocols to the respective treaty or convention, in part as drastically as Protocol No 11 for the ECtHR or the 2005 Protocol for the ECOWAS Court. And the jurisprudence of both courts regarding procedural and substantive aspects have significantly developed as well. As to the domestic legal framework, one could observe the most significant change in the ECtHR context, that concerning the domestic law approach on direct applicability of the Convention and the jurisprudence of the court.

Moreover, the assessment does not only demonstrate how the legal factors influence the MOC setting. It also shows when the legal factors *primarily determine* the behaviour of actors, as compared with non-legal factors. This is in particular the case in situations in which *opportunity* is the determining MOC factor, ie, when it is at the lowest level as compared with motivation and unconstrained ability. As mentioned above, this has, for example, been the case for NGOs as applicants before both courts as well as for governmental and legislative actors as respondent actors before the ECtHR. Opportunity has also prominently shaped the behaviour of actors in all situations in which no access existed, as was the case for potential applicants to the ECOWAS Court before the 2005 amendment.

[7] See ch 1 as well as, eg, LR Helfer and A-M Slaughter, 'Why States Create International Tribunals: A Response to Professors Posner and Yoo' (2005) 93 *California Law Review* 899; RO Keohane, A Moravcsik and A-M Slaughter, 'Legalized Dispute Resolution: Interstate and Transnational' (2000) 54 *International Organization* 457.

[8] See ch 3.

However, although law plays a significant role in many situations, it is important to stress that it is not the only relevant element of the MOC setting. In what follows, I summarise the impact of non-legal factors on the behaviour of actors in the context of their authority relationship with international courts.

B. Impact of the Political Setting within the Member States on the Authority of International Courts

The MOC assessment undertaken in this book has shown that the political context in which the respective court operates has an impact on the court's authority relationships with its audiences – although this impact is partial and specific.

Regarding the MOC factors for *applicants*, the political setting can have an influence on the motivation and constraints for these actors. A moderate or even low rule of law standard within a member state can motivate private applicants to bring cases to an international court. For example, when the domestic judiciary lacks judicial independence, this can motivate both individuals and corporate actors to pursue their claims on the international level. Inversely, rule of law deficits within member states can reduce the motivation of certain groups of applicants. This is the case when these deficits lead to more non-compliance and thus reduce the expected effectiveness of bringing cases to the court. Moreover, lower rule of law and good governance standards can also increase constraints for applicants as it becomes more likely that governmental actors exercise pressure on potential applicants not to bring cases to their respective regional courts.

Regarding the MOC factors for *respondents*, the political setting impacts the value-correspondence, both in terms of aspirational and de facto value-correspondence. Whether and to what extent state actors embrace and endorse values such as human rights, the rule of law and judicial independence is influenced by the political setting in their respective member states. That said, as demonstrated by the fact that member states of all political backgrounds – including those with low rule of law, governance and human rights standards – support such values on the international level shows that an aspirational value-correspondence can already constitute a motivating factor for accepting the authority of the respective regional court. However, a lower rule of law and human rights standard can limit the interest of state actors in dispute resolution, in particular because reputational costs are lower. It is especially low when the other member states of the court also have a similar political setting so that the reputation within the in-group is not likely to be strongly affected.

A further observation concerns the political heterogeneity among the member states of a court. The two courts provide examples for rather heterogenous as well as rather homogenous groups of member states: the ECOWAS Court has a rather heterogeneous group and the ECtHR in the post-enlargement period also has some level of heterogeneity. In contrast, the pre-enlargement ECtHR had a rather homogeneous membership. Comparing these settings shows that homogeneity can contribute to a lower motivation for pushback and can make it easier for courts to maintain or increase the motivation of state actors for accepting their authority. Homogeneity makes it less likely for outliers to contest the authority of the court as state actors will more easily agree on how to design the court and what jurisdiction to attribute to it. And, with homogeneous member states, it is easier for the court to take into account the expectations and limits of state actors as to when to give deference to member states as compared with when to adopt a more far-reaching jurisprudence. The way in which the ECtHR had to develop its 'variable geometry' approach to deference when the membership became more heterogenous highlights this aspect. In contrast, a more heterogenous setting can also have beneficial effects for MOC factors. It makes it more likely that states can counterbalance each other in potential pushback situations. This has been very prominent in the context of the pushback attempts by the Gambia against the ECOWAS Court as well as during the pushback against the ECtHR in the Brighton and Copenhagen context.

Even though the political context influences the MOC setting, it is important to note that the political context does not necessarily define the extent to which such authority relationships exist. It is one out of several elements that shape the MOC setting for the courts' constituencies and thus the ensuing authority relationships. Even in the absence of a well-established rule of law practice and good governance in member states, there can be strong authority relationships with certain groups of actors if the MOC setting for these actors is favourable. And inversely, member states of all ranges of practice have engaged in pushback against their respective courts.

Finally, concerning a further aspect discussed in the literature about international courts, the assessment in this book has shown that jurisprudence in 'high-politics' areas plays an ambivalent role for the authority relationships between courts and their constituencies.[9] On the one hand, jurisprudence that touches upon high-politics issues can constitute both a motivational factor and an opportunity factor for pushback. And actors can use decisions in 'high-politics' areas as an opportunity to present the international court as political actors and pushback against it on this basis. On the other hand, both courts have addressed 'high-politics' issues without, in most cases, triggering pushback. The ECtHR regularly decides such cases and nonetheless continues to have a well-developed authority relationship towards its audiences. For the ECOWAS Court, access rules currently constitute a more prominent pushback motivation as compared with the subject matter of the courts' decisions. Further, high-politics cases can also have a positive effect on the MOC setting for potential applicants. They generate attention and thus decrease constraints for applicants that before had little awareness and knowledge about the court. The high-profile cases against the United Kingdom before the ECtHR in its early years and the ensuing development of a human rights law community in this state that in turn led to comparatively high application numbers exemplifies this aspect (see chapter five).

[9] On the high-politics nature of disputes as explanatory factor, MR Madsen, P Cebulak and M Wiebusch, 'Backlash against international courts: explaining the forms and patterns of resistance to international courts' (2018) 14 *International Journal of Law in Context* 197; Caserta and Cebulak (n 2) 737; E Posner and J Yoo, 'Judicial Independence in International Tribunals' (2005) 93 *California Law Review* 1.

C. Development of the Authority Relationship Over Time

One can make two observations as to the development of the authority relationship over time. First, the influence of legal and non-legal factors on the MOC setting is not stable but rather fluctuates throughout the development of the authority relationship. Certain non-legal factors are particularly influential at the beginning of the courts' practice. For example, intrinsic constraints concerning a lack of awareness of the court and its jurisprudence predominantly shape the behaviour of diverse groups such as individual applicants, corporate entities and domestic courts. Further, motivation is in the beginning also primarily determined by non-legal factors, given that the respective court had not yet had the chance to influence the actors' motivation with its jurisprudence. As the courts' practice develops, these non-legal factors are either reduced or are being replaced or at least complemented by legal factors. In contrast, the impact of other non-legal factors increases over time. On the one hand, this concerns the psychological factors as addressed in section II such as inertia, status quo bias and group effects that do not exist at the outset but develop only gradually. On the other hand, the impact of practical difficulties that contribute to the opportunity structure such as the backlog that occurs when courts are understaffed and/or under-financed increases. For other non-legal factors such as those that constitute the political setting, there is no necessary downward or upward trend. Although changes can of course occur, these changes are context-dependent and not structurally predetermined as with the above factors.

The second observation about the development of the authority relationship over time relates to the extent and robustness of this relationship. For the courts assessed here, one can discern similar phases of development. In the initial period, there had been hesitation if not pushback by state actors against their respective regional court. For the ECOWAS Court, this took the form of a strong and visible pushback by the Gambia. Similar strong initial pushback also occurred, for example, in the context of the Southern African Development Community (SADC) Tribunal, yet with more serious consequences for this court.[10] Other courts only face a lighter form of initial pushback. This has been the case for the ECtHR where one could witness not only a slow and reluctant acceptance of the jurisdiction by many of the then Council of Europe member states but also repeated pushback by states making only short-term declarations as to jurisdiction of the court and individual access. And applicants in the initial phase only approached their respective courts in small numbers. The authority of the courts was thus limited within both groups. In a second phase, the acceptance by applicants and respondents increased and authority relationships broadened. As a result, the courts also had to readjust their jurisprudence in order to stabilise both the relationship towards applicants and towards respondents. This meant reducing certain MOC factors for applicants in view of maintaining the acceptance by respondents. In conclusion, after initial hesitancy and then a rise in the authority relationship, this relationship did not remain invariable but rather seems to

[10] On the backlash against this tribunal, KJ Alter, JT Gathii and LR Helfer, 'Backlash against International Courts in West, East and Southern Africa: Causes and Consequences' (2016) 27 *European Journal of International Law* 293.

have developed in a way that is akin to a pendulum movement. This movement reflects how courts constantly readjust their strategy to maintain and increase their authority relationships towards all groups of actors involved.

Despite these similarities in development, both courts have evolved at different speeds through these phases. What took the ECtHR many decades, happened much quicker for younger courts such as the ECOWAS Court. The reason for that are the different expectations with which these courts were faced. While the ECtHR was initially designed only as a backup mechanism to ensure that the human rights standard in Europe did not slip below a minimum level and only later developed into a forum with transformative function, this was different for younger courts. The ECOWAS Court was created against the backdrop of such transformative expectations. Due to these high expectations, it could not afford decades of 'sleeping beauty' as the ECtHR has had.[11] It was necessary for it to become effective much faster, at least in its role as a human rights court, because the structural rule of law and human rights issues in the member states were much greater than was the case in the initial ECtHR member states.

In contrast, for the regional integration context, this need was less pressing so that the strategies of the court are less developed in this regard. Here, the development continues to be slow. The coexistence of human rights and regional integration jurisdiction also has a limiting effect on the latter. This becomes clear when one compares the ECOWAS Court with courts such as the CJEU that was initially designed only with jurisdiction for regional integration matters. Whereas the CJEU only had the 'economic route' to establish itself as an authoritative regional court, the ECOWAS Court does not depend on this strand of its jurisdiction. It can – and has indeed chosen to – establish its authority via the human rights route, to the detriment of the regional integration route.

D. Insights on the Relationship between Certain MOC Factors

A final set of insights concerns the relationship between certain MOC factors.

A first observation relates to the interest in dispute resolution and compliance as motivational factors for applicants. The assessment has illustrated that an authority relationship between applicants and the court can develop, even when, due to compliance issues, the expected effectiveness of dispute resolution before a court is limited.[12] As highlighted by the assessment of the ECOWAS Court, NGOs and political actors in particular, but also certain other individual applicants, are motivated by considerations that go beyond dispute resolution. For these actors, a limited expected effectiveness regarding dispute resolution does not hinder them in engaging with the court because other interests and values can motivate them sufficiently. Dispute

[11] On this notion, see E Bates, *The Evolution of the European Convention on Human Rights: From its Inception to the Creation of a Permanent Court of Human Rights* (OUP 2010) 257; J Frowein, 'European Integration through Fundamental Rights' (1984) 18 *Michigan Journal of Law Reform* 5, 8.

[12] Also particularly stressing this point, JT Gathii (ed), *The Performance of Africa's International Courts* (OUP 2020).

resolution and compliance aspects are thus not necessarily decisive for shaping the authority relationship with applicants.

Second, the assessment has highlighted the role of values as motivational factors. Values can motivate applicants to bring cases to the court; and inversely, a lack of value-correspondence can motivate pushback. The role of values as a positively motivating factor has been illustrated, for example, for state applicants before the ECtHR as well es for NGOs before both courts. In contrast, a lack of value-correspondence as to the role of courts and to their relationship to the legislative branch has made several state actors initially reluctant to accept international court authority.

A further aspect of the relationship between MOC factors concerns the link between factors for acceptance and factors for pushback. The book has highlighted the differences between the respective MOC settings as well as the overlaps. This stresses that the MOC factors for pushback are not only a negative of the MOC factors for acceptance. For state actors, the opportunity and constraints for pushback generally differ from the opportunity and constraints for accepting the courts' authority. This includes aspects such as the legal framework for withdrawals and treaty amendments, social opportunity elements for pushback such as the 'true partner effect' and the constraints stemming from supporting actors. For motivational factors there is a closer connection, for example, regarding high value-correspondence as a motivation for acceptance and low value-correspondence as a motivation for pushback. However, there are also several motivational factors that are not merely a negative of a factor that motivates acceptance. The access rules that motivate pushback in the context of the ECOWAS Court and that have no equivalent when it comes to motivation for acceptance illustrate that point.

Moreover, the assessment has also highlighted the inter-actor effects that exist between the MOC factors of different groups of actors (see also chapter three). Opposing effects are most prominent between motivational and opportunity factors for applicants on the one hand and pushback motivation for state actors on the other. For example, when the access opportunity for applicants is high as before the ECOWAS Court, this can contribute to the pushback motivation for member states. Other links do not have opposing effects but make the MOC setting for different groups more favourable. For example, when the courts broadened the opportunity of respondent actors by issuing more demanding remedies, this also increased the effectiveness interest of applicants and thus their motivation to address the court. Both courts have taken such inter-actor effects into account when deciding on their strategies concerning the MOC setting for applicants and respondents.

In conclusion, from this overview, insights have become apparent that help to situate, to corroborate or to challenge certain claims made in the legal and political science scholarship on international courts. The multifaceted assessment that the MOC framework makes possible provides both a tool to analyse such claims and a theoretical model which explains the interplay of the many factors that shape the behaviour of the relevant groups of actors. Further, the MOC framework can be used to assess past developments, including by comparing different international courts, and to predict the future behaviour of these courts' audiences. It is thus a framework that helps to shed light on the authority of international courts and the reasons for when and how it emerges.

IV. GOING FORWARD: MOC ASSESSMENT FOR OTHER INTERNATIONAL COURTS

In view of future research, the assessment undertaken in Part II of this book has shown how to assess the authority relationship between an international court and its relevant groups of actors. It has demonstrated the applicability of the MOC framework and the insights that it generates. This framework can be applied to all other international courts both individually and in a comparative manner.

From the analysis undertaken in this book, one can foreshadow certain expectations. In the first place, it is likely that the MOC settings for actors in their relationship towards other international courts are heterogeneous with diverging determining factors both among groups and among courts. Fully identical settings are unlikely to exist. Using the MOC framework allows us to capture the existing differences. Further, it can be expected that MOC settings have changed, or will change, over time. As the above analysis has highlighted, MOC settings are variable both in favour of the respective authority relationship and to its detriment. For all international courts, such changes can be brought about by state actors and by the international courts themselves and, to a lesser extent, by non-state actors such as NGOs, international or regional institutions and private actors.

As to the MOC analysis for 'old style' international courts as compared with the 'new style' courts assessed in Part II of this book, the insights for state actors in relation to the latter can foreshadow expectations for these courts. This includes the finding that motivation is more likely to be the determining factor for state actors as applicants than for other actors considering that opportunity and unconstrained ability for state actors are often favourable. Yet opportunity elements such as limited jurisdiction as well as constraining factors such as financial constraints or competing authority relationships also play a role, and should thus not be overlooked. In contrast, for state actors as respondents, one can expect the MOC settings to be diverse.

Further, it can be expected that the trend towards broadening the opportunity structure that has been observed for the two courts assessed in this book also exists for other international courts. This concerns in particular an expansion brought about by the courts' jurisprudence as to jurisdiction and remedies. For 'old style' international courts, an important difference is that they do not need to uphold such a broad variety of authority relationships as 'new style' international courts concerning their different groups of actors. However, different 'sub-groups' among state actors can exist which would require similar strategies.

Moreover, the insights on the psychological factors outlined in section II can also be expected to have relevance for most international courts. Effects such as inertia and the status quo bias that develop over time are likely to play a role, albeit to a varying extent, for all international courts that have been in existence for a sufficiently long period. Similarly, group effects can also become relevant for all international courts. This is not only the case for courts that entertain authority relationships with a wide range of actors – here, group effects among domestic courts, governmental actors and NGOs are the most likely – but also for 'old style' international courts in the context of which member states and their respective actors can be affected by group effects. Further, although depending on the jurisprudential practice of the respective court, a 'foot-in-the-door' effect can also occur for all groups of courts and actors. It is, however, most likely for courts with jurisprudence that is at least in part activist. Finally, the 'true partner effect' is, in principle, possible in many backlash situations. Yet as the comparison of the two courts assessed in this book has shown, it is neither a necessary element of pushback nor does it occur in all instances and forms of pushback.

With regard to the MOC setting for pushback, it is worth stressing again that all three MOC factors can be the determining factor for such behaviour in relation to international courts. It is not only the motivation for pushback and constraints against pushback by supporting actors that shape the behavioural setting for pushback. Rather, the opportunity structure in particular with its legal components as well as the social dimension with psychological effects are crucial yet often overlooked factors for pushback. They should be included in any analysis of pushback against other international courts. Further, as for the two assessed courts, it is likely that for other international courts as well, the determining factor diverges significantly among forms of pushback such as pushback by withdrawal, treaty amendment, norm contestation or non-compliance. It is an insight from the present study that, to fully understand pushback, the MOC settings for these forms of pushback should be assessed individually.

Taken together, the present book does not only develop a conceptual framework for the authority of international courts but also provides analytical insights that can serve as a blueprint for assessing other international courts as part of future research. Such research will further strengthen our (comparative) understanding of the factors that determine whether and to what extent actors accept the authority of international courts.

Index

www.ingramcontent.com/pod-product-compliance
Ingram Content Group UK Ltd.
Pitfield, Milton Keynes, MK11 3LW, UK
UKHW020238290926
15470UKWH00002B/615